CHALLENGING ETHNIC CITIZENSHIP

German and Israeli Perspectives on Immigration

Edited by
Daniel Levy
and
Yfaat Weiss

Berghahn Books
NEW YORK • OXFORD

Published in 2002 by

Berghahn Books

www.berghahnbooks.com

Library of Congress Cataloging-in-Publication Data

Challenging ethnic citizenship : German and Israeli perspectives on
immigration / edited by Daniel Levy and Yfaat Weiss.
     p. cm.
     Includes bibliographical references and index.
     ISBN 1-57181-291-1 (cloth : alk. paper) — ISBN 1-57181-292-X (pbk.: alk.
paper)
     1. Germany—Emigration and immigration—Government policy.
2. Immigrants—Government policy—Germany. 3. Minorities—Government
policy—Germany. 4. Israel—Emigration and immigration—Government
policy. 5. Immigrants—Government policy—Israel. 6. Minorities—Government policy—Israel. I. Levy, Daniel. II. Weiss, Yfaat.

JV8033 .C48 2002
323.6'2'0943—dc21
                             2002018265

British Library Cataloguing in Publication Data

A catalogue record for this book is available from
the British Library.

Printed in the United States on acid-free paper

CONTENTS

ACKNOWLEDGMENTS

Both the idea for this book and half of its contributions are the results of an international conference, "Citizenship and Identity: German and Israeli Perspectives," held at Haifa University in March 2000. The conference was made possible by the generous help of the Heinrich Böll Foundation. Particular thanks are due to Claude Weinber, whose enthusiasm and ongoing support for the enterprise greatly contributed to its success. We would also like to thank Haifa University and, in particular, the Faculty of Humanities for their hospitality and organizational support. Yfaat Weiss is grateful for the financial support provided by the Zeit Foundation during the final stages of the editorial process. In 2001 the funding of the Bucerius Center for Research of Contemporary German History and Society at the University of Haifa facilitated the employment of Bea Schroettner, whose diligent work on all of the manuscripts vastly improved the quality of the book and deserves a special thanks. During the latter stages of the manuscript process, Martin Dobeš's assistance with transliterations and other editorial matters were of great value. The editors also want to express their appreciation to Dick Bruggeman, whose editorial and translation skills have made this book more accessible. Daniel Levy would like to express his gratitude to the Center for European Studies at Harvard University. His fellowship at the center during the 1999–2000 academic year provided a congenial environment in which to conceive of and work on this book. Many thanks are also due to his colleagues at Stony Brook, whose kind welcome and ongoing support have been an invaluable resource. We also wish to thank Berghahn Books for its outstanding professional assistance during all of the stages of this project. Last but not least, we wish to thank the contributors of this volume, who have made our editorial work as pleasurable as it could possibly be.

INTRODUCTION

Changing Configurations of German and Israeli
Immigration Regimes—a Comparative Perspective

Daniel Levy

Citizenship and immigration are valuable prisms through which to analyze conceptions of collective identification because they entail deeply ingrained cultural self-understandings of nationhood. To be sure, the claim is not that collective identities are fixed in time. Hence, combining the study of citizenship with that of migration alerts us to the malleability of identities. Changes in the relationship between, say, national majorities and minorities, are highly contingent on political and historical junctures challenging the prevailing assumptions about the boundaries of the collectivity. Not only does citizenship reveal how self-conceptions of nationhood are culturally inscribed; it also reflects the ways in which they are intertwined with institutional realities and political changes, and respond to migratory trends. In other words, debates about immigrants institutionalize the ways in which strangers are perceived. Conversely, they serve as a measure of how a society perceives itself. Citizenship legislation may thus be viewed as a pervasive system of classification, organizing society into "us" and "them." This distinction links the institutional dimension of citizenship to cultural perceptions of otherness. That is, almost by definition migration constitutes a challenge to one's own identity insofar as one perceives of migrants as "others." They do not belong to the same "ethnos." Conceptions of what it means to belong to a collective at times even exclude those who are formally considered to be citizens—some of the immigrants in our case studies are formally part of the ethnos and yet they are perceived as strangers.

Immigration is at the forefront of the current research agenda in the social sciences. However, this literature has largely focused on the incorporation of labor migrants. This book proposes to examine the issue of immigration from a different but no less salient angle, viz., immigrants who are formally part of the nation. Both Germany and Israel have descent-based conceptions of nationhood and have granted members of their nation (i.e., ethnic Germans and Jews) who wish to immigrate automatic access to their respective citizenship privileges. We look at the integration of these "privileged" immigrants and compare it with the experiences of other minority groups involved (e.g., labor migrants, Palestinians). Central themes in this volume hinge on three dimensions of citizenship: sovereignty and control; the allocation of social and political rights; and questions of national identification. Furthermore, the range of interdisciplinary research we have been able to bring together here allows us to approach these topics from a rewarding variety of perspectives. These include the historical developments of respective citizenship legislation and their immigration flows; the demographic changes in the size and composition of immigrant groups; the sociological problems these transformations have brought about; the anthropological givens upon which collective identities are negotiated; and the implications these processes carry for policy makers.

In most countries where differences surface in debates about citizenship and immigration, controversies are particularly strong where national self-understanding is based on ethnic conceptions. There are, of course, no pure models as all states consist of a mix of ethnic and civic components, but the proportions between the two can vary considerably. Globalization and the growing recognition of civic democratic values have strengthened the apparent tension between ethnic and civic claims. Countries with civic traditions, such as those of North America or France, may conduct debates about ethnicity, but have, for the most part, managed to rely on the assimilatory power of their institutions, even when, as in the United States, the latter have recently taken on a more multicultural character. On the other hand, countries with ethnic traditions, where institutional and cultural mechanisms to cope with heterogeneity are limited, face a more problematic situation when confronted with an increasingly heterogeneous population. Germany and Israel are two countries where tensions between ethnic (particularistic) and civic (universalistic) dimensions are part of their self-definition and an expression of their continuing search for shared identifications.

The national idioms of Germany and Israel conspicuously lack consensual codification, reflecting recurrent tensions between ethnic and civic understandings of nationhood. While collective understandings of the nation frequently arise before the consolidation of nation-states, this sequence was particularly notable in the German and Israeli cases. In its formative phase, the German concept of nation centered on the *Volk*, signifying organic relationships among a people rather than a political organization. This emphasis on cultural cohesion was a response to the fragmentation of the German states between 1815 and 1871. After the unification of Germany in 1871 a new, state-centered conception of nationhood was introduced. Ever since, German politics have been shaped by tensions between ethno-national and state-national conceptions—between the *Kulturnation* and the *Staatsnation*—which has led to shifting policies toward members of the German *Volk* resident in Eastern Europe. In Israel, a comparable tension arose with the founding of the Jewish state. Zionism's concept of Jewish nationality emerged within a broader debate about Jewish identity in the modern world. Influenced by Central European nationalist models, Zionist ideology selectively shaped a national myth from the materials of Jewish history, in order to affirm the claims of an ethnos to a territory, thus to establish statehood. Zionism's attempts to "nationalize" Judaism in ethnic-organicist terms produced competing claims about ethnic, religious and civic definitions of nationhood: secular Jewish nationality conflicts with religious understandings; and organicist views are in tension with civic-democratic understandings of the state.

The Federal Republic of Germany and the state of Israel share a considerable number of originating similarities. To begin with, they were officially established around the same time and both were the immediate product of the consequences of World War II. For both, the Holocaust constitutes a formative symbolic moment. From the outset, they were confronted with large waves of migration (initially mostly from Eastern Europe) brought about—in different measure—by persecution and expulsion. Their migration policies were shaped in the context of different conditions of war. For West Germany this meant the Cold War and the claim—following division and the ensuing conflict with East Germany—to be the legal successor state of the German nation. Israel's migration policy was shaped in the context of actual wars and the pursuit of demographic supremacy vis-à-vis the Arab citizens within its borders. Despite, or perhaps precisely because of, their ethno-cultural conceptions of citizenship, both countries have been eager to legitimize their policies democratically. In the Federal Republic this dynamic was largely determined in reference to the events of World War II. It justified restrictive descent-based citizenship conceptions by largely limiting the application of *ius sanguinis* to those it considered to be victims of expulsion or other measures of persecution. Furthermore, to "make good" for past atrocities in its treatment of minorities, Germany instituted liberal asylum provisions. Israel too was eager to underscore its democratic character, if only to ensure the support of the West vital for the formation of its nation-state. Like Germany, Israel ultimately justified its reliance on *ius sanguinis* conceptions of immigration by giving its Law of Return an ideological slant that (rhetorically) transformed all Jews into uprooted people whose true home, at least potentially, was the newly founded state of Israel.

The large migrations precipitated by the end of the Cold War resulted in public debates about immigration in Germany and Israel. As we saw, tensions between ethnic and civic conceptions are constitutive for the self-understanding of both countries, but are subject to change. Each country has passed through historical conjunctures in which these aspects of nationhood have come into conflict. German reunification in the context of European integration, and political settlements between

Israel and Arab countries, have challenged, reasserted or altered prevailing national understandings. In Germany, new vocabularies of identity have arisen. A strategy of strong alliances and engagement in the European Union goes hand in hand with a commitment to European identity, particularly among the younger generation. Emerging in competition with traditional understandings of nationhood, this new orientation has been further complicated by the ongoing antagonism between West and East Germans after unification. In Israel, the immediate effect of the post–Cold War era was an unprecedented massive influx of immigrants from the former Soviet Union (FSU). In the way it reset the parameters of the Arab-Israeli conflict, the temporary demise of the latter prompted a new political situation in the Middle East. According to some, the dominance of the ethnos is being challenged by more civic perspectives, with national priorities moving from military toward economic concerns (Shafir and Peled 1998). However, given the intractability of the Arab-Israeli conflict, the balance between ethnic and civic conceptions of society remains ever so fragile. Recent mass migration into Israel has not only worsened the relationship between Jews and Arabs, but also exacerbated ethnic tensions among the country's Jewish population, between Ashkenazim (who are of European origin) and Mizrahim (who are of North-African and Middle Eastern origins). This makes it imperative to keep the distinction between the "external borders" of the state and the "internal frontiers" of society in mind. Consequently, this volume traces the emergence of new relations among different immigrant groups (e.g., the relatively recent phenomenon of non-Palestinian labor migrants in Israel), the impact their presence has on debates about national citizenship (e.g., the introduction of partial *ius soli* in Germany) and their relationship to global processes (e.g., the significance of transnational ties).

"Uniqueness" and Other Myths Preventing Comparisons

These structural and historical similarities provide unusual opportunities for the analysis of a range of themes that are frequently treated in isolation. Despite the fact that both cases are well documented in the literature on immigration, they have rarely been situated in a comparative framework. It is instructive to take a brief look at the reasons for this, if only to underscore the advantages for juxtaposing German and Israeli incorporation regimes in a comparative context. To begin with, explicit comparisons between these two countries almost inevitably lead one into a politically and culturally charged terrain. This relates, of course, to the impact the memory of the Holocaust exerts in each country (Levy 1999). For example, there are constraints on discussing the impact the German tradition of romantic nationalism had on the articulation of Zionist ideas. There are similarities between the German and the Jewish imagination of nationhood that have to do with, among other things, the way Zionism historically has mimicked German nationalism. The absence of an explicit comparison of their respective immigration regimes is further explained by the fact that each case emphasizes uniqueness in terms of its distinctive diaspora, and claims incomparability for its ethnic migration. In the Israeli case, Zionist ideology perceives immigrants, not as people leaving one home for another, but as people "returning" to their historic homeland from a place where they had always been strangers. The same holds for ethnic Germans who are coming home (*in die Heimat*), even though they have never lived there. In both cases, the Zionist and *völkisch* definition of immigration, have long precluded the recognition of other groups as immigrants. In Germany this long found its expression in the recurrent insistence that "we are not a country of immigration," a trope that is beginning to fade. In Israel the immigration of non-Jews has only recently become a topic of public debate (and even then more as a problem of human rights rather than as one of citizenship rights).

To be sure, the political and cultural circumstances in which these debates about membership and immigration take place in our two cases differ considerably and we do not seek to flatten out these differences. However, as evidenced by the contributions to this volume, we find that a range of comparable features for many aspects of membership, boundary maintenance, changing conceptions of territoriality and nationhood come to the fore. To start with, their respective laws of return are legal-normative reactions to their historical "incompleteness" as nation-states: *ius sanguinis* (i.e., descent-based citizenship) comes in response to two interrelated aspects: one, a long condition of statelessness—in both cases, the nation concept is prepolitical insofar as it antedates the formation of the state; and two, dispersion—that is, not all members of the nation reside in the nation-state. Furthermore, not all citizens or residents (both de jure and de facto) belong to the same nation, that is, significant portions of the population are excluded from participating in the culturally dominant discourse of belonging. Consequently, they share a certain territorial ambiguity. The civil-ethnic dichotomy extends itself to normative and political conceptions. In the Israeli case it revolves around the distinction of *Medinat Israel* (the state of Israel) and *Eretz Israel* (the land of Israel), in the German context around the *Staatsnation* and the *Kulturnation*. Both are struggling with tensions between particularistic self-understandings (i.e., Jewish state and *deutsches Volk*) and universalistic (i.e., democratic) commitments. In both, the continuous significance of nationalism on the one hand, and the redrawing of boundaries, both territorial and imagined, on the other, point up a growing concern with the establishment and maintenance of collective identities. Germany's central role in the political process of consolidating a supranational Europe and the insecurities called up by the expansion of the EU, reveal a delicate balancing act. In Israel, postnational manifestations are largely confined to academic debates and public disputes pitting so-called post-Zionists against the prevalent assumptions of Jewish nationhood. Both countries are engaged in an ongoing search for normality. It does not really matter what this normality entails, it is the very search that is symptomatic of ongoing negotiations over the nature of the polity. And in both countries, following the end of the Cold War, migratory developments evoked debates about the original meanings citizenship has for their national self-understanding.

The Structure of the Book

In the first section, Rainer Münz and Yinon Cohen cover demographic developments in Germany and Israel between 1945 and the present. They address the shifting policies instigated in the two states vis-à-vis different groups of immigrants. Particular emphasis rests on the differential treatment of privileged immigrants (viz., Jews and ethnic Germans), homeland minorities (viz., Palestinians) and labor migrants. Both scholars explore how continuities and changes in citizenship laws and basic assumptions of nationhood are related to changes in migration flows and the growing number of nonethnic immigrants. Münz provides a comprehensive overview of immigration trends in the Federal Republic of Germany and the ways in which social scientists have studied them. He points to the apparent contradiction of Germany's self-proclaimed ethos of "not being a country of immigration" and the large-scale de-facto presence of immigrants. This tension is also reflected in the rather compartmentalized approach we find in the field of immigration studies where different groups (e.g., labor migrants and ethnic Germans) have, for the most part, been studied separately. The integrated analysis Münz provides highlights the changes in Germany's incorporation regimes. He "relates to the few attempts to look at migration as a whole, that is, to analyze the stocks and flows of expellees, ethnic Germans, and foreign immigrants alike and to look at the demographic and societal impacts." In addition, he introduces "the criterion 'place of birth' which is regularly used in U.S. research and statistics but so far is not common to the German research tradition." From this perspective a picture emerges that points to the increasing salience of immigration in utilitarian terms (e.g., to balance a low birth rate) and political changes pertaining to the criteria of citizenship and naturalization. As a member of the Federal Commission on Immigration Reform, Münz complements his analytic presentation with an insider's view on the policy formation process.

The importance immigration has retained for the Zionist project can hardly be exaggerated. As Cohen tells us, "by the end of 1999 nearly 40 percent of Israel's Jewish residents were immigrants (i.e., foreign-born), and over 70 percent were either immigrants or children of immigrants (i.e., second-generation immigrants)." While immigration is almost exclusively Jewish, he reminds us that demographic transformations have their origin in the period from 1947 to 1949, when about 750,000 indigenous

Palestinians were expelled from their homes and villages to make room for the Jewish state. According to Cohen, the demographic balance between Jews and Arabs is consolidated in the context of three main periods of immigration, each characterized by a corresponding set of motivations (refugees, economic and ideological), specific ethnic compositions (Jews from Europe, or Ashkenazim, from North Africa, or Mizrahim, and recently "Russians" from the FSU), and varying educational skills. With the recent influx of non-Arab, non-Jewish labor migrants and a growing proportion of immigrants from the FSU who are not Jewish, Israel faces new challenges to the Zionist ethos of a Jewish state that claims democratic commitments.

The second section traces the political circumstances under which German and Israeli citizenship laws originated and developed. Rather than viewing their respective citizenship legislations as inevitable products of national self-conceptions, Dieter Gosewinkel, Ralf Fücks and Yfaat Weiss illustrate how political, social, and cultural factors informed the original implementation and subsequent modifications of their respective codifications of citizenship. Through a study of changing naturalization practices, Gosewinkel shows how German citizenship evolved in conjunction with an increasingly exclusionary nationalism. He analyzes a broad time span covering the period from 1830 to the promulgation of the Basic Law in 1949. The inclusion and exclusion of Jews from Eastern Europe provides a special test case for the changing boundaries of German national identity in the period under investigation. Fücks extends the question of naturalization and integration to developments of citizenship laws in the Federal Republic. Pointing up the social and political conditions for the recent implementation of a new citizenship law, Fücks discusses recent legislative changes. He is particularly interested in the impact the new law has for the naturalization and incorporation of labor migrants who currently do not hold a German passport. Weiss explores the developments and debates surrounding Israel's Law of Return. This descent-based law constitutes the central mechanism for the reproduction of Israel's dominant Zionist ideology and the differential treatments of Jews and non-Jews. While Weiss recognizes the inequalities that inhere in Israel's citizenship legislation, she cautions us not to view the present situation as the inevitable outcome of the lawmakers' original intentions. She contends that the central incentive for the drafting of Israel's citizenship law was not so much the possibility it offered to insure a non-Arab majority, but was primarily guided by the formative geopolitical experiences of ethno-nationalism the Israeli lawmakers brought with them from Central and Eastern Europe.

The third section deals with the impact these legislative measures and the differential incorporation regimes have vis-à-vis minorities in Germany and Israel. Both countries have a perturbed relationship with respectively their non-German and non-Jewish minorities. In the German context this has, until recently, manifested itself in the refusal to grant

German citizenship to resident nonnative immigrants. The Israeli case is marred by similar shortcomings in its treatment of non-Jewish minorities. Generally speaking, the concept of immigration is confined to Jewish immigration. The Hebrew word commonly used for immigration reflects how ideologically charged the issue is in the context of the Zionist project. Rather than using the term *Hagira* (migration), researchers have long addressed issues of immigration and emigration in terms of *Alyia* (ascendance) and *Yerida* (descent), both terms carrying strong evaluative connotations. Most Israeli scholars have viewed their professional work as part of or even underpinning the Zionist nation-building project. Thus, they provided the scientific apparatus for an ideology that construed the immigration process in Israel as an "ingathering of exiles." Beholden to structural-functionalist modernization theories, they minimized problems of dislocation and conflict among new immigrants as temporary phenomenon that would subside once they had assimilated into the dominant (Western) culture (Shuval and Leshem 1998).

The research included here presents a shift in both empirical and conceptual focus and pays particular attention to the marginal treatment of immigrants, the allocation of social and political rights and the ongoing conflicts created by the quest for integration. The authors of this section challenge previous assumptions of assimilation, acculturation and the counterpart of failing integration. Instead they highlight the persistence of ethnic identities, the multiplicity of integrative arenas in the urban context, the institutional and political constraints of integration, and the formation of transnational forms of identification.

Gilad Margalit explores various state policies toward Sinti and Roma in Germany during the nineteenth and twentieth centuries, with particular emphasis on state practices and adaptation strategies in the Federal Republic. His historical overview underscores the arbitrary nature of citizenship legislation and the extent to which the implementation of these laws functions as a mechanism of social closure when applied to certain minorities. This historical background also helps explain the strategies that German Sinti have chosen to pursue their rights as citizens in the Federal Republic in light of ongoing discrimination. Margalit shows how the refusal to admit Sinti and Roma into the German collectivity has recently been mirrored by their efforts to cultivate their ethnic heritage. Questions of assimilation and related theories on the prospects of second-generation immigrants inform Levent Soysal's ethnographic study of Turkish youth in Berlin. In contrast to those who unquestionably accept the linear assumptions underlying assimilation theories (i.e., from tradition to modernity), Soysal challenges "the axiomatic acceptance of generational categories and the (implicit) contention of in-betweenness (cultural or otherwise) in studying and writing about migrant youths." He argues "that the generational categories hide, rather than reveal, the conditions, participation, and diverse cultural productions of migrant youths in their countries of residence by rendering their experience as an unceasing and unremitting journey 'in between' tradition and modernity." Soysal's thick description of youth experience provides a multicultural perspective, as envisioned by a minority group, rather than the frequently misleading assumptions that inform the deployment of multiculturalism by the majority group.

Similar nonlinear assumptions inform most of the studies of immigration in Israel. The ideological focus on Jewish immigrants has recently been challenged by the phenomenon of large-scale labor migration. Along with the rise of a new generation of ideologically more detached scholars, there has been growing attention to non-Jewish migrants and the emerging phenomenon of labor migrants, in particular. Zeev Rosenhek is among the early voices in this emerging field. He examines the politics of exclusion and inclusion of migrant workers in the Israeli welfare state. His findings underscore the restrictive character and the exclusionary practices of the Israeli migration regime toward non-Jews. At the same time, he indicates that some state agencies at the local (municipal) level, endorse more inclusionary policies, usually in pursuit of organizational interests of their own. Rosenhek's institutional approach yields important empirical and conceptual insights about the partial inclusion of migrant workers in the welfare state.

Questions of assimilation also loom large in the rapidly growing field of studying immigration from the FSU, which now constitutes almost 20 percent of the population in Israel. In contrast to the Soviet immigrants of the 1970s, the arrivals of the last decade have been portrayed as less willing to integrate into Israeli society. This is commonly inferred from their desire to retain their ethnic culture through a variety of cultural and educational institutions, and from their persistence in maintaining ties with their countries of origin (Leshem and Lissak 1999). For some scholars these transformations challenge the basic assumptions about immigration in Israeli society and they speak about a "separatist phenomenon" (Shuval 1998: 33). Dimitry Schumsky's insightful analysis of the organizational structures of Jews from the FSU and the dominant tropes in the Russian-language press directs our attention to a complex situation in which ethnic retention and integration are not mutually exclusive processes. He shows how the awareness of ethnic traits among these immigrants actually facilitates their participation in the Israeli collective. Contrary to notions that this group of immigrants harbors merely sectoral interests, Schumsky points to the fact that their preconceived notions of minority-majority relations (the product of a highly developed nationality discourse and their own minority status in the Soviet Union) inform their self-perception as defenders of traditional Zionist values. His analysis points to their gradual movement into the mainstream of Israeli society and politics.

The fourth section situates the findings of the preceding chapters within a broader debate about the relationship of citizenship, membership, and related aspects of national identification. The focus here is on the negotiation of boundaries of belonging within the context of an increasing pluralization of group identifications. Rogers Brubaker (1992) has highlighted the close connection between citizenship and questions of national belonging. Attempts to change citizenship regulations and the conditions for immigrants problematize questions of collective identification and national belonging. This explains, among other things, why recent changes to Germany's citizenship legislation have caused so many heated political debates. Conversely, it also explains how Israel's citizenship legislation has remained largely intact, and why the extent of occasional debates remains confined to the provision of "Who is a Jew," rather than the general premises upon which the Law of Return is based. Overall then, questions of national self-understanding are framed in a tense relationship of ethnic and civic dimensions of citizenship.

Baruch Kimmerling elucidates these tensions between civic and primordial ties by analyzing a debate between two intellectuals, both Israeli citizens, one Jewish, the other Palestinian. The former ultimately insists on the exclusive Jewish character of the state, while the latter demands equal shares for his local Arabness, under a reshaped universal Israeli nationality based on civic rather than ethnic criteria. Underlying this debate, which took place in 1985, is another tension, namely, that between group and individual rights. The Palestinian challenges the view that these are mutually exclusive categories. Instead, he advances the view that "citizenship can be shaped and reshaped by an interaction between the individual (as a part of a community) and the community (that makes individuals)." On this view, rights accrue not merely to individuals but also to members of minority communities.

Hassan Jabareen elaborates on this tension. He focuses on the legal system and the continuous deployment of a dominant Zionist-Jewish discourse, which predicates the acceptance of individual Arab citizens on the negation of their shared Palestinian self-understanding as a nation. Through a close reading of various recent legal cases, Jabareen shows how the duality between Israel as a Jewish state and its claims to be democratic is suspended by denying Palestinians their status as a national minority. Drawing comparatively on the theoretical literature of polyethnic states, he illustrates how juridical narratives treat Palestinian citizens as an ethnic minority rather than as a homeland minority. Formal equality on the individual level does not challenge the dominant assumptions of the Jewish state. But, he poignantly concludes, this equality only applies if Palestinian citizens subscribe to the same dominant assumptions of the state's Jewishness, which leads to their experiencing discrimination in the first place.

A comparable tension between ethnos and demos also informs Daniel Levy's chapter on changing perceptions and policies toward ethnic German immigrants from East and Central Europe. Levy examines the transformation of Germany's ethno-cultural self-understanding in the Federal Republic, with a particular focus on post–Cold War developments. Rather than serving as a vestige of an ethno-cultural past, the author suggests that recent representations of ethnic German immigrants reflect and reinforce a political and cultural shift to a more pluralistic conception.

The last section of this volume seeks to overcome the nation-centric focus that has dominated the discourse on citizenship during much of the nineteenth and twentieth centuries. At the beginning of the twenty-first century, issues of transnational migration and the growing recognition that homogeneous nations are giving way to multicultural societies have raised new conceptualizations of citizenship (see, for example, Soysal 1994; Kymlicka 1995). By that we do not imply that the nation-state model is no longer relevant, but rather that its previously exclusive and dominant status is being challenged by competing visions of the "good society." This process forms the backdrop for Diana Pinto's and Natan Sznaider's attempts to explore the potentialities of new forms of citizenship in Germany and Israel. Pinto discusses the recent emergence of a European Jewish space that transcends the conventional assumptions about the nation-state. While her main focus is on the developments within Jewish communities of Europe, her assessments also bear on the formation of Europeanness in general. In this view, the Jewish experience in Europe becomes paradigmatic for a broader transnational conception of citizenship. According to Pinto, the Jewish experience is central to a "future oriented role ... in a continent coming to grips with democratic, pluralist and multicultural challenges." Sznaider also proposes an alternative conception of citizenship, one that relies no longer on the nation-binding powers of wars, but instead on market-binding forces of indifference and consumption. The ideological imperative of the "nation in arms" is here replaced through the formation of a sociological habitus based on consumption. Sznaider explores the historical and ideological origins of this transformation by juxtaposing two ideal types: the warrior and the consumer. His analysis carries valuable interpretive and political implications. More importantly perhaps, it provides an additional perspective on the social and cultural destructiveness that accompanies the ongoing conflict between Jews and Arabs.

Based on the interdisciplinary texture of these findings, the concluding essay of this book seeks to provide an overview of new conceptualizations of citizenship and emerging immigration trends, with a particular focus on the conditions of possibility as they manifest themselves in Germany and Israel respectively. At stake are ideological constellations, institutional circumstances, and the transformation or reproduction of specific geopolitical conditions.

References

Brubaker, Rogers. 1992. *Citizenship and Nationhood in France and Germany.* Cambridge, Mass.: Harvard University Press.

Kymlicka, Will. 1995. *Multicultural Citizenship: A Liberal Theory of Minority Rights.* Oxford: Clarendon Press.

Leshem, Elazar, and Moshe Lissak. 1999. "Development and Consolidation of the Russian Community in Israel." In *Roots and Routes: Ethnicity and Migration in Global Perspective,* ed. S. Weil, 135–171. Jerusalem: The Magnes Press.

Levy, Daniel. 1999. "The Future of the Past: Historiographical Disputes and Competing Memories in Germany and Israel." *History and Theory* 38 (1): 51–66.

Shafir, Gershon, and Yoav Peled. 1999. "The Dynamics of Citizenship in Israel and the Israeli-Palestinian Peace Process." In *The Citizenship Debates: A Reader*, ed. Gershon Shafir, 251–262. Minneapolis: University of Minnesota Press.

Shuval, Judith T., and Elazar Leshem. 1998. "The Sociology of Migration in Israel: A Critical View." In *Immigration to Israel: Sociological Perspectives,* ed. Elazar Leshem and J. T. Shuval, 3–50. New Brunswick: Transaction Publishers.

Soysal, Yasemin N. 1994. *Limits of Citizenship: Migrants and Postnational Membership in Europe.* Chicago: University of Chicago Press.

PART ONE

CITIZENSHIP AND MIGRATION

Chapter 1

ETHNOS OR DEMOS?

Migration and Citizenship in Germany

Rainer Münz

Introduction

In Germany, as in many other European democracies, immigration and citizenship are contested and contentious issues. In the German case it was both the magnitude of postwar and recent immigration as well as its interference with questions of identity that created political and social conflict. As a result of World War II, the coexistence of two German states, and the persistence of ethnic German minorities in Central and Eastern Europe, (West) Germany's migration and naturalization policy was inclusive toward expellees, citizens of the German Democratic Republic (GDR), and co-ethnics. At the same time, despite the recruitment of several million foreign labor migrants and—until 1992—a relatively liberal asylum practice, the Federal Republic of Germany did not develop similar mechanisms and policies of absorption and integration of its legal foreign residents. The late 1980s and 1990s first saw a rise in the number of ethnic German and foreign immigrants, then growing skepticism and even hostility toward immigrants. The political answer to this was the implementation of measures restricting the inflow of ethnic Germans, asylum seekers and some other categories of foreigners, and the reduction of their access to both the labor market and public benefits. At the same time, several attempts were made to liberalize naturalization procedures and to install a more inclusive citizenship law in spite of serious opposition from the conservative part of the political spectrum. The most important change was the introduction of a new citizenship law in the summer of 1999 by the SPD/Green government. What remains unresolved is the politically and economically marginal position of the majority of foreign immigrants from Mediterranean countries and also of those ethnic Germans who came during the 1990s from Russia and Kazakhstan.

Since World War II, Germany has received substantial numbers of foreign and ethnic-German immigrants. Over the last few years, immigration has declined, and in 1997 and 1998 there were more foreigners emigrating than immigrating. A considerable part of the German public still perceives immigration more as a burden than as an enrichment for the country and is afraid of a lack of control over immigration. In recent years, however, the focus of the debate has shifted more to demographic aging, to the foreseeable shrinking of Germany's population, the sustainability of the public pension system and the shortage of highly skilled labor. In this context, a growing number of people see immigration as a possible solution rather than as a problem. There is a growing consensus among Germany's political and economic elites that the country has to prepare for a new migration regime.

Research Traditions

In the past, German research on migration and integration has mainly used immigrants' nationality as a point of orientation. In the 1950s the field was dominated by research on ethnic German expellees (that is, German citizens originating from former German territory annexed to Poland, and the Soviet Union; and noncitizens expelled by Poland, Czechoslovakia, Hungary, and Yugoslavia). In addition to analyzing the history, the circumstances of expulsion, and the contemporary life of this group, there was also an underlying attempt to demonstrate that this group had experienced a grave injustice (Lemberg and Edding 1959). In contrast, the life, biographies, and contemporary living conditions of Jewish emigrants expelled during the Nazi era, of former forced laborers, survivors of concentration camps, and other "displaced persons" were not themes of social science research in postwar Germany.

In the 1960s and early 1970s, research on "guest workers" started both in Germany and Switzerland.[1] In contrast to the postwar migrants, labor migrants from the Mediterranean were portrayed as a problematic group. The phrases "guest worker problem" or "guest worker question" were generally used to refer to migration-related political and social problems in the receiving countries, and not to the difficulties and constraints of the migrants themselves.

From the early 1980s until approximately 1988 there was little political discussion about immigration to Germany and the social integration of immigrants. Neither continuing chain migration through family reunion nor the existence of a "second generation" of migrants received much attention in the public sphere. Consequently, research during that time concentrated less on the current socioeconomic situation of migrants, and more on the history of migration from and to Germany (Bade 1984; Dohse 1981; Herbert 1986; Heyden 1986; Luettinger 1986). The focus of research has changed dramatically since 1988–89. The ongoing debate on the consequences of immigration is a direct result of the dramatic changes in Central and Eastern Europe, and their impact on massive out-migration from this region (Fassmann and Münz 1994). It is also a result of massive refugee flows caused by the wars and forced expulsions in Bosnia, Croatia, and Serbia (including Kosovo). Suddenly, the question of asylum seekers, refugees, and temporary protection was pushed to the forefront of the agenda (Blahusch 1994; Morokvasic 1993; Münch 1993).

Political scientists also began to discuss and analyze several aspects of international migration. Facing a manifest increased demand for control, questions concerning possible state actions to limit immigration were and are increasingly being pushed onto the agenda at both the national and European levels (Hailbronner, Martin and Motomura 1998a; 1998b; Klos 1998; Santel 1995). Some authors increasingly portrayed migration as a problem of national and international security (Angenendt 1997a; 1997b; Münz and Myron 1997; Widgren 1990).

There has been an interest in the North American debate on multiculturalism since the 1980s. Some expected that Germany would be enriched by more "diversity" (Leggewie 1990). For some authors, foreign migrants and their children were no longer viewed as migrants, but as members of ethno-cultural minorities in Germany (Heckmann 1992; Schmalz-Jacobsen and Hansen 1995). Others pointed to the growing social and economic integration of labor migrants and their children (Seifert 1995; Herrmann 1993; Boos-Nünning 1990). Certainly, though, there were also a few increasingly skeptical voices that pointed to a continuing marginalization and (self)isolation of the foreign population, especially the so-called "second generation" (Grüner 1992; Kurthen and Fijalkowski 1989). Some even identified a considerable potential for conflict and inter-ethnic violence (Heitmeyer 1996). In addition, the 1990s saw the introduction of research on ethnic German migrants (that is, *Aussiedler*) (Bals 1994; Beer 1991; D. Blaschke 1991; J. Blaschke 1991; Heinelt and Lohmann 1992; Koller 1993; Dietz and Hilkes 1994; Sterbling 1994; Münz and Ohliger 1998). Ultimately, Jewish immigration from the former Soviet Union (Schoeps 1996) and the increasing mobility of highly qualified workers also received some attention (Hillmann and Rudolph 1996). Since the 1980s, interest in the topic of migration has also increased among economists studying the positive and negative effects of immigration (Hof 1989; Steinmann and Ulrich 1994; Zimmermann 1992; Ulrich 1994); the impact of immigration on the labor market (Zimmermann 1998; Reyher and Bach 1989; Velling 1994); the financing of social security (Dinkel and Lebok 1994; Sprink and Hellmann 1989); and the demand for welfare benefits (Ulrich 1994).

Interestingly, the various traditions of German migration research mentioned above overlapped only minimally. Interactions remained an exception both at the theoretical as well as at the empirical level. In research on labor migrants ("guest workers"), almost no attention has been paid to the research done on expellees. The research on foreigners of the 1990s owes very little to the research on "guest workers" of the 1960s and 1970s, and neither has had much influence on the analysis of immigration and the lack of integration of ethnic German *Aussiedler*. The main reason for this is the general reluctance (even in scientific analysis) to put expellees and ethnic Germans from Central and Eastern Europe on an equal footing with foreign migrants. Therefore, comparing the two groups either did not come to mind or appeared to be politically incorrect as long as expellees and ethnic German *Aussiedler* successfully claimed not to be "immigrants" at all while foreign immigrants and their children were portrayed in many instances as being of "transitory" status to German economy and society (compare the terms *Gastarbeiter* and *Asylanten*). The sole exception to this are the works of Bade (1992; 1994), Bethlehem (1982), and Gugel (1990), as well as a study by the ministry of employment, health and social services of North Rhine-Westphalia (Ministerium für Arbeit 1992).

The research summarized in this article relates to the few attempts to look at migration as a whole, that is, to analyze the ebbs and flows of expellees, ethnic Germans, and foreign immigrants alike and to look at the demographic and societal impacts. Furthermore, we have tried to introduce the criterion "place of birth" which is regularly used in U.S. research and statistics but so far is not common in the German research tradition. The main criterion used by German administration and reflected in the available statistical information is citizenship, not place of birth. This has to do with the fact that Germany does not view itself as an immigration country. Both the political and administrative apparatuses, as well as most researchers in Germany, use the criterion of nationality as their main point of orientation. This same criterion of citizenship is used in official statistics. National and other statistics provide information about the German and foreign populations in Germany according to age, sex, marital status, and birth rate. But no information can be found about place or country of birth for either Germans or non-Germans. Using nationality as a central defining criterion increases the tendency to see non-Germans, regardless of their place of birth, as the "true immigrants," whereas ethnic Germans from Central and Eastern Europe (*Aussiedler*) are not readily identified as such. Our attempt to reverse this research tradition not only has scientific implications (for example, making German data comparable to U.S. and Canadian data), but also could influence the general debate on immigration by making clear that a considerable number of Germany's citizens are foreign-born while many of its legal foreign residents are German-born.

Germans and Foreigners, Immigrants and German-Born

In 1999 Germany had 82 million inhabitants: 74.7 million were German citizens, including those holding dual citizenship, and 7.3 million residents did not have German citizenship. The share of the foreign nationals was therefore just below 9 percent of the total population. Of the German citizens, at least 2.2 million people hold a second citizenship (2.7 percent of the population).[2]

The status of "foreigner" does not automatically mean that the person in question has immigrated to Germany, although this is now generally the case. In 1999 of the 7.3 million foreigners in Germany, approximately 5.8 million were foreign-born and therefore immigrants. Nevertheless, 1.5 million foreigners were born in Germany as the children (or grandchildren) of immigrants, but because of prevailing *ius sanguinis* (based on descent) citizenship (until 1999) they hold only the nationality of their parents. Therefore, only 79 percent of the foreign population in Germany are immigrants. The other 21 percent are German-born.

In contrast, most German citizens were born in Germany, but there are also German immigrants; the largest group is people who once belonged to ethnic German minorities (*Volksdeutsche*) in Central and Eastern Europe, and who have come to Germany as *Aussiedler* since the 1950s. *Aussiedler* automatically acquire German citizenship upon immigration to Germany. Approximately 3.2 million *Aussiedler* currently live in Germany (3.9 percent of the total population). In addition, some 800,000 legal foreign residents have become naturalized German citizens over the past three decades.[3]

Finally, Germany has a unique feature associated with population relocations during the Nazi period,[4] the change in borders after 1945, and the escape and expulsion of ethnic Germans (*Ostdeutsche* and *Volksdeutsche*) between 1944 and 1948–49. The approximately 625,000 to 650,000 people (*Umsiedler*) who were relocated under the auspices of ethnic "return" programs organized by Nazi Germany (*Heim-ins-Reich*) all came from what was then and is now foreign territory, among them 525,000 to 550,000 from East Central and Eastern Europe. In addition, approximately 55 percent of the 12 million expellees from that period originally came from Germany's former eastern provinces.[5] Their place of birth lay within the 1937 prewar borders of the German Reich. Today these places belong to either Poland or Russia (Kaliningrad).

Some 40 percent of the expellees were citizens of other countries (at least prior to 1938–39) or stateless persons who had ethnic German origins (*Volksdeutsche*). They originally came from regions that, at least before 1938, had not belonged to Germany. Their place of birth lay both then and today in foreign territory (that is, former Yugoslavia, Poland including Danzig, former Czechoslovakia, Hungary, and to a small extent also Romania). Another 525,000 people originally came from these regions and from the former Eastern provinces, but were already living in 1945 in Germany within its present-day borders or had become prisoners of war (POWs). They could not return to their regions of origin and were also considered expellees in postwar Germany (5 percent of all expellees). Although their migration was forced rather than voluntary, in a wider sense of the term these people can be considered to be immigrants. It is estimated that in the late 1990s approximately 3.6 million of the 1944–49 expellees and refugees from the East (*Vertriebene*) as well as 170,000 of the displaced ethnic Germans (the *Umsiedler* of 1939–44) were still alive and living in Germany.[6]

TABLE 1.1 German Expellees (1944 to 1948–49) by Country of Origin and Area of Residence after the Expulsion; Transferred Ethnic Germans (1939 to 1944) by Country of Origin

Country	Expellees Total	(1944–49) percent	West Germany	East Germany with Berlin	Austria and Other Western Countries	Transferred Ethnic Germans 1939–1944[1]
	in 1,000s	percent	in 1,000s	in 1,000s	in 1,000s	in 1,000s
Former German territories	6,980	55.8	4,380	2,600	–	–
Poland (with Danzig)	980	7.8	630	335	15	150
Czechoslovakia	3,000	24.0	1,900	850	250	–
Soviet Union (with the Baltics)[2]	270	2.2	180	55	10	1,555
Hungary	210	1.7	175	10	25	–
Romania	250	2.0	145	60	45	200
Yugoslavia	300	2.4	150	35	115	35
Italy	–	–	–	–	–	100
Subtotal	11,990	95.8	7,560	3,945	460	2,040
Quasi-expellees[3]	525	4.2	385	125	15	–
Total	12,515	100.0	7.945	4,070	475	2,040

[1]Some 625,000 to 650,000 ethnic Germans were transferred in 1939–44 to Germany; another 1.4 million were internally deported to the Asian part of the USSR.

[2]From 1939 to 1942 some 130,000 ethnic Germans from the Baltics and a relatively small number of Germans from the Crimean peninsula and from the Caucasus were transferred to Germany.

[3]Quasi-expellees are persons originating from territories where the expulsion took place, but who themselves in 1945 already lived in Germany (within its present-day borders) or had become POWs.

Sources: Data from Wolfgang Benz, ed., *Die Vertreibung der Deutschen aus dem Osten: Ursachen, Ereignisse, Folgen* (Frankfurt, 1995); Rainer Münz, "Deutschland und die Ost-West-Wanderung," in *Ost-West-Wanderung in Europa*, ed. Heinz Fassmann and Rainer Münz (Vienna/Cologne/Weimar, 2000), 49-82; Gerhard Reichling, *Die Deutschen Vertriebenen in Zahlen*, vol. 1: *Umsiedler, Verschleppte, Vertriebene, Aussiedler* (Bonn, 1986).

When one adds up all these groups (*Aussiedler*, naturalized foreign migrants, and those expellees and displaced ethnic Germans, that is, *Vertriebene* and *Umsiedler* who are still alive) then 9.6 percent of the German citizens living in Germany (7.2 million people) immigrated from what today is foreign territory. Of them, five million were born outside both today's and former German territories (6.7 percent of all German citizens) and some 2.2 million in former German territories annexed to Poland and Russia (2.9 percent of all German citizens).

In sum, this analysis shows that in 1999 approximately 13.3 million inhabitants of Germany (16.2 percent of the population) were born outside the borders of today's Germany. Naturally, not all of these people would consider themselves to be immigrants. Most expellees and post-war refugees of the years 1945 to 1948 would probably reject this categorization even though the fate of forced migration has shaped their lives and identities in many ways. Only some 40 percent of them, however, were de facto born in a third country. In any case, *Aussiedler* as well as naturalized citizens and foreigners born outside of Germany can certainly all be counted as immigrants. All together these three groups consisted of 9.6 million people or 11.7 percent of the population of Germany in 1998. If expellees born in a third country are included, the foreign-born population, at the end of the 1990s, reached 10.9 million or 13.3 percent of the total population.

Immigration of Foreigners to Germany

Even prior to World War II, there were phases of increased immigration of laborers from other European countries. The 1910 census counted 1.3 million foreigners in Germany. Of this group, 50 percent were Austrian citizens (mainly from Bohemia, Moravia, and Galicia), 11 percent were Dutch and 11 percent were citizens of Czarist Russia (mainly from the Russian parts of Poland and the Baltics). Migration from neighboring countries also took place during the interwar period. Of the one million foreigners in 1925, 27 percent came originally from Poland, 23 percent from Czechoslovakia and 14 percent from Austria (Münz, Seifert and Ulrich 1999).

During World War II, the German war economy could to a considerable extent only be maintained through the employment of foreign workers and forced laborers (Bade 1992; 2000; Dohse 1981). By 1944–45 the number of foreigners who had been forced to work in Germany had risen to almost eight million (Herbert 1986). In addition to this group of foreigners, there were also the prisoners of war and the survivors of concentration camps. The majority of these foreigners, either voluntarily returned or were forcibly returned to their homelands in 1945 and 1946 (Fassmann and Münz 1994; 2000).[7] Others emigrated to Israel or overseas. Only a few remained as displaced persons in Germany. At the same time, return migration of Jewish and other emigrants who had left the country during the years 1933 to 1940 was very low.

In the first years after World War II, the shortage of housing and high unemployment rates made the economic and social integration of expellees and war returnees difficult. However, with the start of the unprecedented economic growth (the "economic miracle"), the demand for labor grew sharply in the 1950s. Unemployment quickly fell, and both expellees and citizens of the GDR, who had migrated to West Germany, were integrated in large numbers into the West German economy (Luettinger 1986).

Despite the large number of expellees and the annual immigration of 200,000 to 300,000 GDR citizens, by the 1950s some sectors of the West German economy were already not able to satisfy their demands for workers in the domestic labor market. West German industry thus began to recruit workers in Southern Europe (Fassmann and Münz 2000a).[8] In

TABLE 1.2 Germany's Population According to Place of Birth and National Citizenship (estimates for 1999)

Citizenship	Place of Birth			Population (in millions)
	Germany	German territory at time of birth; foreign territory today	Foreign territory both now and in the past	
German citizenship only	Majority of Germans (with place of birth inside today's borders of Germany) Naturalized children of foreign migrants (who have relinquished their original citizenship)	The majority of expellees (people born as German citizens with place of birth in the German Reich's 1937 borders)	Ethnic German expellees (*Volksdeutsche* with place of birth outside the German Reich's 1937 borders) Displaced ethnic Germans of the period 1939 to 1943 (*Umsiedler* with place of birth outside the borders of the German Reich) Ethnic German immigrants from Central and Eastern Europe (*Aussiedler* who have come between 1950 and 1989 and who had to relinquish their original citizenship) Naturalized foreign immigrants (who have relinquished their original citizenship)	72.5
German and a second citizenship (dual citizenship)[1]	Germans by birth with one non-German parent Naturalized children of foreign immigrants (who were naturalized with toleration of dual citizenship) Naturalized children of foreign immigrants (who were naturalized after having reacquired their original citizenship)		Ethnic German immigrants from Central and Eastern Europe (*Aussiedler* who have come since 1989–90 and who have retained or reacquired their original citizenship) Naturalized foreign immigrants (who were naturalized with toleration of dual citizenship) Naturalized foreign immigrants (who have reacquired their original citizenship)	2.2
Solely foreign citizenship	Children and grandchildren of foreign immigrants (with place of birth inside today's borders of Germany)		The majority of foreign immigrants (with place of birth in their country of origin)	7.3
Total (in millions)	68.7	2.2	11.1	82.0

[1]Since the year 2000, Germans with *ius soli* citizenship (i.e., German-born children with foreign parents and at least one parent who has been a legal foreign resident for eight or more years) also fall into this category.

Source: Author's estimates.

1955 the Federal Republic of Germany concluded a bilateral agreement with Italy, and in the 1960s, in short succession, with Spain (1960), Greece (1960), Turkey (1961), Morocco (1963), Portugal (1964), Tunisia (1965), and Yugoslavia (1968) (Münz, Seifert and Ulrich 1999).

At first these agreements were of little relevance. During Germany's "economic miracle" of the 1950s, employment expanded initially through a decrease in unemployment rates and through the integration of ex-GDR citizens. In 1950 there were only approximately 72,000 foreign workers in Germany. In 1960 there were 329,000, and almost half were Italians (144,000). Only after the construction of the Berlin Wall was there a noticeable increase in the employment of foreigners as the West German economy stepped up the recruitment of foreign workers. By 1964 we saw the arrival of the one millionth guest worker, a Portuguese national, and he received a warm and widely publicized welcome. In addition to Italy (296,000), Greece (155,000) and Spain (151,000) also became important countries of recruitment. By the end of 1964, the total number of foreigners in Germany was around 1.2 million (2.1 percent of the total population). By 1970 the number of foreigners had reached three million (5 percent of the total West German population). In 1973 almost four million foreigners lived in West Germany (7 percent of the population).

The aim of recruitment was not the formulation of a coherent migration policy similar to the French or American model, but rather to counterbalance the bottlenecks in the West German labor market created by a conjuncture of both economic and demographic trends. Foreigners were recruited for particular work places and brought to Germany on a temporary basis. This policy explains the high annual level of immigration and return migration in the 1960s and early 1970s (see fig. 1.1).

FIGURE 1.1 Migration of Foreigners to and from Germany, 1955–1999 (in thousands)

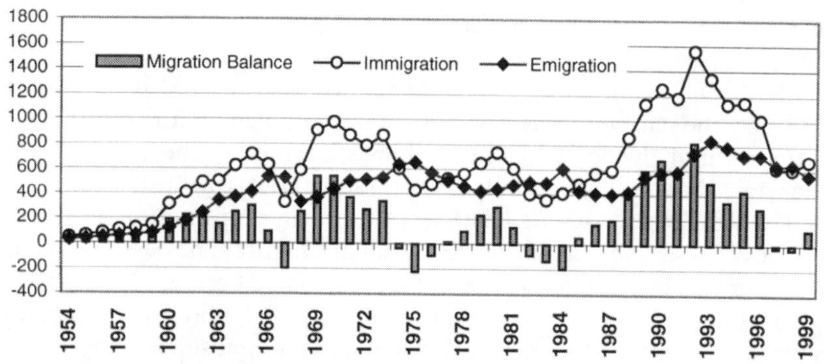

Note: Emigration includes return migration. Until 1991, immigration to and emigration from West Germany only.

Source: Statistisches Bundesamt.

The year 1973 became a drastic turning point in the migration of foreigners to Germany. The German government first tripled the fees that employers had to pay for the recruitment of guest workers. After the OPEC oil embargo, the West German government ended the recruitment of foreigners in October 1973.

The recruitment stop did limit migration in the short term, but in the medium term it did not produce the desired results. In some cases, the measures produced some completely unintended consequences. This is especially true with regard to both the structure of immigration and its dependence on economic cycles (Höhn and Rein 1990).

During the recession of 1974 and 1975 there was once again a decrease in immigration and a slight increase in return migration. But already by 1976 the level of immigration began to increase, and return migration decreased.

In 1980, 4.5 million foreigners lived in Germany (7 percent of the population). There were 2.1 million foreign workers; most numerous were those from Turkey (592,000), Yugoslavia (357,000), and Italy (309,000). In the following years, the number of foreigners declined only slightly, despite the recession of the early 1980s (in 1985 there were 4.4 million foreigners), although the number of foreign workers sank significantly (in 1985 there were 1.6 million). In this period (1983–84) the German government attempted to promote the return migration of labor migrants by offering financial incentives.

A new wave of immigration set in after 1987, spurred by a rising number of asylum seekers, the fall of the Iron Curtain, war and ethnic cleansing in former Yugoslavia, and the growing violence in Kurdish regions of Turkey and northern Iraq. For these reasons, the bulk of migration was for a time shifted from labor migration and family reunion to asylum seekers. At the beginning of the 1970s, the portion of those seeking asylum was less than 1 percent of total foreign migration to Germany. By the beginning of the 1990s, its share had risen to more than 30 percent. The wave of arriving asylum seekers reached its peak in 1992: during that single year 438,200 people, 63 percent of all asylum seekers in Western Europe, applied for asylum in Germany.

After the annual number of asylum applicants surpassed 100,000 in the late 1980s, the nature of this migration and the potential for controlling it became central themes in German domestic politics. The result of this debate was the so-called Asylum Compromise of 1993 (Blahusch 1994; Bade 1994), which created two new barriers to applying for political asylum in Germany. These restrictions were the result of a highly controversial change in the German constitution (*Grundgesetz*) negotiated between the then-ruling coalition of Christian Conservatives (CDU/CSU) and Free Democrats (FDP), and the Social Democrats (SPD), the main opposition party of that period. The change abolished the unconditional access to formal asylum procedures. First, asylum seekers who traveled to Germany from other EU member states or other "safe third states" could be sent back immediately and without a court hearing. Second, a simplified asylum procedure was instated for applicants from countries that were considered to be "free of persecution,"[9] which in most cases meant an immediate rejection of the application and possible deportation. During the 1990s, most European countries have introduced similar restrictions. And the EU member countries have agreed to gradually harmonize their asylum regulations and some aspects of their systems of migration control.[10]

The change in the German constitution and the more restrictive practices obviously had the desired effect: the number of asylum applications was already down by the second half of 1993. Whereas 224,000 asylum seekers had come to Germany in the first half of 1993, only 98,000 asylum applications were registered in the second half of the year. In 2000 only 78,000 people applied for asylum, less than 10 percent of that year's total immigration.

The conflicts in former Yugoslavia, in southeastern Turkey, and in northern Iraq were not only reflected in the statistics on asylum applications; in the case of Turkey and former Yugoslavia, the conflicts also prompted a larger number of legal foreign residents of both countries to bring more of their family members to Germany.

Economic growth during the late 1980s, the short economic boom of 1990 to 1991 resulting from German unification, and emigration incentives in the originating countries all led to the recruitment of new foreign workers. It is within this context that new groups of foreign workers appeared in Germany. These workers came primarily from Poland and the Czech Republic, but also from other Eastern European states, and included people with a limited employment contract, seasonal workers (that is, harvesters), cross-border commuters, and those who came (and come) to Germany explicitly for professional training. New possibilities for legal migration and temporary employment were created for Central and Eastern European seasonal workers, contract labor, guest workers or cross-border commuters (Hönekopp 1997; Münz 2000; Velling 1994). Most of these programs are seen as a means to stabilize Germany's eastern neighbors by creating additional income for their citizens and by transferring skills. In any case, during the 1990s, remittances of Central and Eastern European labor migrants temporarily working in Germany exceeded direct foreign investment.

The late 1990s again reversed the migration pattern. Both in 1997 and in 1998 the number of foreigners emigrating or returning from Germany exceeded the number of foreign immigrants for the first time since 1984. In 1964 one million foreigners lived in Germany; in early 2000 the number of foreigners was already 7.3 million. Between 1954 and 1999, a total of 25.3 million foreigners migrated to the Federal Republic of Germany. Approximately 18.6 million foreigners left Germany during this period. The resulting migration balance is a net gain of 6.7 million people since the mid-1950s. By subtracting the number of naturalized citizens[11] and the number of deaths, this is the foreign-born foreign population of Germany (in 1999 this was 5.8 million people). Some 1.5 million foreigners living in Germany are born in the country.

TABLE 1.3 Migration between Germany and Other Countries, 1954–1999 (in thousands)

	Immigration			Emigration/Return Migration			Migration Balance		
	Total	German	Foreign	Total	German	Foreign	Total	German	Foreign
1954–1961	1.923	633.000	1.290	1.440	818.000	622.000	483.000	-185.000	668.000
1962–1973	9.137	830.000	8.307	5.953	832.000	5.121	3.184	-2.000	3.186
1943–1987	7.389	1.266	6.124	6.968	795.000	6.172	421.000	471.000	-49.000
1988–1991	4.450	1.274	3.176	2.130	370.000	1.760	2.320	904.000	1.416
1992–1999	8.435	2.061	6.374	5.853	940.000	4.913	2.582	1.121	1.461
1954–1999	**31.334**	**6.064**	**25.271**	**22.344**	**3.755**	**18.589**	**8.990**	**2.309**	**6.682**

Note: "German" includes ethnic Germans (*Aussiedler*). "Foreign" includes asylum seekers and Bosnians with temporary protection (TPS).
Sources: Statistisches Bundesamt; Münz et al. 1999.

Structure of the Foreign Population

Until 1970, almost half of all foreigners in Germany were originally from one of today's EU member states, in the early days especially from Italy, Greece, Spain or Austria. Only after 1970 did Turks and ex-Yugoslavs become the two most important groups of foreigners. In 1999, citizens of other EU countries constituted no more than 25 percent of the foreign population. By far the largest group of foreigners in 1999 were the 2.1 million Turkish citizens (28 percent of the foreign population); next were the 1.1 million citizens of former Yugoslavia, Bosnians, Croats (15 percent, including Bosnian war refugees living in Germany under temporary protection),[12] followed by Italians (8 percent) and Greeks (5 percent). Since the mid-1970s the percentage of Greeks and Italians has decreased substantially. In contrast, the proportion of Poles living in Germany in recent times has grown to almost 4 percent.[13]

Today, the foreigners with the most secure legal status are those 25 percent who come from other EU countries.[14] They have almost unlimited access to the German labor market, and have the right to settle in Germany, provided they have either a regular income or other means of support, and are not dependent on social welfare. Other groups with a similar status include foreigners who have a permanent residence permit (*Aufenthaltsberechtigung*, from 1996 to 1997 this was 12 percent of all foreigners) or those who have a limited or unlimited residence permit (*Aufenthaltserlaubnis*, which during the same period was 17 percent, excluding EU citizens). In 1996–97, another 3 percent of all foreigners were in Germany for a specific purpose and could legally reside in the country for a limited period of time;[15] 5 percent of all foreigners were waiting for a decision on their asylum application;[16] approximately 7 percent of all foreigners in 1996–97 had a temporary right to residence (*Aufenthaltsbefugnis*) because of humanitarian reasons (among them, "humanitarian quota" refugees), or were tolerated as de facto refugees who could not be deported for

FIGURE 1.2 Foreigners in Germany According to Citizenship, 1999 (by percentage)

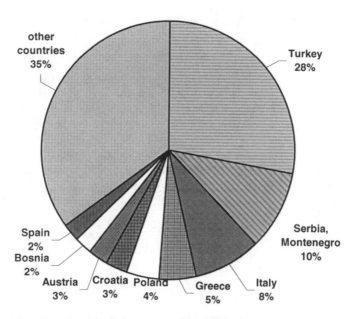

Source: Data from Beauftragte der Bundesregierung für Ausländerfragen, *Daten und Fakten zur Ausländersituation,* 19th ed. (Berlin, 2000).

humanitarian, political or legal reasons.[17] Another 3 percent of foreigners in 1996–97 were, in the view of the authorities, required to leave the country, but had not yet done so.

Migration and Structure of Ethnic German Immigrants

At the end of World War II and in the immediate postwar years, most of the migrants who came to the country were refugees and expellees from the former eastern provinces of the German Reich, as well as from Poland, Czechoslovakia, Hungary, and Yugoslavia. By the end of the 1940s, a total of approximately 12 million Germans (both German citizens and ethnic Germans) had come to the Federal Republic of Germany, the GDR and Austria (Benz 1995; Lemberg and Edding 1959; Stanek 1985). In relative terms, these immigrants played a somewhat larger role for the GDR (3.6 million, or 19 percent of the total population) than for the FRG (7.9 million, or 16 percent of the total population; see table 1.1).[18]

The immigration of ethnic Germans from Central and Eastern Europe (*Aussiedler*) continued at a lower level between 1950 and 1987 (see fig. 1.3).

FIGURE 1.3 Immigration of Ethnic Germans to the FRG by Country of Origin, 1950–1999 (in thousands)

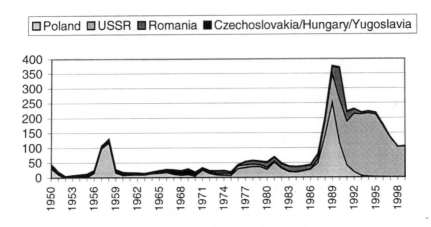

Sources: Statistisches Bundesamt, Rainer Münz; Ralf Ulrich, "Migration und zukünftige Bevölkerungsentwicklung in Deutschland," in *Migrationsreport 2000*, ed. Klaus Bade and Rainer Münz (Frankfurt am Main/New York, 2000), 25.

Only the late 1980s and early 1990s brought a substantial increase in the number of *Aussiedler*. Until 1999, some four million *Aussiedler* had immigrated to Germany. Upon arrival, *Aussiedler* have a legal claim to German citizenship. They are entitled to a number of social benefits. Thus, at least in the past, *Aussiedler* were in a better position than most foreign immigrants.[19]

For most *Aussiedler*, the possibility of migrating was made possible prior to 1988–89 by bilateral agreements between the Federal Republic of Germany and the Polish, Romanian, Czechoslovak and Soviet governments. Migration was characterized by a higher degree of voluntarism than that of those expellees during 1945 to 1948, and generally only came about when the persons concerned had applied for it. In this context, it is meaningful to make a distinction between ethnic German expellees (*Vertriebene*, 1945 to 1948), earlier ethnic German immigrants (*Aussiedler*, 1950 to 1992), and the last generation of ethnic German immigrants (*Spätaussiedler*, since 1993). Prior to 1990, a large portion of the German public interpreted the decision of ethnic Germans to leave their traditional settlement areas as a response to political and social discrimination, combined with their strong identification with the German culture and the West German political system. Only a few scholars saw them as primarily motivated by greater opportunities in the West (Bethlehem 1982; Delfs 1993; Ronge 1993).

After the end of organized relocation and expulsion during the 1940s, there was a period of time in which ethnic German migration was reduced to a few cases of family unification. In 1950, it still stood at 47,000, but by

1952, had dropped to only 5,000 cases. During the next thirty-five years (from 1953 to 1987), a yearly average of 37,000 *Aussiedler* came to Germany. Fluctuations in the annual number of ethnic German migrants was, on the one hand, due to periods of domestic liberalization (Poland in the second half of the 1950s; Czechoslovakia 1967 to 1968; USSR after 1986) and on the other, was attributable to the governments of Poland and Romania using permission to emigrate as a lever with which they could either improve their political relationship with West Germany or acquire economic and financial assistance. At the same time, there was seemingly the hope that ethnic minority groups in the country would be weakened through emigration. All of these factors played a role in the 1950s, when approximately 250,000 people of German or mixed ethnicity were allowed to leave Poland for Germany. Also, in the periods before and immediately following the conclusion of the State Treaty (*Grundlagenvertrag*) between Bonn and Warsaw (1970 to 1971), the number of *Aussiedler* from Poland was almost five times what it was in the period from 1968 to 1969. In the case of Romania, the Federal Republic in 1978 even started to pay for every *Aussiedler* who was allowed to leave for Germany.

Between 1950 and 1987, 62 percent of the *Aussiedler* came from Poland (848,000), and a further 15 percent came from Romania (206,000). Although there was also a strong German minority in the Soviet Union, during that period (1950 to 1987) only 110,000 (8 percent of *Aussiedler*) were allowed to leave the country (see fig. 1.3). Even with emigration, the largest portion of the German minorities continued to live in their traditional areas of settlement (Upper Silesia, Transylvania, Banat), or in regions to which they were forcibly displaced during World War II (that is, Siberia, Kazakhstan, Kyrgyzstan).

With the fall of the Iron Curtain and the removal of administrative restrictions on travel in Central and Eastern Europe, barriers to migration for *Aussiedler* in the late 1980s also disappeared. As a consequence, their number increased significantly. From 1988 to 1999, a total of 2.6 million *Aussiedler* immigrated to Germany. During this phase, the majority of *Aussiedler* came from the former Soviet Union and the successor states (1,775,000 *Aussiedler* or 69 percent).[20] The second most important country of origin for ethnic German *Aussiedler* during this period was Poland (from 1988 to 1999, 574,000 or 22 percent), while ethnic Germans from Romania formed the third largest group (from 1988 to 1999, 219,000 or 8 percent).

For decades, those belonging to German diasporas in Central and Eastern Europe had not been allowed to leave their countries legally, but according to German law had been free to travel to Germany and apply for German citizenship. The fast and nonbureaucratic process of acquiring citizenship made it possible for *Aussiedler* to stay in the country right away, even if they had not entered as regular immigrants. With the beginning of the 1990s, Germany reacted to the liberalization of migration regimes in Central and Eastern Europe, and the strong increase in the number of *Aussiedler*, by instating a number of restrictions. Since 1 July 1990, ethnic

Germans must apply for an entry permit for Germany before they leave their home countries. Additionally, application decisions are no longer made quickly or without red tape. By 1991, these regulations reduced the immigration of *Aussiedler* to 221,000 (in 1990 there were 397,000), and produced a backlog of pending applications. In 1992 an annual quota for the immigration of *Aussiedler* (220,000 per annum) was set; and in 2000 this quota was reduced to 110,000 per annum Indeed, in 1994, 222,000 *Aussiedler* came to Germany; in 1996 only 178,000; in 1997, 134,000; and in 1999 only 105,000 (see fig. 1.3). There are several reasons for this decrease.

According to the new laws, only ethnic Germans who live in the successor states of the former Soviet Union have an unconditional claim to immigration to Germany. The requirement that ethnic Germans demonstrate their knowledge of the German language before leaving their country of origin also serves to restrict the flow of *Aussiedler* to Germany. If they are unable to do so, their status as *Aussiedler* can be denied (Ohliger 1998).[21] An end to ethnically privileged migration to Germany is also foreseeable. The so-called law dealing with late consequences of World War II, the *Kriegsfolgenbereinigungsgesetz* of 1992, states that only people who were born before 1 January 1993, are entitled to individually apply for admittance to Germany. This provision will only have an effect, however, when ethnic Germans born after 1 January 1993, reach adulthood, which will occur beginning in the year 2010. But even after 2010, many of these people will still be able to come to Germany within the context of family reunion.

Conclusion

Between 1954 and 1999, a total of 31.3 million Germans and foreigners migrated to Germany. Of this number, four million were ethnic German *Aussiedler* and 2.7 million were asylum seekers and refugees. During the same period, 22.3 million Germans and foreigners left the country. In the case of Germans, emigration dominated in the 1950s, 1960s, and early 1970s. Since that time, immigration has become dominant, because of the privileged access of ethnic Germans (*Aussiedler*) from Eastern Europe. For foreigners, there was more emigration than immigration in the mid-1970s, the first half of the 1980s, and in 1997 to 1998. In all other periods since 1954, immigration dominated over emigration. Net foreign immigration was especially high from 1962 to 1973, and between 1988 and 1996. On balance, the net number of foreign citizens who have migrated to Germany is 6.7 million (in the period from 1954 to 1999), and the net number of Germans (including *Aussiedler*) is 2.3 million. Altogether, this means that since the mid-1950s Germany has gained a net number of nine million new residents through international migration. Since a considerable portion of immigrants, especially foreign immigrants, have had children, migration has also made a significant indirect contribution to population growth in Germany.

The positive migration balance compensates for Germany's low fertility and the declining number of births. Had it not been for immigration, Germany's population would already have been in decline since the mid-1970s. The impact of immigration on the size and structure of the population will only become stronger in the coming decades. Regardless of this trend, the decline of Germany's native population, due to low fertility rates, is almost inevitable in the coming decades. The number of people with German citizenship will probably also shrink, even though the trend of increased naturalization and of *ius soli* citizenship for German-born children of many foreigners may slow down this process. The number of foreigners, or of people with foreign origins, however, will further increase through immigration, but also through a growing number of children born in Germany whose parents or grandparents are of foreign origin.

Germany would need a net immigration of 23 million people in the first half of the twenty-first century in order to stabilize its population size. Given emigration of Germans and return migration of foreign migrants, the gross intake would have to be in the range of 30 to 35 million immigrants. It is unclear where to recruit immigrants, who would fit Western European labor market requirements, in such large numbers. At least for now, it is also unclear whether German society will be able and willing to accept immigrants on such a large scale. A legal basis to regulate immigration will certainly not be able to completely change this perception. But it might serve as a framework for Germany's native population to come to terms with the fact that this country will be in need of immigrants during almost the whole twenty-first century.

Notes

1. For example, Esser 1980; Hoffmann-Nowotny 1970; Hoffmann-Nowotny 1973; Mehrländer 1987.
2. This is significantly more than the 520,000 people who indicated in the Microcensus that they had dual citizenship. The ALLBUS survey also shows too few people by far with dual citizenship (in 1996, 0.5 percent of those surveyed). The largest group of dual citizens are *Aussiedler*, who since the collapse of the Soviet Union and political liberalization in Poland and Romania are no longer required to (and no longer do) give up their citizenship before leaving for Germany (in 1999, approximately 1.3 to 1.4 million). The second largest group are Germans born in Germany who have one German and one non-German parent (from 1960 to 1999, more than 1 million people). Of this group, approximately 700,000 (1999) may hold dual citizenship. In third place are those of foreign descent naturalized under conditions that tolerated multiple citizenship (by 1999, ca. 230,000 people).
3. It is surmised that approximately one-third of naturalized citizens were born in Germany, and two-thirds are immigrants.

4. From 1939 to 1944 this affected primarily ethnic Germans from the Baltics, South Tyrol (i.e., the Italian province of Alto Adige), Volhynia, Bukovina, Bessarabia, Dobrudja, the Crimean peninsula, and the Caucasus.

5. Pommerania, East Brandenburg, Upper and Lower Silesia, and East Prussia.

6. This estimate is based on information gathered from German respondents to the 1996 ALLBUS survey who were 47 years old or older and whose place of birth is in the regions mentioned (12.1 percent Germans born prior to 1949 in the ALLBUS random sample). This ratio was then projected onto the overall German population aged 47 years and older, creating information that cannot be found in official statistics. An estimated 2.2 million expellees still alive in the late 1990s were born as German citizens within the 1937 borders of the German Reich, and 1.4 million were born in a third country. At birth, most of the latter were citizens of these third countries.

7. Many of the forced laborers, expellees, prisoners of war, and concentration camp inmates from the Soviet Union who were forcibly repatriated by the Western allies were, upon their return to the USSR, imprisoned in labor camps—some were even executed. The forced repatriation to the Soviet Union came to a halt only at the end of 1946, i.e., with the beginning of the Cold War. Fassmann and Münz 1994; Fassmann and Münz 2000b.

8. Without a formalized recruiting procedure at that time, Austrians also entered the country. Fassmann and Münz 2000a.

9. A positive list of these countries has been established by the German parliament (Bundestag).

10. This harmonization started as intergovernmental cooperation (Dublin and Schengen II agreements). Since the ratification of the Amsterdam Treaty, the EU has the right to regulate some aspects of migration and asylum policies. But at least until the year 2004, the decisions have to be taken unanimously by the EU council of interview and justice ministers.

11. Of the 800,000 foreigners (excluding *Aussiedler*) who were naturalized between 1970 and 1999, approximately two-thirds were born outside of Germany and therefore belong to the group of foreign immigrants.

12. Of the 1.27 million citizens of (former) Yugoslavia in Germany (1997), 721,000 were citizens of Yugoslavia (i.e., Serbs, Montenegrans, and Kosovo Albanians), 281,000 were citizens of Bosnia-Hercegovina (of which almost all were Bosnian Muslims), and 207,000 were Croatian citizens. Those who had an old Yugoslav passport and had not yet applied to one of the successor states for citizenship were counted as citizens of Yugoslavia. Most Bosnian war refugees lost their status of temporary protection in 1997 and 1998, and were subsequently forced to return to their home country.

13. This figure does not include ethnic German immigrants (*Aussiedler*) from Poland.

14. Citizens of the other countries of the European Economic Area (EEA: EU-15 plus Iceland, Liechtenstein, and Norway) are in a similarly privileged position, as they can freely move within this economic space and settle in each of these countries so long as they can economically sustain themselves. Because of the 1963 Association Agreement between Turkey and the European Community, Turkish citizens have an easier entry to the German labor market and a permanent resident status after a minimum of a five-year stay in the country. Since the year 2002, Swiss citizens get privileges similar to those of citizens of EEA countries.

15. These include foreign students from non-EU countries as well as so-called "new guest workers."

16. If asylum applicants are constitutionally recognized as refugees, they are given a permanent residence permit. According to the Geneva Convention, recognized refugees (i.e., humanitarian quota refugees) are to be given a right to residence.

17. Included in this group are foreigners in refugee-like situations who have not applied for asylum (e.g., temporarily tolerated Bosnian war refugees) and asylum seekers whose application has been rejected.

18. In the West, expellees predominantly found refuge in the British and American occupation zones. French military officials gave only approximately 300,000 expellees the right to settle in the portion of Germany that they controlled. See Lemberg and Edding 1959.
19. For a detailed discussion, see also Münz and Ohliger 1998.
20. Of the *Aussiedler* from the post-Soviet successor states (from 1992 to 1998), 55.5 percent came from Kazakhstan, 33.7 percent from Russia (most of these from Siberia), 4.9 percent from Kyrgyzstan, and 6.0 percent from other countries.
21. See the decision of the Federal Administrative Court (BVwG Az 9c.8.96).

References

Angenendt, Steffen. 1992. *Ausländerforschung in Frankreich und der Bundesrepublik Deutschland. Gesellschaftliche Rahmenbedingungen und inhaltliche Entwicklung eines aktuellen Forschungsberichtes.* Frankfurt am Main/New York: Campus.

———. 1995. *Deutsche Migrationspolitik im neuen Europa.* Opladen: Leske and Budrich.

———, ed. 1997. *Migration und Flucht. Aufgaben und Strategien für Deutschland, Europa und die Internationale Gemeinschaft.* Bonn: Deutsche Gesellschaft für auswärtige Politik.

Bade, Klaus J. 1994. *Ausländer, Aussiedler, Asyl.* Munich: Beck.

———. 2000. *Europa in Bewegung.* Munich: Beck.

———, ed. 1984. *Auswanderer – Wanderarbeiter – Gastarbeiter.* Ostfildern: H. Scripta Mercaturae.

———. 1992. *Deutsche im Ausland – Fremde in Deutschland. Migration in Geschichte und Gegenwart.* Munich: Beck.

Bals, Christel. 1989. "Aussiedler – Erneut ein räumliches Problem?" *Informationen zur Raumentwicklung* 4: 305–317.

Beer, Mathias. 1991. "'Das unsichtbare Gepäck'. Drei Thesen zur kulturellen und sozialen Integration der Aussiedler aus Rumänien in der Bundesrepublik." *Aktuelle Ostinformationen* 23: 49–60.

Benz, Wolfgang, ed. 1995. *Die Vertreibung der Deutschen aus dem Osten. Ursachen, Ereignisse, Folgen.* Frankfurt am Main: Fischer.

Bethlehem, Siegfried. 1982. *Heimatvertreibung, DDR-Flucht, Gastarbeiter, Zuwanderung, Wanderungsströme und Wanderungspolitik in der Bundesrepublik Deutschland.* Stuttgart: Klett-Cotta.

Blahusch, Friedrich. 1994. "Flüchtlinge in Deutschland nach der Asylrechtsänderung im Grundgesetz." In *Internationale Wanderungen (Demographie aktuell 5),* ed. Rainer Münz, Hermann Korte, and Gert Wagner, 143–157. Berlin: Humboldt University.

Blaschke, Dieter. 1991. "Sozialbilanz der Aussiedlung in den 80er und 90er Jahren." In *Integration von Vertriebenen,* ed. Hans-Peter Baumeister, 35–77. Weinheim: Juventa.

Blaschke, Jochen. 1991. "International Migration and East-West Migration: Political and Economic Paradoxes." *Migration* 11/12: 29–46.

Boos-Nünning, Ursula. 1990. "Einwanderung ohne Einwanderungsentscheidung." *Aus Politik und Zeitgeschichte* (Beilage zur Wochenzeitung Das Parlament), B 23–24, 90: 16–31.

Dietz, Barbara, and Peter Hilkes. 1994. *Integriert oder isoliert? Zur Situation rußlanddeutscher Aussiedler in der Bundesrepublik Deutschland.* Munich: Olzog.

Dinkel, Reiner Hans, and Uwe Lebok. 1994. "Demographische Aspekte der vergangenen und zukünftigen Zuwanderung nach Deutschland." *Aus Politik und Zeitgeschichte* (Beilage zur Wochenzeitung Das Parlament), B48/94: 27–36.

Dohse, Knuth. 1981. *Ausländische Arbeitnehmer und bürgerlicher Staat.* Königstein: Hain.

Esser, Hartmut. 1980. *Aspekte der Wanderungssoziologie. Assimilation und Integration von Wanderern, ethnischen Gruppen und Minderheiten. Eine handlungstheoretische Analyse.* Darmstadt-Neuwied: Luchterhand.

Fassmann, Heinz, and Rainer Münz. 1994. "European East-West Migration, 1945–1992." *International Migration Review* 3: 520–538.

———. 2000a. "Österreich und die Ost-West-Wanderungen." In *Ost-West-Wanderung in Europa,* ed. Heinz Fassmann and Rainer Münz, 83–94. Vienna/Cologne/Weimar: Boehlau.

———, eds. 2000b. *Ost-West-Wanderung in Europa.* Vienna/Cologne/Weimar: Boehlau.

Grillmeister, Helmut, Hermann Kurthen, and Jürgen Fijalkowski. 1989. *Ausländerbeschäftigung in der Krise? Die Beschäftigungschancen und -risiken ausländischer Arbeitnehmer am Beispiel der West-Berliner Industrie.* Berlin: Sigma.

Grüner, Hans. 1992. *Mobilität und Diskriminierung. Deutsche und ausländische Arbeiter auf dem Arbeitsmarkt.* Frankfurt am Main/New York: Campus.

Gugel, Günther. 1990. *Ausländer, Aussiedler, Übersiedler.* Tübingen: Verein für Friedenspädagogik.

Hailbronner, Kay, David A. Martin, and Hiroshi Motomura, eds. 1998a. *Immigrations Admissions: The Search for Workable Policies in Germany and the United States.* Providence/Oxford: Berghahn Books.

———. 1998b. *Immigration Control: The Search for Workable Policies in Germany and the United States.* Providence/Oxford: Berghahn Books.

Heckmann, Friedrich. 1992. *Ethnische Minderheiten, Volk und Nation. Soziologie interethnischer Beziehungen.* Stuttgart: Enke.

Heinelt, Hubert, and Anne Lohmann. 1992. *Immigranten im Wohlfahrtsstaat am Beispiel der Rechtspositionen und Lebensverhältnisse von Aussiedlern.* Opladen: Leske and Budrich.

Heitmeyer, Wilhelm, ed. 1996. *Was hält eine multi-ethnische Gesellschaft zusammen?* Frankfurt am Main: Suhrkamp.

Herbert, Ulrich. 1986. *Geschichte der Ausländerbeschäftigung in Deutschland 1800–1990.* Berlin/Bonn: J.H.W. Dietz Nachf.

Herrmann, Helga. 1993. *Ausländische Jugendliche in Schule, Ausbildung und Beruf.* Cologne: Deutscher Instituts Verlag.

Heyden, Helmut. 1986. "Kontinuität und Diskontinuität der Ausländerpolitik." In *Strukturwandel des Ausländerproblems,* ed. Johannes C. Papalekas. Bochum: Ruhr University.

Hillmann, Felicitas, and Hedwig Rudolph. 1996. *Jenseits des brain drain. Zur Mobilität westlicher Fach- und Führungskräfte nach Polen.* Berlin: Sigma.

Hof, Bernd. 1989. "Modellierung zu den Auswirkungen einer verstärkten Aussiedler-Zuwanderung auf Bevölkerung, Wirtschaftswachstum und Arbeitsmarkt." In *Die Integration deutscher Aussiedler – Perspektiven für die Bundesrepublik Deutschland,* ed. Institut für deutsche Wirtschaft, 38–72. Cologne: IW.

Hoffmann-Nowotny, Hans-Joachim. 1970. *Migration. Ein Beitrag zu einer soziologischen Erklärung.* Stuttgart: Enke.

———. 1973. *Soziologie des Fremdarbeiterproblems. Eine theoretische und empirische Analyse am Beispiel der Schweiz.* Stuttgart: Enke.

Höhn, Charlotte, and Detlev B. Rein, eds. 1990. *Ausländer in der Bundesrepublik Deutschland.* Boppard: Boldt.

Hönekopp, Elmar. 1997. "The New Labor Migration as an Instrument of German Foreign Policy." In *Migrants, Refugees, and Foreign Policy: U.S. and German Policies Towards Countries of Origin,* ed. Rainer Münz and Myron Weiner, 165–182. Providence/Oxford: Berghahn Books.

Klos, Christian. 1998. *Rahmenbedingungen und Gestaltungsmöglichkeiten der europäischen Migrationspolitik.* Constance: University of Constance.

Koller, Barbara. 1993. "Aussiedler nach dem Deutschkurs. Welche Gruppen kommen rasch in Arbeit?" *Mitteilungen aus der Arbeitsmarkt- und Berufsforschung* 3: 207–221.

Leggewie, Claus. 1992. *MultiKulti. Spielregeln für die Vielvölkerrepublik.* Berlin: Rotbuch.

Lemberg, Eugen, and Friedrich Edding, eds. 1959. *Die Vertriebenen in Deutschland.* Kiel: Hirt.

Luettinger, Peter. 1986. "Der Mythos der schnellen Integration. Eine empirische Untersuchung zur Integration der Vertriebenen und Flüchtlinge in der Bundesrepublik Deutschland bis 1971." *Zeitschrift für Soziologie* 1: 20–36.

Mehrländer, Ursula. 1987. *Ausländerforschung 1965 bis 1980. Fragestellungen, theoretische Ansätze, empirische Ergebnisse.* Bonn: Friedrich-Ebert-Stiftung.

Ministerium für Arbeit, Gesundheit und Soziales des Landes Nordrhein-Westfalen, ed. 1992. *Ausländer, Aussiedler und Einheimische als Nachbarn. Ermittlung von Konfliktpotentialen und exemplarischen Konfliktlösungen.* Wuppertal.

Morokvasic, Mirjana. 1993. "Krieg, Flucht und Vertreibung im ehemaligen Jugoslawien." *Demographie aktuell 2.* Berlin: Humboldt University.

Münch, Ursula. 1993. *Asylpolitik in der Bundesrepublik Deutschland. Entwicklung und Alternativen.* Opladen: Leske and Budrich.

Münz, Rainer. 2000. "Deutschland und die Ost-West-Wanderung." In *Ost-West-Wanderung in Europa,* ed. Heinz Fassmann and Rainer Münz, 49–82. Vienna/Cologne/ Weimar: Boehlau.

Münz, Rainer, and Rainer Ohliger. 1998. "Deutsche Minderheiten in Ostmittel- und Osteuropa, Aussiedler in Deutschland." *Demographie aktuell 9.* Berlin: Humboldt University.

Münz, Rainer, Wolfgang Seifert, and Ralf Ulrich. 1999. *Zuwanderung nach Deutschland. Strukturen, Wirkungen, Perspektiven.* 2nd ed. Frankfurt am Main/New York: Campus.

Münz, Rainer, and Weiner Myron, eds. 1997. *Migrants, Refugees, and Foreign Policy: U.S. and German Policies Toward Countries of Origin.* Providence/Oxford: Berghahn Books.

Ohliger, Rainer. 1998. "Rückgang des Zuzugs von Aussiedlern." *Migration und Bevölkerung* 3: 4–5.

Reyher, Lutz, and Hans-Uwe Bach. 1989. "Der Potential-Effekt der Zuwanderungen – Eine Arbeitskräfte-Gesamtrechnung für Aus- und Übersiedler." *Mitteilungen aus der Arbeitsmarkt- und Berufsforschung* 4: 468–471.

Santel, Bernhard. 1995. *Migration in und nach Europa. Erfahrungen, Strukturen, Politik.* Opladen: Leske and Budrich.

Schmalz-Jacobsen, Cornelia, and Georg Hansen, eds. 1995. *Ethnische Minderheiten in der Bundesrepublik Deutschland.* Munich: Beck.

Schoeps, Julius H., ed. 1996. *Russische Juden in Deutschland. Integration und Selbstbehauptung in einem fremden Land.* Weinheim: Juventa.

Seifert, Wolfgang. 1995. *Die Mobilität der Migranten. Die berufliche, ökonomische und soziale Stellung ausländischer Arbeitnehmer in der Bundesrepublik. Eine Längsschnittanalyse mit dem Sozio-Ökonomischen Panel, 1984–1989.* Berlin: Free University.

Sprink, Joachim, and Wolfgang Hellmann. 1989. "Finanzielle Belastung oder ökonomisches Potential – Regional unterschiedliche Konsequenzen des Ausländerzustroms." *Informationen zur Raumentwicklung* 5: 323–329.

Steinmann, Gunter, and Ralf Ulrich, eds. 1994. *The Economic Consequences of Immigration to Germany.* Heidelberg: Springer.

Stanek, Eduard. 1985. *Verfolgt – verjagt – vertrieben. Flüchtlinge in Österreich 1945–84.* Vienna/Munich/Zurich: Europa Verlag.

Sterbling, Anton. 1994. "Die Aussiedlung der Deutschen aus Rumänien. Motive, Randbedingungen und Eigendynamik eines Migrationsprozesses." In *Internationale Wanderungen (Demographie aktuell 5),* ed. Rainer Münz, Hermann Korte, and Gert Wagner, 66–74. Berlin: Humboldt University.

Ulrich, Ralf. 1994. "Foreigners and the Social Insurance System in Germany." In *The Economic Consequences of Immigration to Germany,* ed. Gunter Steinmann and Ralf E. Ulrich, 61–80. Heidelberg: Physica.

Velling, Johannes. 1994. *Zuwanderer auf dem Arbeitsmarkt. Sind die neuen Migranten die "Gastarbeiter" der neunziger Jahre?* Mannheim: ZEW.

Widgren, Jonas. 1990. "International Stability and Regional Stability." *International Affairs* 4: 749–766.

Zimmermann, Klaus F., ed. 1992. *Migration and Economic Development.* Berlin: Springer.

———. 1998. *The Economics of Migration.* Aldershot: Edward Elgar Publishing.

Chapter 2

FROM HAVEN TO HEAVEN

Changing Patterns of Immigration to Israel

Yinon Cohen

Introduction

At the end of 1919, the Jewish population of Palestine was estimated to be about 56,000 people.[1] By May 1948, when the Jewish State was established, the number of Jews had increased by a factor of twelve, to around 650,000. Most of the population growth during this period was due to immigration—the most important factor in the development of the Jewish community during the British Mandate period. Indeed, the history of the Zionist colonization of Palestine is to a large extent the history of Jewish migrations. In fact, Israeli historiography of the pre-state years employs periodization that follows five, well-defined migration waves from 1882 to 1938, and an additional wave for those arriving illegally between 1939 and 1948. During statehood, immigration continued to be a major source of Jewish population growth (Della Pergola 1998). In the fifty-two years between 1948 and 2000, an additional 2.8 million immigrants came to Israel. Consequently, by the end of 2000, nearly 40 percent of Israel's Jewish residents were immigrants (i.e., foreign-born), and over 70 percent were either immigrants or children of immigrants (i.e., second-generation immigrants). Surely, the demographic history—and to a large extent the social, cultural, political and economic history—of Israel has been shaped by its migration patterns.

In the following pages I will provide an overview of the immigration patterns to Israel in the last half century, with a special emphasis on post-1967 immigrants. The chapter consists of two main parts. The first part examines immigration patterns to Israel since 1948 and their effect on the national and ethnic structures of Israeli society. The migration patterns of the last decades, as well as the long term effects of the pre-1967 migrations, resulted in a population structure whose ethnicity and nationality is no longer a simple matter to classify. The current classificatory system, based on country of birth, fails to capture the changing nature of the Israeli population. The second part of the chapter focuses on the skill levels with which immigrants arrived in Israel during the past five decades. I will argue that the increase in immigrants' schooling levels between pre- and post-1967 immigrants is mainly due to changes in immigrants' selection patterns (i.e., changes in the type of people who immigrated to Israel) within source countries.

Immigration Patterns

In order to understand the making of Israel's ethnic composition, it is useful to distinguish between three main periods of immigration: the mass migration of the years from 1948 to 1951; the North African immigrations of the 1950s and 1960s; and the post-1967 immigrations (including two main waves, one in the 1970s and the other in the 1990s).

The Demographic Transformation, 1947–1951

The mass migration of the years from 1948 to 1951 brought nearly 700,000 Jews to a Jewish population base of approximately the same size. Most writers analyze this wave with little or no reference to the Arab exodus of 1947 to 1949. Yet the period between December 1947 and August 1951 is the most crucial in Israel's demographic history. During these forty-four months Israel underwent what I call a demographic transformation. The transformation involved two migration processes of about equal size: the (forced) emigration of the Palestinians, on the one hand, and the mass immigration of Jews, on the other hand. The exodus of Palestinians started in December 1947, and lasted nearly two years. During that period, approximately 760,000 Palestinians fled or were expelled from their homes in the cities and villages, and about four hundred Arab villages were destroyed (Morris 1987). The Jewish mass migration started in May 1948. In the following three years, 678,000 Holocaust survivors and Middle Eastern Jews were brought to Israel. Until the middle of 1949, 124,000 Jewish immigrants were housed in vacant Arab houses, mostly in cities (Lissak 1999). In 1948 to 1949 alone, 144 new Jewish communities were established (Naor and Giladi 1990), many of them on or near the lands of destroyed Arab villages. While these processes hardly affected the total size of Israel's population (fig. 2.1), they radically transformed its national composition. The proportion of Jews in the area to become Israel in 1949 increased from 44.7 percent[2] in 1947 (Bachi 1974), to 89 percent at the end of 1951 (Central Bureau of Statistics, CBS 2001), resulting in a record-high Jewish majority that has not been surpassed since.

FIGURE 2.1 The Demographic Transformation of Israel—National and Ethnic Composition, 1947–1951

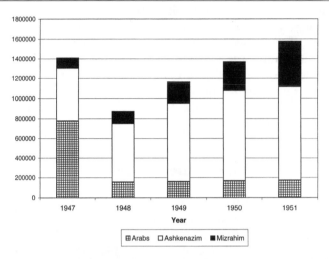

Sources: For the number of Jews and Arabs, see Bachi (1974), and Statistical Abstract of Israel (2001). For the number of Mizrahim and Ashkenazim, see my estimates based on Goldscheider (1989, 1996), and Statistical Abstracts of Israel (different years).

The demographic transformation not only secured the Jewish majority in the new state, but it also altered the ethnic composition of its Jewish population. Before 1948, 90 percent of Jewish immigrants arriving in Israel during the thirty-one years of the British Mandate (1917–48) were born in Europe (most of them in Poland and Russia), and only 10 percent in Asia (most of them in Yemen and Turkey) and Africa (Bachi 1974: 93). The mass migration equalized the proportions. About half the immigrants came from countries in Asia and Africa, and the other half were mostly European-born survivors of the Jewish Holocaust. Three source countries—Iraq, Romania, and Poland, each with over 100,000 immigrants—accounted for about half the immigrants arriving in the mass migration. The other major source countries were Yemen, Turkey, Libya, Morocco, Iran, and Egypt in the Middle East, and Bulgaria, Hungary, and Czechoslovakia in Europe. Consequently, the proportion of Mizrahim (the present-day label for Jews of Asian or African origin) among Israel's Jews, increased from about 12 percent in 1948 (Goldscheider 1996: 30), to about 33 percent in 1951 (Goldscheider 1989).

Most immigrants who arrived in Israel during the mass migration were refugees who were brought by the state with the help of Jewish organizations. What can explain the desire of the state to bring so many immigrants in such a short time? Surely, the fear for the fate of Jews in some countries played a role, as did the desire to fulfill the core theme of the Zionist ideology—bringing Jews to Israel in a short time,[3] thereby sealing or at least securing the demographic transformation by increasing the Jewish population. Finally, the 1948 war (that lasted well into 1949) demanded human resources that were expected to be met by the new immigrants (Lissak 1999; Friedlander and Goldscheider 1979: 92). Thus, some Holocaust survivors were issued military draft orders while still in Displaced Person camps in Europe, even before they had become Israeli citizens (Grodzinsky 1998).

The North African (Mostly Moroccan) Immigrations, 1952–1967

The "mass migration" ended in the second half of 1951. In part, this was the result of Israel's policy, as the major operations of the mass migration period were completed, bringing to Israel the entire Jewish communities of Yemen, Bulgaria and Iraq. In some other countries Jews were no longer allowed to emigrate. In addition, a restrictive migration policy was adopted in 1952 for a short time. However, available evidence suggests that the decline in immigration preceded the policy change (Friedlander and Goldscheider 1979). Moreover, the effectiveness and success of the restrictive policy is questionable. At any rate, following three years of low immigration rates (in 1953 net migration was negative), immigration continued, albeit at a slower pace. In the fifteen years between 1952 and the end of 1967, 582,000 immigrants arrived. This migration wave accentuated the ethnic transformation of the Jewish state, and helped maintain the Jewish majority in the face of the higher fertility rate of the Arab minority. Immigrants from Asia and especially North Africa comprised about 60 percent of this wave. Moroccan Jews alone numbered 210,000 in this period, and an additional 60,000 immigrants came from other North African countries. Romanian Jews were the largest European group with about 109,000 immigrants. In fact, in all years during this period (1957 being the exception) Moroccan and Romanian Jews together outnumbered immigrants from all other source countries combined.

The pre-1967 immigration has had a long-term effect on Israel's ethnic composition. Since Mizrahi immigrants in the 1950s and 1960s were younger and had a higher fertility rate than the Ashkenazim, the proportion of Mizrahim in the Jewish population grew, reaching parity with the Ashkenazim in the early 1970s and maintaining it at least until 1990 (Goldscheider 1996: 30)[4]. A comparison between the sizes of Romanian and Moroccan groups illustrates this point. As shown in table 2.1, these are the top two source countries for Jewish immigration during the pre-1967 period, sending a similar number of immigrants to Israel (Romania 227,000; Morocco 238,000). In 2000 there were about 500,000 Moroccan Jews in Israel (167,000 Moroccan-born, and 333,000 second-generation), but only about 250,000 Romanians (121,000 Romanian-born, and 126,000 second-generation).[5] Differential fertility rates in Israel are the main reason for the dramatic increase in the relative size of Moroccan-Israelis during the past thirty-three years, a period in which only about 28,000 Moroccan and 39,000 Romanian immigrants came to Israel. In short, in order to understand the making of the ethnic mosaic of the Israeli society,

TABLE 2.1 Immigrants by Country of Birth, 1948–2000

Period of Immigration	1948–51	1952–67	1968–88	1989–00	Total 1948–00	1919–48
Country						
Total Asia	237,704	67,722	57,122	14,078	376,626	40,776
Iran	21,910	28,811	23,539	1,708	75,968	3,536
Iraq	123,371	3,838	1,955	291	129,455	–
Turkey	34,547	13,499	10,908	1,303	60,257	8,277
Yemen	48,315	2,118	142	90	50,665	15,838
Syria[1]	2,913	4,862	3,703	93	11,571	–
India-Pakistan	2,176	11,312	11,684	1,041	26,213	–
Other Asia	4,472	3,282	5,191	9,552	22,497	13,125
Total Africa	93,285	279,213	72,759	53,935	499,192	4,033
Morocco	28,264	210,115	24,420	3,290	266,089	994[2]
Algeria	3,811	10,566	7,331	1,655	23,363	
Tunisia	13,294	32,84	1 6,239	1,610	53,984	
Libya	30,976	3,329	1,430	72	35,807	873
Ethiopia	10	82	14,691	41,854	56,647	–
South Africa	666	2,457	11,143	3,366	17,632	259
Egypt-Sudan	8,760	19,198	1,899	243	30,100	–
Other Africa	7,504	625	5,606	1,845	15,580	1,907
Total Europe	332,802	213,479	290,798	931,603	1,768,682	377,487
USSR	8,163	23,851	172,043	885,435[3]	1,089,492	52,350
Poland	106,414	47,143	13,543	3,126	170,226	170,127
France	3,050	3,699	20,074	11,903	38,726	1,637
Romania	117,950	109,273	31,000	7,583	265,806	41,105
Hungry	14,324	11,559	2,353	2,542	30,778	10,342
Bulgaria	37,260	2,359	292	3,965	43,868	7,057
Czechoslovakia	18,788	2,417	2,103	522	23,830	16,794
Germany[4]	10,842	3,755	7,061	2,437	24,095	52,591
UK	1,907	3,479	14,469	5,538	25,393	1,574
Other Europe	14,104	5,944	27,860	8,560	56,468	23,910
Total America	3,822	22,239	112,065	40,205	178,331	7,579
Argentina	904	10,138	27,224	11,686	49,952	238
USA	1,711	5,111	56,182	17,693	80,697	6,635
Brazil-Uruguay-Chile	418	4,194	13,182	4,020	21,814	–
Oceania	119	348	2,994	1,157	4,618	72
Other America	670	2,448	12,483	5,649	21,250	634
Unknown	19,129	671	1,656	523	26,979	52,982
Total	**686,739**	**583,327**	**534,391**	**1,040,344**	**2,844,801**	**482,587**

[1]Until 1972 with Lebanon.

[2]Including immigrants from Algeria and Tunisia.

[3]Since 1995, including 52,000 immigrants who were born in Asian Republics. Before 1955, all immigrants from the former Soviet Union were classified as Europeans.

[4]Until 1972 with Austria.

Sources: Central Bureau of Statistics. Special Series No. 489; 457; 503; 528; 547; 580; 632; 642; 672; 706; 723; 747; 773; 790; 808; 833; 858. Statistical Abstract of Israel, different years.

fertility patterns are as important as numbers of immigrants. Interestingly, the differences in total fertility rates between Mizrahi and Ashkenazi women have been attenuated over the years, and among the second generation the gap was entirely closed by 1995 (CBS 2001: 3.15).

The Post-1967 Period: Ideological and Economic Immigrants

The migration waves following the 1967 war were different from those preceding the war. Israel's economic development has made it an increasingly attractive destination country for immigrants seeking to improve their economic situation, rather than a haven for refugees. With the exception of about 56,000 Ethiopian immigrants arriving in two waves in 1984 and 1991, entire groups are no longer being brought to Israel in military-like operations, nor are there refugees who have no choice but to come to Israel. Rather, most of the 1.5 million immigrants who came to Israel in the post-1967 period elected to do so for economic, political, ideological or religious reasons. The Israeli victory in the 1967 war and its aftermath attracted nearly 200,000 Jewish immigrants from the developed countries of North America, Western Europe (mostly France and Britain), Australia, and South Africa. These immigrants, especially the North Americans (about 70,000) and to a lesser extent the West Europeans, included a disproportionate number of ideological immigrants—mostly right-wing religious zealots, as evidenced by their crowding into the Jewish settlements in the West Bank.[6] Immigrants from South America also started to come after 1967, and until 2000 about 60,000 of them, mostly from Argentina, arrived in Israel. They too, should not be viewed as refugees, although some of them—mostly those with left-wing affiliations—fled the repressive regimes in South America in the 1970s and 1980s. Likewise, the 160,000 Soviet Jews arriving in the 1970s could have gone to the U.S. where they were offered refugee status, but most of those leaving the USSR during the 1970s decided to immigrate to Israel (Dominitz 1997). Although refugee status in the U.S. is not available to the current wave of immigrants from the former USSR, they too, must not be viewed as stateless refugees. Rather, the 885,000 immigrants arriving during the years from 1989 to 2000 are rational decision makers who elected to leave the former Soviet Union and reside in Israel, where they believe that they and their offspring will fare better than in their source countries.

The impact of the post-1967 wave, and especially the post-1989 wave on Israel's ethnic and national composition cannot be exaggerated. Less than 12 percent of the immigrants arriving since 1989 were born in Asia or Africa (including those born in the Asian republics of the former Soviet Union). Consequently, the proportion of first- and second-generation Mizrahim among Israeli Jews declined from 44 percent in 1983 to 31 percent in 2000, while the proportion of their Ashkenazi counterparts remained stable at about 40 percent. The remaining 16 percent in 1983 and 29 percent in 2000 are third-generation Israelis (Israeli-born to fathers who were also born in Israel), defined in official statistics as being of "Israeli origin." Origin is defined in Israeli statistics strictly by one's country of birth, and for the Israeli-born, by father's country of birth. The reliance on an objective definition of country of birth as the sole indicator of ethnicity, together with the decision to trace it only one generation, results in the elimination of ancestry and ethnicity from official statistics within two generations, or about fifty years. Whether such administrative rulings affect identities or change the role of ethnicity in Israel remains to be seen. So far, available evidence suggests that the role of ethnicity has not diminished in the past twenty years, at least with respect to voting patterns,[7] and, in particular, in determining social and economic standing.

Unlike their Jewish counterparts, Arab citizens of Israel, some 1.2 million in 2000, are unable to attain the status of having an "Israeli origin" no matter how many generations their ancestors have resided in Israel. Rather, they are referred to as "Arabs" (until 1995 they were referred to merely as "non-Jews" or as "other religions"), and are divided in official statistics by their religion—Muslims (the largest group, comprising about 80 percent of all non-Jews in Israel), Christians, and Druze. Following the 1967 war, Israel

FIGURE 2.2 Ethnic Composition of the Jewish Population—percent Mizrahim, Ashkenazim, and Third-Generation Jews, 1961–2000

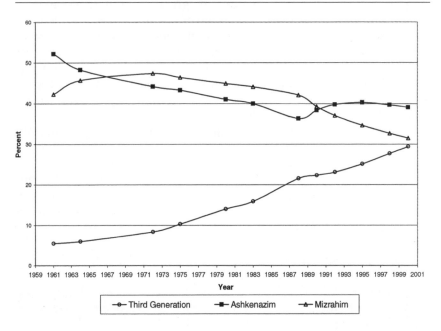

Ashkenazim: Jews born in Europe or America and Israeli-born Jews to fathers born in Europe or America. Mizrahim: Jews born in Asia or Africa and Israeli-born Jews to fathers born in Asia or Africa. Third-Generation Jews: Israeli-born Jews to Israeli-born fathers.
Source: Statistical Abstract of Israel (2001, table 2.24).

unilaterally annexed East Jerusalem, thereby, increasing the proportion of Arabs in the Jewish State from 11.8 percent to 14.1 percent overnight. The proportion of Arabs continued to climb and reached 18.5 percent in 1989. Thus, between 1967 and 1989 Jewish immigration to Israel lagged behind Arab fertility, reducing the Jewish majority to 81.5 percent.

The 1990s brought to Israel new kinds of immigrants, some of them non-Jews. Thus, despite the mass migration of the 1990s, the proportion of Jews continued to decline and reached 77.8 percent in 2000. Ironically, the decline in the Jewish majority during the 1990s is due, at least in part, to the Law of Return. Many of the immigrants from the former USSR in the 1990s were not Jews, but had Jewish relatives that enabled them to immigrate to Israel under the Law of Return.[8] Consequently, in 1995 a new religious category—"religion unclassified"—was added to Israel's official statistics, and the group of Christians was divided to "Arab Christians" and "other Christians." Both groups were labeled as "others," and consequently, by the end of 2000, 3.5 percent of the Israeli population were defined in official statistics as "others": 201,500 persons without religious classification, and 3,500 non-Arab Christians. If we add all "others" to the group of Jews, as has been the CBS practice in recent years,[9] the proportion of "Jews and others" in 2000 was 81.3 percent (CBS 2001), which essentially amounts to the proportion in 1989 just before the beginning of the current immigration wave. However, the fate of these non-Jews in Israeli society is still unclear, and their proportion is rising. They

FIGURE 2.3 National Composition of Israel's Population—percent Jews, 1948–2000

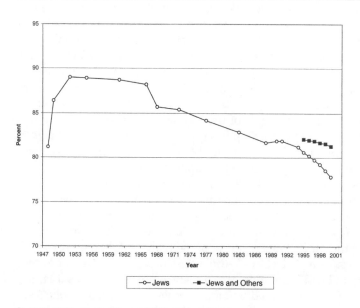

Source: Statistical Abstract of Israel (2001, table 2.1).

may face legal and administrative problems that will align them with other non-Jewish groups, including the growing population of labor migrants (Lustick 1999). Alternatively, their exposure to the main Zionist socialization agents—schools and the military—may prevent such alliances, at least for the time being.

The second kind of non-Jewish immigrants arriving in the 1990s are temporary labor migrants from Southeast Asia (mostly Thailand and the Philippines), Eastern Europe (mostly Romania), South America, and Africa who were recruited to replace Palestinian Arabs from the occupied territories. As in most developed countries, it is impossible to estimate the number of labor migrants with any precision. Available estimates for the end of the 1990s range between 150,000 to 200,000 legal and illegal immigrants (Rosenhek and Cohen 2000).[10] Experience from other labor importing countries in Europe and America suggests that a large proportion of labor migrants and their families will stay in Israel. So far, they are unable to gain citizenship due to Israel's immigration and citizenship laws. Nevertheless, with time they are likely to gain some rights (Kemp and Raijman 2000), become a permanent sector in Israel society, and influence its national and ethnic composition.

The above discussion leads to one surprising conclusion: it is no longer a simple matter to classify the Israeli population by national and ethnic categories. What was possible twenty years ago—when all immigrants were Jews, all non-Jews were Arabs, all labor migrants were Palestinian commuters, and all or at least most third-generation Israelis were Ashkenazi—is no longer the case in contemporary Israel. Rather, at the turn of the millennium, the proportion of non-Jews among immigrants from the former Soviet Union exceeds the proportion of Jews; the proportion of labor migrants in Israel's labor market (about 13 percent) is larger than in most European countries. Finally, not much is known of the ethnicity of the growing group of third-generation Israeli Jews. In 1972 this was a homogeneous group of less than 230,000 persons of mostly Ashkenazi grandparents, comprising 8 percent of the Jewish population. Ignoring this group, or considering it a part of the Ashkenazi ethnicity was unproblematic, as most grandparents of third-generation Jews were born in Europe. In 2000 the size of this group has grown to 1.5 million, or 29 percent of the Jewish population. While it is impossible to estimate precisely the proportion of those having Mizrahi grandparents, it is known that the older age cohorts are mostly Ashkenazim, while the younger age cohorts of third-generation Jews are predominantly Mizrahim (i.e., they have grandparents who were born in Asia or Africa).[11] Given that the median age of third-generation Israelis is less than fifteen (CBS 2001), it is no longer possible to assume that in 2000 the majority of them are of Ashkenazi origin.

To be sure, an "objective" ethnic classification by father or grandfather's country of birth is an important dimension of ethnicity, as it largely determines how one is treated by others, as well as influences one's subjective identity. It (country or continent of birth) cannot, however, serve as the sole indicator for ethnicity, especially if the people involved do not view themselves as such (Mizrachim or Ashkenazim). The ethnic identity literature of the past decade emphasizes that nationality and ethnicity are multidimensional dynamic identities, having both objective and subjective elements that are likely to interact (Jenkins 1996). Relying on grandparent's country of birth is not only theoretically problematic, but also practically nearly impossible, as each person has two grandparents who could have been born in two different countries. In short, for both theoretical and practical reasons it is time for Israel to ask its residents (not only its citizens) to define their ancestry and (ethnic) identity. Other migration countries where most of the population are descendants of immigrants do so. For example, in the U.S. Americans are asked about their ancestries, allowing each respondent to name two ancestries.[12] Having information on ethnic identities is necessary for describing and understanding Israeli society. As things currently stand, we are unable to assign an ethnic identity to 1.2 million Arabs and 1.5 million third-generation Jews. The former are classified by their religion only, and the latter are considered as having one, unequivocal "Israeli" origin.

Throughout this chapter I have followed the classification of Mizrahim and Ashkenazim, which is a common dichotomy used by both popular and scholarly writers in describing Israel's Jewish population. This binary view of Israel's Jewish population has been sustained in the 1980s and early 1990s by indicators of education, occupational status, and income for second-generation immigrants. Interestingly, the dichotomy of Mizrahim and Ashkenazim or continents of birth was not the best way to describe pre-1967 immigrants' socioeconomic status. For example, the pre-1967 immigrants from Egypt and Iraq had schooling levels that were more similar to those of Romanian and Polish immigrants than to immigrants from other Asian or African groups (Khazzoom 1998). By 1983, the dichotomy of the two ethnic groups adequately describes the socioeconomic standing of the second generation (Amit 2002). Apparently, with time and generations, Israeli society has constructed this ethnic dichotomy along social, economic and cultural lines. In the 1990s, however, there are indications that the dichotomy is weaker than it used to be in the 1980s. Specific countries of birth are once again important for understanding the socioeconomic fortunes of second-generation immigrants (Amit 2002). In short, it appears that the current classificatory system (based either on continents of birth or on the aforementioned ethnic dichotomy) is no longer adequate, and fails to capture the structural complexities and the changing nature of the Israeli population.

Selection Patterns and Socioeconomic Assimilation

While admittedly crude, the ethnic dichotomy still serves an important function when measuring social and economic inequalities among immigrants. In the melting pot model of immigrant absorption one expects social, cultural, political, and economic differences between immigrants and natives to gradually narrow and eventually disappear in one or two generations. On the basis of voting patterns and especially of socioeconomic gaps between Mizrahim and Ashkenazim, most scholars view the Israeli melting pot as a failure (Lissak 1999). This assessment is probably true, especially in light of the socioeconomic fortunes of the pre-1967 waves of Mizrahi immigrants and their offspring. The schooling and income gaps between second-generation Mizrahim and Ashkenazim have hardly changed during the past twenty years. In 1975 one in every four Ashkenazi men was a university graduate, compared to one in twenty among Mizrahim. In 1995 the education gap narrowed, but not by much: one out of three Ashkenazim was a university graduate, compared to one in ten among Mizrahim (Cohen 1998). Despite narrowing the schooling ethnic gap, the income gap among second-generation Jews increased during the past twenty years. In 1975 the average Mizrahi man earned 79 percent of the earnings of his Ashkenazi counterpart. By 1995 this proportion dropped to 69 percent (Cohen 1998). In sum, pre-1967 Mizrahim have failed to catch up economically with their Ashkenazi counterparts. While in other spheres of life (fertility, marriage patterns, labor force participation rates) the ethnic gap narrowed significantly or even disappeared in the second generation (Goldscheider 1996), the schooling and income gaps among the second generation of pre-1967 immigrants hardly changed. Unfortunately, the lack of ethnic information regarding the third generation, as well as their relatively young ages, prohibit analyses of the income gaps in the third generation.

The failure of the melting pot to absorb pre-1967 Mizrahi immigrants is exacerbated by the relative success of (the mostly Ashkenazi) post-1967 immigrants (Lewin-Epstein and Semyonov 2000). The immigrants of the 1970s and 1980s (with the exception of the Ethiopians) fully assimilated in the Israeli labor market and economy within a short time. There are no income or schooling gaps between them and the native population. Moreover, by 1983 the income of post-1967 immigrants surpassed the income of Mizrahi veteran immigrants arriving in the pre-1967 period. For example, in 1983, recently arrived Romanian immigrants earned more than pre-1967 Moroccan immigrants, and as much as Iraqi Jews who arrived in 1950–51. In 1983 Russian Jews who arrived in the 1970s, earned more than pre-1967 immigrants from any Mizrahi source country (Cohen and Haberfeld 2000). Likewise, the economic absorption of the current wave of immigrants from the former Soviet Union appears to be successful. Their schooling level is high, and in relatively short time they find jobs that enable them to join the Israeli-Ashkenazi middle class (Sikron 1998).

The success of post-1967 immigrants is largely attributed to the high skills with which they arrived in Israel compared to pre-1967 predecessors, both Mizrahim and Ashkenazim. This assessment is, for the most part, true, although another factor, institutional discrimination (Swirski

1990), played a central role in the failure of Mizrahi immigrants and their children to fully assimilate in Israel's economy and society.[13] Notwithstanding the existence of institutional and other forms of discrimination against Mizrahi immigrant groups, educational level upon arrival is arguably the single most important determinant of immigrants' economic progress, as well as the main predictor for the educational attainment of their offspring (Friedlander et al. 2001). This being the case, the next section presents analyses that track changes in the skill levels of successive immigrant cohorts arriving in Israel in the past five decades.

The Educational Levels of Successive Immigrant Cohorts

In order to estimate the skills with which immigrants arrive, their education level, (which is considered the best proxy for immigrant labor market skills), should be measured in the first few years after they arrive in Israel, before they had a chance to acquire more schooling in their new country.[14] The trend in mean years of education reveals a relative improvement in immigrants' schooling over time. The average immigrant

FIGURE 2.4 Mean Years of Schooling upon Arrival of Recent Immigrants and of Native Jews, 1951–1995

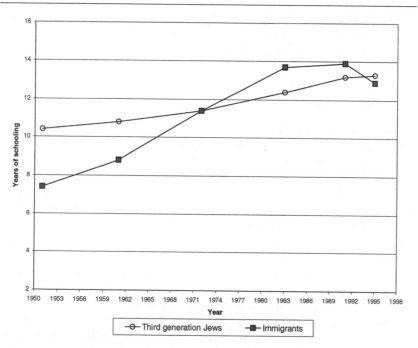

Recent immigrants: immigrant men arriving in Israel during the three years preceding the year of observation. Native Jews: third-generation Jewish men.

Source: Cohen and Haberfeld, 2000.

coming to Israel in the mass migration in the years from 1948 to 1951 had 7.4 years of schooling, compared to 10.4 years among natives. This gap between recently arrived immigrants and native Jews gradually narrowed over the years until 1972, when recently arrived immigrants and natives had the same average years of schooling. Eleven years later, in 1983, recent immigrants surpassed natives by 1.3 years, but by 1995 (the date of the last Israeli census) recent immigrants (arriving in 1992 to 1995) fell behind again, although not by much.

Years of schooling, however, is only one measure of educational level. Academic degrees have increasingly become important in the labor markets of developed countries including Israel. Comparing recent immigrants and natives on that measure—the proportion with at least a B.A. degree—reveals even more impressive progress among immigrants. During the mass migration of 1948 to 1951, less than 5 percent of immigrants were university graduates, compared with nearly 9 percent among natives. Twenty years later, in 1972, the proportion among recent immigrants (27 percent) was more than twice the proportion among natives. In the years 1979 to 1983, nearly 40 percent of immigrants had a college degree (compared to less than 20 percent among natives), and by 1989 to 1991 nearly half the immigrants were university graduates. Those arriving in 1992 to 1995 also had a higher proportion of university graduates than natives, but the gap was not as wide as in 1983 or 1991. In sum, both measures of schooling indicate that the educational level of recent immigrants to Israel has increased over the years, from the periods of 1948–51 to 1989–91, and somewhat declined since 1992.

Explaining the Rise in the Educational Level of Successive Immigrant Cohorts

Contrary to popular and scholarly beliefs, these changes—the rise in immigrants' educational levels during the period from 1948 to 1991, as well as the decline since 1992—are mainly due to educational changes within their country of origin rather than to shifts in source countries from which most immigrants come. In other words, while shifts from low to high education countries (e.g., from Yemen to the USSR) contributed to some of the overall rise in immigrant schooling during 1948 to 1991, most of the rise occurred because of changes over time in the education level of successive immigrant cohorts coming from the same countries (i.e., within-country changes). Consider, for example, Moroccan immigrants. Most of them, about one-quarter of a million, came during the period from 1948 to 1969, and had low schooling levels. In 1972, the average Moroccan immigrant man who immigrated to Israel during the preceding four years had little more than eight years of schooling, and only one in twenty-five immigrants had a university degree, compared to one in eight among native Jews. Eleven years later, in 1983, the average Moroccan immigrant who arrived during the years from 1979 to 1983 had about fourteen years of schooling, and one in three was a college graduate, twice the rate among natives. The increase in schooling level among successive cohorts of Romanian immigrants is even more striking. Their mean years of schooling increased from 9.7 for the cohort arriving during 1957 to 1961 to 13.8 for the cohort of 1968 to 1972, and to a peak of 15.6 for those arriving during 1979 to 1983. Apparently, in all decades, within-country changes were responsible for over one-half of the total rise in the schooling of successive cohorts of immigrants. Thus, while shifts from low to high education countries contributed to some of the overall rise in immigrant schooling, most changes during the period from 1948 to 1991 were due to rises in the educational level of immigrants coming from specific countries.

The decline in immigrant skills in the post-1991 period is also due to the same type of changes within countries. Since 1989, the top two source countries sending immigrants to Israel are the former Soviet Union (85 percent), and Ethiopia (4 percent). While the (low) educational level of successive cohorts of Ethiopian immigrants has not changed over time, a close examination of immigrants coming from the former USSR in the 1990s reveals a decline in their schooling starting in 1992. Those arriving in 1989 to 1991 belong to the first wave that brought some 400,000 immigrants to Israel. In subsequent years, the annual number of immigrants from the former USSR was around 40,000 to 70,000. The schooling levels of those arriving in the first wave were significantly higher than that of those arriving during the years 1992 to 1995. Mean years of schooling of those arriving during the years from 1989 to 1991 is fourteen, and 51 percent of them are university graduates. The respective figures among those arriving between 1992 and 95 are thirteen years and 36 percent,[15] far below the previous cohort, and similar to the educational level among Israeli Jews.[16]

What could explain changes in the educational level of successive cohorts of immigrants from the same country? There are two processes, not mutually exclusive, that are responsible for these changes. First, it is possible that the type of selectivity for immigration has changed over the years. Second, it is possible that the characteristics of the populations at risk (i.e., potential immigrants) in some source countries have changed, mainly due to prior nonrandom immigration to Israel and other countries.[17] Consider, for example, the rise in the schooling of Moroccan immigrants. It is reasonable to assume that immigration from Morocco to Israel until 1972 was negatively selected for education (i.e., immigrants were disproportionately less educated than the Moroccan Jewry from which they were drawn). Apparently, in those years, the more educated Moroccan Jews either stayed in Morocco or immigrated elsewhere, especially to France and Canada (Toledano 1984; Bensimon and Della Pergola 1986). Since the mid-1970s, the schooling of the 12,000 Moroccan immigrants coming to Israel has risen dramatically. It is possible, however, that these immigrants' schooling represents the average schooling among the remaining Moroccan-born Jews outside Israel. There are no readily available data to test this possibility. I wish to emphasize, however, that even if this is the case, (self)selection processes in the 1950s and 1960s are in large part responsible for the dramatic rise in the average schooling of Moroccan immigrants to Israel starting in the mid-1970s.

Other source countries from which major changes in the level of schooling over time were detected are Romania, Iran, the former Soviet Republics, and the U.S. In both Romania and Iran the first waves were negatively selected for education. In Romania, the selectivity for education improved dramatically until 1983, after which it declined again. In Iran, the selectivity of the first wave (1951) was negative (Hacohen 1994), and a major rise occurred in 1979, at the time of the Iranian revolution. However, it is not clear that positive selectivity brought Iranian Jews to Israel. The more educated and wealthy Iranians emigrated to the U.K. and the U.S. Likewise, in the 1970s the educational levels of Soviet immigrants were relatively high compared to the levels among third-generation Jews. It is unclear, however, whether their schooling was high compared to that of Soviet Jewry. What is known, however, is that Soviet Jews who immigrated to the U.S. during the 1970s were younger and had about two more years of schooling, on average, than those who came to Israel (Schwartz-Shavit 1995). Interestingly, the same pattern is observed among Russian immigrants of the 1990s. Those arriving in Canada in 1990 to 1991 were of higher educational levels than those who immigrated to Israel (Kogan 2000). Apparently, during the 1970s and 1990s, the best and the brightest among Soviet Jewry elected to immigrate to countries other than Israel, where the risks of failure are higher than in Israel, but so are the potential economic gains from successful assimilation in the labor market.[18]

In this context the selectivity of U.S. immigrants is of interest for two reasons. First, the U.S. is the third largest source country for immigrants in the post-1989 area. Second, in the U.S. there is readily available information on the schooling level of the population at risk, namely, U.S. Jews. Analyses of the General Social Surveys, suggest that from 1970 to 1990 the proportion of college graduates among American Jews increased by 25 percentage points, from 48 percent to 73 percent. At the same time, the proportion of college graduates among American Jews that self-selected themselves to immigrate to Israel declined by 13 percentage points, from 77 percent among those coming immediately after the 1967 war, to 64 percent among those arriving during the early 1990s. In short, the selectivity of U.S. Jews for immigration to Israel, which was very positive in the first few years after the 1967 war, has deteriorated and become negative over time, as the less educated among American Jews decide to reside in Israel.

Conclusions

Thus far, Zionism has been a demographic success. In 1947, just before Israel was established, only 6 percent of the Jews of the world (about

600,000) resided in the area that became Israel in 1949, comprising less than half the population in that area. By 2000 Israel had become the home for about 5 million Jews, comprising nearly 40 percent of world Jewry and about 80 percent of the state's citizens (CBS 2001). For the most part, immigration patterns are responsible for the three dimensions of Zionism's demographic success—increasing the proportion and the absolute number of Jews in Israel, as well as their share in world Jewry.

With some exceptions in the early 1950s, Israel has always attempted to bring as many Jews as possible to Israel, and there seems to have been no upper limit to the number of immigrants it has been willing to admit in a given period. Moreover, unlike other migration countries that prefer skilled and young immigrants, Israel's declared policy is to admit all Jewish immigrants, with no regard to age, educational level, ethnic origin, and skin color. On the face of it, it looks as if actual migration patterns are consistent with this declared policy. However, when potential Jewish immigrants choose to go to a country other than Israel, Zionist values and goals led Israel to adopt a less humanitarian policy. Such was the case in the 1970s, when Israel asked the U.S. to stop granting refugee status to Soviet Jews who were permitted to leave the USSR, but preferred the U.S. over Israel as their new home. In sum, in the last half-century migration patterns to Israel suggest that the state has been consistently fulfilling the core Zionist mission—populating the land with a multitude of Jews. Whenever this goal contradicted humanitarian goals, such as helping Jews reach safe destinations other than Israel (or, alternatively, when it encountered racist attitudes against immigrants of certain ethnicity or color), Zionist values and goals prevailed.

While Israel actively attracts and accepts all Jews, not all Jews chose to immigrate to Israel. With time, however, the demographic success of Zionism manifested itself also in the type of people who chose Israel as their destination. In the early years of the mass migration and the North African migration, many immigrants were stateless refugees. Others fled repressive regimes in Eastern Europe and Arab states that were in conflict with the new Jewish state. Many of those who could have gone to a more developed state went there rather than to Israel,[19] or left Israel after a short stay. Those residing in developed countries in Western Europe, North America, and Australia did not consider immigrating to Israel. Consequently, the immigrants arriving in Israel in the first twenty years after statehood had lower educational levels than the resident Jewish population of Israel.

Following the 1967 war the type of immigrants choosing Israel as their country of destination changed. For religious, ideological and economic reasons, immigrants from Western Europe and America, mostly highly educated, have begun coming to Israel. Immigrants arriving from the Soviet Union and other countries in Eastern Europe, Africa and Asia were of higher educational levels than their predecessors coming from the same countries in the 1950s and 1960s. Apparently, Israel of the post-1967 period has become a more attractive destination for educated immigrants, although not as attractive as the U.S., as evidenced by highly educated Soviet Jewish emigrants in the 1970s preferring the U.S. to Israel as their country of destination. To be sure, it is not a simple matter for a conflict-ridden, less affluent country such as Israel to compete with the U.S. and other Western countries for skilled Jewish immigrants. Yet one of the main demographic achievements of contemporary Zionism is not only attracting Jews to come to Israel, but also retaining immigrants and their offspring, including the highly educated, in the country.[20]

The current demographic picture, however, is more complex. Since 1992, the immigrants coming from the former Soviet Union (and since 1970 those coming from the U.S.) are of lower educational level than their predecessors, and if the decline in the schooling of immigrants continues, Israel will soon face immigrants whose educational levels will be lower than that of native Israelis. More troubling for the Zionist mission is the monotonic rise in the proportion of non-Jews among immigrants from the former Soviet republics. Moreover, as in other labor-importing countries, many temporary workers who were recruited by Israel since 1993 have rapidly become undocumented, that is de facto permanent residents. This being the case, contemporary migration patterns are not as conducive as previous patterns to winning the demographic race with Israel's Arabs. In addition to about 1.2 million Arab citizens and three million Arabs under occupation (some of them in the semi-autonomous territories ruled by the Palestinian Authority), Israel now faces a challenge it has never faced before: dealing with over 300,000 (and growing) non-Jewish, non-Arab residents (some of whom are not citizens). It is ironic that Zionism's very success—military, economic, and demographic—has led to an incipient challenge to the original mission it set out to accomplish.

Notes

I wish to thank David De Vries, Yosef, Grodzinsky, Yitzhak Haberfeld, Alexandra Kalev, Tali Kristal, Gideon Kunda, Ronny Talmor, and the editors of this volume for their comments on an earlier draft of this chapter, and Tali Kristal for her excellent research assistance.

1. Between 1882 (when Zionist immigration to Ottoman Palestine first began) and 1900, the Jewish population of Ottoman Palestine increased from about 25,000 to 50,000. It reached over 80,000 before World War I. During the war, net migration was negative, leading to the estimated figure for 1919 (Bachi 1974).
2. This figure is obtained using Bachi's (1974: 401f.) estimate that in 1947, 778,700 Palestinians and 630,000 Jews resided in the area that would become Israel in 1949.
3. "The very essence of Zionism," says David Ben Gurion, in 1944, "is populating. To populate Eretz Israel with multitudes of Jews" (Weitz 1994: 81).
4. Goldscheider's estimates are based on CBS statistics for first- and second-generation Jews, and on his estimates regarding the ethnic origin of third-generation Jews.
5. These estimates include only first- and second-generation immigrants (CBS 2001). Since there are likely to be third-generation Moroccan and Romanian immigrants, the sizes of these groups are larger than reported above.
6. In 1995 the share of U.S.-born in Jewish settlements in the occupied West Bank and the Gaza strip (4.0 percent) was approximately 4.1 times its share in the Jewish population. In 1983, when the settler population was smaller, yet more ideological, the share of U.S.-born in the territories (4.3 percent) was 4.8 times their share in the population (the respective figure among those born in Western Europe is 2.3). These figures, which are based on my analyses of Israeli censuses of 1983 and 1995, are underestimates, as they include only the territories defined by Israel as "Judea, Samaria, and the Gaza Area." These do not include territories that were annexed to Jerusalem in 1967, nor the occupied Golan Heights.
7. In the last general elections in 1999, Shas—a religious-Mizrahi party—received about 500,000 votes. Apparently, the party's insistence on being both Jewish-religious and Mizrahi (all its seventeen parliament members are religious Mizrahim) is central for explaining its success among poor Mizrahim (Peled 1998). Unfortunately, it is not known how many third-generation of Mizrahi ancestry voted Shas.
8. In 1970 the Law of Return was amended to include not only Jews, but also non-Jewish children and grandchildren (and their spouses) of Jews. See Weiss in this volume.
9. Until 1994 the basic classification of the population was according to religion, between "Jews" and "non-Jews." The latter were further classified into Muslims, Christians, and "Druze and others" (CBS 1994: table 2.1). In the 1995 Statistical Abstract, when the word "Arabs" first appeared, the basic distinction was between "Jews" and "Arabs and others," whereby "others" included a few hundred "Buddhists, Hindus, Samaritans etc" (CBS 1995, page 21). With the increase in the number of non-Jewish immigrants, the original "others" were reclassified, and together with the new "others" were added to the Jewish group. Thus, beginning in the Statistical Abstract of 2000, the basic classification is between "Jews and others" and "Arab population" (CBS 2000: table 2.1). See Lustik (1999)for the difficulties of the CBS following the rise in the number of non-Jewish immigrants.
10. The total number of labor migrants in Israel's labor market (including Palestinians from the occupied territories) is estimated at about 290,000, comprising 13 percent of the labor market (*Haaretz*, 4.4.01).
11. Special pooling of the 1983 and 1995 censuses enabled researchers to estimate the proportion of Mizrahim and Ashkenazim among some birth cohorts of third-generation Jews. Analyses provided to me by Yossi Shavit, suggest that in 1995 Ashkenazim outnumbered Mizrahim by a ratio of roughly two to one among those twenty-seven to thirty-four years old, but only by a ratio of four to three among those twenty years old

in that year. It is thus reasonable to assume that the proportion of Mizrahim is higher among younger age cohorts.

12. Only 37 percent of Israeli-born Jews residing in the U.S. in 1980 chose "Israeli" as their first ancestry (Cohen and Tyree 1994). The respective figure in the 1990 census was appreciably the same (Cohen and Haberfeld 1997).

13. Mizrahim suffered from discrimination in many spheres of life, including the labor market, where both the state and private employers valued their human capital as inferior to the human capital of Ashkenazim. Khazzoom (1998) have demonstrated that in the 1950s the educational levels of immigrants from some Mizrahi source countries were very similar to the educational levels of Polish and Romanian immigrants. Nevertheless, the Romanian and Polish immigrants fully assimilated in Israeli economy and society, while the educated Mizrahi immigrants failed to do so.

14. The findings regarding trends in the educational level of successive immigrant cohorts are based on Cohen and Haberfeld (2000) who compared the schooling of recent immigrants from twenty source countries to a benchmark of third-generation Israeli Jews ("natives") of the same ages.

15. There are no differences in the schooling levels between men and women immigrants from the former Soviet Union, nor between Jews and non-Jews. Those coming from the Asian republics have somewhat lower schooling levels than their European counterparts (Haberfeld, Semyonov, and Cohen 2000).

16. While experts are in agreement with respect to the economic assimilation of the new immigrants from the former Soviet Union (Sikron 1998), there are debates regarding their social and cultural assimilation. Some (e.g., Lissak 2001) argue that this immigrant group views Israeli culture and society as inferior to Russian culture, and resists cultural assimilation. The evidence for such attitudes are survey research, the number of Russian-language newspapers (including the contents of the articles published in these newspapers), the success of Russian political parties, and the continuing connections between the immigrants and their country of origin. Others (e.g., Smocha 2001) expect the new immigrants from the former Soviet Union to integrate into the Ashkenazi middle class in relatively short time. The Russians, argues Smocha (2001), do not want to become a distinct sector in the Israeli society. They do not demand that Russian become an official language, nor do they ask for a special educational track. Without a state-supported school system, Smocha concludes, it is nearly impossible to maintain the original culture. The demands of the Russian parties are far from being separatist. Rather, they ask for resources and integration into Israeli society.

17. The mean schooling of populations of source countries rises also due to expansion of the educational systems.

18. These preferences are consistent with economic migration theory (Borjas 1994), which expects skilled immigrants to prefer high inequality countries such as the U.S., where skills are compensated generously, whereas less skilled immigrants prefer more egalitarian countries (such as Israel), where they are protected by a net of social services.

19. Only about 40 percent of the Jews in DP camps during the period from 1945 to 1951 immigrated to Israel (Grodzinsky 1998).

20. See Cohen and Haberfeld (1997, 2001) for the number of Israeli Jews in the U.S. in 1990 (less than 130,000), their high rate of return migration to Israel, as well as for evidence that those returning to Israel are of higher educational level than those staying in the U.S.

References

Amit, Karin. 2001. "The Binary Ethnic Classification and the Economic Assimilation of First- and Second-Generation Immigrants in the Israeli Labor Market." Ph.D. diss., Tel Aviv University. [Hebrew]

Bachi, Roberto. 1974. *The Population of Israel*. Jerusalem: The Institute for Contemporary Jewry.

Bensimon, Doris, and Sergio Della Pergola. 1986. *La population juive de France: socio-demographie et identité*. Jewish Population Studies No. 17. Paris: The Institute of Contemporary Jewry, the Hebrew University, and Centre National de la Recherche Scientifique. [French]

Borjas, George. 1994. "The Economics of Immigration." *Journal of Economic Literature* 32: 1667–1717.

Central Bureau of Statistics (CBS). 2001. *Statistical Abstracts of Israel No 52*. Jerusalem.

Cohen, Yinon. 1998. "Socioeconomic Gaps among Jews, 1975–1995." *Israeli Sociology* 1: 115–134. [Hebrew]

Cohen, Yinon, and Yitchak Haberfeld. 1997. "The Number of Israeli Immigrants in the U.S. in 1990." *Demography* 34: 199–212.

———. 2000. "Selectivity and Economic Assimilation of Israeli Immigrants Since 1948." Paper presented at the RC28 meeting in Lieborne, France, May.

———. 2001. "Self-Selection and Return Migration: Israeli-Born Jews Returning Home from the United States during the 1980s." *Population Studies* 55: 79–91.

Cohen, Yinon, and Andrea Tyree. 1994. "Palestinian and Jewish Israeli-Born Immigrants in the U.S." *International Migration Review* 28: 243–255.

Della Pergola, Sergio. 1998. "The Global Context of Migration to Israel." In *Immigration to Israel: Sociological Perspectives*, ed. E. Leshem and J. Shuval, 51–92. New Brunswick: Transaction Publishers.

Dominitz, Yehuda. 1997. "Israel's Immigration Policy and the Dropout Phenomenon." In *Russian Jews on Three Continents: Migration and Resettlement*, ed. Noah Lewin-Epstein, Yaacov Ro'I, and Paul Ritterband, 113–127. London: Frank Cass.

Friedlander, Dov, and Calvin Goldscheider. 1979. *The Population of Israel*. New York: Columbia University Press.

Friedlander, Dov, et al. 2000. "Religion, Ethnicity, Type of Locality and Educational Attainment Among Israel's Population: An Analysis of Change over Time." Working Paper Series. Jerusalem: The Hebrew University.

Goldscheider, Calvin. 1989. "The Demographic Embeddedness of the Arab-Jewish Conflict in Israeli Society." *Middle East Review* 21 (3): 15–24.

———. 1996. *Israel's Changing Society: Population, Ethnicity, and Development*. Boulder: Westview Press.

Grodzinsky, Yosef. 1998. *Good Human Material: Zionists vs. Jews, 1945–1951*. Tel Aviv: Hed Artzi. [Hebrew]

Haberfeld, Yitchak, Moshe Semyonov, and Yinon Cohen. 2000. "Ethnicity and Labour Market Performance among Recent Immigrants from the Former Soviet Union to Israel." *European Sociological Review* 16: 287–299.

Hacohen, Dvora. 1994. *Immigrants in Turmoil: The Great Wave of Immigration to Israel and Its Absorption, 1948–1953*. Jerusalem: Yad Ben Zvi. [Hebrew]

Jenkins, Richard. 1996. *Social Identity*. New York: Routledge.

Kemp, Adriana, and Rivka Raijman. 2000. "Foreigners in the Jewish State: The New Politics of Migrant Labor in Israel." *Israeli Sociology* 3 (1): 79–110. [Hebrew]

Khazzoom, Aziza. 1998. "The Origins of Ethnic Inequality among Jews in Israel." Ph.D. diss., University of California, Berkeley.

Kogan, Irena. 2000. "Labor Market Attainment of Immigrants from the Former Soviet Union in Canada and Israel." Master's thesis, Tel Aviv University.

Lewin Epstein, Noah, and Moshe Semyonov. 2000. "Immigration and Stratification in Israel." In *Society in Perspective*, ed. Hanna Herzog, 95–106. Tel Aviv: Ramot. [Hebrew]

Lissak, Moshe. 1999. *The Mass Immigration in the Fifties: The Failure of the Melting Pot Policy.* Jerusalem: Bialik Institute. [Hebrew]

———. 2001. "The Russian Immigration." Paper presented at the Rabin Center, Tel Aviv, 5 March. [Hebrew]

Lustick, Ian. 1999. "Israel as a Non-Arab State: The Political Implications for Mass Immigration of Non-Jews." *Middle East Journal* 53: 417–433.

Morris, Benny. 1987. *The Birth of the Palestinian Refugee Problem, 1947–1949.* New York: Cambridge University Press.

Naor, Mordechai, and Dan Giladi. 1990. *Eretz Israel in the 20th Century: From Yishuv to Statehood, 1900–1950.* Tel Aviv: Ministry of Defense. [Hebrew]

Peled, Yoav. 1998. "Toward a Redefinition of Jewish Nationalism in Israel? The Enigma of Shas." *Ethnic and Racial Studies* 21: 354–367.

Rosenhek, Zeev, and Erik Cohen. 2000. "Patterns of Migrant Workers' Incorporation and the Israeli Migration Regime: A Comparative Analysis." *Israeli Sociology* 3 (1): 53–78. [Hebrew]

Schwartz-Shavit, Miri. 1995. "Quality Examination of Jewish Emigrants from the USSR to Israel and to the U.S.A. between the Years 1975–1980." Master's thesis, Tel Aviv University. [Hebrew]

Sikron, Moshe. 1998. "The Human Capital of the Immigrants and Their Absorption in the Labor Market." In *A Profile of a Migration Wave,* ed. Moshe Sikron and Elazar Leshem, 127–181. Jerusalem: Magnes. [Hebrew]

Smocha, Sammy. 2001. "The Russian Immigration: An Assessment." Paper presented at the Rabin Center, Tel Aviv, 5 March.

Swirski, Shlomo. 1990. *Education in Israel.* Tel Aviv: Breirot. [Hebrew]

Toledano, Joseph. 1984. *At the Time of the Mellah.* Jerusalem: Ramtol. [Hebrew]

Weitz, Yechiam. 1994. *Awareness and Helplessness.* Jerusalem: Yad Ben Zvi. [Hebrew]

PART TWO

CITIZENSHIP AND NATURALIZATION

— *Chapter 3* —

CITIZENSHIP AND NATURALIZATION POLITICS IN GERMANY IN THE NINETEENTH AND TWENTIETH CENTURIES

Dieter Gosewinkel

Introduction

The history of the modern state is inextricably linked to the development of our current conception of citizenship.[1] Citizenship defines the people who constitute the state and, at the same time, the historical transition of the foundation of membership in the modern state from territory to the individual. With the intensification and concentration of state power, the importance of citizenship with regard to individual rights and duties has steadily increased. Finally, the character of citizenship as a political institution of the modern democratizing state system is now fully developed. It—virtually exclusively—extends the opportunity for political participation on the state level.

In the climate of nationalism at the end of the nineteenth century, citizenship became more sharply defined—both territorially and personally—and came to distinguish those affiliated with a state from those outside its conceptual as well as physical boundaries. Thus, citizenship became the institution within the nation-state that was charged with determining the extent of a national citizenry's "inclusiveness" or "exclusiveness."

It is my *first thesis* that an increasingly close relationship and, ultimately, an institutional connection, developed between citizenship and the conception of the nation in modern German history.[2] The focus of this chapter will be an analysis of the politics of citizenship and naturalization in modern German history, centered on the German Citizenship Law of 1913.[3] To naturalize means to create new members of the state, that is, citizens.

It is my *second thesis* that citizenship as a means of conceiving of national identity is reflected in the way in which particular groups are included in, or excluded from, naturalization policy. I will illustrate this by examining the naturalization of Jews in Germany.[4]

My *third thesis* is that there is no straight ethno-cultural line of development inherent in the concept of German citizenship that dominated from the outset and merged seamlessly into the racist citizenship law of National Socialism. Certain segments of the literature on the subject cause this impression. It is asserted that the *ius sanguinis* prepared "fruitful ground for the National Socialist seed of genocide," since it nourished the belief that membership in the nation was a matter of descent and thus of biology. The transformation of the principle in racist National Socialist law also rather recedes behind the ideal of a *"völkisch* reinterpretation."[5] A functional continuity is also assumed because of the continued existence of the legal principle (Wippermann 1999: 141). Rogers Brubaker (1992: 166), who makes a differentiated argument speaking of the "radical novelty of Nazi citizenship policy," at the same time wholly ignores the Weimar Republic, the phase of radicalization and thus fails to explain the break.

In contrast, I distinguish between a juridical principle and the way it became politically charged over the course of changes in the national discourse. The dominance of the principle of descent in German citizenship law did not arise naturally from an ethno-cultural conception of the German nation, but rather was the product of specific historical constellations, which determined the political decision in favor of the principle of descent, thus providing the institutional point of departure for an ethno-cultural interpretation.[6]

The historical survey extends from the time of the first codification of civil rights and citizenship in the prerevolutionary period between 1815 and 1848 to the promulgation of the German constitution or Basic Law (*Grundgesetz*) of 1949. The Citizenship Law (*Reichs- und Staatsangehörigkeitsgesetz*) of 1913 possessed outstanding significance for the development of national German citizenship. Its advent and effects will thus be discussed in a longer passage, which forms the center of my contribution. The German defeat in World War I, the interlude of the first democratic Weimar Republic (1919–33) and the National Socialist regime (1933–45) mark stages in the development of the German nation-state. After a period of deformation and destruction under National Socialism, the constitution of the Federal Republic restored German citizenship law to its traditional form, which had been shaped over the course of the nineteenth century. The following outline covers the history of the German nation-state, its rise, unfolding and temporary decline after World War II. In contrast to France and England, Germany did not enter the nineteenth century as an established nation-state with centralized structures and a consolidated territory. In the course of the nineteenth century, it developed from a loose federation of states into a powerful nation-state, the German Reich of 1871.

The Essential Traits of Prenational Citizenship in Germany

The rise of modern citizenship in Germany reflects a fundamental revolution in political and socioeconomic processes during the first half of the nineteenth century. Through the end of the eighteenth century, German states based citizenship on adherence to a territorial state and to the person of the feudal sovereign rather than on descent from a subject of the state.[7] The economic and social consequences of the early nineteenth-century reforms—the mass migration of an impoverished rural population[8]—forced the states to define such adherence more precisely. In the light of inter-state migration, birth within the borders of a state no longer represented a sufficiently stable criterion by which to define adherence to a state. In contrast to the older criteria, the quality of physical "descent" from a citizen of the state was held to be less ambiguous (Grawert 1973: 136ff., 184). It was introduced as a legal principle in inter-state treaties.

This development was accompanied by an increasing need within states to standardize their criteria for membership and to distinguish adherence to a state from adherence to local or municipal bodies. Economic, social and administrative requirements all contributed to the 1842 reform bill on Prussian citizenship (Koselleck 1989: 631f.), which came to serve as a model for citizenship laws among the states of the German Federation. It established a territorially uniform and direct relationship between the state and its members that was comprehensive, i.e., not confined to certain groups or classes. This new legislation sprang from a fundamental modernizing impulse that was at once prenational and transnational: "subjects" of the Prussian crown, be they of German or Polish nationality, had equal rights and were mutually indistinguishable under Prussian law.[9]

Citizenship in the Developing German Nation-State, 1848–1871

The relationship between the liberal and national constitutional movements in prerevolutionary Germany was increasingly expressed in a modern conception of citizenship. The connection began to become legally and politically manifest in the constitution of 1849. The founding of the German nation-state made a definition of membership in the new state necessary, and therefore required that German citizenship be defined. The concept, however, remained ambivalent. For the time being, a federalist definition of the "German people" with reference to the state seemed to be effective: the "German people" should consist of "adherents to the states that form the German Empire." In addition to that definition, however, the important cultural concepts of "Germanness" and the "German nation" influenced the constitutional assembly's debates over the text of the constitution. This structural ambivalence shaped the further development of the institution of German citizenship.

The first attempt to establish a comprehensive German citizenship failed in 1849. Within the states of the German Federation, however, there was an increasing trend toward the adoption of the "modern" Prussian, descent-based model of citizenship (*ius sanguinis*) over the traditional, territorial one (*ius soli*), which was deeply rooted in feudal legal tradition. This process was accompanied by the development in political theory of the concept of the state as an "organism," which was equated with the family as the embodiment of the idea of a community of descent.

Citizenship in the Powerful Nation-State: The German Empire

The 1871 constitution of the German Empire and the accompanying legislation took the Prussian citizenship law of 1842 as a model, setting a uniform canon of fixed minimum criteria both for the primary acquisition of citizenship and for naturalization. In so doing, they advanced the homogenization of citizenship; descent from a citizen became the guiding principle of citizenship throughout the German Reich. Naturalization was linked to two main conditions: a) minimum socioeconomic criteria of integration into the local community (e.g., proof of the applicant's ability to support himself and his family, and consent of the municipality to his settling there), and b) proof of "respectability." The calculated vagueness of the latter criterion allowed for the inclusion of political, moral and economic considerations. The reality of inclusion and exclusion in German naturalization policy depended on federal practice on the sub-legislative level. The authorities kept secret the criteria they used to determine an applicant's desirability as a citizen. These arcane politics combined with the discretionary powers of the naturalization authorities to make their decision-making process akin to an act of grace. It was a standardized procedure, sanctified by special documents, comparable in form and symbolic meaning to documents certifying baptism, marriage or the appointment of civil servants.

The new citizenship legislation had a unifying effect on the practice of naturalization in the Reich. Moreover, through diplomatic pressure and a complicated consent procedure, the most restrictive naturalization policy in the German Empire—that of the hegemonic Prussian state—became the standard for all the federal states.[10]

The homogenizing effect of citizenship, however, was eroded by the pressures exerted by political and structural changes in the German Empire as well as by a new quality of nationalism. During the economic boom of the last decade of the nineteenth century, the Reich became the second-largest labor-importing country in the world. The immigrant labor force, predominantly Polish Jews from Russia and the non-German parts of Austria-Hungary, faced increasing nationalistic and anti-Semitic prejudice in German society. [11]

Under the influence of the nationalistic movements in Europe at the turn of the twentieth century, national minorities in Germany became politically more active. Thus, with regard to a common citizenship, the political, social and religious differences deepened along "national" lines, especially in Alsace-Lorraine, northern Schleswig, and the Polish east of Prussia. These tensions were eventually sharpened by structural conflicts within German society. Bismarck's battle against internal "enemies of the Empire" demonstrated the increasing symbolic force of citizenship through the will to expatriate those regarded as political enemies of the "community of citizens." These expatriation measures were planned against socialists and Catholics deemed disloyal to the German state. They were only applied in a single case, against a Catholic bishop. The mere existence of expatriation plans, however, shows their potential to be instrumentalized as the most extreme measures—aside from physical destruction—that a constitutional state could take to define its own identity by closure.

In addition to expatriation plans and measures, the Prussian state took restrictive legal and administrative action against its ethnic minorities. Prussian citizens of Danish and especially Polish descent were discriminated against by means of laws regulating the use of their national languages, the organization of schools, the right of assembly and the distribution of land.[12]

Both the naturalization practices and the erosion of rights reveal how the formal claim to homogeneity and equality inherent in the legal institution of citizenship increasingly diverged from an underlying, more restrictive and more substantive conception of adherence. In addition to the social and religious arguments, nationality proved to be the weak link in the defense against internal discrimination. De facto discrimination divided citizens of the same state into separate legal classes, with unequal social and political opportunities.

To come back to naturalization politics: how were the strictly secret criteria according to which candidates for naturalization were ranked put into practice? First, economic and social suitability for naturalization represented minimum criteria, to which the desire to avoid unwanted economic rivalries set partial limits. Fitness for military service was a highly important factor, as was being politically "above suspicion" (particularly for foreign clergymen and journalists). The investigation also included a test of the candidate's knowledge of the German language and a declaration of religious affiliation. The latter point posed a particular problem for Jews seeking naturalization. For many years, they constituted a separate category in that the final decision regarding their eligibility had to be made by the minister of the interior rather than by municipal or local authorities (Wertheimer 1987: 55).

Jewish applications for citizenship also represented the main impetus for the systematic statistical record-keeping on naturalization and its secrecy in

Prussian Germany. The administrative recording of naturalizations according to religious affiliation was introduced in connection with a tightened Prussian defensive policy against Jews, and in response to anti-Semitic calls for a religious census. It was kept secret from the public in order to conceal the role that naturalization played as an instrument of selection, in violation of the guarantee of religious neutrality in the constitutions of the German states. Thus, it would hardly be an exaggeration to trace the birth of Prussian naturalization policy to the spirit of anti-Semitism.

A general profile of "desirability" for applicants would include the following: those regarded as "nationally harmless," meaning they were members of Western nations "of related blood," were at the top of the list. Former citizens seeking re-naturalization, especially if they were fit for military service and morally "respectable," occupied approximately the same rank. Their privileged position was justified with reference to their knowledge of the German language and their proximity to the "German character." Slavs, particularly Czechs and Poles, were toward the bottom of the scale, being regarded as "unwanted elements" for reasons of national homogeneity. The lowest rank in the naturalization hierarchy was clearly occupied by Jews, who faced rejection on economic, national and religious grounds.

To recapitulate some essential traits of Prussian naturalization policy in the German Empire: obstacles to naturalization were, in principle, still surmountable if applicants demonstrated their willingness to assimilate linguistically and culturally and to perform military service. In the long run, naturalization policy worked as a defense mechanism, particularly against Jewish applicants: one can speak of a "blocked naturalization" (*Einbürgerungsstau*) of Jews. More than one-third of the approximately 100,000 Jews who lived in Germany in 1933 had been born or brought up in the territory of the German Reich, but had not been naturalized. The statistics of the Prussian State, where more than two thirds of the "foreign" Jews lived, demonstrated that Jews accounted for 10 percent of the "foreign" population, but only 1 percent of naturalizations at the end of the German Empire.

The Reinforcement of an Institution: The Citizenship Law of 1913

A long-term analysis of the development of citizenship in the German Empire reveals a shift in the criteria used to determine a person's "desirability" for naturalization. Over time, economic and social indicators became less important and linguistic or cultural affinity more so. This development found expression in, and was to some extent reinforced by, the German *Reichs- und Staatsangehörigkeitsgesetz* or citizenship law for the empire and the federal states.[13] The legislating process, which took some twenty years, reflected the nationalization of politics in the last decades of the German Empire.

Nationalities' struggles within the German Empire and transformations in the national self-understanding altered the practice of naturalization policy. The deep transformation revealed itself in the changes in the foundations of the federal law of 1870, which had defined German citizenship for more than a generation after the founding of the Empire. In the course of the nineteenth century, the ground rules of German citizenship had been defined either by reform efforts on the part of the state bureaucracy or attempts at a revolutionary refounding of the state—in the Paulskirche in Frankfurt. On the whole, citizenship had remained a construct of a narrow political or administrative elite. This changed at the end of the nineteenth century. For the first time, organized political forces from within German society pressed for a new organization of the basic rules of membership in the German nation-state to ensure national homogeneity.

The initiative for a reform of German citizenship law came from the parliament. A group of mainly national-liberal and conservative Reichstag deputies pursued a dual objective: on the one hand, to make it easier for Germans living abroad to retain their citizenship, and on the other to make it more difficult for foreign nationals living in the German Empire to acquire German citizenship. The parliamentary initiative was introduced by Ernst Hasse, chairman of the Pan-German League (Alldeutscher Verband).[14] It corresponded to the program of this radically *völkisch* and nationalist association, which was devoted to the cultivation of *Deutschtum* (Germans and Germanness) abroad, particularly to a *völkisch* minorities policy in Central Europe, as well as to fighting the "Slavic menace" on the empire's frontiers.

Under the influence of these objectives, citizenship became for the first time an instrument of national policy, which was to strengthen *Deutschtum* at home and abroad and defend it against dilution, dissolution, and the encroachment of foreigners. The initiators of the legislation painted a picture of peril. The "homogeneity" of the German nation was under threat from a flood of "people of alien tongues and races." Thus, as few foreigners as possible should be naturalized. Only "members of the German people" (*deutsche Volksgenossen*) should have a right to German citizenship, while foreigners of "inferior nationalities" should be excluded.[15] In international terms, this venture was aimed at compensating for a sense of national inferiority: the German Empire should, like other self-assured colonial and nation-states, particularly England and France, retain authority over its citizens living abroad, thus demonstrating its strengthened interest as a "self-confident and powerful empire." In domestic terms, the experience of growing struggles between nationalities within the empire played a significant role. The intensified pressures of state Germanization policy beginning in the 1890s increased the desire for national self-determination among the Danish and Polish minorities in the German Empire. National minorities responded to expulsions and discrimination in educational and language legislation with increased national self-organization, boycotts and secessionist tendencies. Finally, the parliamentary initiative coincided with Germany's above-mentioned transformation in the mid-1890s from a country of emigration to one of immigration. Increased immigration from Eastern Europe unleashed a sense of threat to which citizenship law, as a means of closure, was intended to respond.

At the same time, and for similar reasons as the parliamentary initiative, in 1894 the administration of the most powerful German state, i.e., Prussia, concluded a fundamental decision-making process, which helped set the course of German citizenship law. In the two decades after the founding of the German Empire, the governments of Alsace-Lorraine and the Prussian border provinces repeatedly considered introducing the territorial principle into German citizenship law. The point of departure for this reform movement was the unjust distribution of military duties primarily concerning "colonies of foreigners" of Danish or French citizenship that had formed in Alsace-Lorraine and the northern regions of Schleswig.[16] On the one hand, these people had lost contact with their "home" countries, and on the other they were not subject to German compulsory military service, which aroused anger among the German population. Were birth in German territory to suffice for the acquisition of German citizenship, the descendants of these foreigners could be drafted for military service. Proponents of this reform also argued in terms of military competition with France, which since the late 1880s had strengthened the territorial principle in its citizenship law, thus also strengthening its military forces. The territorial principle also met with support among the leading civil servants of the western Prussian provinces of the Rhineland and Westphalia. The foreigners resident there were mainly immigrants from neighboring Belgium and Holland. They were considered well-integrated both socially and economically, generally spoke German, and often volunteered for military service. From the viewpoint of the senior administrators of these provinces, granting German citizenship to these German families and their descendants, who were long-time residents of the region, was merely the conclusion and thus recognition of a social and cultural assimilation that had already taken place.

The introduction of the territorial principle ran up against the resistance of the leading civil servants of Prussia's eastern provinces, who unanimously feared the potential substantial economic and national disadvantages that might arise from the integration of "Eastern" immigrants. They regarded the national stance of the Poles, who had successfully resisted all efforts at Germanization, as the most significant obstacle. Their naturalization would not cause them to feel "German," but rather would leave untouched their "sense of Polish identity." The naturalization of immigrants of mainly "Jewish-Polish nationality" was also deemed undesirable from the standpoint of Prussian state interests. This group of immigrants was considered incapable of naturalization-worthiness and loyalty to the German state, even after naturalization. Senior administrators in the Prussian east saw an unbridgeable gap between state-legal and cultural-national membership. The civil servants, for their part, deepened this ambivalence by stressing pre-state and pre-political assessment criteria of a national, social and religious nature. From their perspective, "naturalization-worthiness" took precedence over "naturalizability." Alongside obvious anti-Jewish and anti-Polish resentments, the social gap between the desire for well-to-do foreigners and the economic reality of Eastern European immigrants who were regarded as "proletarian" played an important role.

Pre-state, ethnic and religious arguments against the territorial principle were of central significance. At the same time, to assume an absolute primacy of ethno-cultural arguments would be to oversimplify the political decision-making process and ignore the economic and above all political context in which the administrative discourse took place. The cultural and religious misgivings regarding "Eastern" immigrants were always connected with concerns about their economic and social status. In contrast to the more prosperous "Western" immigrants, the authorities did not consider them to be "valuable" additions to the population in a material and utilitarian sense. The authorities' lack of faith in the assimilatory power of German citizenship also did not mirror an ahistorical constant of national self-perception, but rather emerged from contemporary political experience. From the perspective of the Prussian state, the heightened struggles between nationalities, although members of the German majority and the Polish minority almost always shared the same citizenship, necessarily aroused skepticism regarding the political integrative power of its citizenship. In contrast to France, the German Empire had to contend with organized movements of national minorities, which were gaining in strength, enjoyed political support abroad, and developed secessionist tendencies (Gosewinkel 2001c). In this situation, the introduction of state elements into German citizenship law was viewed as a relinquishing of state decision-making powers over the naturalization or expulsion of foreigners who were deemed to be potentially dangerous. The decision of the Prussian leadership not to introduce the territorial principle thus did not follow a preexisting ethno-cultural model of the nation, but rather remained essentially a *political* decision in a specific historical situation of internal instability within the empire. In political deliberations, the disadvantages of introducing the territorial principles in the eastern border regions, the main source of immigration, outweighed the potential advantages in the state's western provinces.

It is one of the peculiarities of the establishment of a juridical principle that it takes on a life of its own beyond the political occasion of its emergence. The assertion of the pure principle of descent over the territorial principle was directed against particular groups of immigrants, but set the tone for immigration policy more generally, particularly since it coincided with Germany's transformation into a country of net immigration. Germany's road to a reluctant nation of immigrants began with the administrative decision and parliamentary initiative opposing an integrative concept of citizenship.

After confirming the status quo in citizenship law, the imperial administration showed little inclination to bow to the demands of the Reichstag initiative. There was, to be sure, a basic agreement that it would be made easier in future for Germans living abroad to retain their German citizenship. The question of the legal means, however, elicited fundamental differences of opinion between the imperial ministries (Gosewinkel 1995: 373–374). A minority of ministers who supported the national political reform project were prepared to accept two fundamental departures from existing citizenship law: in order to ensure that Germans living abroad could pass their German citizenship on to their children, limitations on the fair distribution of military service would have to be accepted, along with dual citizenship. In particular, the head of the Imperial Navy Office, Admiral Tirpitz, the political and military brain behind the German naval movement, supported this attitude in order to strengthen Germans abroad in the service of an imperial German "world politics." Tirpitz, who wholeheartedly adopted the cause of the parliamentary reform initiative, embodied a new form of aggressive imperial nationalism, which placed more emphasis on technological process, individual achievement, and political and military utility than on communal values such as the maintenance of compulsory military service. The contrary position, which was shared by the majority of ministers, proceeded from a primacy of reason of state over what was opportune for the nation: according to this view, citizenship rested on the notion of the state as a defense community, which was based on equal duties, and clung to the principle of unambiguous citizenship (Gosewinkel 2001b: 317). In the government draft, which was finally presented to the Reichstag in 1912 after long debates, the etatist standpoint had asserted itself over the nationalist one: according to the principle "no national community without a defense community," a German living abroad lost his citizenship if he violated his duty to perform military service.

The central debate over legal reform flared up around the principle of the acquisition of citizenship: should the pure principle of descent be upheld, as in the law of 1870, or should it be modified by the territorial principle? The Social Democratic minority in the Reichstag demanded the latter solution, which was also favored by left liberals and representatives of the Danish and Polish minorities. The opposition sought to give German citizenship to all persons born and raised in Germany, even if their parents were foreigners. They justified their position in terms of the reciprocity of rights and duties in a state community, and of the concept of the state as a "working community" (*Arbeitsgemeinschaft*).[17] The parliamentary majority composed of conservatives, National Liberals and the Center Party, won out, however. Arguing just as definitely as the minority, the majority championed the organicist position of the state as a family. The analogy between the state and the family attributed a hereditary quality to ethnic and national differences and fit quite neatly with the conception of the "Christian state" promoted by the Center Party and segments of the conservatives.

The Imperial Citizenship Law of 1913 codified the pure *ius sanguinis* as both a legal and political institution of German citizenship. The decision in favor of the pure principle of descent confirmed the administrative decision of 1894 against the *ius soli* and elevated its political intentions into law. The *ius sanguinis* was deliberately strengthened as a regulative measure in order to control undesirable immigrants from Eastern Europe, who were regarded as ethnically and culturally alien and inferior as well as threatening to national homogeneity. Thus a historically specific notion of national protection became structurally cemented. The principle of the inheritance of citizenship through descent corresponded to ideas of ethnic homogeneity, which proceeded from the "objective," genetically transferable quality of Germanness. To this extent the ethnic-*völkisch* ideas of the original Reichstag initiative succeeded in asserting themselves.

Would it therefore be correct to interpret the imperial law of 1913 as the single-minded triumph and indeed embodiment of the primacy of the ethno-cultural, which set the stage for a blood-based racist principle of German citizenship? This opinion is widespread in the literature, but does not stand up to a closer analysis of the law's genesis and structure.[18]

Firstly, the introduction of permanent and heritable German citizenship outside Germany—seventeen years after the parliamentary initiative—no longer stemmed from a specifically ethno-cultural understanding of the nation, as Rogers Brubaker (1992: 118f.) would have it. Instead, this regulation was based on a broad consensus among all parties regarding the value of the nation, which, despite a diversity of political and social motives, contained a core of agreement: four decades after the founding of the empire, German citizenship represented an established symbol of the national honor. The common ground here was not a feeling of national superiority, although this certainly existed, particularly in conservative circles, but rather the aspiration to the oft-cited model of the English and French nation-states and national pride. It was characteristic of this primarily compensatory national pride that it imposed legal and ethical boundaries on itself—in the form of the citizen's obligation to the defense community. This also proved an obstacle to demands to promote dual citizenship for ethnic and national reasons in order to preserve a German community and culture abroad. The duty to maintain loyalty to a single defense community forbade the general acceptance of multiple citizenship.[19]

Secondly, a comparison of the motives behind the original parliamentary initiative of 1895 with the text of the 1913 law reveals that significant demands for an ethnic homogenization of the "national community" remained unrealized. The restriction of naturalization to specific "desirable" groups was not adopted in law. To be sure, Jews in particular faced serious discrimination, for example within Prussian naturalization policy, which Jewish civil rights organizations did not succeed in having outlawed (Gosewinkel 1998: 78–83, 90–97). On the other hand, this political practice of exclusion could be stopped at any time and was precisely not adopted in the 1913 law. Such a regulation would have aroused the ire of

the liberal public, as the Minister of the Interior Bethmann Hollweg realized quite clearly in 1908, and would not have found a parliamentary
majority.[20] *Völkisch* demands for the exclusion of so-called colored persons of alien race (*rassefremder Farbiger*) from German citizenship likewise
failed. Rather, the law expressly allowed for the possibility of giving citizenship to "natives in the protectorate," i.e., the empire's colonial subjects.[21] Certainly, naturalization practice continued to discriminate
against Jews and "natives" (Gosewinkel 1998: 97–106). It is important,
however, that this was not mandated nor even legitimated by law, and
thus was subject to change if the political will was present. The law of
1913 did not forbid a restrictive and discriminatory naturalization practice—but it did not demand it either. It also left scope for a liberal naturalization policy. It remained an *institution of a potentially closed state entity*.
Even after 1913, political decisions and mentalities, to which the law
merely lent an institutional framework, continued to be the ultimate
determinants of the restrictive or liberal granting of German citizenship.

Thirdly, and finally, the cementing of the exclusive *ius sanguinis* did not
signal the adoption of a blood-based biological racial theory in German
citizenship law. This assumption may be terminologically tempting, since
representatives of the nationalist and anti-Semitic associations and parties repeatedly used terms such as "blood" and "race" to bolster their
construction of ethnic homogeneity. The same did not apply to the construction of the principle of descent. German citizenship was acquired by
descent, to be sure. However, as long as naturalizations continued in a
manner that did not—or did not necessarily—follow racist criteria, German citizenship could also be passed on to applicants who were considered to be of foreign race. Once naturalized, they bequeathed their
citizenship to their children like other Germans. To this extent the principle of descent remained a formal legal construction, since it was wholly
uninterested in the biological or racial quality attributed to the blood
being passed on. The blood in the principle of *ius sanguinis* was formal
and instrumental, not substantial in intention. That it was interpreted as
substantial by the apologists of biological racial ideology says much more
about the propagandistic flexibility of the word "blood" in the early
twentieth century than about the factual accuracy of this loading of terms
(Gosewinkel 2001b: 326).

The Destruction and Reconstruction of an Institution: From the Citizenship Law of 1913 to the German Basic Law of 1949

The law of 1913, which still determines the structure of the new German
Staatsangehörigkeitsgesetz of 2000, embodies the essential traits of modern
German citizenship. It assumed the quality and continuity of a political
and legal institution. As a result, the reinforcement of the principle of

descent was used as institutional confirmation of the ethno-cultural strand of German nationalism. The new law could be and was used to exclude nonethnic Germans from the institution of citizenship.

At the same time, it became clear that the ethno-cultural principle of German citizenship was not determined by a specific concept of the nation, but rather managed to assert itself because of political decisions in specific historical situations, and remained dependent upon changing political circumstances. Hence, the transition from an ethno-cultural to a racial conception of homogenization, which took place between the Weimar Republic and the racist Nuremberg Laws, was not the inevitable result of tendencies inherent in the institution of German citizenship, but rather one of several possible outcomes.

Decisive for this development was the political caesura of the First World War, the defeat of the German Empire, the loss of large territories, and the shock to and growing radicalization of the German national consciousness. During Germany's war with Russia, people—many of whom had left German territories for the Czarist Empire centuries before, were integrated there, and had never possessed German citizenship—were virtually constructed as "Russian Germans" (*Rußlanddeutsche*). In the conflict with enemy nation-states they were identified as ethnic Germans (*deutsche Volkszugehörige*), politically annexed to their state of origin and relegated to its protection. In the large territories of the Prussian east, which fell to Poland after 1918, and in Eastern Europe millions of people were identified as "Germans" according to ethnic and cultural criteria. As ethnic Germans who, however, did not enjoy the protection of German citizenship, they became objects and justifications for the revisionist aspirations of the German Empire. From now on, German citizenship would follow the primacy of ethnically and culturally defined "membership in the German people" (*Volkszugehörigkeit*).

Hence, it becomes evident that in the political reality after the defeat of the German Reich in World War I, citizenship became a highly political flash point. Conflicts arose over discrimination against ethnic minorities: former German citizens in the ceded German territories (especially in Poland), on the one hand, and minorities of the victorious powers among German citizens (e.g., German citizens of Polish nationality in the Ruhr area) on the other hand (Kleßmann 1978: 161–168). These conflicts affected naturalization policy, leading to more restrictive policies toward the growing number of new arrivals from the East, who were classified as "ethnically foreign." In certain cases, applications for naturalization were rejected with explicitly racist arguments.

Jews from Eastern Europe (*Ostjuden* in the contemptuous terminology of the time) were at the center of the debate. They represented 90 percent of the foreign Jews in Germany and were identified in public not just with foreign Jews, but with undesirable foreigners as such. A conflict over the treatment of Jews within German naturalization policy revealed the narrow scope for a reform of the traditional principle of excluding Jews from

German citizenship. The Prussian state tried to liberalize the criteria of nationalization by introducing the term *Kulturdeutscher* (cultural German) as a preferential category of naturalization. This was explicitly meant to include Jews who had maintained "German customs and language" abroad. However, this initiative met with firm and ultimately successful opposition from Bavaria and other German states. In view of the increasing number of applications by "Austro-Galician and Russian-Polish Jews," the Bavarian government feared inundation by foreigners (the untranslatable German word is *Überfremdung*). According to this position, one could not be both a Jew and a German by ethnic origin (*Deutschstämmiger*). In this view, the attempt to protect the German economy from unwanted competition fused with an underlying mentality concerned with defending national identity. Eastern European immigrants were regarded as representatives of a deeply alien, mainly urbanized culture that could not be integrated. In 1932, in the middle of the final Weimar crisis, the conservative German Minister of the Interior, Freiherr von Gayl, restored the traditional principles of naturalization policy. He proposed more restrictive policies against the "rootless characters of foreign states," particularly against "foreigners of an inferior or totally alien culture, especially against the members of Slavic states and Eastern Jews."[22]

The National Socialist regime drove the standardization of citizenship to total centralization, homogenization and racial segregation. The symbolic value of German citizenship came to be employed as a weapon. The mass expulsion of opponents of the regime and "racially undesirable elements" from the national community of citizens demonstrated a new, restrictive national identity. These measures were also intended to humiliate those expelled, a tactic that generally succeeded.

That Jews in particular were the targets of these measures illustrates the failure of attempts to emancipate Jews as German citizens. From that point on, Jews could neither be nor *become* Germans. Their lasting integration was thwarted by a new, radical model of national homogeneity that was no longer ethno-cultural but racial. Jews were—essentially, if not without exception—regarded as "elements undesirable" to the community of the German state. More than any other group, they represented the German state's definition of Germanness by means of negation. The exclusion and final expulsion of Jews from German citizenship went to the heart of German national identity: Jews did not belong to it.

The Nuremberg Laws of 1935 destroyed citizenship as an instrument and institution of modernization that had been directed toward a "civil society" based on equality.[23] The creation of the category of "full citizens of German or related blood" reduced "plain citizenship" to a secondary status, distinguished from full citizenship. The National Socialist regime broke with the continuity of German citizenship law. An institution of *potential* exclusion, as embodied in the imperial law of 1913, became an instrument of *absolute* exclusion according to pseudo-biological racist criteria.

The German Basic Law of 1949 returned to a modern construction of citizenship based on individual equality. At the same time, it retained elements of continuity, with the full restoration of the 1913 law, most notably of Article 116, which explicitly legitimates the ethnic component of German citizenship. Thus, the ambivalent and potentially strained relationship with a political, state-related conception of citizenship was maintained.

Notes

1. For a fundamental analysis of these structural lines cf. Marshall 1950; Bendix 1977.
2. I agree here with Rogers Brubaker's pioneering analysis of the subject (1992: 52, 119).
3. The theme is treated in detail in Gosewinkel 2001b.
4. For a detailed analysis, see Gosewinkel 1998.
5. Cf. above all Turner 1996: 147; Mommsen 1996: 138.
6. Regarding terminology, a conceptual clarification might be useful. When I use the word "citizenship" here, I do so to refer exclusively to the legal institution regulating membership in the state, which is precisely denoted by the German term *Staatsangehörigkeit*. For a detailed, comparative analysis, see Gosewinkel 2001a. I am not referring to the democratic and participatory connotations of citizenship/*citoyenneté*, which include the material rights and obligations expressed by the German term *Staatsbürgerschaft*. For this distinction, see Preuss 1993: 22ff., 36.
7. For this whole subject, see the thorough analysis by Grawert 1973.
8. Koselleck 1989: 630–637, exemplifying the early process of industrialization in Prussia.
9. Members of the Polish minority saw themselves as "Prussian subjects," not as "Germans"; see Schieder 1992. This went together with the fact that federal patriotism (*Landespatriotismus*) disregarded ethnic origin and was based on people's common quality as subjects; see Wehler 1987: 396.
10. This practice was based on § 9 of the *Reichs- und Staatsangehörigkeitsgesetz* of 22 July 1913 (Citizenship Law for the empire and the federal states), which gave the federal states the right of veto in each and every case of naturalization.
11. For statistical details, see Bade 1983: 25.
12. For a detailed analysis, see Schieder 1992: 33–40.
13. For a detailed account, see Gosewinkel 2001b: 278–327, idem 1995.
14. On this organization and its program, see Peters 1992.
15. On the quotations from the Reichstag debates of 1895, see Gosewinkel 2001b: 278–294.
16. Letter of 16 July 1892 from the governor of Alsace-Lorraine Prince Hohenlohe-Schillingsfürst to Imperial Chancellor Caprivi, 16.7.1892, Preußisches Geheimes Staatsarchiv Dahlem, Rep. 77, Tit. 227, Nr. 53, Bd. 2; on the debate more generally, see Gosewinkel 2001b: 285–294.
17. Cf. "Bericht der 6. Reichstagskommission," *Protokolle der Verhandlungen des Reichstags, 13. Legislaturperiode (1912/1914)*, Anlagen, Bd. 301, 1421; Gosewinkel 2001b: 321.
18. Cf., for example, Turner 1996: 147; Hoffmann 1990: 91; for the different positions, see Gosewinkel 2001b: 324–327.
19. § 25 Abs. 1 *Reichs- und Staatsangehörigkeitsgesetz* of 22 July 1913, exceptions with written authorization only (paragraph 2). The elementary significance of the defense community—despite the easing of regulations on compulsory military service for Germans abroad—as a limitation on the ethno-national people's community is also overlooked by Brubaker 1992: 115.

20. Letter of 25 July 1908 from the Minister of the Interior to the Imperial Chancellor, Bundesarchiv Berlin, Reichsministerium des Innern, Nr. 8010.
21. § 33 Abs.1 *Reichs- und Staatsangehörigkeitsgesetz* of 22 July 1913.
22. Letter of 3 October 1932 from the Reich Minister of the Interior to the governments of the federal states, Preußisches Geheimes Staatsarchiv Berlin-Dahlem, Rep. 90, Nr. 2555; Gosewinkel 1998: 100–104.
23. Reichsbürgergesetz vom 15. September 1935 (*Reichsgesetzblatt* I, 1146).

References

Bade, Klaus J. 1983. *Vom Auswanderungsland zum Einwanderungsland?* Berlin: Colloquium.

Bendix, Ralf. 1977. *Nation-Building and Citizenship.* 2nd ed. Berkeley/Los Angeles/London: University of California Press.

Brubaker, Rogers. 1992. *Citizenship and Nationhood in France and Germany.* Cambridge/London: Cambridge University Press.

Gosewinkel, Dieter. 1995. "Die Staatsangehörigkeit als Institution des Nationalstaats. Zur Entstehung des Reichs- und Staatsangehörigkeitsgesetzes von 1913." In *Offene Staatlichkeit. Festschrift für Ernst-Wolfgang Böckenförde,* ed. Rolf Grawert et al., 359–378. Berlin: Duncker and Humblot.

———. 1998. "'Unerwünschte Elemente' – Einwanderung und Einbürgerung der Juden in Deutschland 1848–1933." *Tel Aviver Jahrbuch für deutsche Geschichte* 27: 71–106. Gerlingen: Bleicher.

———. 2001a. "Citizenship, Subjecthood, Nationality: Concepts of Belonging in the Age of Modern Nation States." In *European Citizenship: National Legacies and Transnational Projects,* ed. Klaus Eder and Bernhard Giesen, 17–35. New York: Oxford University Press.

———. 2001b. *Einbürgern und Ausschließen. Die Nationalisierung der Staatsangehörigkeit vom Deutschen Bund bis zur Bundesrepublik Deutschland.* Göttingen: Vandenhoeck and Ruprecht.

———. 2001c. "Staatsangehörigkeit in Deutschland und Frankreich im 19. und 20. Jahrhundert." In *Staatsbürgerschaft in Europa. Historische Erfahrungen und aktuelle Debatten,* ed. Christoph Conrad and Jürgen Kocka, 48–62. Hamburg: Edition Körber Stiftung.

Grawert, Rolf. 1973. *Staat und Staatsangehörigkeit.* Berlin: Duncker and Humblot.

Herbert, Ulrich. 1993. *Geschichte der Ausländerbeschäftigung in Deutschland 1880 bis 1980.* Berlin: Dietz.

Hoffmann, Lutz. 1990. *Die unvollendete Republik.* Cologne: Papyrossa.

Kleßmann, Christoph. 1978. *Polnische Bergarbeiter im Ruhrgebiet 1870–1945.* Göttingen: Vandenhoeck and Ruprecht.

Koselleck, Reinhart. 1989. *Preußen zwischen Reform und Revolution.* 3rd. ed. Munich: DTV Klett-Cotta.

Marshall, Thomas H. 1950. "Citizenship and Social Class." In *Citizenship and Social Class—and other Essays,* ed. Thomas H. Marshall, 1–85. Cambridge: Cambridge University Press.

Mommsen, Wolfgang J. 1996. "Nationalität im Zeichen offener Weltpolitik." In *Nation und Gesellschaft in Deutschland,* ed. Manfred Hettling and Paul Nolte, 128–141. Munich: C. H. Beck.

Peters, Michael. 1992. *Der Alldeutsche Verband am Vorabend des Ersten Weltkrieges (1908–1914).* Frankfurt am Main: Peter Lang.

Preuss, Ulrich K. 1993. "Zum verfassungstheoretischen Begriff des Staatsbürgers in der modernen Gesellschaft." In *Staatsbürgerschaft und Zuwanderung*, ed. Ulrich K. Preuss, 21–37. Bremen: Zentrum für Europäische Rechtsgeschichte.

Schieder, Theodor. 1992. *Das Deutsche Kaiserreich von 1871 als Nationalstaat.* 2nd ed. Göttingen: Vandenhoeck and Ruprecht.

Turner, Henry A. 1996. "Deutsches Staatsbürgerrecht und der Mythos der ethnischen Nation." In *Nation und Gesellschaft in Deutschland*, ed. Manfred Hettling and Paul Nolte, 142–150. Munich: C. H. Beck.

Wehler, Hans-Ulrich. 1987. *Deutsche Gesellschaftsgeschichte.* Vol. 2. Munich: C. H. Beck

Wertheimer, Jack. 1987. *Unwelcome Strangers.* New York: Oxford University Press.

Wippermann, Wolfgang. 1999. "Das 'ius sanguinis' und die Minderheiten im Deutschen Kaiserreich." In *Nationale Minderheiten und staatliche Minderheitenpolitik in Deutschland im 19. Jahrhundert*, ed. Hans H. Hahn and Peter Kunze, 133–143. Berlin: Akademie Verlag.

Chapter 4

REFORM OF THE CITIZENSHIP LAW

The Debate over Dual Citizenship in Germany

Ralf Fücks

Introduction

The federal coalition of Social Democrats (SPD) and Greens that has been in power since the autumn of 1998 has faced no more intensely controversial reform project in its first year at the helm than that of the citizenship law. The main point of contention raised by the opposition, organized by the recently ousted Christian Democrats (CDU), was the intention to accept dual citizenship for migrants as a step to facilitate their taking German citizenship. Under the pressure of a plebiscitary mobilization by the CDU, and a surprising defeat of the so-called "red-green" coalition of SPD and Greens in the Hesse state elections, the SPD made a turnabout and withdrew the dual citizenship proposal.

With that step, a major point in the "red-green" coalition agreement had been annulled. Let me cite the decisive passage in this agreement:

> Our integration policy shall be centered around the creation of a modern citizenship law. In particular, two relaxed regulations are to be implemented:
>
> 1. Children born in Germany of foreign national parents shall automatically receive German citizenship if [at least] one parent was born here or came to Germany as a minor before his or her fourteenth birthday and has a residence permit for Germany.[1]
>
> 2. The following persons shall be entitled to naturalization, provided they have no criminal record and have means of support: Foreign nationals who have legally resided in Germany for eight years. Underage foreign nationals, if at least one parent holds at least an unlimited residence permit and if the minor has been living together with this parent as a family in Germany for at least five years.

In both cases, the granting of German citizenship shall not be dependent on the renunciation of the former citizenship.

This proposal was withdrawn. Instead, it was resolved that children born in Germany under the above-named conditions would automatically receive German citizenship, but they would have to decide between German citizenship and the citizenship of their parents by their twenty-third birthday. Multiple nationality is only permitted if the country of origin poses unreasonable conditions or does not decide in due time regarding a petition for release from the former citizenship. There were also further restrictions in the legislative procedure. Prerequisites to naturalization are the ability to support oneself and competence in the German language, to be verified by a language test.

Despite this setback, which was difficult especially for the Greens to accept, the new naturalization law is a major step forward for the political culture of the Federal Republic of Germany. Up to now, citizenship was granted according to *ius sanguinis*, the right of blood, or parentage, as the justification for German citizenship. Now this has been supplemented by a "birth right" (*ius soli*, or right of the soil). This has paved the way for a new, republican understanding of nation and citizenship.

The Social Point of Departure

A democratically constituted society can only function in the long term if no large segments of the society are excluded from full participation. As long as the determinant political unit is the nation-state, however, equal participation by migrants can only be assured through the acquisition of German citizenship.

In the future, national citizenship will be subsumed by a fully valid European citizenship within the scope of the European Union, just as national currencies will be replaced by the Euro as a common currency. We are already in the middle of this transitional process. Citizens from all EU member states already enjoy active and passive voting rights in every member state at a local level and at the level of the European Parliament. The right to set up permanent residence, the labor market, and freedom of trade have already been Europeanized.

To this extent, from today's legal perspective, there are two classes of migrants within the European Union: those from "within" the Union, and those who come from "without." Here are a few figures in order to illustrate the magnitude of the issue:

- There are 7.5 million foreign nationals living in Germany.
- Despite the large number of refugees who have applied for political asylum or war refugees who have temporary permission to stay in the country, 30 percent of all foreign nationals in Germany have

lived there for twenty years or more. Approximately half have been in Germany for over ten years.

- Roughly 100,000 foreign national children are born in Germany annually, a majority of whom will grow up, attend school, marry, and work in the country of their birth. They nevertheless have the legal status of aliens.

According to the old legal situation, naturalization was also possible, and this did have some impact, even though the barriers were relatively high. The naturalization rate (that is, the number of naturalizations relative to the total number of foreign residents) was 0.3 percent in 1986, increasing to 1.2 percent in 1996. This naturalization rate was far too low to make millions of foreign nationals into citizens with equal rights.

The Federal Republic of Germany prior to unification, that is, the former West Germany, gradually developed into an immigration country over decades, without having deliberated or reflected on this process politically or psychologically. Germany is in actual fact an immigration country, but it does not perceive itself as one.

Contrary to real conditions—and counterproductive to the interests of an aging and shrinking society—leading politicians, especially from the CDU, have been proclaiming for years that "Germany is not an immigration country." Yet all demographic studies have emphasized that in the future the Federal Republic of Germany will urgently need immigration in the magnitude of several hundred thousand immigrants per year in order to maintain a relative balance between old and young, that is, between retirees and workers.

This conflict has extended into the current debate on providing residence permits for a limited number of computer specialists, in an attempt to make up for the deficit in innovative experts in the high-tech economy. Major segments of the trade unions and conservative opposition have formed a united front against any move to open the labor market to Eastern European or Asian specialists. Some fear that this will open the door to a steady flow of immigrants, and others view the foreign experts as unwelcome competition for jobs. Chancellor Gerhard Schröder and the Social Democratic minister of labor have responded to this resistance by expressly announcing that this would involve only temporary high-tech guest workers, by no means immigrants who would receive permanent, unlimited residence status.

This discussion shows the wariness of Germany regarding migrants and immigration. In times of globalization, in which a mixture of cultures is the key to innovation, these mental barriers will increasingly lead to competitive drawbacks.

Psychological and Political Resistance

"Alien" or "foreigner" status represents a legal and psychological obstacle to achieving true integration. It maintains distance, from both sides: "foreigners" do not truly belong. If Germany does not want to have to accept a two-class society in the long run, with all the social and political conflicts that are fueled by ethnic-based exclusion, German citizenship must become easier to obtain.

Toleration of dual citizenship is intended to reduce the existing hurdles by acknowledging the fact that migrants feel strong ties both to their home country and to the country to which they have immigrated. Recognition of dual citizenship has led to an open conflict with the long-standing defensive strategy of conservative political and social forces in Germany.

Although the CDU also has its rhetoric for simplified naturalization, it always includes the clause that naturalization can only represent the completion of the integration process. In this context "integration" virtually means "assimilation." This implies that the immigrants should take on the majority culture, and those affected also understand it that way: "The majority society only wants us if we are willing to renounce our Turkish, Yugoslavian, or Russian heritage."

Behind this lies the desperate attempt to answer the question "who is a German?" by claiming a national identity that is not defined in a republican sense that is, by recognizing common political values and the active affiliation to a political community. Instead, it is defined culturally, through common cultural traditions and lifestyles. The opinion that Germany must remain a Christian country is a standard tenet of this position, as is the attitude that opposes school instruction for immigrant children in their native language. Although English lessons are to be introduced in primary school in the future, and even Chinese is offered in school curriculum, there is great resistance to allowing children from Turkish families to receive school instruction in Turkish.

Demanding commitment to a clearly defined "national culture" is simply anachronistic in times of global migration, multiethnic societies, and multinational identities. Even with respect to the German majority population, one can no longer speak of a homogeneous majority culture. The lifestyles and cultural traditions even of native-born Germans have gone through strongly divergent developments, as in all modern societies. This applies to opinions on marriage and the family as well as religious issues. Germany has become a thoroughly secular country, since for most Germans affiliation to a Christian church is more a traditional relic than it is a question of lived faith. The Muslim faith held by immigrants from Turkey is thus often questioned, not so much because it challenges the Christian monopoly, but because religion per se plays such a large role in the lives of many immigrants.

Dual Rights and Loyalties

A diffuse mixture of arguments, are used in opposing dual citizenship-for instance, that anyone who is also a citizen of another country cannot be loyal to Germany. And it is claimed that dual citizenship leads to dual rights and thus privileged status vis-à-vis the majority German population. But experience has proven otherwise; namely, that multiple nationality leads neither to deficient loyalty nor to privileges or disadvantages for the person involved. The number of people in Germany with multiple nationalities is presently estimated at far more than two million. (Children resulting from binational partnerships receive the citizenship of both parents; ethnic Germans immigrating from Eastern Europe are not required to renounce their previous citizenship; and there are also a considerable number of individual cases in which the multiple nationality of foreign nationals is tolerated when they are naturalized.) This has not let to any practical problems, either for the person involved or for society.

In Germany, citizens holding more than one passport have the same rights and duties as other Germans. Also, foreign national residents in Germany are subject to German law and they pay taxes and make social security contributions, like all other citizens, although they lack the general voting rights necessary to influence conditions. The German Federal Constitutional Court has determined that, corresponding to the "idea of democracy," "congruence is to be created between the holders of democratic, political rights and permanent subjects of a certain political sovereignty." Whether or not dual nationals living in Germany are also allowed to vote in another country is the decision of the respective country and does not affect their status in Germany. The question of conscription into military service has been clarified through international and bilateral agreements.

A Look beyond the Border

The new German citizenship law has once again linked Germany to the development of citizenship rights in other European countries. Great Britain originally had an almost purely *ius soli* model, granting citizenship on the basis of birth in Great Britain. Great Britain still has a rule, according to which a child born there receives British citizenship if the parents have permanent residence status. Thus there are no second or third generation "British residents with foreign passports." Neither in the naturalization process nor in the case of *ius soli* must a second nationality be renounced in order to hold British citizenship in Great Britain.

France also has strong elements of *ius soli* in its citizenship law. Originally, any child born in France received French citizenship, at the latest when he or she came of age. This principle was restricted in 1993 to the effect that a child born in France also had to submit a declaration between his or her sixteenth and twenty-first birthdays, expressing the wish to obtain French citizenship. The new French government has since reverted to the former law. The question of multiple nationalities is irrelevant when acquiring French citizenship. As a result, in France as well, there are no comparably large groups of immigrants who are excluded from full political and social participation.

Belgium and the Netherlands grant citizenship by birth if the parents were born in the country. For other foreign national children born in these countries, flexible regulations for acquiring citizenship exist, in which a declaration must be submitted once they come of age.

I assume that in the not-all-too-distant future a European citizenship will evolve, creating a new type of so-called supranational citizenship that will definitively abandon ethnic definitions and will instead be based on the conscious and active affiliation to a political union.

Notes

This article was translated from the German by Allison Brown.

1. The right to refusal provided for in item 5 and 6.1 of the proposal for the "Revision of the Citizenship Law" submitted by the SPD parliamentary party has been eliminated (File ref. 13/2833, 30 October 1995).

Chapter 5

THE GOLEM AND ITS CREATOR, OR HOW THE JEWISH NATION-STATE BECAME MULTIETHNIC

Yfaat Weiss

Introduction

The Law of Return, which was passed by Israel's Parliament, the Knesset, in 1950, and the Law on Citizenship, enacted in 1952, constitute the legal groundwork for migration and naturalization in the state of Israel. Both laws are a fundamental expression of the fact that Israel was created as the Jewish state. "The laws of return and citizenship," writes jurist and former Israeli Justice Minister Amnon Rubinstein, "can be seen to have been drafted in a spirit of ideological fervor, while overlooking the problems generated by the categorical form of words" (Rubinstein 1991: 61). When one reads the discussions of the government, the Knesset and the Constitution, Law and Justice Committee that drafted the details of the law, one comes away with the inescapable impression that all involved felt driven by the historical import of the task they had been entrusted with, that of turning the state of Israel into the home of the Jews by virtue of their Jewishness. The semantic debate that took place in the committee between those who advocated the term "return" and others who were in favor of calling the law the "Ingathering of the Exiles Law" reflects different levels of awareness vis-à-vis the historical symbolism of the law.[1] But on the whole it is this pervading sense of fulfilling a historical mission that became the bedrock for the wording of the Law of Return, and is responsible for the great weight attached to origin in the model of Israeli citizenship, that is, to Jewish ethnic affiliation, and less to territory, that is, the state. It was not simply that legislators gave preference to Jewish migrants over other, non-Jewish migrants; they also made the civil status of Jews born in what was now the state of Israel equal to that of those who immigrated to the country on the basis of the Law of Return. They thereby created a clear-cut differentiation between what counts as civil rights for Jews and what counts as such for Arabs. In 1970 the state of Israel further consolidated the implications of ethnic affiliation when in a significant step the Knesset passed an amendment to the Law of Return, under which the non-Jewish third-generation descendants of Jews were also entitled to immigrate to Israel and obtain citizenship there.

The fact that over the last ten years around one million immigrants have come to Israel from countries of the former Soviet Union (FSU) had of course much to do with the push factor of the USSR's collapse in 1989. But it was the pull factor of the widened scope of the Law of Return in 1970 that made these large numbers possible. When one looks at the backgrounds of the new immigrants one finds that the number of non-Jewish immigrants who have been able to immigrate under the Law of Return reaches several hundred thousand, with their proportion among the total body of FSU immigrants increasing from one year to the next, reaching around 40 percent in recent years (Al-Haj and Leshem 2000: 25).[2] This paradoxical reality, in which every year more and more "non-Jews"—irrespective of the criteria one uses to define them besides the orthodox, halachic yardstick—are immigrating to Israel, was brought home recently by Ian Lustick who claims that the Law of Return as it now stands has become a law promoting the immigration of "non-Arabs" (Lustick 1999).

Lustick takes great pains to try to reconstruct the alleged number of non-Jews among the immigrants, figures that official circles in Israel are eager to conceal. Lustick sees in this cover-up a conspiracy of silence, with differing and even conflicting vested interests existing side by side. One of these is the sense of survival displayed by the Jewish Agency's bureaucracy, which for Lustick ties in with the ambitions of the Russian immigrants' party "Yisrael Ba'aliya" (and of course also of "Israel Beitenu"—another "Russian" party) to expand their political electorate. Other considerations have to do with maintaining the Jewish demographic edge in Israel and the significance this has for the state's ability to continue to influence the future of the Palestinian territories it has held under occupation since 1967. Given the way information about numbers of non-Jewish immigration is being withheld or even obstructed, one might have expected a liberal lobby to have emerged setting itself up as some kind of a watchdog. This has not happened, possibly, because a genuinely liberal position would hesitate to attack immigrants because of their being "non-Jews." Another reason may well be that liberal Israelis do not want to be identified with "post-Zionist" positions. Neither are they interested in opening up the question of "Who is a Jew," because— given Israel's political constellation—this would mean running the risk of having an ultra-Orthodox interpretation imposed upon the country to the detriment of liberal, conservative or reform interpretations.

Lustick's article is fascinating for the picture he paints of the contemporary situation. With his—admittedly—sweeping interpretation of the

Law of Return as a law enabling the immigration into Israel of "non-Arabs" he succeeds admirably, for example, in showing how the facts and dynamics of the recent developments he exposes serve the demographic, and thus the political, interests of Israel's Jewish majority vis-à-vis the country's Palestinian minority. But he is less convincing, I think, when he claims that it was the Israeli legislator's original intention to ensure Israel's population would be ethnically cleansed of its Palestinian component so as to become non-Arab. In other words, I accept the picture Lustick draws for us of the current situation, and I am even inclined to follow him in the "conspiracy of silence" thesis he puts forward. But I would like to suggest that the Israeli legislators at work in 1950 and 1970 could not have anticipated the geopolitical upheavals of the 1990s and thus with the measures they were taking could not have intended "Israel's transformation from a state clearly divided between a Jewish majority and an Arab minority into a country where identity categories are multiple, blurred, and uncertain, and whose 'Jewish' majority is more accurately and meaningfully regarded as 'non-Arab'" (Lustick 1999: 418). Lustick chooses to focus on the reality of the 1990s and naturally bases his argument on the contemporary press and face-to-face interviews. Interested as he is in "considering the changing meaning of traditional Zionist categories, and of the concepts 'Jew' and 'Jewish state,'" for him "the complexities of the present are as important and as interesting as those of the future" (Lustick 1999: 433). But this also means that he leaves out any historical analysis of how the laws developed.

In the following pages, I set out to contextualize the agenda of the Israeli legislators who framed the Law of Return in 1950 and its Amendment in 1970, and try to reconstruct the ethno-cultural assumptions that underpinned their motivations. Comparing the position Arabs have been given in the structure of Israeli citizenship with that of "non-Jews," I will try to determine whether the exclusion of the Arabs is the result of a deliberate policy of consolidating a "non-Arab majority," come what may, or whether it was the chance result of different considerations, which then cumulated in the reality of the 1990s. It is my assumption that the political experience molding the mind-set of the Israeli legislator was primarily Central and East European. When drafting both these laws—the Law of Return and the Law on Citizenship—the lawmakers were copying East European thought patterns and a political experience they were familiar with. In other words, they were not looking forward, to the 1990s, but backwards, to the 1920s.

Ius Soli vs. Ius Sanguinis

"As a country which absorbs immigrants," notes Amnon Rubinstein, "Israel is an exception, because countries which absorb migrants, since they wish to rapidly create a common attachment with all their residents, give priority to *ius soli*; in contrast, countries whose residents emigrate from them want to maintain the emigrants' ties with their first homeland, and therefore prefer *ius sanguinis*. Israel is a country which absorbs immigration, but because of its special position as a Jewish state, it has given preference to *ius sanguinis*, and its recognition of *ius soli* is very limited—so much so that even a person born in Israel does not acquire citizenship of the country merely by being born there" (Rubinstein 1991: 672).

Israel is not, however, an absolute exception. It is not a country of immigration in the classical sense, but rather, by virtue of its self-definition, of immigration for a specific ethnic group only, and to this extent—notwithstanding the irony of the similarity—it is not much different from Germany. The unequivocal preference of the element of *ius sanguinus* (origin) over that of *ius soli* (territory) as we find it in the wording of the Law of Return resembles the German model to a very large extent. Legal scholar Claude Klein has highlighted the similarities and differences as follows: "Technically, it might be said that the main reason for all these 'parallels' between Germany and Israel lies in the imperfect character of the two nation-states. It may be suggested that the perfect nation-state is a state wherein two conditions are fulfilled: a) all the citizens of the state belong to the same nation and b) all the members of that nation reside in that nation-state" (Klein 1997: 54).

The second condition, of course, is present in neither country: Germany as well as Israel have large-scale ethnic diasporas outside the borders of the nation-state, which play a key role in shaping their national outlooks. And though there are some contrasts—the German nation-state maintains ties with migrants and German settlers who migrated to the New World or to parts of Eastern Europe, while the Jewish nation-state is the product of migration by settlers—there are certainly some affinities between German nationalism and its Israeli counterpart. For example, neither has clearly defined borders, while both share a "frontier" outlook (Diner 1980: 87–148; Kemp 1991). Even leaving aside instances of direct influence, one can find similarities between Zionist frontier nationalism and its German counterpart in how they dealt with questions of citizenship on the eve of World War I.

While the reality of a large-scale diaspora outside the borders of the nation-state is a key element manifestly shared by both Israel and Germany, there is a difference when it comes to the first obstacle that prevents them from being perfect nation-states, viz., the fact that not all of the state's citizens belong to the nation. As a result of the partition of Poland, German citizenship—taking the place of "Prussian" citizenship—now also covered Polish citizens. Although the political and social rights of the latter did not equal that of German citizens, the process of naturalization was the same for them as for individuals of ethnic origin (Blanke 1981). According to the German model, in the light of the 1913 legislation individuals who were not part of the majority ethnic group were still able to naturalize and automatically pass on their German citizenship to their children. In this sense, the citizenship of Jews or Poles in Imperial Germany can be said to be equivalent to that of the contemporary Arabs in Israel. Another point of similarity is that, like the Poles in the eastern areas of Germany, the Palestinians in Israel are not migrants but part of the indigenous population of the country who formed the numerical majority before the Jewish state was established (Shafir and Peled 1998: 252 f.). Similar to Prussia's measures against the Poles in the eastern areas, Israel adopted procedures targeting the Palestinians in order to maintain the demographic advantage it had obtained through the 1948 war. But this is where the comparison stops, as the demographic conditions in Israel are utterly different—Israel has a Palestinian minority that makes up 18 percent of the total population while Germany is practically homogeneous in ethnic terms (Klein 1997: 54 f.).

Moreover, the changes affecting German citizenship as a result of the collapse of the Eastern bloc have further shifted the German model away from its Israeli equivalent, even showing opposite trends. While Israel, for reasons that we will examine below, opened its doors to absorb hundreds of thousands of East European Jewish migrants, Germany has displayed a growing lack of interest in absorbing the masses of East European migrants of ethnic German origin, going so far as to abolish the automatic naturalization process and to lay down stringent new criteria. In other words, Germany is adopting territorial principles and downplaying ethnic principles.

Any discussion that posits a similarity between the principles of Israeli citizenship as it still exists today and its German equivalent as it existed from 1913 until recently necessarily attaches key importance to geographic space in shaping views of citizenship. Thus, for example, the American sociologist Rogers Brubaker has compared and contrasted this German view of citizenship with its French equivalent taking as his starting point the fundamental difference in the creation of the two countries in terms of geographical structure, viz., location and geographic cohesiveness. Lacking borders in Central Europe, Germany developed a form of citizenship based on the German ethnos, while France, with its clearly defined geographical borders and centralist tradition, was able to allow itself a demos-based model (Brubaker 1992: 3–6). Geographer Oren Yiftachel writes along similar lines when he identifies the limitations on Israel's democracy with its system of government without clear borders (Yiftachel 2000: 93). [3] As Yiftachel argues, Israel's political structure—i.e., land ownership arrangements and the Zionist policy of rural settlement accompanied by discrimination against the country's Palestinian citizens as practiced by extraterritorial Jewish bodies such as the Israel Lands Administration and the Jewish Agency—as well as its settlement policies in the occupied territories on the West Bank and the Gaza Strip—conflict with the basic conditions for democracy. This contention is backed up in an article he wrote with Kedar, in which they link the country's migration policy "which is designed to strengthen the Judaization of the state through Jewish migration" to "the adoption of a new spatial-land policy" (Yiftachel and Kedar 2000: 87). Yiftachel and Kedar's instructive contention introduces a host of many questions about Israel's democratic character. However, it is a moot point whether the growing group of immigrants who entered the country under the Law of Return but who are not Jewish can be located in the field of contrast they outline between a Jewish ethnos and an Israeli demos, the latter made up of Jewish and Palestinian citizens and residents. Yiftachel and Kedar do show convincingly how the policy of Jewish rural settlement gave rise to regressive processes of ethnic separation and stratification within Jewish society, primarily reproducing the gap between Ashkenazim and Mizrahim. Yiftachel also emphasizes the stratification processes that took place as a result of the geographical dispersion between the two groups in the course of the various waves of immigration, as different forms of rural settlement characteristic of each of the two were instituted and encouraged. In this process the immigrants from the Soviet Union and Ethiopia have been identified as new groups, which like other groups also develop markers of ethnicization according to the "basic rationale of the Jewish ethnocracy" (Yiftachel 2000). However, for the first time since the establishment of the state of Israel, the wave of migration of the 1990s has brought to the country, under the Law of Return, several hundred thousand migrants who are not Jewish, creating the question, not of where, but whether they can be positioned within the strata of Jewish society in Israel.

Given the significance of the growing presence of this group of people who are neither Jews nor Palestinians, I would like to propose a relational and comparative model that differs from its German equivalent. Unlike Lustick, who claims that for the purpose of Israeli citizenship a Jew is somebody who is not an Arab, and also differing from Yiftachel and Kedar, whose reading contrasts demos and ethnos, i.e., majority and minority, I wish to examine a theoretical model derived from the geopolitical reality of Eastern Europe. It seems to me that if we compare the structure of Israeli citizenship not with West European democracies, as is standard practice among most researchers in the field, but with East European models, we should be able to expand the framework of the sociohistorical analysis of how Israeli citizenship has evolved and thus throw some light on the discriminatory practices so firmly in place today.

There are many links between Israel's reality in the early decades of the state and the political traditions of Central Europe. The pattern of behavior demonstrated by Israel's political leadership in the country's formative years was predominantly East European. As such, it permeated practically all aspects of Israeli politics (Shapiro 1984: 15–26). Besides playing a major part in the biographical background of most Israeli politicians, Eastern Europe was also central in the realm of Zionist operational activities as early Zionism was primarily concerned with finding solutions for the Jews living in the areas of Central and Eastern Europe. How and when the state came into being furthermore makes Israel similar to the new states in Central and Eastern Europe, not Germany. Israel was part of the legacy of British imperialism, set up in a divided Palestine, and its self-definition as the nation-state of the Jewish people stood in stark contrast with the multiethnic reality it erased. The East European orientation of Israel's legislators then also is reflected in the enactment and amendment of the Law of Return, not in the least in the expectation they harbored of future immigration from the Soviet Union. But reality as we know it today, one can argue, exceeds even the wildest expectations anyone could have had at the time. The mass immigration that followed the disintegration in 1989 of the Soviet Union, and the ensuing national atomization there, has been changing the face of Israel beyond recognition.

For my comparison between the structure of Israeli citizenship and the East European models, I shall apply the distinctions the American sociologist Rogers Brubaker set out in his discussion of the relationship between nationalism and citizenship. A systematic examination of the history of Central and East European states in the interwar period and a comparison with the post-1989 emergence of nationalism in the same geographical areas allows Brubaker to identify three main variables that he defines as a "triad linking national minorities, the newly nationalizing states in which they live, and the external national 'homelands' to which they belong, or can be construed as belonging, by ethno-cultural affinity though not by legal citizenship" (Brubaker 1996: 4).

The Israeli reality can easily be read into the triadic nexus proposed by Brubaker: Israel is applying a nationalizing nationalism to the Palestinian national minority within Israel, i.e., those Palestinians who are Israeli citizens and who maintain close ties with the "homeland nationalism" of the neighboring Arab states, but primarily, of course, with the Palestinians in those areas of the West Bank and the Gaza Strip over which Israel has "ceded" control to the Palestinian Authority and in those territories that remain under Israeli occupation. Brubaker defines the characteristics of nationalizing nationalism as follows:

> Nationalizing nationalism [of newly independent (or newly reconfigured) states] involves claims made in the name of the "core nation" or nationality, defined in ethno-cultural terms, and sharply distinguished from the citizenry as a whole. The core nation is understood as a legitimate "owner" of the state, which is conceived as the state of and for the core nation. Despite having "its own" state, however, the core nation is conceived as being in a weak cultural, economic, or demographic position within the state. This weak position—seen as a legacy of discrimination against the nation before it attained independence—is held to justify the "remedial" or "compensatory" project of using state power to promote the specific (and previously inadequately served) interest of the core nation. (Brubaker 1996: 4f.)

Nationalizing nationalism as outlined here by Brubaker effectively acts in a framework of dissonance: the ethnic majority's position of superiority in its country is perceived as fragile and inadequate given the profound need for historical compensation. Thus, despite its superiority, the nationalizing nation applies governmental practices to further consolidate its power. From the Jewish and Israeli perspective, the dissonance revealed between the de facto numerical superiority and political supremacy of the Jewish majority in Israel and the need for "historical self-compensation" is particularly glaring, since the state of Israel must compensate not only the Jews living in Israel but also the "Jewish people" as a scattered and persecuted minority. This is a minority that has become a majority in a Jewish nation-state, that perceives itself in historical terms as completing a process of repatriation. But this repatriation, which is the basis of the Law of Return, can be considered as such only in terms of an ideological position. In practice, the "returning" Jews are simply migrants or refugees who have escaped or been expelled from their countries of origin to their new country. Furthermore, given the presence of these refugees who are "returning" to a—for them—new and unknown country, another genuine repatriation is being blocked: that of the original inhabitants of that "new and unknown" country, the Palestinian refugees who are denied the right to return to their own homeland.

Stage One: The 1950 Law of Return

The discussions that preceded the passing of the Law of Return in 1950 provide a telling glimpse of the political and cultural frame of reference of the generation that established the state, both because of what was said but also because of what was not said. While the law as a whole was presented as a piece of repatriation legislation—however problematic—so that it could not therefore be considered discriminatory as such (Klein 1997: 56; Gans 1998), one section of the law, Section 5, does explicitly discriminate against Israel's Arab residents. This section creates equality under the Law of Return between Jewish immigrants who had immigrated to Israel before the law was enacted and Jews born in the country, to the effect that: "Every Jew who has immigrated into this country before the coming into force of this Law, and every Jew who was born in this country, whether before or after the coming into force of this Law, shall be deemed to be a person who has come to this country as an *oleh* (immigrant) under this Law." What this section meant to avoid was discrimination between immigrants and long-established Jewish inhabitants, but in doing so it introduced clear discrimination between the new nation-state's Jewish and Arab citizens.

One looks in vain, however, for any intensive discussion, let alone awareness, of this discriminatory aspect of the Law of Return. But this indifference on the part of Israeli legislators did not mean they failed to understand the issues. Haim Cohn, the then attorney-general, was more candid than most when he explained to the Knesset's Constitution, Law and Justice Committee: "We do not wish to introduce discrimination between Jews and non-Jews in any *other* law. This is the only law to lay down special rights for a Jew because he is a Jew. This is the reason why we are including Section 5 here in the Law of Return, the law that discusses the special rights of Jews—and not in the Law on Citizenship, even though from the purely legal point of view, it might be better to do so."[4]

Cohn himself recognized the fact that "these rights are of importance mainly, but not solely, for the Law on Citizenship."[5] Not surprisingly, the only committee member who objected to giving equal status to immigrants under the Law of Return and the country's native-born Jews as to the Jewish veteran settlers, was MK Tawfiq Toubi. As an Israeli citizen and an Arab, Toubi understood only too well what significance the section would have for his community. None of the committee's members supported the amendment he proposed, which was rejected by an absolute majority.[6] Neither was there any discussion of the law's discriminatory aspects at the Knesset session that debated the law. Here objections came from MK Meir Vilner, like MK Toubi a member of Israel's Communist Party. Examining the Law on Citizenship and the Law of Return in tandem, Vilner stressed how both laws worked to heighten discrimination against the Arabs, something he could only call "racist."[7] In the Knesset debate Vilner's objection went the same way as MK Toubi's in the Constitution, Law and Justice Committee—it was duly rejected by an absolute majority.

The Law on Citizenship, which came into force in 1952, was an equally discriminatory piece of legislation (Kretzmer 1990: 37f.) because it was intended to curtail the practical possibilities of obtaining the legal status of Israeli citizens for Palestinians who had been living within those areas of Palestine that became the state of Israel in 1948. It did so by binding entitlement to citizenship to a list of conditions—registration in the Israel Population Register of 1 March 1952, continuous presence within the territory of the state of Israel in the 1948 to1952 period, or entry to Israeli territory with proper papers—that made it impossible to regularize the status of most Palestinians who during or after the war had come back to their villages or homes but who, for fear of being expelled again, kept low as the authorities considered them "illegal infiltrators." A number of researchers have rightly pointed out that until the 1980 amendment of this law, the close connection between the Law of Return and the Law on Citizenship prevented Israeli citizenship from being granted to many of the Palestinians not included among the 143,000 Palestinians who immediately acquired citizenship in 1952 (Peled 1993: 26). The Law of Return thus includes a section that discriminates against Israel's Arab residents, while the 1952 Law on Citizenship provided no counterbalancing mechanism. But in the 1950 debates we do not find any intention on the part of the Israeli legislators to define Israel as a state of "non-Arabs." In other words, we should not equate the political practice of those years—when Israel was anxious to consolidate the gains it had been able to achieve through the war of 1948—with the country's legislative procedure. The legislators focused on curtailing and restricting the ability of the country's Arabs to participate in Israel citizenship as equal partners because they wanted to safeguard Israel's character as a Jewish state, not as a "non-Arab" state.

This comes into even sharper focus when we look at yet another group —the non-Jewish spouses of Jews immigrating under the Law of Return. Here it was decided to include the issue of their civil affiliation under the Law on Citizenship and not the Law of Return. "What will happen to the non-Jewish wife? Abroad they had a civil marriage, and where a Jew has a non-Jewish wife, is the law to apply to him and not to her?" asked MK R. Cohen in a meeting of the Constitution, Law and Justice Committee.[8] The reaction of the other Knesset members was uniform, showing a marked lack of tolerance for this issue. The matter of mixed marriages should not fall under the Law of Return, and including it in the Law of Return would mean mingling the secular with the profane and thus spoil its symbolism, they thought. "The principle is a historical one. And so, if we accept the proposal of Member of Knesset Cohen, we shall ruin this principle,"[9] declared MK Prof. Benzion Dinur, soon to become education minister. MK Ami Assaf added, "There are laws on immigration and there will be more laws on immigration, and if we go into all these details here, we will ruin the essence of this law which addresses one issue: the right of a Jew, as a Jew, to return to the Land of Israel in a special fashion."[10] Haim Cohn was in favor of making the status of the Jews born in the country comparable to that of Jewish immigrants by virtue of the Law of Return, i.e., he supported the principle of discriminating against Arabs, and equally refused to include the non-Jewish spouses in the Law of Return, pointing out that these dilemmas would be resolved in the framework of the Law on Citizenship and the Law on Migration.[11]

Nobody truly thought that this human problem could remain unresolved. But if we look at the discussions the Knesset's Immigration Committee held about the problem of non-Jewish spouses during the years of 1948 to1950 and prior to the enactment of the Law of Return, we find an obvious lack of enthusiasm, with most of the Israeli legislators recoiling at the possibility of immigration to Israel by non-Jewish spouses (Hacohen 1998: 298ff.). Given the uncertainty about the number and composition of the expected immigrants, there were widespread rumors about especially large numbers of mixed couples. The religious representatives rejected mixed marriages for religious reasons, but in fact, had it not been for international criticism, almost all of the committee's members would have preferred to make immigration conditional upon conversion. Religious MKs then tried to instigate a discussion of the identity-based and historical context of non-Jewish immigration. About German wives, suspicions were voiced that they might have had a Nazi past and were using immigration to Israel in order to escape from Germany. For mixed Jewish-Polish couples, too, committee members thought that only those couples should be allowed to immigrate who could prove that they had actively helped to save Jews. While the Immigration Committee concentrated on Germany and Poland, the attention of the Cabinet was focused on the Soviet Union. Given high expectations of Soviet immigration, this meant that they refused to accept a blanket ban on the immigration of mixed families, but during the period from 1948 to 1950 left matters up to the discretion of the head of the immigration committee.

A comparison of the legislators' attitudes to non-Jewish spouses in 1950 with the attitude they took up vis-à-vis the country's Arab population shows that, at a time when the legislators adopted a clear-cut position on Arabs, choosing to discriminate and give preference to the country's Jewish residents, they decided to also shift to the Law on Citizenship and the Law on Migration arrangements governing the status of the non-Jewish spouses of Jews immigrating under the Law of Return. Though there are great differences, the Israeli legislators' two dilemmas have a common aspect. By undermining the principle of endogamy, the mixed couples constituted not only a halachic problem, but also a fundamental test for the definition of Jewish nationality in Israel. By allowing religious marriages only and imposing endogamy—marriages solely within the different religious communities—Israeli legislation not only serves the religious establishment, as is habitually thought, but also encourages and creates ties with that national outlook that is interested in preserving the Jewish nation and restricting possibilities of "assimilating" and "integrating" members of different national groups in Israel (Smooha 1996: 283). The sweeping refusal to regularize the status of non-Jewish spouses under the 1950 Law of Return constitutes proof of the mutual dependency between religious and nationalist circles in the framework of Zionism and state. "The secular Jewish system [needs] a religious system which in its eyes represents historical Judaism," Yigal Elam writes, "and here it was prepared to pay the full price required in order to preserve the general Jewish character" (Elam 2000: 10). It is this mutual dependence or even the blurring of the distinction between religion and nationality in Israel that comes to the fore so strongly in the discussions about the Law of Return in 1950, and again—albeit in an entirely different fashion—in 1970.

The Israeli legislators understood "return" as repatriation, with all its attendant historical and symbolical significances—in the words of David Ben-Gurion, the Law of Return is "the fulfillment of Israeli history."[12] This legal framework included depriving the Palestinians of key rights, primarily, the ability to acquire citizenship, that did not derive from territorial affiliation, i.e., by framing the law such that most of them had been "outside the country" as a result of the war. However, addressing the status of the non-Jewish spouses of Jewish immigrants in the same manner would have "spoiled" the law's historic status, and thus it was shifted to another piece of legislation.

Still, in terms of the overall debate the above issues remained utterly marginal. The main focus was on semantic nuances concerning the concept of *oleh* (immigrant), the status of the minister of the interior, the ability of the latter to disqualify applicants, reservations concerning elements who allegedly formed a danger to the country's security, questions relating to "enemies of democracy," and the problem of "dual citizenship" that arose out of the law. What is crucial is that the Law of Return in its 1950 version was framed as a law of repatriation for Jews and for Jews only, until we come to the decisive expansion that was introduced in 1970.

Stage Two: The 1970 Amendment to the Law of Return

Neither the 1949 Population Registry Ordinance nor the 1950 Law of Return contain a definition of who was and who wasn't a "Jew." During the 1950s and 1960s, a number of interpretations were offered that ranged from a person being a Jew who defined himself or herself as such, on the one hand, to someone being Jewish only when he or she could produce halachically authoritative and valid documents on the other (Elam 2000: 12–29). As a result of ambiguities when it came to registration, a number of legal cases were brought, and there was one coalition crisis.

The 1970 Amendment of the Law of Return started out as an attempt by the government to prevent a coalition crisis in the wake of the so-called "Lieutenant Shalit case." Shalit, who had married a non-Jewish French woman, had petitioned the Supreme Court in 1969, after an interior ministry registration clerk had rejected his statement that his third newborn was Jewish and had refused to record it as such in the Population Registry. By a slim majority (five to four), the Supreme Court decided in favor of the petitioner but expressed itself dissatisfied at having to rule in a matter in which the legislator ought to have provided sufficient clarity—it was the Knesset's task to solve the Population Registry issue as a matter of principle. The true significance of the issue revolved around the question of "who is a Jew," a decision the Knesset had managed to evade until then. The fact that this was to be dealt with now had to do with the special political constellation of the day. The Law of Return was expanded to the effect that the right of return applied also to the non-Jewish child, grandchild and spouse of a Jew, as well as to the spouses of children and grandchildren (Section 4A). In other words, the right of "return" and citizenship was automatically extended to also include people who were not Jewish, halachically or otherwise. Section 4B determined that "For the purposes of this Law, 'Jew' means a person who was born of a Jewish mother or has become converted to Judaism and who is not a member of another religion." At the same time, the 1970 amendment made the civil definition subject to the Orthodox one.

While in 1950 the Knesset refused to "spoil" the historical significance of the "return" by discussing such "trifles" as the fate of mixed couples, in 1970 these were no longer trifles. Absorption for "mixed" families was particularly difficult when different members had different statuses.[13]

Moreover, coinciding with the 1970 debate, Israel was preparing itself for the possibility of massive emigration from the Soviet Union following the Jewish "national awakening" there. Many of those taking part in the discussion were convinced that, given the realities of Jewish life in the Soviet Union, they could expect large numbers of mixed couples,[14] and there was a desire to make immigration easier for them. However, facilitating the immigration of mixed families was likely to be interpreted as though Israel was encouraging mixed marriages, which in turn would weaken the struggle of Jewish communities in the diaspora against assimilation.

But other paradoxes faced Israel's legislators. Given the status quo to which she had committed herself, Golda Meir, by then prime minister, was forced to find a way to appease her National-Religious government partner. As the NRP had been willing to allow for the scope of the Law of Return to be widened, the other partners were put in a position that left them with no choice but to agree to a religious definition of "who is a Jew" for the purpose of both the Law of Return and the Population Registry. Although for the ultra-Orthodox parties, which wanted to impose exclusive recognition of Orthodox conversion, this was not enough, the new Law of Return did accept the religious principle of matriarchal descent—i.e., a Jew is the son or daughter of a Jewish mother—and of conversion. Rubinstein comments that it is of interest that this essential extension of the right of return, and to citizenship by virtue of such return, did not lead to a public debate when the law was changed, unlike the less important matter of the definition of the term Jew for the purpose of registration in accordance with Section 3A of the Population Registry Law 5725–1965 (Rubinstein 1991: 675).

Most of the political struggles that followed in the year the law was passed focused on the attempts of the ultra-Orthodox parties to restrict recognized conversions to Orthodox ones only, and to invalidate other conversion procedures, while the debate on the extension of the right of return came to an end.[15] Anyone searching the Knesset debates and the discussions of the Constitution, Law and Justice Committee for voices pointing out the significance that broadening the law might have demographically (i.e., vis-à-vis future population relationships of Jews versus Arabs) will find none. The Committee discussed the law as a purely internal Jewish affair. The reason for this might be that, in 1970, the law was of theoretical significance only: admittedly, mention was made of anticipated large-scale immigration from the Soviet Union, but that was not expected to materialize in the near future. On the other hand, what most Knesset members as well as most of Israeli society were concerned about in 1970 was not any discussion of "return," but the need to maintain the Population Registry in its current form.

While the law prevented discrimination between Jewish and non-Jewish family members when it came to immigration, it preserved the Population Registry: in other words, while the non-Jewish immigrants immigrated with a status identical to that of their Jewish family members, in the Population Registry only children of a Jewish mother or those who had undergone conversion could be registered as Jewish. The continued existence of a Population Registry therefore threatened to preserve discrimination between family members—the same discrimination that the broadening of the law was supposed to abolish. At this point a number of voices were heard calling for the abolishment of the nationality clause in the Population Registry—a clause that in Western democracies, in any case, is not standard practice. However, those who wanted to delete the nationality clause in the Population Registry were quickly sidelined by others who reasoned from the argument of "security needs." The latter is an indelible part of Israel's political discourse and can be traced to an 1958 statement by David Ben-Gurion to the effect that

> security and other considerations have to date prevented us, and will continue to prevent us in the near future, from accepting these proposals. In the light of our special situation, it being impossible in practical terms to provide permanent and effective monitoring of the country's borders against people infiltrating into Israel from our hostile neighbors, and constituting an acute and perpetual source of danger to the country and its residents, it is imperative that a legal resident of Israel should be able to identify himself at all times by means of a notice provided to him by a competent authority.[16]

Not only were Israel's security needs not reexamined, but no onus of proof was demanded. Obviously, the "infiltrators" that Ben-Gurion referred to in his arguments in 1958 had no relevance in the post-1967 war reality. Given the fact that against the background of the Shalit Affair, the security establishment proved willing to revoke the nationality section in the Population Registry, David Kretzmer concludes that insisting on maintaining the Population Register in its old format "results from the basic philosophy of the State of Israel which is working actively not to encourage an assimilationist approach to the Arab minority" (Kretzmer 1990: 44). To bolster his argument, Kretzmer makes the point that the Population Registry has no significance whatsoever for the rights and duties of the country's citizens: its sole purpose is to heighten the contrast between the state as the political framework for the aggregate of its citizens, and Israel as the particularistic nation-state for the Jewish people. In other words, the Register is an external marker that helps accentuate Israel's character as a republican democracy vis-à-vis its Jewish citizens. But as, at the same time, no actual active discrimination can be deduced from it vis-à-vis its Arab citizens, this serves as proof of Israel's character as a liberal democracy.

The recurring but by now irrelevant reference to "infiltrators" in the discussions about the Population Registry are meant to camouflage the real—identity-based—reason why it is there, and provides additional evidence of the duality attached to the "border" and the way it is represented in the Israeli collective consciousness. When Ben-Gurion went on to further strengthen the security argument—encountering the dissent of only a small number of Knesset members—he advanced an additional—but for him obviously a major—argument, as follows: "The suggestion to delete nationality from the Population Registry may perhaps suit the outlook of the 'Canaanites,' if any are still around, but not the Jewish citizen of the State of Israel. The Jewish people in Israel is for the time being (and will remain for a long time if not for ever) part of the Jewish people, and deleting nationality from the documents of a Jew in Eretz Israel is the beginning of deleting our being part of the Jewish people."[17]

Significantly, when the issue of the Population Registry was debated in 1970, the overwhelming majority of the people involved saw nothing wrong with having nationality recorded in the Population Registry. A number of MKs argued that recording nationality was not accepted practice in Western Europe, but only in Eastern Europe, and even if problematic, this was the reality familiar to them.[18] The historical irony here is that while many of the contributors to the discussion maintained the need for a registry of religion and nationality in Israel, they were forced to come to terms with the consequences of what it meant that the Soviet population registry used the entry "Yevrei" (Jew) (Kimmerling 1998: 273f.).[19] Critics became increasingly vociferous when some suggested that the Soviet record might sometimes prove useful, e.g., when potential candidates needed to be located for immigration, in particular in cases where, given the absence of diplomatic relations between Israel and the Soviet Union, this was up to foreign consular representatives. When the critics complained about the moral blemish attached to using Soviet documents, whose primary purpose appeared to be discriminatory,[20] MK Menachem Begin rose to the challenge:

> We have a list of charges against Bolshevik wickedness, against Communist evil, against Soviet animosity, but precisely because these charges are correct, let us not add anything to them which is not correct. It is a mistake which naive people also make sometimes to argue that because it says in the identity document of a Jew who is a Soviet citizen: "Nationalnost yevreiska" or "Yevrei," this is like the contaminated "J" applied by hands soaked in Jewish blood, in the sense of "Jude," so that they would know what the person's origins were. It is not true, and it should not be asserted. On the contrary: in the past, the recognition of "Nationalnost yevreiska" since Lenin's time was considered a major achievement. It is true that the Russians, the Communist rulers, stripped this concept of all substance relative to the Jews. However, what concepts did they not so strip?… Consequently, it is not true that the reference is as if to the Nazi "Jude," and one should not say something which is not true about this regime.[21]

From Begin's observation it is clear that he insists on a clear distinction between Soviet ethno-nationalism and Nazi racism: the former, notwithstanding reservations, should be acceptable to most Israeli lawmakers, and could not be viewed as racist. But there were other Knesset members who were especially sensitive that people would criticize the amendment of the Law of Return as a racist modification.[22] Admittedly, it is difficult to prove that the expansion of the Law of Return was intended "to constitute 'positive discrimination' in respect to those who suffered from the definitions of 'Jewishness' under the Nuremberg Race Laws" (Kimmerling 1998: 284), but some remained worried. In the Jewish historical memory, counting back three generations for immigration purposes was reminiscent of the Nuremberg Laws, but its unmistakable roots were related to the Bolshevik Revolution and the resulting rupture that took place between Soviet Jewry and the other Jewish communities in Europe in 1922—a time span of three generations prior to the 1970 debate.

The Law of Return 2000

In 1970, Israeli legislators opened the country's gates to the non-Jewish relatives of Jews down to the third generation, making their civil status comparable to that of Jewish immigrants and leaving just one restriction—the Population Registry. To what extent, however, was this legislation designed to encourage "non-Arab immigration"? A reading of the various discussions—of the Constitution, Law and Justice Committee and of the Knesset plenum—shows that most of the Israeli lawmakers assumed that once the immigrants arrived, they would rapidly become assimilated. Many pointed a finger at Israel's religious establishment, demanding it make the conversion process easier. The assumption was that the majority of the non-Jewish immigrants would opt for conversion of their own free will, particularly if the Rabbinate were to facilitate the conversion process. There was also a concomitant belief in the power of the institutions of the state, and the ability of the Zionist ethos to turn those selfsame immigrants into Jews.[23] Naturally, they were not assuming large-scale "non-Jewish" immigration, and it is equally doubtful whether they could have anticipated the creation of a non-Jewish milieu within the state of Israel. As one member of the Constitution Committee put it: "What are we doing? We are expanding the scope so greatly that even I, who favor expansion, am beginning to hesitate, because all of us are thinking of the immigration of Jews coming to Israel because they are Jews, but not of the immigration of people who will want to come in order to enjoy certain economic benefits which the state gives to immigrants, and in order to put this into practice they will go looking for some distant Jewish origins."[24]

But then in his very next sentence, he already hastens to take back the basic apprehension he had just raised, stating: "[True], I do not at the moment see a problem of migrants, particularly in light of the war situation that we are currently experiencing." In 1970, it is safe to say, there was no obvious reason to assume that anyone not connected with Jews and Jewishness through family ties would chose to migrate to Israel for purely utilitarian reasons. Even less was there any intention to encourage the immigration of non-Jews because they were "non-Arabs." What does stand out, though, is the absence in the discussions of any awareness of the nature and vitality of ethnic identities that we have witnessed so prominently all through the second half of the century (Kymlicka 1995). The Israeli lawmakers appear to have proceeded along the limited axis between authentic identity and assimilation. Given the assimilationist perception they adopted,[25] they assumed that changing the Law of Return would facilitate the immigration of mixed families, thereby stemming the threat of assimilation looming over Jewish spouses. Alternatively, they imagined that the expanded Law of Return would contribute to the absorption of non-Jewish spouses into Israel's Jewish society. At the same time, the state, of course, never thought of offering its Palestinian citizens a similar possibility of assimilation.

A reexamination of the relationship between nationalism and citizenship in Eastern Europe, as sketched by Brubaker (1996), should make it easier to understand the process followed by Israeli legislators. As already pointed out, Eastern Europe was central in the political experience of Israel's political elite, and it was from Eastern Europe that most of those involved in the debate derived their historical examples. We can find striking similarities between certain aspects of Polish history in the interwar period and its Israeli counterpart since the 1950s that can be, inter alia, explained by the repercussions the Jewish-East European political world of concepts has had for Israeli reality. As in interwar Poland, Israeli politics has always distinguished between various types of minorities—those earmarked for assimilation, with whom closer ties should be fostered, and those who are to be sidelined. Brubaker makes the point that the Polish state had no intention of bringing the Jewish minority closer to center stage, nor did it think that it could do this for the German minority, but it invested relatively major efforts in trying to do so for the Ukrainians and Ruthenians (Brubaker 1996: chap. 4).

The same applies to the case at hand: Israel already began discriminating against its Arab citizens under the 1950 Law of Return, and this de facto discrimination was then endorsed again in the decision not to drop the "nationality" rubric in the Population Registry. In contrast, after avoiding the issue in 1950, in 1970 Israel's lawmakers moved to acceptance, when they decided to include the third generation of non-Jewish immigrants as Jews according to Halacha, i.e., as being entitled to immigrate under the Law of Return with a status equal to that of Jewish immigrants. As early as the 1950 Law of Return and the 1952 Law on Citizenship, Israel had already put in place the institutional rejection and exclusion of the Arab population within the state's borders. Demographical statistics for Israel in the period from 1950 to 1970 show that while the proportion of migrants in the overall population growth totaled dozens of percentage points among the Jews, it was zero or mainly negative among the Arab population for the same period (Israel Statistical Yearbook 1970/1971: 24).[26] In 1970 it was no longer necessary for Israel to address the Arab question, because this aspect had been settled by earlier legislation blocking the return of all Palestinian refugees. A careful reading of documentation relating to the lawmaking process clearly shows that the 1970 amendment to the Law of Return was aimed not at "non-Jews," but at Jews, and specifically and unmistakably at the special situation of Soviet Jewry. Given the highly hierarchical stratification of Israeli society, one possible underlying interest the state may have had was to attract Ashkenazim as a counterweight to the Mizrahim. As the discussions contain no hint of this, it remains difficult to claim that the argument has any base in reality. In later years, too, one cannot really maintain that the expanded Law of Return was activated in order to bring about the immigration of "non-Jews," as shown by the way it has been applied to the non-Jewish relatives of Ethiopian immigrants. In their case, a slow and individual approach is applied on the basis of family unification, not at all in accordance with any broad-based principle (Kimmerling 1998: 299). Leaving aside the question as to what extent one can speak here of another form of disguised racism, this disparity between the acceptance of Russian immigration and of its Ethiopian counterpart cannot be readily included in a dichotomous model of "non-Arabs." Instead, it can be more convincingly explained in the framework of the model of nationalizing nationalism developed by Brubaker.

Poland's fate between the two world wars constitutes a clarion call warning us about the limitations of nationalizing nationalism in many domains: in time, those minorities that Poland chose to marginalize became irredentist. In the Israeli context, this might well become a self-fulfilling prophecy, unless Israel fully acknowledges and begins eliminating the large-scale discrimination against the country's Palestinian citizens.

Conclusion

The overwhelming majority of scholars writing about the structure of citizenship in Israel measure constitutional reality in the country against Western models of democracy. Irrespective of whether they are addressing the tension between the principles of liberal democracy and those of republican democracy, whether they come up with intermediate models of Israel as a consociational democracy or an "ethnic democracy," decline to see Israel as a democracy and instead perceive it as a model of a different—"ethnocratic"—system of government, or seek alternatives in the framework of a multiethnic democracy, the discussion generally remains Western-oriented and basically normative. The historical discussion that I have introduced in this essay is intended to broaden the picture—as I argue, it is the Central and East European experience from which the Israeli political elite derived its understanding. The internal contradictions between "Jewish state" and "democratic state" are not exhaustively explained by pointing to the tension between religion and nationality in the democratic tradition of the West. Rather, the contradictions have their origin in the East European "forge" that most Israeli lawmakers drew upon for their political values. Unlike in Western Europe and North America, the relationship between nationality and citizenship in Eastern Europe derived, not from the tensions between a single national majority of the established population and a minority group of migrants, but from the power relations between large ethnic populations in transition between multinational empires and new nation-states. The Central and East European Jewish experience was multifaceted, and it led many of the legislators to be haunted by existential fears that were then translated in the wording of the Law of Return, as though it were designed to deal with asylum seekers. At bottom is the transformation of the experience of a minority into the politics of a majority—most of the lawmakers and most of those who immigrated under the expanded Law of Return were automatically meant to become part of Israel's majority population. The way that many of the legislators understood the relationships between Jews and Palestinians, and consequently the relationship between nationality and citizenship, between demos and ethnos, was bound up with their own background and experience (Bishara 1993: 18). Hence, this involved not only the dual tension between majority and minority, but entailed the complexity of a Jewish majority—through a minority in the region—confronting an Arab minority—but belonging to the majority in the region—in the way that center confronts periphery. More specifically, the Arabs constituted a danger that had to be held in check by preventing repatriation (vide: Law of Return, Law on Citizenship) vis-à-vis the Jews whose "repatriation" was welcomed and encouraged by means of the Law of Return and 1970 Amendment. The latter were, of course, put in place to engender high levels of motivation for people who were Jewish by origin but not by religion to convert to Judaism.

The Law of Return is a manifest product of a particular ethno-cultural tendency. It was introduced so as to strengthen the Jewish ethnic majority in Israel, out of a belief in Israeli-Jewish culture's power to turn family members from a foreign ethnos into an integral part of the Jewish majority. As I pointed out above, there was never a parallel intention to enable the possible assimilation of Palestinians in Israel; in this sense, the Law of Return was from the outset and has remained until today a discriminatory law.

Only a few years ago, Gershon Shafir and Yoav Peled advanced the hypothesis that as the then peace process and the manifest economic advantages it was advertised to bring would enhance Israel's orientation toward the West, liberalization was likely to prevail over ethno-cultural tendencies (Shafir and Peled 1998: 260f.). At the moment, this possibility appears more remote than ever. Moreover, in the new multicultural and global reality of today, it is difficult to share the assumption that several hundred thousand ethnic Russians who immigrated and are still immigrating to Israel will fully assimilate into Israeli Jewish society. On the one hand, that society has lost many of its collective and assimilationist characteristics, and, on the other, the new immigrants all share a strong ethnic awareness. In such a reality, it may be hypothesized that they will maintain their collective characteristics. They will not be equal citizens, because in a Jewish state you are not a citizen with equal rights if you are not registered as a Jew in the population registry (Kimmerling 1998: 283f.). Since they themselves are subjected to a certain amount of discrimination, they will not be particularly sensitive to other groups that have suffered or are suffering from permanent discrimination in the state of Israel—the Palestinians and the Mizrahim (Al-Haj and Leshem 2000: 39). This becomes especially salient if we view their attitude against the background of the perceptions of origin in issues of nationalism and citizenship that are the accepted practice in the East European countries from which they come (see Dimitry Shumsky's contribution in this volume). Their considerable numerical weight, which will only grow in the coming years, is likely to hamper the chances of the peace process and of improving the delicate fabric of multicultural relationships in Israel. One can agree with Lustick that de facto, and given the current political reality, the Law of Return has negative implications for the Arabs in Israel. The time may have come to rethink the justifications that were offered for the 1970 amendment to the Law of Return, and it may even be appropriate to consider returning to the original intention, in other words, preserving the element that provided the bedrock for the expansion, i.e., entitlement to asylum, but not as a substitute for legislation on migration as is common in Western democracies.[27]

Notes

My thanks go to Amnon Raz-Krakotzkin, Yinon Cohen, Dan Diner, Rogers Brubaker, Natan Sznaider, and Dick Bruggeman for their helpful comments. I would also like to thank Noa Wertheim and Alon Schwarz for their assistance in gathering archival material. Knesset Archives, meeting of the Constitution, Law and Justice Committee, 3.5.1950–10.8.1950 [hereafter: 1950 Constitution Committee], 3f.

1. The difference between the two concepts—return, and ingathering the exiles—is illustrated by Ben-Gurion's statement: "The Law of Return ... contains a mission on the part of our State, the mission of ingathering the exiles. This law is decisive: it is not the State which confers on the Jew from overseas the right to settle in the country, but this right is inherent in him as a Jew, simply if he wishes to join in the settling of the country." David Ben-Gurion, Knesset Archives: Knesset meeting, Second Session, 3 July 1950, 87. Return as a right that precedes the state takes precedence for Ben-Gurion as a political goal over the "ingathering of the exiles."
2. According to Al-Haj and Leshem's research report, in the 1990–94 period the proportion of non-Jewish immigrants was around 20 percent of all immigrants, while the proportion of non-Jews or those married to non-Jews in the 1995–99 period increased to 41.3 percent.

3. It is interesting that it was Pinhas Rosen (Felix Rosenblueth), a native of Germany and Israel's first minister of justice, who insisted just before the signing of the Declaration of Independence that the document specify the borders of the State. Rosen thought that borders were a "legal matter," while Ben-Gurion, who wanted the borders of the State to include more land than those stipulated in the U.N. Resolution, held that "law is something which is determined by people (Segev 1986: xviii)."
4. Haim Cohn, Knesset Archives: Minutes of the meeting of the Constitution, Law and Justice Committee, 20 Tamuz, 5710: 29 (emphasis added).
5. Ibid.
6. Ibid., 30.
7. Meir Vilner, Knesset Archives: Minutes of the Knesset session on 5 July 1950, 149ff.
8. R. Cohen, Knesset Archives: Minutes of the meeting of the Constitution, Law and Justice Committee, 20 Tamuz, 5710: 5.
9. Benzion Dinburg, ibid.
10. A. Assaf, ibid.
11. Haim Cohn, ibid., 8. On the tension between sensitivity to individual freedoms and "state interests" in Haim Cohn as part of the group of legal experts of German origin in Israel, see Salzberger and Oz-Salzberger 2000: 97, 107–108.
12. David Ben-Gurion, Knesset Archives: Minutes of the Second Knesset session, eighth meeting, Monday, 3 July 1950, 87.
13. Haim Yosef Zadok (Ma'arach—Labor-Mapam), Law of Return (Amendment No. 2), 1970 (First Reading), 10 February 1970 (hereinafter: Knesset Plenary, February 1970), 766.
14. Yitzhak Meir Levin (Agudat Israel), Knesset Plenary, 5730, February 1970, 727f.; Menachem Begin, ibid., 735; Yaakov Hazan (Ma'arach—Labor-Mapam), ibid., 739; Shoshana Arbeli-Almoslino (Ma'arach—Labor-Mapam), ibid., 746; Moshe Nissim (Gahal), ibid., 768; Prime Minister Golda Meir, ibid., 771ff.
15. On this point I agree with Yigal Elam's (2000: 10) contention that "there is no real division between the views of secular and religious circles over Jewish identity, despite the yawning gulf between them."
16. David Ben-Gurion, quoted by the chairman of the Constitution, Law and Justice Committee, Shlomo Ben-Meir, Knesset Plenary, March 1970, 1139.
17. Ben-Gurion, Ma'ariv, 6 February 1970, quoted by Minister of Justice Shapiro: Knesset Plenary, March 1970, 725; previous reference, Ari Ancorion (Ma'arach, Labor-Mapam), Knesset Plenary, February 1970, 777.
18. For example, see the position of Minister Menachem Begin, Knesset Plenary, February 1970, 732; a moderate position was adopted by Haim Yosef Zadok (Ma'arach, Labor-Mapam), ibid., 764; and in particular by Prime Minister Golda Meir, ibid., 772.
19. Uri Avneri (HaOlam haZeh—Koach Hadash) made more pointed comments on the issue, Knesset Plenary, February 1970, 759.
20. Reuven Arazi (Ma'arach, Labor-Mapam), Knesset Plenary, March 1970, 1131–1132; or the furious reaction of Gideon Hausner (Independent Liberal Party): "It is utterly abhorrent to think that that selfsame Soviet identity document, the source and fount of anti-Jewish discrimination and persecution, should be used as proof by people wishing to immigrate to Israel because they are Jewish." Ibid., 1136.
21. Menachem Begin, Knesset Plenary, February 1970, 723.
22. Israel Yeshayahu-Sharabi (Ma'arach, Labor-Mapam), Knesset Plenary, March 1970, 731, Avraham Werdiger (Poalei Agudat Israel), ibid., 751; Israel Kargman (Ma'arach), ibid., 778.
23. Qv: Minister of Justice Y. S. Shapiro, Knesset Plenary, February 1970, 726; MK Meir Avizohar (HaReshima haMamlachtit), Knesset Plenary, March 1970, 1130; Yaacov Hazan (Ma'arach, Labor-Mapam), Knesset Plenary, February 1970, 738ff.; Uzi Feinerman (Ma'arach, Labor-Mapam), Knesset Plenary, February 1970, 753.
24. See MK Meir Avizohar, Constitution Committee, 18 February 1970, 3.
25. On the distinction between an integrative and an assimilative outlook, see Yona 1998: 254f.

26. With the exception of the 1950–51 period, during which a 14.9 percent increase occurred in the non-Jewish population as a result of migration, i.e., the years prior to the Law on Citizenship [Israel Statistical Yearbook 1970/1971: 24].

27. On ideas for possible changes to the Law of Return, see Amir 2000; Gans 1995.

References

Al-Haj, Majid, and Elazar Leshem. 2000. *Immigrants from the Former Soviet Union in Israel: Ten Years Later. A Research Report.* Haifa: University of Haifa.

Amir, Dan. 2000. "New Thinking about Israeli Conventions: The Law of Return. Initial Proposal of Criteria for Redrafting the Law of Return and Naturalization in the State of Israel." *Makom leMachshava—Bashaar* 7: 16–17. [Hebrew]

Bishara, Azmi. 1993. "On the Question of the Palestinian Minority in Israel." *Theory and Criticism* 3: 7–20. [Hebrew]

Blanke, Richard. 1981. *Prussian Poland in the German Empire (1871–1900).* New York: Boulder.

Brubaker, Rogers. 1992. *Citizenship and Nationhood in France and Germany.* Cambridge, Mass.: Harvard University Press.

———. 1996. *Nationalism Reframed. Nationhood and the National Question in the New Europe.* New York: Cambridge University Press.

Canefe, Nergis. 1998. "'Citizens versus Permanent Guests': Cultural Memory and Citizenship Laws in a Reunified Germany." *Citizenship Studies* 2: 519–544.

Diner, Dan. 1980. *Israel in Palästina. Über Tausch und Gewalt im Vorderem Orient.* Frankfurt am Main: Athenäum.

Elam, Yigal. 2000. *Judaism as Status Quo: The 1958 Who is a Jew Controversy and the Light It Shed on Relations between Religious and Secular Circles in the State of Israel.* Tel Aviv: Am Oved. [Hebrew]

Gans, Chaim. 1995. "The Law of Return and Affirmative Action." *Tel Aviv University Law Review* 19 (3): 683–697. [Hebrew]

———. 1998. "Nationalism and Migration." In *Multiculturalism in a Democratic and Jewish State,* ed. Menachem Mautner, Avi Sagi, Ronen Shamir, 341–360. Tel Aviv: Ramot. [Hebrew]

Gosewinkel, Dieter. 1995. "Die Staatsangehörigkeit als Institution des Nationalstaats. Zur Entstehung des Reichs-und Staatsangehörigkeitsgesetzes von 1913." In *Offene Staatlichkeit. Festschrift für Ernst-Wolfgang Böckenförde zum 65. Geburtstag,* ed. Rolf Grawert et al., 359–378. Berlin: Duncker und Humbolt.

———. 1998. "Citizenship and Nationhood: The Historical Development of the German Case." In *European Citizenship, Multiculturalism and the State,* ed. Ulrich K. Preuss and Ferran Requejo, 125–135. Baden-Baden: Nomos.

Hacohen, Dvora. 1998. "The Law of Return: Its Meaning and Implications." *Zionism* 21: 289–319. [Hebrew]

Huber, Ernst Rudolf, ed. 1990. *Dokumente zur deutschen Verfassungsgeschichte,* Bd.3. *Deutsche Verfassungsdokumente 1900–1918.* 3rd, rev. ed. Stuttgart: W. Kohlhammer.

Kemp, Adriana. 1990. *Frontier Nationalism: The Discourse of Israeli Labor Movement on Territories and Borders.* Master's thesis, Tel Aviv University. [Hebrew]

———. 2000. "Borders, Space and National Identity in Israel." *Theory and Criticism* 16: 13–43. [Hebrew]

Kimmerling, Baruch. 1998. "The New Israelis: A Plurality of Cultures without Multiculturalism." *Alpayim* 16: 264–308. [Hebrew]

Klein, Claude. 1997. "The Right of Return in Israeli Law." *Tel Aviv University Studies in Law* 13: 53–61.

Kretzmer, David. 1990. *The Legal Status of the Arabs in Israel.* Boulder: Westview.

Kymlicka, Will. 1995. *Multicultural Citizenship: A Liberal Theory of Minority Right*. Oxford: Clarendon Press.

Levy, Daniel. 2002. "The Politicization of Ethnic German Immigrants: The Transformation of State Priorities." In *Ethnic Migration in 20th Century Europe: Germany, Israel and Russia in Comparative Perspective,* ed. Rainer Münz and Rainer Ohlige.. London: Frank Cass.

Lustick, Ian. 1999. "Israel as a Non-Arab State: The Political Implications of Mass Immigration of Non-Jews." *Middle East Journal* 53: 417–433.

Morris, Benny. 1996. *Israel's Border Wars 1949–1956*. Tel Aviv: Am Oved. [Hebrew]

Peled, Yoav. 1993. "Strangers in Utopia: The Civic Status of Israel's Palestinian Citizens." *Theory and Criticism* 3: 21–35. [Hebrew]

Penslar, Derek J. 1991. *Zionism and Technocracy: The Engineering of Jewish Settlement in Palestine, 1870–1918*. Bloomington: Indiana University Press.

Rubinstein, Amnon. 1991. *The Constitutional Law of the State of Israel*, 4th expanded ed. Tel Aviv: Schocken.

Salzberger, Eli M., and Fania Oz-Salzberger. 2000. "The Hidden German Sources of the Israel Supreme Court." *Tel Aviv University Studies in Law* 15: 79–121.

Sartorius, Carl. 1930. "Erwerb und Verlust der deutschen Staatsangehörigkeit." In *Handbuch des deutschen Staatsrecht*, ed. Gerhard Inschüz and Richard Thoma. Vol. 1. Tübingen: J.C.B. Mohr.

Sassen, Saskia. 1996. *Migration, Siedler, Flüchtlinge. Von der Massenauswanderung zur Festung Europa*. Frankfurt am Main: Fischer.

Segev, Tom. 1986. *1949—The First Israelis*. New York: Free Press.

Shafir, Gershon, and Yoav Peled. 1998. "The Dynamics of Citizenship in Israel and the Israeli-Palestinian Peace Process." In *The Citizenship Debates: A Reader*, ed. Gershon Shafir, 251–262. Minneapolis: University of Minnesota Press.

Shapiro, Yonatan. 1984. *An Elite without Successors: Generations of Political Leaders in Israel*. Tel Aviv: Sifrut Poalim. [Hebrew]

Shumsky, Dimitry. 2002 "Ethnicity and Citizenship in the Perception of Russian Israelis." In *Challenging Ethnic Citizenship: German and Israeli Perspectives on Immigration,* ed. Daniel Levy and Yfaat Weiss, 154–178. New York: Berghahn Books.

Smooha, Sammy. 1996. "Ethnic Democracy: Israel as a Proto-Type." In *Zionism: A Contemporary Controversy,* ed. Pinhas Ginossar and Avi Bareli, 277–311. Sede Boqer: Ha-merkas le-moreshet Ben-Gurion. [Hebrew]

Thedieck, Karl. 1989. *Deutsche Staatsangehörigkeit im Bund und in den Ländern. Genese und Grundlagen der Staatsangehörigkeit in Deutschlands rechtlicher Perspektive*. Berlin: Duncker und Humbolt.

Wippermann, Wolfgang. 1999. "Das Blutrecht der Blutsnation. Zur Ideologie- und Politikgeschichte des *ius sanguinis* in Deutschland." In *Blut oder Boden: Doppel-Pass, Staatsbürgerrecht und Nationsverständnis*, ed. Jochen Baumann, Andreas Dietl, and Wolfgang Wippermann, 10–48. Berlin: Elefanten Press.

Yiftachel, Oren. 2000. "'Ethnocracy,' Geography and Democracy: Notes on the Politics of Judaizing Israel." *Alpayim* 19: 78–105. [Hebrew]

Yiftachel, Oren, and Alexander Kedar. 2000. "Landed Power: The Making of the Israeli Land Regime." *Theory and Criticism* 16: 67–100. [Hebrew]

Yona, Yossi. 1998. "A State of All Its Citizens, a Nation-State, or a Multicultural Democracy? Israel and the Limits of Liberal Democracy." *Alpayim* 16: 238–263. [Hebrew]

PART THREE

MINORITIES AND INCORPORATION REGIMES

— *Chapter 6* —

GERMAN CITIZENSHIP POLICY AND SINTI IDENTITY POLITICS

꧁

Gilad Margalit

Introduction

This chapter explores Sinti identity politics in post-Auschwitz Germany. It traces three phases through which Sinti chose to present themselves differently to the German public. Each phase corresponds to specific changes in the political climate of postwar Germany. In spite of their long history on German soil, they are still not accepted by Germans as fellow citizens who truly deserve equal rights. All of these phases reflect an enduring notion of the Sinti as undesirable foreigners. Before we delve into the distinctive features of each phase, we shall take a brief look at the policies that German states adopted toward this tiny itinerant minority of Indian origin prior to examining their status in postwar Germany.

The State and the Gypsies in the Realm of German Culture

Since the sixteenth century and until the beginning of the nineteenth, the declared policy by most German states toward Gypsies was deportation of this "undesirable" element from the German territories. Gypsy could be neither subject (*Untertan*) nor member of a German community (*Gemeindeangehörige*). The existence of most Gypsies in the German states was not legal. However, pragmatism and the influence of the Enlightenment led to the gradual abandonment of the traditional policy of deportation. Instead Gypsies were tolerated as a marginal group, and certain states attempted to integrate and to settle them in their communities.

The concept of integration of the Gypsies within Central European societies crystallized at the end of the eighteenth century due to the influence of the Enlightenment. It regarded the Gypsies as *homines educandi* and called for their civic correction (*bürgerliche Besserung der Zigeuner*) (Grellmann 1787), as opposed to the concept of civic improvement (*bürgerliche Verbesserung*) applied to the Jews (Dohm 1781). The different appellation of concepts of integration toward these two peoples reveals the difference in Central European attitudes to both minorities. Gypsies were regarded as wilder and much less civilized than Jews.

In sharp contradiction to the rapid modernization process that German Jews underwent since the last quarter of the eighteenth century, which was accompanied by an increased level of acculturation and assimilation into German bourgeois norms and the emergence of a small middle class (Volkov 1993), the Sinti retained to a considerable extent their traditional social and cultural frameworks and their ancestors' trades until the second half of the twentieth century. Only very few German Sinti families entered the lower middle classes. Whenever assimilation took place, it was usually with the German lower classes.

Sinti and Citizenship in the German States

The main obstacle to Sinti access to German citizenship was primarily their itinerant lifestyle and not their ethnic otherness. Precisely *ius soli* (coupled with *ius domicili*) and not *ius sanguinis* prevented their access to citizenship. The German states conducted restrictive citizenship policies toward Sinti, and were not ready to allow special prerequisites regarding their naturalization, which would have accepted their itinerant lifestyle on German soil as a legitimate mode of residence.

During the first decades of the nineteenth century, most German states had changed the traditional policy toward the local Sinti. The German states wanted the Sinti to quit their itinerant lifestyle and settle, but showed no willingness to invest resources by establishing special settlements for them. They sought to restrict Sinti activity as tradesmen and peddlers by limiting the issue of traveling trade licenses (*Wandergewerbscheine*), but they did not give them any alternative means of making a living legally (for example, as farmers). The Gypsies were pushed into the same kind of illegal existence they had known before the nineteenth century. Gypsies who were caught trading without a license were liable to imprisonment or deportation from the Reich.

The outcome of this internal contradiction in official policy, which existed in most German states, was that most Sinti were not granted German citizenship, although they were tolerated by the authorities. Those Sinti who did succeed in becoming German citizens could not enjoy full citizen's rights, and usually remained second-class citizens because of the social stigmatization (Fricke 1991: 37ff.).

Since 1870 the acquisition of citizenship by Gypsies could only be based on naturalization, as they are not ethnic Germans. Due mainly to their itinerant way of life, their low social status and the prejudices against them, the majority of German Sinti found it very hard to comply with all the necessary provisions for naturalization according to the citizenship law (Jansen 1996: 55ff.). A comparison of the figures on the number of holders of German citizenship among two nonethnic German minorities, German Sinti and German Jewry from the 1920s and 1930s, reveals that naturalization in the German Reich was a much easier process for a Jew than for a Sinto (singular for Sinti). The 1933 census indicates that only 19.8 percent of the 499,682 Jews in the German Reich were foreigners, which means the majority of Jews in the German Reich (more than 80 percent, many of whom were immigrants from Slavonic countries) had succeeded in attaining German citizenship since 1871. However, only little more than one third of German Sinti and very few Roma (who had earlier gained the status of Prussian subjects) succeeded in attaining German citizenship. According to a police publication of 1938, 35 percent of the 30,903 registered Gypsies were Reich citizens, 2 percent were stateless and 55 percent had an unresolved citizenship status (Jansen 1996: 81).

Nazi Policy Regarding German Sinti

During the Nazi period, Gypsies who lived in the German Reich were exposed to unprecedented discrimination and harassment. The motives of this Nazi persecution, however, were not identical with the motives of the persecution of the Jews. The Nazi perception of Gypsies lacked the political dimension, which was so central for the persecution of the Jews, and were a much lower-priority problem than the Jews. The Nazi regime defined the Gypsy problem in the German Reich as an integral part of interior problems of antisocial elements (*Asoziale*). The Nazis perceived the persecution of this minority as an integral part of their struggle for the elimination of crime and social deviance in the German national community (*Volksgemeinschaft*). Racial hygienic considerations played a central role in this persecution and not anthropological racism as in the Jewish case. The main Gypsy "expert" of the Third Reich, Robert Ritter, claimed that hardly any of the Gypsies were pure nomads of Indian origin, but were *Mischlinge* (mongrels) of various stocks and races. The *asoziale* properties, which he claimed were prevalent among those who conducted a gypsy way of life, were, he said, a consequence of mixing Gypsy blood with that of disreputable elements in German society. He argued that most of the so-called Gypsies were in fact *asoziale Mischlinge* who had inherited from their German ancestors the inclination to crime. Ritter maintained that there were no longer any truly "pure-race" Gypsies left in Europe. He believed that the *Asoziale* were a hopeless case, and could not be integrated into respectable and productive social circles. He recommended solving "the problem" through compulsory sterilization and incarceration

(Margalit 2001: 60ff.). In January 1943, Himmler issued a circular ordering the deportation of the Reich's Gypsies to a special families' camp at Auschwitz-Birkenau. Fifteen thousand German Gypsies were either murdered or died as result of their incarceration during the Third Reich.

German Policy Regarding the Sinti in the Aftermath of Auschwitz

The Sinti and German Citizenship

During the Allied occupation of Germany, German citizenship was restored to Sinti and Roma survivors. Some stateless Sinti who had lived for generations in Germany were recognized as German citizens and received German passports and identity cards.[1] However, during the 1950s the interior ministries of the German states (*Länder*) revoked the German citizenship of a considerable number of Sinti and Roma. This act relied on a provision of the Passport Law of 1952, which enabled the state to withdraw a passport if its holder could not certify, to the authorities' satisfaction, that he was a German according to Subsection 1 of Section 116 of the Basic Law. This section stated that a German was a person already holding proof of German citizenship, or was himself an ethnic German refugee or deported person, or a spouse or child of such a person who had been living in the domain of the German Reich in December 1937 (Klebe 1974: 61ff.). Usually, it was difficult for the Gypsies to provide such proof; the police generally had taken their papers from them prior to their deportation to Auschwitz.

The position taken by Dr. Mittelstädt, an official of the North Rhine-Westphalia Ministry of the Interior, in January 1954, was typical of the stance of the German bureaucracy regarding the Sinti's German citizenship. *Zigeuner* (Gypsies) were not regarded as fellow citizens but as dubious foreigners who were trying to obtain German citizenship illegally. Mittelstädt had instructed the municipal authorities (the Regierungspräsidenten and the Verwaltung der Landkreise) to investigate the question of the Gypsies' citizenship; he stated that the few cases that had been investigated raised doubts concerning the determination of the Gypsies' citizenship. Reviewing the possibilities and conditions required since 1842 for attaining citizenship in Prussia, and later the Reich, through inheritance or naturalization, he wrongly claimed that it could not be presumed that Gypsies met either the conditions set for the grant of citizenship in Prussia until 1871, or the prerequisites of German citizenship after 1871. He ruled that even when a Gypsy held a German passport, this should not be regarded as a proof of his or her German citizenship as it was known that after World War II citizenship matters were not thoroughly investigated and procedures for awarding citizenship were generous, especially for people released from concentration camps (Jansen 1996: 56–63).[2]

As the acquisition of German citizenship was based on *ius sanguinis,* the citizenship of many Sinti in the Federal Republic of Germany was entirely dependent on the circumstances in which one of their ancestors had gained or lost the status of a subject in certain German states a century ago or earlier. In the 1970s the Bavarian authorities withdrew German citizenship from a Sinto whose family had lived in Württemberg and Bavaria at least since the eighteenth century. The authorities claimed that one of his ancestors had left Württemberg for Bavaria without the authorities' consent so he and his descendants had forfeited their citizenship. In 1979 the Bavarian administrative court rejected the authorities' claim (Jansen 1996: 39ff.).

The West German authorities also relied on the findings of Nazi racial research to annul or confirm citizenship of German Sinti and Roma. In the early 1950s the German citizenship of Roma families, which had been restored after the war, was again revoked in light of the information from the Nazi period provided by the criminal police, which had preserved the Gypsy files from the Third Reich. The racial-hygienic research conducted during the Third Reich deprived most of the German Roma of German citizenship. Robert Ritter, the main "Gypsy expert" during the Third Reich, found out that the ancestors of the German Roma families (mostly Lovara) had illegally immigrated to Germany from Hungary between 1878 and 1880. They adopted German names such as Schubert, Strauss, and Weiss, instead of their original Hungarian names. He claimed that this enabled them to gain unlawfully the status of Prussian subjects. In the early 1940s, they had been accordingly stripped of their citizenship by the Third Reich authorities, and declared stateless.[3] The late lawyer, Paul Jochum, from Cologne who represented Sinti families, claimed that he had succeeded in regaining German citizenship for ten to fifteen Sinti families. He did so by bringing proof, as required by the passport law, from the racial-hygienic genealogical tables prepared by Robert Ritter and his team under the Third Reich. Through these tables the history of certain Sinti families could be traced to the eighteenth century.[4]

Stateless Sinti and Roma could attain German citizenship only by naturalization in the FRG, as if they were newly arrived immigrants. To be eligible for naturalization in Germany, one had to meet several conditions: mastery of the German language, both spoken and written, proof of never having broken any laws, and proof of economic independence, namely no need of welfare. But many Sinti, lacking a regular education, and a permanent occupation, and sometimes possessing a criminal record, could not meet these demands.

Compensation for Sinti Victims of Nazi Persecution

Perversely, the social stigmatization of the Gypsies as *Asoziale,* which had incriminated them during the Third Reich and condemned them to be victims of the Nazi criminal cleansing policy, also adversely affected their prospect of being officially recognized as victims of Nazism after the war. Sinti were treated by the authorities as victims of the second degree. They were not fully recognized as victims of racial persecution as were the Jews. The West German compensation and legal agencies accepted arguments used by the Nazis to legitimize the Gypsy persecution as a legitimate struggle against criminals. Many were deprived of any material compensation for years (Margalit 2001).

Sinti Politics of Identity in the Post-Auschwitz Period

The First Phase

German Sinti started relatively late to found their own organizations for pursuing their interests in the FRG. The first association of the Sinti was founded in 1956. However, noninstitutionalized patterns of collective action could be traced even earlier. As early as 1945, Gypsies in Lower Saxony claimed that they belonged to the "united nations," or to the "friendly nations," i.e., to the Allies who fought Nazism. The Sinti wished to gain this status since it might have enabled them to free themselves of the jurisdiction of German police. Among the policemen, who were in charge of the Gypsy departments in postwar Germany, the Sinti could meet officials who, just a few years earlier, had been responsible for their deportation to Auschwitz. According to the Allies' policy, the citizens of the "united nations" were not subjected to the authority of the German police and judicial system, but instead to the police and legal authorities of the military government, which was the aim of the Gypsies. The authorities in Lower Saxony submitted the matter to be ruled upon by the British military government in Lüneburg, which, in early November 1945, refused the Gypsies' request, thereby authorizing the German police to continue to act against them. Similar claims were made by some Gypsies in 1946 to the Gendarmerie command in Hesse. The American military government maintained that the Gypsies were not recognized internationally as an independent nation, therefore their nationality would be determined according to the rules referring to the establishment of citizenship.[5]

The Jewish Phase

Facing the failure to gain a better status in occupied Germany, Sinti ingenuity led to making use of a concrete identity, which was much harder for the authorities to refute. Certain prominent Sinti families as Rose and Bamberger, who were involved later in the founding of Sinti associations in the FRG, pretended to be Jews for a considerable time since the late 1940s. In June 1950, an official of the Bavarian welfare organization Bayerisches Hilfwerk, complained to the Gypsy department at the Munich police and to the Bavarian compensation office that: "this group of persons has recently pretended to be Jews and Jewish *Mischlinge* (mongrels), and obstinately concealed their Gypsy properties. The camouflage went so far that they let their recently born babies be baptized according to the Jewish rite."[6]

Hans Braun, another Sinti activist, said in an interview during the early 1980s, at the height of the civil right movement for the German Sinti and Roma, that he was ashamed to have pretended to be Jewish in the past. He explained that Germans feared the Jews much more than the Sinti (*Gypsyland* 1983). Even Romani Rose, the present chairman of the Zentralrat (the main Sinti organization), told a German reporter that as a young man he used to wear a Star of David chain while he sold carpets. This was his explanation for his practice: "As a youngster I also wanted to be able to be proud of something, but everywhere I was only the Gypsy. So I wore the Star of David and no one dared to say anything bad to me anymore." (Völklein 1980: 9)

The deprived Sinti victims of Nazi persecution observed the process by which, due to the outbreak of the Cold War and other reasons, Jews became the representative victims of Nazism in West Germany. The public debate on the guilt question (*Die Schuldfrage*) in postwar Germany, concentrated mainly on the fate of Jews without referring to Gypsies (e.g., Stern 1991: 272ff.). The persecution of the Gypsies evoked neither guilt nor shame feelings among the German political establishment, let alone the wider population. Discriminated against by West German compensation policy and denied the official warm and caring treatment bestowed on the small Jewish community in postwar West Germany by prominent state officials, the Sinti could hardly avoid feelings of envy and sorrow as reflected in the words of Vinzenz Rose: "Why do the Jewish victims receive 10 DM per day as compensation for their incarceration in concentration camps and we get only 5 DM? The Gypsy camp at Auschwitz was no different from the Jewish camp there. Are our lives worth only half the price, was the suffering inflicted on us only half as bad, so that one tries to pay us off with only half of the sum, which, in any event, is a ridiculous restitution for the incarceration?" (Spitta 1979: 24).[7]

The first president of the Federal Republic, Theodor Heuss, never referred to the atrocities committed against the Sinti. Public speeches such as "Mut zur Liebe" in December 1949 or "Das Mahnmal" in November 1952 (Heuss 1964: 121–140) were addressed only to Jews (and received prominent coverage in the German media), not to mention his annual gesture of greetings to the Jewish community on the Jewish New Year (Heuss 1964: 113–120). Official philo-Semitism regarded the small Jewish community as a guardian of the pre-Holocaust legacy of German-Jewish elites, although, the new community consisted largely of East European Jews. Official philo-Semitism adopted the Jewish apologetical arguments of the Central Verein deutscher Staatsbürger jüdischen Glaubens (Central Association of German Citizens of the Jewish Faith, founded in 1893), which as late as 1932 desperately tried to convince Germans that emancipation brought them only benefits, such as the German Jewish contributions to German science and culture (Centralverein 1932: 15). It pertained mainly to members of the upper German-Jewish circles, who had contributed immensely to German culture and not to the many Jews of lower classes, who remained in Germany after the war, and, similar to German Sinti, were petty dealers or petty craftsmen, whose contribution to German culture was much less glorious (Stern 1991: 298).

As victims of Nazi racial persecution, most prominent Sinti families pretended to be Jewish after the war so that they could enjoy the special status of the Jews in post-Holocaust Germany. The status of German Jewry in the philo-Semitic climate of postwar West Germany was regarded by the underprivileged Sinti as a lucrative status to which they should aspire. It was not just a trick to manipulate German guilt and shame for the murder of the Jews to win financial and other profits as some officials thought. The Sinti devised these means as a tool to evade discrimination. It also enabled them to proudly demonstrate the non-German side of their identity. At that time they were still ashamed to present their Gypsy identity in public, since they had internalized the contempt Germans felt toward them. The pretense of being Jewish was one of the few avenues by which they could be accepted and respected as non-German by their fellow Germans. Other Gypsies pretended to be Italian or Spanish or even Romanian.[8]

The public philo-Semitic climate created the impression that the new West German leadership did accept the Jews as fellow countrymen, in spite of the Jewish reluctance to call themselves German Jews (*deutsche Juden*). In light of the Nazi instruction to the Reichsvertretung der deutschen Juden (Reich's Association of German Jews) to change its title to Reichsvertretung der Juden in Deutschland (Reich's Association of Jews in Germany) in 1935, the Jewish leadership in postwar Germany regarded the using of this very formula—*deutsche Juden*—as taboo (Brenner 1995: 181). The main Jewish organization in the FRG therefore wished to dissociate itself from the pre-Holocaust concept of German Jews as German nationals, members of the Mosaic persuasion, a notion that acquired its ultimate expression in the name of the aforementioned pre-Holocaust organization, the Central Verein deutscher Staatsbürger jüdischen Glaubens (Central Association of German Citizens of the Jewish Faith). Consequently, the postwar Jewish leadership called its organization Zentralrat der Juden in Deutschland (Central Committee of the Jews in Germany), emphasizing that after Auschwitz Jews in Germany no longer regarded themselves as part of the German nation. Nevertheless they insisted on being an integral part of the German community and of the German polity in the FRG.

The legitimization of an organized Jewish existence in the German political culture afforded the German Sinti a model for the collective existence of a non-German minority in Germany. The next phase was replacing the pretense of being Jews with the ostensible adoption of the Jewish organizational framework in Germany. In 1956, Vinzenz Rose founded the Verband und Interessengemeinschaft rassisch Verfolgter nicht-jüdischen Glaubens deutscher Staatsbürger e. V. (Association and Interest Community of German Citizens of Non-Jewish Faith who have been Racially Persecuted). It was a rather odd name for an organization whose main mission was to represent the Sinti claims, as it totally blurs its members' identity. Such a name pertained equally to "non-Aryan Christians," that is, people of Jewish descent who were persecuted by the Nazis for racial reasons. The choice of name might have been deliberate. In the 1950s the self-appellation Sinti was not known in Germany. Rose probably tried to evade the derogatory association of the term *Zigeuner* (Gypsy), which prevailed among the German public. This title is reminiscent of the above-mentioned Central Verein, and the similarity is certainly not accidental. Both titles truly reflect the desperate quest of the two German minorities to be recognized and accepted as Germans. The association represented a few prominent Sinti families, and was engaged mainly in the matter of compensation of its members for their persecution by the Nazis, as was the Jewish organization of the time, as well as in bringing to trial certain Nazi perpetrators of this persecution.

From the late 1970s, Sinti activists in Germany, influenced by the International Romany Union, started to regard the German term *Zigeuner*, as carrying derogatory connotations. They therefore replaced it with their self-appellation Sinti. Since 1973, Vinzenz Rose's son, Romani, has presided over the reactivated organization that was then called Deutscher Sinti Verband (Association of German Sinti). In 1983 it was renamed Zentralrat deutscher Sinti und Roma, imitating the title of the main Jewish organization in the FRG (Zentralrat der Juden in Deutschland). Despite the pretension to pursue a national struggle in the name of all Romany groups, the Zentralrat is in fact a traditional organization of a few Sinti families with no Roma on its board.

This attempt to define the Sinti organization as German has not been pursued as a strategy by the Roma in Germany. When, in 1960, Walter Strauss and Wilhelm Weiss, two German Roma from Frankfurt, founded the first Roma organization in the Federal Republic, they had no qualms about calling it Zentral Komitee der Zigeuner (Central Committee of the Gypsies) (Hoffmann 1960). This trend could also be traced in the organizations of the second generation after the Second World War. When Rudko Kawczynski, a Rom (singular of Roma) who was born in Poland (to a Roma family of non-Polish origin), and immigrated to Germany as a child, founded an organization for both groups in Hamburg in 1980, he named it Rom und Cinti Union (Romany and Cinti Union).

In sharp contrast to the German Sinti, many Roma, especially activists such as Kawczynski who were the first generation in their family to grow up in Germany, and who have relatives and connections all over Europe, do not regard themselves as Germans and are not so eager to be accepted as German even though for practical reasons they wish to acquire German citizenship. In an interview with the Communist newspaper *Neues Deutschland* in 1993, Kawczynski was asked about the German citizenship he had recently acquired. He replied: "Naturally I am not a German. When I go along the street, no one sees that I have a German passport in my pocket" (Bozic 1993). Rather like the first generation of immigrants of Eastern European Jewish origin in Germany during the postwar period, these activists regard themselves as members of a nation (the Jewish people or the Roma) and not as members of a German minority group (German Jews or *"Gadschkene Sinti,"* which means German Sinti in the Sinti dialect). The present generation at least would never call itself *Gadschkene Roma.*

In contrast to Germany where Romany nationalism appeared as late as the early 1970s, in Eastern Europe it had emerged as early as the 1930s, and Roma intellectuals in Rumania and Yugoslavia were preoccupied with Romani culture and the Romani national movement and published Romany newspapers (Bācanu 1996: 40f.; Djurić 1987: 45). These developments surely have encouraged the emergence of national consciousness and identity among Roma. The different self-appellations and the specific naming of the Roma and Sinti organizations express a different collective consciousness in these two Gypsy groups. The Roma have national consciousness while the Sinti have tribal consciousness.

The Present Phase: Romani Nationalism, the Holocaust, and Sinti's Germanness

During the late 1960s, in England as in other European states, a Romany nationalism started to crystallize, peaking in the convening of the first Romano Kongreso in London in 1971 (Kenrick 1981: 14). Romany nationalism aims at transforming the tribal consciousness and identity of various Romany groups such as the German Sinti into a Romany national consciousness and national identity.[9] It emphasizes their Indian origin and the Romany language. The Romany national flag resembles the Indian flag with the Ashok Chakra (the Indian wheel of destiny) at its center. The Romany anthem emphasizes their Indian origins and wandering as the formative experience of Gypsy existence. Romany nationalism expects and demands all tribal groups, such as the German Sinti, to show solidarity with other Romany tribes, as members of the same Romany nation (Saip 1981: 11ff.).

The influence of Romany nationalism could be traced in all Romany organizations in Europe. However, its impact on German Sinti and their main political organization, the Zentralrat, has been fairly weak. But no other local Romany organization in any European country is so desperately engaged, as is the Zentralrat deutscher Sinti and Roma (the main Sinti organization that was recognized by the federal German government), in an apologetic attempt to persuade the German public that German Sinti truly merit the right to live in Germany. Between 1979 and 1985, Sinti and Roma organizations cooperated in pursuing a public campaign for civil rights and recognition in the FRG. The Sinti did not embark with other groups on a public campaign to promote a political concept aimed at revising the citizenship law of 1913. Instead they have chosen a strategy based on the ethnic-cultural concept of German self-understanding. They have tried to persuade the German public that they, the Sinti, constitute an integral part of the German culture and German nation.

The Zentralrat demanded the federal government recognize "German Sinti and Roma as a German ethnic group (*deutsche Volksgruppe*) with its own 600-year German history, language and cultural identity." Rose argued that "Romani is a language which has been spoken in Germany for 600 years and therefore it forms a part of German culture" (Rose 1987: 11; 1994: 10–20). The Roma by contrast demand that European authorities recognize all Gypsy groups as a nonterritorial European people (Matras 1998: 59ff.).

The Zentralrat has also tried to impress the German public with their patriotism. They have chosen to insert photos of Sinti soldiers in Wehrmacht uniform in some of their publications (Rose 1987: 70, 73), which thereby resemble the apologetic publications of the Jewish veterans' organization of the Weimar period Reichsbund Jüdischer Frontsoldaten (Reichsbund 1935). In some of his public statements, Rose mirrored the West German official philo-Semitic tone regarding Jews. He also depicted the Sinti as guardians of German cultural heritage and emphasized their actual contribution to the German culture: "Sinti are among the foremost people to ensure that old cultural possessions (*Kulturgut*) would remain preserved. They went to the villages and bought or secured their antique things, that other people would just have tossed into the garbage.... Some German citizens, who today possess a Baroque chest of drawers, do not know that they owe it to Sinti."[10]

The Sinti highlight their respectability and "Germanness," and simultaneously represent their Gypsyhood as an aspect of their identity that belongs to the private domain alone, and has nothing to do with the public sphere. This conduct claiming the Sinti function exactly like their fellow Germans, calls to mind the interpretation in liberal German-Jewish circles of their Jewishness and "Germanness," and reflects the demands of the German citizenship law for those who wish to become naturalized in Germany.

In contrast to Romany nationalism, the Sinti refrained from showing solidarity and support for Roma refugees from Eastern Europe. In the early 1980s, Roma refugees arrived in Germany, and sought the help of Sinti organizations in their own legal struggle for the right to stay there and escape deportation to their countries of origin. The Zentralrat claimed that growing numbers of foreign Roma who "abused their guest status in our country" might harm the image of German Sinti and Roma and thus ruin many of the achievements of the organizations. This policy of the Zentralrat brought to an end the cooperation between the Sinti's main organization and the Rom und Cinti Union, which consisted mainly of Roma (Matras 1998: 56ff.).

In retrospect, the adoption of "Jewish" organizational structures and action strategies by the Zentralrat since 1983, and the emphasis on the victimization of the Sinti during the Holocaust and in its aftermath, has proved to be the most effective element of the campaign for equal civil rights of Sinti and Roma in German political culture. In a relatively short period, the claim that the persecution of the Gypsies was identical with the Jewish Holocaust, which had consistently been denied by the German establishment until the 1960s, has become widely accepted. The ultimate expression of its adoption by the German political culture was the announcement by the president of the Federal Republic, Roman Herzog, on 16 March 1997 at the opening of the Documentation and Culture Center of the German Sinti and Roma in Heidelberg, an institution operated by the Zentralrat. He said: "The genocide inflicted upon the Sinti and Roma was conducted out of the same motive of the racial madness, and [pursued] with the same intention and with the same will for systematic and final extermination as that of the Jews." (Sander 1998: 12)

However, this alleged "philo-Gypsyism" is restricted to official German political culture. Public polls have consistently indicated that during the last decade Gypsies have been the most resented "others" in Germany. A poll conducted in 1992 by the Demoscopic Institute of Allensbach, indicated that 64 percent of Germans do not want to have Gypsy neighbors. This constitutes a much higher rejection rate than for other ethnic, religious, and racial categories (Arabs, 47 percent; Africans, 37 percent; Turks, 36 percent; Muslims, 17 percent; Hindus, 14 percent; foreign laborers, 12 percent; dark-skinned, 8 percent; Jews, 7 percent) and is equal only to the rejection rates concerning drug addicts (66 percent), drunkards (64 percent), and leftist extremists (62 percent).

The downplaying of the Gypsy component and the highlighting of the German component in Sinti identity are clear indicators of the lack of acceptance of the Sinti as fellow citizens by the German public. The uniqueness of Romany nationalistic positions among the German Sinti in comparison to Romany groups in France or Britain might attest that this situation is the outcome of the ethno-cultural perceptions of German society regarding their belonging to the German community, which, until recently, was reflected in the *ius sanguinis* principle of the acquisition of German citizenship. But the discrimination against German Sinti does not derive solely from prejudice against a nonethnic German element. After all, the rate of objection to living in a neighborhood with Jews is only 7 percent (and 22 percent in Emnid polls from 1994). It seems that social prejudice against Sinti, which stigmatize them as an *asoziale* group play an important factor in the negative attitude toward them in the past and in present. It will probably take at least one generation until the ethnocultural German self-understanding will give way to the new political concept of *ius soli*, which is incorporated within the new citizenship law. However, it might take the average Germany much longer to overcome his or her social prejudice against Sinti. To a certain extent, this also depends on the ability of Sinti to free themselves of the vicious circle of misery, poor education and poverty in which many of them have been caught for generations. Such changes will probably create a new phase of Sinti identity politics.

Notes

1. Hess. MInn Abt. III 22 e 30 Bekämpfung der Zigeunerwesen Dr. Mittelstädt Nord-Rhein Westfälischen Innenminister, 13.1.1954.
2. See Fn no. 1; Gesetz über die Erwerbung und den Verlust der Bundes- und Staatsangehörigkeit 1.6.1870 (RGBl, 355).
3. HStA Düsseldorf Rep. 231 1535 Bl. 101–102 Leo Karsten, Kriminal Obermeister Ludwigshafen 12.3.1959; Bundesarchiv Koblenz B 106 5271 Bundesministerium des Innern. Dr. Eggendorfer Bayer. Staatsministerium für Wirtschaft und Verkehr 16.3.1953.
4. Interview with Paul Jochum, Cologne, 27.10.1992.
5. Nieders. HSTA Hannover Nds. C 100 Acc. 60/55 Nr. 1103: A copy of a letter from the British military government at Lüneburg to the local German administration of November 1945; Hess. Minn 22 e 30 Zinnkann to the Office of Military Government, 20.9.1946.
6. Herr Koch, Bayerisches Hilfswerk an Abt. Zigeunerpolizei Munich, 14.6.1950. *Pogrom* 80/81 (March/April 1981): 80.
7. Rose's highly subjective claims against German compensation authorities, attributing official preferable treatment of Jews in comparison to Sinti, has no factual basis.
8. "Gespraech mit Rudko Kawczynski und S. Tornado Rosenberg," *Pogrom* 80/81 (March/April 1981): 129. Kawczynski: "I had very little problems, as I did not go to school as a Gypsy but as a Romanian."
9. "Vorwort des Präsidenten der Romani-Union." *Pogrom* 80/81 (March/April 1981): 6. Jan Cibula: "If we continue to regard ourselves only as Lovar, Kalderasch, Sinto, or Gitano, we could not appear together.... We do not want to operate in a manner that will split our people."
10. "Bei Sinti und Roma gibt es noch viel zu tun. Ein Interview mit Romani Rose," in Dieter Galinski et al., *Nicht irgendwo sondern hier bei uns!* (Hamburg, 1982), 89.

References

Băcanu, M. Ţigannii. 1996. *Minoritate Natpionlă sau Majoritate Infracpională*. Bucuresti.
Brenner, Michael. 1995. *Nach dem Holocaust. Juden in Deutschland 1945–1950*. Munich: Beck Verlag.
Centralverein Deutscher Staatsbürger Jüdischen Glaubens, ed. 1932. *Wir Deutsche-Juden 321–1932*. Berlin: Centralverein Deutscher Staatsbürger Jüdischen Glaubens.
Djurić, Rajko. 1987. "Die Roma in der Sozialistischen Föderativen Republik Jugoslawien." *Pogrom* 130 (6): 45.

Dohm, Christian W. 1781. *Über die bürgerliche Verbesserung der Juden*, Berlin/Stetin: Nicolai.

Fricke, Thomas. 1991. *Zwischen Erziehung und Ausgrenzung. Zur württembergischen Geschichte der Sinti und Roma im 19. Jahrhundert*. Frankfurt am Main: Peter Lang.

Grellmann, Heinrich Moritz Gottlieb. 1787. *Historische Versuch über die Zigeuner, betreffend die Lebensart und Verfassung Sitten und Schicksale dieses Volkes seit seiner Erscheinung in Europa und dessen Ursprung*. Göttingen: Dieterich.

Gypsyland – It Doesn't Exist. A film by the BBC. 1983

Heuss, Theodor. 1964. *An und über Juden*. Düsseldorf: Econ.

Hoffmann, Volkmar. 1960. *"Sie wollen keine Bürger zweiter Klasse sein." Frankfurter Rundschau* 15 (3).

Jansen, Michael. 1996. *Sinti und Roma und die deutsche Staatsangehörigkeit*. Aachen: Shaker.

Kenrick, Donald. 1981. "Die britischen Roma heute." *Pogrom* 80/81 (12): 14.

Klebe, Thomas. 1974. "Staatsangehörigkeit – unbekannt." *Nachrichtendienst des Deutschen Vereins für öffentliche und private Fürsorge* 54 (3): 61–63.

Margalit, Gilad. 2001. *Die Nachkriegsdeutschen und "ihre Zigeuner." Zur Haltung der deutschen Gesellschaft im Schatten von Auschwitz*. Berlin: Metropol.

Matras, Yaron. 1998. "The Development of the Romani Civil Rights Movement in Germany 1945–1996." In *Sinti und Roma in German-Speaking Society and Literature*, ed. Susan Tebbutt, 49–64. Oxford: Berghahn Books.

Reichsbund Jüdischer Frontsoldaten e.V., ed. 1935. *Gefallene Deutsche Juden. Frontbriefe 1914–1918*. Berlin: Reichsbund Jüdischer Frontsoldaten e.V.

Rose, Romani. 1987. *Bürgerrechte für Sinti und Roma. Das Buch zum Rassismus in Deutschland*. Heidelberg: Zentralrat deutscher Sinti und Roma.

———. 1994. *"Konkreter* Minderheitenschutz fuer die Sinti und Roma." In *Minderheitenschutz für Sinti und Roma in Rahmen des Europarates, der KSZE und der UNO*, ed. Zentralrat Deutscher Sinti und Roma, 10–20. Heidelberg: Zentralrat deutscher Sinti und Roma.

Saip, Jusuf. 1981. "Das Rad des Schicksals – Die Roma heute und morgen." *Pogrom* 80/81 (12): 10–12.

Spitta, Arnold. 1979. "Der Verband Sinti Deutschlands e.V." *Pogrom* 68: 22–24.

Stern, Frank. 1991. *Im Anfang war Auschwitz. Antisemitismus und Philosemitismus in deutschen Nachkrieg*. Gerlingen: Bleicher Verlag.

Van Rahden, Till. 2000. "From Idea into Practice: Is There a Social History of Antisemitism after the 'Linguistic Turn'? Breslau as an Example." In *German Antisemitism*, ed. Jacob Borut and Oded Heilbronner, 293–318. Tel Aviv: Am Oved. [Hebrew]

Völklein, Ulrich. 1980. "Lästig ist das Zigeunerleben." *Die Zeit*, 7 March: 9.

Volkov, Shulamit. 1993. "The *'Verbürgerlichung'* of the Jews as a Paradigm." In *Bourgeois Society in Nineteenth-Century Europe*, ed. Jürgen Kocka and Allan Mitchell, 367–391. Oxford: Berg Publishers.

Zimmermann, Michael. 1996. *Rassenutopie und Genozid. Die nationalsozialistische 'Lösung der Zigeunerfrage.'* Hamburg: Christians.

Chapter 7

BEYOND THE "SECOND GENERATION"

Rethinking the Place of Migrant Youth Culture in Berlin

Levent Soysal

The Discrete Charm of the "Second Generation"

In his introduction to the special issue of *International Migration Review* on "The New Second Generation," Alejandro Portes urges the practitioners of immigration scholarship to turn their attention from "adult immigrants" to the "growth and adaptation of the second generation" (1994: 632). He rightly complains that "the dearth of accessible census data" has been used to "[compress] the second generation youth into a classificatory scheme that obliterates their history"—that is, a scheme that groups the youth under "pan-ethnic labels" such as "Hispanic," "Black," "Asian," and "non-Hispanic white," and hence "hopelessly obscuring the character and implications" of the data. His concern emanates from a sense of loss under the current labeling system of accurate indicators that reveal the "adaptation of the second generation," which will, for Portes, "be decisive in establishing the long-term outlook for the contemporary immigration" to the United States.

The "new" in Portes's definition of the second generation refers to a distinction made between the "post-1965" immigration and earlier waves. In this new second generation, Portes sees the keys to understanding the "recent evolution of the American society," as manifested by a plethora of social issues such as "the continuing domination of English, the growth of a welfare-dependent population, the resilience of culturally distinct urban enclaves, and the decline or growth of ethnic intermarriages." In studying the second generation, Portes seeks evidence as to the state and unfolding of these social issues in order to solve the "puzzle" of evolution he sets up for immigration scholarship. The puzzle is seemingly simple enough: whether or not "today's children of immigrants will follow their European predecessors and move steadily into the middle-class mainstream, or on the contrary, their ascent will be blocked and they will join children of earlier black and Puerto Rican migrants as part of an expanded multiethnic underclass" (Portes 1994: 634). Of the outcome, Portes (1994: 635f.) is not so certain: "today's second generation finds itself somewhere between these extremes," "abstracted in academic theories" of "linear assimilation" and the "culture of poverty and urban underclass." Hence, Portes proposes extensive studies to recover evidence from the available second-generation data. Accordingly, the studies collected in the aforementioned IMR volume probe the economic conditions, family arrangements, ethnic and racial identities, self-esteem, social capital, language competency, and labor-market achievement of the second generation.

In *Between Cultures*, a study that takes its cues from similar concerns as those of Portes, Mohammad Anwar (1998) attempts to catalogue the indicators of "continuity and change in the lives of young Asians" in Britain. Like Portes, Anwar's point of departure is also the "new" immigration, postwar immigration to Britain. Parsing statistics of settlement patterns, education, family and marriage, religion and mother tongue, Anwar sets out to determine the place of Asian youths, the second generation of postwar immigration, in comparison with the parameters of "normal" in British society. In this endeavor, the assessment of where youth stand in between two "cultures' (home and host country cultures) ultimately becomes the benchmark of progress achieved in terms of "race relations" in Britain. The extensive study carried out by Tariq Modood and his colleagues (1997; based on the fourth national survey of ethnic minorities in Britain conducted by the Policy Studies Institute) is another example of extant exercise in measuring the condition of the second generation vis-à-vis the society within which they live as a means to appraise the degree of progress (read adaptation or integration) achieved in the host country. Compared to Anwar, Modood finds in his assessment more evidence for a positive reading of the statistical data in question and places less emphasis on the in-betweenness of the second generation. In similar work, Tribalat (1996) sifts through massive life cycle data on the Magrebin second generation in France in order to delineate their place in French society in terms of religious orientation, education, unemployment, and other customary indicators of integration, while Wilhelm Heitmeyer and his colleagues (1997) in Germany amass data on the indices of crime, religion, and nationalism as a means to portray a Turkish youth locked in fundamentalism, with no sign of integration in sight.

I cite these studies not so much to doubt the nature and reliability of the data collected or dispute the conclusions and interpretations advanced by the authors in question (such debates abound in the literature). My point of departure is to interrogate the axiomatic acceptance of generational categories and the (implicit) contention of in-betweenness (cultural or otherwise) in studying and writing about migrant youths. In the social scientific literature, as well as policy documents and popular conversations, "second generation" emerges as a taken-for-granted, self-evident operational category, without any questioning of the axiomatic frameworks of ethnic or religiously defined cultural differences and time-honored, worn-out models of linear progressive transition from tradition to modernity, which singularly underline the seeming materiality and factualness of the category. This is irrespective of the degree to which the above-mentioned studies in particular—and migration research in general—attribute an explanatory prowess to the category "second generation." I argue that the generational categories hide, rather than reveal, the conditions, participation, and diverse cultural productions of migrant youths in their countries of residence by rendering their experience as an unceasing and unremitting journey "in between" tradition and modernity. When advanced as self-evident and without critical scrutiny, statistical exercises to establish the empirical conditions and integration (adaptation, adjustment) of migrant youths inevitably and inadvertently become complicit in perpetuating the fictions of in-betweenness, isolation, and maladjustment. Absent from the analytical, policy, and popular narratives are connections of migrant youths not only to their places of residence but also to transnational flows of youth culture and their competencies in exercising their citizenship in a world we increasingly imagine as "global."

In this essay, I counter the conventional narratives of second generations and in-betweenness, by locating migrant youth in the social and cultural spaces within which they realize their life stories, make and have cultures, and converse and cooperate with their peers from other places and cultures in conjuring up dreams and futures for themselves and the world at large.[1] First, I will advance a critique of the foundational assumptions of in-betweenness and paradigmatic dexterity of generational approaches to studying migrant youth. Subsequently, I situate migrant youths in the institutional settings, which afford the means and constraints for their participation and productions of culture. Then, deriving ethnographic evidence from the cultural projects of Turkish migrant youths in the public spaces of Berlin, I will provide a narrative of migrant youth culture that assigns primacy to the institutional resources afforded by the newly projected metropolis, Berlin, for the culture and leisure of migrant youths. The narrative of migrant youth culture I provide is also sensitive to the affinities of youthful productions of culture with the contemporary organizing discourses of plurality, tolerance, and multiculturalism. In the public spaces of metropolitan Berlin and in dialogue with global discourses and cultural flows, I contend, we can capture meaningful stories of youth culture and civic participation, beyond the limitations of the unrelenting narratives of generations and in-betweenness.

Despite their significance in shaping migrant youth culture, much of the literature overlooks the promises, and adversities, offered by the city and simply concerns itself with the location of migrant youths in a scale of generations and vis-à-vis timeless (Turkish) traditions and cultural formations. In generational terms, while the first generation is identified with origins (in Turkey, traditions, the past), the second generation is simultaneously associated with hope (of breaking old ties and immersing in the culture of the host country) and suspended in a state of neither-here-or-there. The third generation is expected to inherit the norms of the new culture (of Germany, modernity, the future).

This seemingly intuitive scheme of change derives its potency from the territorial closure of culture within the nation-state. The borders of the state enclose the nation, and its culture as one cohesive entity collapsing all useful categorical and historical distinctions between place, nation (ethnicity) and culture.[2] Without allowing for historical predicaments, the terrain of Germany becomes congruent with Germanness (the land of natives) and the contemporary geography of Turkey embodies Turkish-ness (the place from which the foreigners come). For the migrant, the roots and homes immanently remain elsewhere. She, the Turk, *brings* her *home* culture to her *host* country, into the *center* of the culture of her *host*, the German. Her presence, praxis, and culture effectively remain tempo-rary and restless against the inherent, and prevailing, permanence of the "native" existence.[3]

Furthermore, her presence is committed to categories of "typological time" in which home and host places occupy differential modernizations, developments, and civilizations (Fabian 1983). As a "distancing device," typological time conjures not "time elapsed" but intervals between "qual-ity of states" that are "unequally distributed among human populations of this world" (Fabian 1983: 23). In units of typological time, *home* (not where she lives but from where she comes) is located in tradition, whereas host country (where she is the foreigner) denotes modernity. Although the units of tradition and modernity suggest a movement in "evolutionary time" (Fabian 1983:17), from the former to the latter, this movement is only virtual; tradition and modernity are spatialized thus arrested in Turkey and Germany, respectively. Her *"co-evalness,"* her belonging to the "same age, duration, or epoch" (Fabian 1983), is denied in an a priori fashion. The Turkish migrant brings her tradition, not her modernity, to Germany and lives her culture and otherness within but outside of modernity.

When it comes to migrant youth, the unequivocal "second generation" of migration studies and policy papers, their location in time and space has no coordinates: they are deemed to be *in-between*, or *betwixt and between*—between two cultures (Turkish and German), two places (Turkey and Germany), and two states of being (tradition and moder-nity). The inventory of binary oppositions, which are employed to describe their situation, comprise an interminable list of self-fulfilling prophecy. Migrant youths are invariably portrayed as stranded and torn between tradition—that which is of home, parents, and distant places and pasts—and modernity—that which is of streets, social workers, and the here and now. Home is inside, oppression, night, and darkness, whereas the street is outside, freedom, day, and brightness. Moreover, as I have stated, typological time works as a device of a priori differentiation between migrants and natives the first occupying tradition and the second, modernity. Neither migrants (the first generation) nor natives (Germans), the migrant youths have no categorical place in the taxonomy. So proceeds the logic of classification: they are neither here nor there, neither Turkish nor German, neither traditional nor modern. *By fiat, they become in-between.*

For migrant youths, in-betweenness also designates a state of perpetual liminality, from which there seems no plausible escape. In Turnerian terms, the "social drama" of migration is nationally structured and "crisis" occurs when nationally ordered social relations are "breached" "by the infraction of a rule ordinarily held to be binding" (Turner 1987: 34). That is, crisis happens when the migratory move unsettles the rule of nationness, "which is itself a symbol of the maintenance of some major relationship between persons, statuses, or subgroups held to be a key link in the integrality of the widest community" (Turner 1987: 34), presumably the nation. However, the crisis of in-betweenness is not taken to be the predicament of the nation (Germanness or Turkishness) but of the "second-generation" migrant youth. She is in-between, in crisis, twice removed from the "nationally governed" social life. As a migrant, she is deemed "outside, or on the peripheries of everyday life" in Germany, where she was born (Turner 1974: 47). Yet as a "second-generation" youth, she is no longer inside Turkishness, since she was born in Germany. She enters the realm of the "ambiguous, neither here nor there, betwixt and between all fixed points of classification," having "few or none of the attributes of [her] past or coming state" (Turner 1974:232).[4]

Being evicted from everyday life and placed in the "nowhere" of in-betweenness is a punishing occupation. In endless tales of integration, scholarly attempts are made to define their social and cultural condition by way of furnishing empirical content to an otherwise inventive category, the second generation. The science of psychology explores the degree of their adjustment and the ways that they cope—or rather, the ways they do *not* cope—with the changes that they encounter in their new (German, Western, modern) culture. Other social sciences set to measure their "integration" (or its earlier incarnations, "assimilation" or "acculturation") in units of educational attainment, employment, types of accommodation, language competency, respect for parents, religious activity, and others as if these variables self-evidently reflect "cultural" conflict or disengagement from social life. In more sinister versions of statistical exercise, the migrant youths appear as relentless agents of radical or criminal otherness. The charm of the (categorical) "second generation" is indeed discrete—and relentless.

For this, I argue we should "write against" in-betweenness and generational narratives (Abu-Lughod 1991). Firmly anchored in daily rhythms of school, work, and street, the condition of migrant youth defies assertions of in-betweenness. They are not located in the shadows of a precarious NoWhere as the model dictates. On the contrary, as Berlin's migrant youths, they inhabit the (un)familiar of NowHere in Berlin, Germany, Turkey, and the transnational spaces of youth culture. They confidently conduct their daily life in the social spaces of Berlin, negotiate tensions and anticipations inscribed in life-course narratives, and engage in the (in)tangible civic and cultural projects of their times. As participants at several social and cultural borders, they generate their visions of political and cultural identity from a repertoire of contemporary identity politics, through processes of selection, modification, and enactment. Particularly significant for their cultural projects and productions are the affinities of transnational cultural flows and local social spaces, which engender their presence in the public spaces of Berlin and complicate "national" configurations of belonging and conventional conceptions of otherhood.[5]

The Place of Migrant Youth Culture: "Open City" Berlin

Since the unification of the two Germanys a decade ago, Berlin, "the City," has come to occupy an increasingly glamorized place in the fin-de-siècle imagination of Europe, as well as the world. As projected in official and popular visions, Berlin is a (trans)national actor in its own right. It is officially named "the Open City," with a proper definition: "'Open' means: ready for change, receptive, forward-looking, open to what is strange, different, new. Open doors and buildings—so to speak a metaphor for the processes of transformation intended to create a redesigned European metropolis of mediation, communication and exchange" (Berlin 1999). As is the case with any actor, the Open City of Berlin has many yet equally pronounced identities: *Hauptstadt* of the unified Germany, *Kulturstadt* in a unified Europe, and *Weltstadt* in a cosmopolitan world. And, in its many guises, Open City Berlin underwrites utopias and dystopias, past and present, invoking a thematic spectrum of diversity, pluralism, tolerance, and racism: a capital for Nazi grandiosity and destruction, a monument to the tyranny of the socialist GDR, a beacon of progress for a unified Germany, and a multicultural haven for Europe in the twenty-first century.

As a public social space, Berlin is the site within which the ethnographic sights are located and acquire meaning and specificity. Its architectural layout (i.e., office towers, shopping centers, palaces, museums, statues, low-income houses, and government buildings) identifies social cleavages and hierarchies; its public transportation system and the opening hours of shops orient and prescribe daily routines; and the posters and graffiti that decorate the streets and metro stations communicate messages about political and commercial possibilities (e.g., elections, demonstrations, and summer sales) and provide cultural maps (e.g., operas, cabarets, and street shows).

Berlin is also the symbolic and physical site of German unification—and a proxy for unifications of East and West the world over. As the unification of the two Germanys has progressed, the public debates have necessarily involved and accentuated questions of cultural conflict and identity, both between Germans and others (migrants, refugees, and gypsies), and between Germans themselves (Ossies and Wessies). Thus, in the context of unified Berlin, the struggle over identity readily goes beyond the simple dichotomy of us (Germans) and them (migrants = Turks). The politics of, and claims to, identity blur the demarcations of "Germanness," fraction "national" boundaries, and open the way for new local and transnational imaginations: inclusive or exclusive "Europeanness," pluralisms of various sorts, and new migrant identities.

This Berlin, the City, in its capacity as the locale and the actor, simultaneously delimits and conditions the lives of Turkish migrant youths, whose diverse experiences, and experiences of diversity, will underline my arguments in this essay. Turkish youths are citizens of this cosmopolitan metropolis in contact with peoples and cultural flows from around the world. They live in Berlin, a place that is distinct from Germany. This distinction is partly a legacy of divided Germany, in as much as it is an extension of Berlin's projected cosmopolitanism. In everyday conversations, citizens of Berlin still refer to the rest of Germany as "the West," while the former East Germany is still "the East." In this Berlin, Turkish youths occupy Kreuzberg, a district known for its eccentricity and where one is sure to find the "real" action. As prescribed "marginals," Kreuzberg is said to belong to them, for it epitomizes the exotic, the ghetto, and the hip. Living at the heart of Berlin, where the local, national, and global intersect and coalesce, they respond to the challenges and discourses offered by the urban cosmopolis, ranging from conformity to social protest. In other words, Berlin's urban landscape accommodates, and colors, the everyday experiences and life cycle projections of the Turkish migrant youth.

In Berlin, approximately 12 percent of the population is foreign, with migrants from Turkey comprising approximately 4 percent of the total population. Not only do foreigners statistically constitute a sizable portion of the total population, but they are also extensively involved in the economic, political, and cultural life of the city. Migrant youths are especially visible as participants in the social and cultural scenery of Berlin. Of the foreigners in Berlin, 20 percent are under the age of twenty-five. Of the Turks in Berlin, 36 percent are between the ages of ten and twenty.

Particularly significant for the cultural projects of migrant youths are the organizational resources available to them as youths—cultural and recreational centers, clubs, cafés, sports associations, and numerous social and educational programs. In fact, Berlin is the Holy City of youth organizations. They have many members and, despite recent budget cuts, most receive ample support from the Berlin Senate, financially and otherwise. According to a 1997 survey conducted by Berlin's Foreigners' Office, on the average every fourth Turkish youth in Berlin is a member of an association or club. While the membership figures for male youths are quite high (about 38 percent), the same does not hold true for females (only 8 percent) (Pressemitteilung 1997).

Let me cite a few institutions from the many scattered over the urban map of Berlin. In one of their publications, for instance, the Foreigners' Office of the Berlin Senate lists about 180 "inter-cultural" associations in East and West Berlin (Ausländerbeauftragte Berlin 1992). Of these, forty-five are specifically youth organizations, and Turkish youths comprise the majority of membership. *BERTA*, a widely distributed handbook designed for young women, registers the addresses of more than four hundred youth clubs, about half of which are specifically women's organizations or provide special services for them (Berta 1995). A booklet called *Jugendarbeit*, published by the Municipal Government of Kreuzberg, proudly mentions twelve youth centers that it operates, along with a street work outfit called Koko, a job-exchange center, and a mobile team for condom distribution (Bezirksamt Kreuzberg 1990). And in a properly titled hip pamphlet, *Jungle Info 1995* (*Dschungel Info 95: Wegweiser für junge Bands in Berlin*), one finds the addresses of music and dance studios, rock and hip-hop mobiles, music schools, graffiti workshops, and alternative cafés and clubs. To get a sense of the subcultural scene in Berlin, from Techno-logie, Smells like Crossover, and I kissed a girl to Multikulti, Spraycity, and finally Total Normal, a glance into the youth guide *Der ÜBerliner* (The Super-Berliner) suffices (Kurzweil and Hein 1996).

These institutional spaces of youth culture are inhabited by Turkish youths, as well as Germans, Kurds, Arabs, Russians, rappers, writers, feminists, the unemployed, students, and others. In these spaces, migrant youths participate in the production of youth subcultures that Berlin—the metropolis, the global city of hip and underground youth action—proudly offers to nonchalant natives, curious visitors, and inquisitive researchers. These teeming projects of youth culture are woven into the fabric of the spectacle, which is named Berlin, the Culture City. They are constituents of the informal scene of art and politics in Berlin. Like so many others staged every day in the City, they occupy a landscape outside the formal outlets for high culture and public display. Their publicity posters adorn the walls in districts of the hip and alternative, namely Kreuzberg and Prenzlauer Berg. They take place in small venues in forsaken factories and old buildings that are turned into youth centers, association halls, mosques, and public places of all kinds. They taciturnly comprise the City's image as Culture City.

In what follows I present a brief ethnographic rendition of two events from the world of migrant youth culture in Berlin—*Street '94* and *Multinationales Anti-rassistiches Performance Project* (MAPP), the first a hip-hop festival and the second a multinational antiracist music performance, both organized under the auspices of NaunynRitze, an after-school youth center in Kreuzberg. These events are in no way "typical" and do not exhaust the range and diversity of migrant youth experience in Berlin. They do, however, allude to different images than the instinctive sketches of a lost and dis-Oriented second generation, which one invariably encounters in media and academic accounts of generations and in-betweenness. In recounting these examples, my aim is to expose the fact that Turkish youth do not form isolated, marginalized islands of subculture in a foreign land, but rather take part in the artistic and discursive practices representative of their times and environs. They perform and advocate diversity and plurality, they rap and rock against racism, and they call upon their peers to engage against intolerance and prejudice. In exercising their membership and otherness in public spheres of Berlin and Europe, I argue, their enactments of subculture and identity are shaped by the resources and climate afforded by the *habitus* (Bourdieu 1977) of culture in Berlin, while at the same time their performances shape the very fabric of the City's cultural habitus.

Making Youth Culture in Kreuzberg, Berlin, Europe

In March 1994, Berlin was a stage for a youth festival called *Street '94*. Publicity posters and graffiti in Kreuzberg radiantly displayed the mottoes of the festival: "TO STAY IS MY RIGHT" and "WE ARE ALL ONE." The prominence of English in the name and mottoes of the project was intriguing but not surprising, if one was attentive to the global currents of youth culture, with its de facto attribution of coolness and hipness to the exploitation of English in naming orientations and styles. The festival, two months of extensive activity, revolved around a street art exhibition, workshops on graffiti writing and rap music, dance parties with rap and ethno-pop bands, and open-air screening of films such as *Boyz 'N the Hood* and *Menace II Society*.

The festival, a showcase for NaunynRitze's commitment to multicultural youth action, was co-sponsored by Kreuzberg's municipal government and Berlin's Ministry of Youth and Family. *Street '94* was listed as a special project in the program of another Berlin-wide youth project, which was going on at the time—an upscale "Youth Art + Culture" project called *X-'94*, with the subtitle "50 Days to Blow Your Mind," set in motion by (formerly East) Berlin's Academy of Arts. In the grand design of *X-'94*, *Street '94* represented the cool art of the street, subcultural undercurrents of the metropolis, and the raw skill of ghetto boys and girls. And *Street '94* was true to its projected image. It was located in Kreuzberg, the ghetto, with a touch of hipness and the avant-garde. The day-to-day activities of the festival were carried out by a group of youths from NaunynRitze. Neco, a Turkish youth, and Gio, an Italian, were responsible for running the show. They were both self-made street artists, who expanded their repertoire as painters. It was Neco's dream to make a film on the migrant youth experience in Germany—a film just like the award-winning French ghetto story, *Hate*. Gio had his works exhibited in a major Berlin gallery as part of *X-'94*.

During the festival, various rap and graffiti workshops took place, attracting renowned local street artists and numerous rappers and writers-to-be. Also present were prominent graffiti writers from other metropolitan centers, such as T-KID from New York and JAY-ONE from Paris. They were in Berlin as invited artists and conversed with their Berliner hip-hop brothers on the aesthetics of graffiti, and on the ethics of hip-hop. In one panel discussion on style with T-KID and JAY-ONE, the hip-hop community was heralded as a multicultural community, extending beyond borders and delivering the message of peace and brotherhood. In their interpretation of the "imagined community" (Anderson 1991) of hip-hop, graffiti on the walls were messages addressed to society at large, as well as being artistic expressions of individual writers. In this world, styles were many and varied, and so were the cultures and writers.

The hip-hop boys and girls of Berlin were indeed innovators of style and meaning. They aspired to be street writers and donned street wear. They preached rhyming against violence and espoused respect and multiculturalism. But their enactments of hip-hop community were not simply imitations of the ghetto bravado of other places. With resourcefulness, they appropriated styles and discourses, dominated the scenes of youth culture, and disturbed the terms of the debate about migrant youth. More importantly, with the imaginative tag of their posse, To Stay Here is My Right, they intervened in civic spaces and prophesied *their right to stay*, whoever they were and from wherever they were. Taken together with their explicit and expressive connections to the world and brotherhood of hip-hop, their intervention was an implicit endorsement of a notion of belonging to a nondescript place (here) without any reference to the predictable signs of timeless cultures and nations—a youthful and unelaborated celebration of cosmopolitanism of sorts.

It should be noted that this celebration of cosmopolitan pluralism by the posse was completely synchronous with the efforts of Berlin's Foreigners' Office in promoting diversity. In 1992, a poster published by the Office covered the billboards of the city and pronounced "Wir sind Berlin" (We are Berlin). The Berlin in the poster comprised the portrait photos of persons of diverse professions, ages, colors, and genders, without any identifiable reference to the nationalities/ethnicities of the persons in the poster. In the late 1990s, Berlin's Foreigners' Office launched another campaign called "Was ist deutsch?" (What is German). The poster of the campaign listed numerous stereotypical images of Germanness: "Bureaucracy? Sauerkraut? Uniforms? Humor? Beer?..." Posed against the larger question, "What is German?" the aim was to problematize Germanness for the sake of plurality. Between "We are Berlin" and "What is German?" the Foreigners' Office was (and still is) involved in other campaigns, all in the service of achieving a cosmopolitan Berlin, tolerant and diverse.[6]

Street '94 was not the only megaproject undertaken by NaunynRitze. There was the *Multinationales Anti-rassistiches Performance Project* (MAPP) in 1995. Like *Street '94*, MAPP was designed by the social workers and administrators of the youth center as a vehicle to actualize the productive potential of the youths. Despite this similarity in pedagogical orientation, MAPP marked a significant departure from *Street '94* in terms of content, scope, and outlook. In the first place, as a project, MAPP was not an obvious enactment of the ghetto narrative. It was not a celebration of hip-hop as *the authentic* artistic expression of ghetto youths and was not concerned with ghetto problems per se. Rather than being an exhibit of impromptu street art, MAPP followed the standard production routines of artwork proper—written scripts, set designs, auditions, and rehearsals. It was managed with semiprofessionalism, employing the talents of a selected group of young dancers, designers, musicians, and actors, as well as experts and established artists. The themes with which MAPPP dealt—antiracism, diversity, and tolerance—were set as societal problems inasmuch as they are problems facing the youths at large. Moreover, with this project, NaunynRitze was shifting its focus from the ghetto scenes of Kreuzberg to European stages. The project was achieved as an international coproduction, under the sponsorship of the European Union, and was meant to bring together European youths in multicultural and antiracist performances. MAPP was a joint production with three other youth organizations from Sheffield, Rotterdam, and Luxembourg. The project was part of the European Council Initiative, the "Campaign on combating Racism, Xenophobia, Anti-Semitism and Intolerance," and was sponsored through the European Union's Youth for Europe program. The funds for the project came primarily from the European Union, with supplementary funds from the local governments of each city. The event had a budget of ECU 142,500 ($128,250 U.S.), whereas the program at large had a budget of ECU 126 million ($113.6 million U.S.) for the years 1995 to 1999.

In the summer of 1995, the show traveled to all four participating cities, with a cast of sixty youths and their social workers. The other three youth organizations that took part in MAPP were the Sheffield Youth Center, Centrum de Heuvel (Rotterdam), and Maison des Jeunes et de la Culture and Maison des Jeunes (Bettembourg and Differdange, Luxembourg). The tour was the high point of their collaborative work, which had started in 1993. After five days of joint rehearsals in Luxembourg, the MAPP company staged their show, "Twenty-four Hours through the City," a total of ten times in front of multicultural audiences—estimated to be a total of five thousand youths in all four cities. The tour was named differently in each country, keeping a thematic commonality and attention to hipness. In Germany, it was called "Gegen Rassismus – Auf Kultur Tour" (Against Racism—Culture on Tour); in England, "Challenging Racism through Performance and Participation"; in the Netherlands, "Jongeren in Aktie Tegen Racisme door Middel van Theater, Muziek en Dans" (Youth in Action against Racism through Theater, Music, and Dance); and in Luxembourg, "'Cool-Tour': Géint Rassismus" (Cool-Tour: Against Racism).

The show was a multigenre performance, a mix of dance, theater, graffiti, acrobatics, and music. The brief leaflet distributed before the show in Berlin addressed the audiences in a voice of social responsibility and explained the purpose of the project. In their own words, "Through their show, [they were] seeking to achieve communication in order to prepare themselves to revolt against hate directed at foreigners, to be ready to have respect for learning from others, and to learn that only with the cooperation of all youths can peace, solidarity, and togetherness be achieved."

As envisioned by its performers and producers, MAPP was an investigation of "intolerance and boundary-making in abstract, concrete, and symbolic ways." Its story was "based on a classic story of two lovers, whose love becomes impossible because of their different origins." At one level, with its easily recognizable, formulaic story line of unrequited love between two youths from different ethnic backgrounds, MAPP was yet another youthful production, variants of which were (and have been) abundantly performed in Berlin's public spaces year after year. At another level, however, MAPP's relevance exceeds the modest and episodic place it occupies in the ever-changing world of youth art. With MAPP, the migrant youths of NaunynRitze were (and have been) connecting Kreuzberg to Europe in (in)tangible ways. MAPP linked Kreuzberg, Berlin, to Sheffield, Rotterdam, and Luxembourg on a map of Europe and Europeanness by way of elaborate bureaucratic exercises and perpetual invocations of "European" principles of antiracism and diversity. Writing grant applications, competing for European funds, receiving awards for intercultural understanding, traveling and performing as members of multicultural troupes, for instance, were acts and enactments that, albeit implicitly, facilitated the spatialization of Kreuzberg as European space or a space of Europeanness.

Youth, Belonging, and the Cosmopolis

Speaking of Berlin, the reunified cosmopolis at the end of the century, we picture cityscapes and urban masquerades and converse about projecting futures and forging transnational connections. In and around Potsdamer Platz, where the Wall once divided Berlin, we see the largest construction site in the world and envision a *Hauptstadt, Kulturstadt, Weltstadt* in the making. In our narratives, a captivating Berlin welcomes its residents and visitors as a place of diversity and cosmopolitanism for the new Europe—even though our captivation with the place is afflicted by disconcerting episodes of its past and present.

In this Berlin of diversity and cosmopolitanism, when it comes to migrant youth, however, we still prefer to discover timeless traditions and unbridgeable cultures. We carry the burden of seeing natural and exotic formations in the making. In our scholarly and everyday conversations, and policy debates, youths appear in tales of second generation and integration—disoriented on street corners and disconnected from the larger society and its institutions, resources, and discourses. The tales of integration, whose definition turns into a mystery even in the narratives of those who perpetually speak of ways to achieve it, rely on taken-for-granted conceptions of identity that singularly take "national" as the defining parameter of identity and belonging. As de facto Turks, they are expected to become Germans, the content of which is impossible to be foreclosed except through a processing of othering whereby the imaginary Turk is located in tradition, in the past and the Orient, and at an incommensurable distance from the modernity and present of the West. Their *co-evalness* (Fabian 1983) denied, they become second-generation Young Turks in narratives of criminality, isolation, and disintegration.

When we see young Turkish rappers and graffiti writers in baggy clothes or Turkish girls donning the latest fashions or wearing headscarves, we conveniently forget the social settings within which they enact identities and assert claims. We disregard the place of contemporary discourses of tolerance, equality, and diversity in the language and content of their claims. They are, however, active participants in the societal projects of their environs and times, and cultivate youthful imaginations. They are inhabitants of Berlin, and the cultural projects they are engaged in contribute to the constitution of the city as a diverse, cosmopolitan metropolis in the new Europe. As Berlin changes, they too talk about, interact with, negotiate, and enact change.

In this chapter, I have presented cultural productions of Turkish migrant youths on the stages of *Street '94* and MAPP, traversing local places (Berlin, Sheffield, Luxembourg, and Rotterdam) and connected to the transnational spaces (Europe) and global flows of youth culture. None of these episodic displays of youth culture and politics is singularly representative of the orientations and political aspirations of Turkish youths in Berlin. With this rudimentary venture into ethnographic narration, I aimed to disrupt customary "integration" narratives, seasoned with dire statistics on displacement and segregation, and the compulsory recitations of cultural differences, such as being Muslim or Turkish.

My reliance on ethnography and avoidance of countering numbers with numbers derive from the apparent ineffectualness of statistical exercise as intervention. After all, "statistics" (as self-evident measurement) is one of the primary instruments of governmentality (Foucault 1991; Anderson 1991, 1998). In order to escape the bind of self-fulfilling integration narratives and explicate the potentialities (and limits) of the cultural performances of migrant youths, we need to be attentive to the institutional spaces that afford the organizational and discursive resources for the enactments of, and encounters with, youth (sub)cultures. It is in the public spaces of Berlin and through episodic productions, conversations, and dreams that migrant youths speak of their conditions, expectations, and resolutions, and speak to the world at large, articulating utopias against, and because of, the uncertain eventualities encompassing their lives. Thus, it is in the civic stages of the City that we capture the terms and conditions of their participation in the social and cultural life of the cosmopolis. They belong to the Open City: Berlin, Europe.

Notes

1. This essay draws upon my field research in Berlin, Germany, on youth culture and formations of identity among migrant youth groups (between 1990 and 1996, I spent three years in Berlin for my fieldwork). My research focuses primarily on Turkish youths organized in various cultural and political associations and cultural/recreational youth centers in Berlin. The outcome of this ethnographic analysis of migrant youth culture, which explicates and reflects upon the experiences of migrant youth in such organizational settings, is compiled in Soysal 1999.

2. For critical treatments of culture-territory and culture-ethnicity closures, see Abu-Lughod 1991; Gupta and Ferguson 1992; Herzfeld 1987; Malkki 1992; Moore 1989; Soysal Nuhoğlu 1994; Stolcke 1995; and Wallman 1978.

3. Not that Germany and Germanness have been without their contingencies and discontinuities. It is sufficient to cite the grand temporal breaks in German history and spatial disconnections of German *Heimat*—beginning with Imperial Germany in the last century, and proceeding in this century through the convulsions of the Weimar Republic, Nazi Germany, the Federal Republic, and East Germany, and ending with the Berlin Republic just before the new millennium.

4. For an application of Turner's model to the case of refugees, see Mortland 1987.

5. My argumentation in this essay takes its cues from, and expands on, the body of critical commentaries and interventions advanced in the following studies on youth and (sub)culture: Amit-Talai and Wulff 1995; Baumann 1996; Cohen 1988; Gilroy 1993; Griffin 1993; Hafeneger 1995; Hall and Jefferson 1983; Hebdige 1979; McRobbie 1994; Pilkington 1994; and Willis 1977, 1990. For a sample of studies on Turks in Germany, with varying degrees of emphasis on—and a critical stance against—culture, see Çağlar 1997; Horrocks and Kolinsky 1996; Mandel 1990, 1996; Schiffauer 1987, 1991; White 1997; and Wolbert 1995. For literature specifically on Turkish youth, see Bröskamp 1994; Çağlar 1998; Heitmeyer et al. 1997; Kaya 1997; Nohl 1996; Soysal 1999; Tertilt 1996; and Zaimoğlu 1995, 1998.

6. On the pluralist policies and efforts of Berlin's Foreigners' Office, see Soysal Nuhoğlu 1994 and Vertovec 1996.

References

Abu-Lughod, Lila. 1991. "Writing Against Culture." In *Recapturing Anthropology: Working in the Present*, ed. Richard G. Fox, 137–162. Santa Fe: School of American Research Press.

Amit-Talai, Vered, and Helena Wulff, eds. 1995. *Youth Cultures: A Cross-cultural Perspective.* London: Routledge

Anderson, Benedict. 1991 [1983]. *Imagined Communities.* London: Verso.

———. 1998. "Nationalism, Identity, and the World-in-Motion: On the Logics of Seriality." In *Cosmopolitics: Thinking and Feeling beyond the Nation*, ed. Pheng Cheah and Bruce Robbins, 117–133. Minneapolis: University of Minnesota Press.

Anwar, Muhammad. 1998. *Between Cultures: Continuity and Change in the Lives of Young Asians.* London: Routledge.

Ausländerbeauftragte Berlin. 1992. *Kulturübergreifende Arbeit in ganz Berlin.* Berlin.

Baumann, Gerd. 1996. *Contesting Culture: Discourses of Identity in Multi-ethnic London.* Cambridge: Cambridge University Press.

Berlin. 1999. *Berlin: Open City, The Guide.* Berlin: Nicolaische Verlag.

Berta. 1995. *Berliner Taschenwegweiserin für Mädchen.* Berlin: Verband für sozial-kulturelle Arbeit.

Bezirksamt Kreuzberg. 1990. *Jugendarbeit in Kreuzberg: Dokumentation der Entwicklung.* Berlin: Nicolaische Verlag.

Bourdieu, Pierre. 1977. *Outline of a Theory of Practice.* Cambridge: Cambridge University Press.

Bröskamp, Bernd. 1994. *Körperliche Fremdheit: Zum Problem der interkulturellen Begegnung im Sport.* Sankt Augustin: Academia Verlag.

Çağlar, Ayşe. 1998. "Popular Culture, Marginality and Institutional Incorporation: German-Turkish Rap and Turkish Pop in Berlin." *Cultural Dynamics* 10 (3): 243–261.

———. 1997. "Hyphenated Identities and the Limits of 'Culture.'" In *The Politics of Multiculturalism in the New Europe: Racism, Identity and Community*, ed. Tariq Modood and Pnina Werbner, 169–185. London: Zed Books.

Cohen, Stanley. 1988. *Against Criminology.* Oxford: Transaction Books.

Fabian, Johannes. 1983. *Time and the Other: How Anthropology Makes It Object.* New York: Columbia University Press.

Foucault, Michel. 1991. "Governmentality." In *The Foucault Effect: Studies in Governmentality*, ed. Graham Burchell, Colin Gordon, and Peter Miller, 87–104. Chicago: University of Chicago Press.

Gilroy, Paul. 1993. *The Black Atlantic: Modernity and Double Consciousness.* Cambridge, Mass.: Harvard University Press.

Griffin, Christine. 1993. *Representations of Youth: The Study of Youth and Adolescence in Britain and America.* Cambridge: Polity Press.

Gupta, Akil, and James Ferguson. 1992. "Beyond 'Culture': Space, Identity, and the Politics of Difference." *Cultural Anthropology* 7: 6–23.

Hafeneger, Benno. 1995. *Jugendbilder. Zwischen Hoffnung, Kontrolle, Erziehung und Dialog.* Opladen: Leske and Budrich.

Hall, Stuart, and Tony Jefferson. 1983 [1975]. *Resistance through Rituals: Youth Sub-cultures in Post-war Britain.* London: Hutchinson and Co. Publishers.

Hebdige, Dick. 1979. *Subculture: The Meaning of Style.* London: Routledge.

Heitmeyer, Wilhelm, Joachim Müller, and Helmut Schröder. 1997. *Verlockender Fundamentalismus. Türkische Jugendliche in Deutschland.* Frankfurt am Main: Suhrkamp.

Herzfeld, Michael. 1987. *Anthropology through the Looking-Glass: Critical Ethnography in the Margins of Europe.* Cambridge: Cambridge University Press.

Horrocks, David, and Eva Kolinsky, eds. 1996. *Turkish Culture in German Society Today.* Providence: Berghahn Books.

Kaya, Ayhan. 1997. "Constructing Diasporas: Turkish Hip-Hop Youth in Berlin." Ph.D. diss., University of Warwick, United Kingdom.

Kurzweil, Linda, and Markus Hein, eds. 1996. *Der ÜBerliner: JugendSzeneStadtführer für Berlin*. Berlin: be-bra Verlag.

Malkki, Liisa. 1992. "National Geographic: The Rooting of Peoples and the Territorialization of National Identity among Scholars and Refugees." *Cultural Anthropology* 7: 24–44.

Mandel, Ruth. 1996. "A Place of Their Own: Contesting Spaces and Defining Places in Berlin's Migrant Community." In *Making Muslim Space in North America and Europe*, ed. Barbara Daly Metcalf, 147–166. Berkeley: University of California Press.

———. 1990. "Shifting Centers and Emergent Identities: Turkey and Germany in the Lives of Turkish *Gastarbeiter*." In *Muslim Travelers: Pilgrimage, Migration, and the Religious Imagination*, ed. Dale F. Eickelman and James Piscatori, 153–171. Berkeley: University of California Press.

McRobbie, Angela. 1994. *Postmodernism and Popular Culture*. London: Routledge.

Modood, Tariq, Richard Berthoud, Jane Lakey, James Nazroo, Patten Smith, Satnam Virdee, and Sharon Beishon. 1997. *Ethnic Minorities in Britain: Diversity and Disadvantage*. London: Public Policy Institute.

Moore, Sally F. 1989. "The Production of Cultural Pluralism as a Process." *Public Culture* 1: 26–48.

Mortland, Carol A. 1987. "Transforming Refugees in Refugee Camps." In *Urban Anthropology* 16 (3–4): 375–404.

Nohl, Arnd-Michael. 1996. *Jugend in der Migration. Türkische Banden und Cliquen in empirischer Analyse*. Baltmannsweiler: Schneider Verlag Hohengehren.

Pilkington, Hilary. 1994. *Russia's Youth and Its Culture: A Nation's Constructors and Constructed*. London: Routledge.

Portes, Alejandro. 1994. "Introduction: Immigration and Its Aftermath." *International Migration Review* 28 (4): 632–639.

Pressemitteilung. 1997. *Berliner Jugendliche türkischer Herkunft*. Berlin: Die Ausländerbeauftragte des Senats von Berlin.

Schiffauer, Werner. 1987. *Die Bauern von Subay. Das Leben in einem Türkischen Dorf*. Stuttgart: Kleff-Cotta.

———. 1991. *Die Migranten aus Subay. Türken in Deutschland, eine Ethnographie*. Stuttgart: Kleff-Cotta.

Soysal Nuhoğlu, Yasemin. 1994. *Limits of Citizenship: Migrants and Postnational Membership in Europe*. Chicago: Chicago University Press.

Soysal, Levent. 1999. "Projects of Culture: An Ethnographic Episode in the Life of Migrant Youth in Berlin." Ph.D. diss., Harvard University.

Stolcke, Verena. 1995. "Talking Culture: New Boundaries, New Rhetorics of Exclusion in Europe." *Current Anthropology* 36 (1): 1–24.

Tertilt, Hermann. 1996. *Turkish Boys. Ethnographie einer Jugendbande*. Frankfurt am Main: Suhrkamp Verlag.

Tribalat, Michele. 1996. *De l'immigration à l'assimilation*. Paris: La Découverte.

Turner, Victor. 1974. *Dramas, Fields, and Metaphors: Symbolic Action in Human Society*. Ithaca: Cornell University Press.

———. 1987. *The Anthropology of Performance*. New York: PAJ Publications.

Vertovec, Steven. 1996. "Berlin Multikulti: Germany, 'Foreigners' and 'World-Openness.'" *New Community* 22 (3): 381–399.

Wallman, Sandra. 1978. "The Boundaries of 'Race': Processes of Ethnicity in England." *Man* 13: 200–217.

White, Jenny B. 1997. "Turks in the New Germany." *American Anthropologist* 99 (4): 754–769.

Willis, Paul. 1977. *Learning to Labor*. New York: Columbia University Press.

———. 1990. *Common Culture: Symbolic Work at Play in Everyday Cultures of the Young*. Boulder: Westview Press.

Wolbert, Barbara. 1995. *Der getötete Pass. Rückkehr in die Türkei*. Berlin: Akademia Verlag.

Zaimoğlu, Feridun. 1995. *Kanak Sprak: 24 Misstöne vom Rande der Gesellschaft*. Hamburg: Rotbuch Verlag.

———. 1998. *Koppstoff. Kanaka Sprak vom Rande der Gesellschaft*. Hamburg: Rotbuch Verlag.

Chapter 8

MIGRATION REGIMES AND SOCIAL RIGHTS

Migrant Workers in the Israeli Welfare State

Zeev Rosenhek

Introduction

Beginning in 1993, substantial numbers of migrant workers have been admitted into Israel to replace the Palestinian workers from the occupied territories. Simultaneously, growing numbers of undocumented migrant workers have entered the country spontaneously, becoming illegal residents. In 1999, some 70,000 documented migrant workers and between 50,000 and 100,000 undocumented workers resided in Israel, all employed in the least desirable occupations in the secondary labor market. The employment and living conditions of these labor migrants, as well as the social and political significance of their presence for Israeli society, are becoming a significant theme of public and political attention. This chapter examines how the Israeli state is facing this new phenomenon, focusing on the politics of exclusion and inclusion in the welfare state.

The welfare state is an important research site for the study of inclusionary and exclusionary processes, and the creation of social hierarchies. In recent years, growing attention has been paid to the status of subordinate groups—especially women and ethnic minorities—in the system of entitlements and distribution (O'Connor 1996; Quadagno 1994; Rosenhek 1999a; Sainsbury 1996). Due to the historical link between the emergence of the concept of social rights, processes of extension of citizenship and the consolidation of the nation-state, noncitizen migrant workers present an especially interesting case of incorporation. Their presence in Western countries as well as that of their families, represents a basic challenge to the exclusionary character of the welfare state. The position of migrants in the system of the distribution of social right has emerged, therefore, as an important topic in the analysis of the dynamics of the welfare state and in the study of the constitution of differential categories of membership in democratic polities.

The aim of this chapter is to explore the politics of exclusion and inclusion of migrant workers in the Israeli welfare state within the context of its dominant migration regime, which has a highly restrictive disposition toward the immigration of non-Jews as a fundamental characteristic. My claim is that while the policy implemented is marked by strong exclusionary practices, some state agencies implement inclusionary measures that contradict the basic assumptions of the Israeli migration regime. I examine the specific modes of operation of different state agencies and the divergent institutional interests within the state apparatus that shape policy formulation and implementation.

Before proceeding with the examination of the Israeli case, I introduce some analytical and empirical links between the dynamics of the welfare state and the incorporation of labor migrants that have emerged mainly from the experience of Western welfare states with labor migration after World War II. I then refer to the replacement of Palestinian frontier workers with migrant labor during the early 1990s and to the challenges this process presents to the Israeli state. Next I assess the extent to which migrant workers—both documented and undocumented—have been included in various fields of social security and services, describing the diverse institutional arrangements through which the services are provided and analyzing the intra-state politics of policy formulation and implementation.

The Welfare State and Labor Migration

Migration flows to Western countries have raised important questions concerning the functioning of the welfare state and its links to processes of political, economic, and social incorporation. As noted by Freeman (1986), the principle of closure is a key factor in the functioning of the national welfare state. As a consequence of the close connection between the emergence of the welfare state and the nation-state, access to social services and benefits was generally articulated in terms of membership of the national polity. Yet the presence of labor migrants posed a basic challenge to this articulation, making the exclusionary character of the welfare state increasingly difficult to maintain (Bommes 1995: 133; Faist 1994: 440; Freeman 1986: 63; Soysal 1994: 28). The challenge became more significant when, mainly as a consequence of family reunification processes, the maintenance and reproduction needs of the migrant population came to the fore of the public agenda.

The general trend in Western countries has been one of gradual assumption of responsibility by the states for the living conditions of their noncitizen residents and a concomitant inclusion of these populations into the welfare state structures. There is, of course, significant variance between different countries, between the diverse legal categories to which migrants are assigned, and between different types of welfare programs. Notwithstanding these differences, however, it is possible to assert that all Western welfare states grant certain social rights to migrants concerning contributory programs of social security and access to social services—such as education and health services (Dorr and Faist 1997; Faist 1995a; Heinelt 1993). In certain cases, even undocumented migrants enjoy certain access to welfare programs and to basic social services (Marcelli and Heer 1998; Schuck 1987). The position of migrant workers in the welfare state is significantly improved when they attain the status of permanent residents in the host countries—a status that most of the former "guestworkers" residing today in Europe have acquired. Although these "denizens" are not granted formal citizenship, and hence do not enjoy full political rights, they are entitled to social rights that are almost identical to those of nationals (Dorr and Faist 1997; Faist 1995b). This inclusionary trend has been interpreted as an indication of the decreasing importance of national citizenship in determining legitimate access to societal resources and as a basic transformation in the articulation of the notion of membership in these polities (Jacobson 1996; Soysal 1994).

It should be stressed that the process of inclusion is not complete, and labor migrants' real access to resources distributed by the welfare state is generally lower than the access enjoyed by citizens. Diverse informal exclusionary practices restrict their de facto access to social services and limit their chances to actualize their formal social rights (Dorr and Faist 1997; Schuck 1987). Moreover, the inclusion of migrants faces strong political opposition. Indeed, this has become a central issue in the politics of the welfare state: significant political forces oppose the granting of social rights to migrants, presenting them as taking over jobs and welfare resources from nationals and as a burden to the host societies (Castles 1986; Faist 1994; Schoenwaelder 1996).[1]

Notwithstanding these limitations, the entitlement of migrant workers to social rights has had significant impact on their incorporation in the host society. Since the welfare domain is one of the most important sites in which membership in the polity is constituted and actualized, their inclusion into the welfare state has not only contributed to an improvement in their living conditions and in their life chances, but has also had broad political significance, decisively reshaping their status in the host polities. The extension of social rights to labor migrants implies recognition and legitimization of their presence by the state, substantiating the accountability of its welfare agencies for their living conditions. Once these populations are defined as having rights in the domain of distribution of societal resources, the way is open for their recognition as legitimate participants in the polity. Hence, by making the state accountable to all of its residents, their inclusion in the welfare state has enabled migrant workers to participate in the political sphere by raising demands upon the state formulated in the language of rights (Freeman 1992; Miller 1981; Schmitter Heisler 1992).

Until now I have referred to general inclusionary trends that characterize Western welfare states. It is important to recognize, however, that these processes are conducted according to the institutional and political principles and modes of action of specific migration regimes. This concept refers to the relatively enduring set of goals, agencies and procedures—including both formal legal provisions and informal institutionalized practices—employed by states to deal with migratory flows. It includes the formulation and implementation of both policies of regulation and control of entry to the national territory, and policies related to the economic, social and political status of immigrants (Freeman 1992: 18). Migration regimes tend to be relatively coherent and stable. Nevertheless, the analysis of concrete modes of operation of these regimes can reveal complex pictures of inner tensions and conflicts, which are reflected in the diverse approaches and practices of specific state agencies. As Calavita (1992) demonstrates in her analysis of the immigration policy in the U.S., the state does not necessarily function as a monolithic entity. Different state agencies with diverse fields of action and clienteles develop divergent, and sometimes contradictory, institutional interests, ideologies and practices. Some of these practices, moreover, can deviate from the dominant migration regime. This does not mean that the state does not exist as an institutional complex or that it is merely a collection of agencies with no common logic of action (Evans, Rueschemeyer and Skocpol 1985: 360; Calavita 1992: 10). The concept of a heterogeneous state implies, rather, an institutional system potentially exposed to inner inconsistencies. In the following analysis of the Israeli case, I examine how these intra-state tensions and conflicts function, along with the dominant migration regime, as crucial factors in the politics of exclusion and inclusion of migrant workers.

Palestinian Frontier Workers, Migrant Workers, and the Israeli Migration Regime

The employment of noncitizens in the Israeli secondary labor market is not a new phenomenon. The construction and agriculture sectors have been dependent upon the employment of noncitizens since the late 1960s, when following the 1967 War, Palestinian commuter workers from the occupied territories were incorporated as a cheap and unprotected labor force (Semyonov and Lewin-Epstein 1987). This situation began to destabilize as a consequence of the breakout of the Palestinian uprising (*intifada*) in late 1987. Due to periodical strikes organized by the Palestinian leadership and closures imposed by Israel, the supply of Palestinian workers became uncertain, causing labor shortages and probably inducing wage increases in those occupational sectors in which Palestinian workers were concentrated (Bank of Israel 1990: 75). At this stage, the Israeli government successfully resisted pressure from employers to authorize the recruitment of foreign workers, proposing instead diverse programs to attract Israeli workers by offering subsidies to both employers and employees (Ministry of Labor 1990).

Following the signing of the Oslo accords between Israel and the Palestine Liberation Organization in 1993 the situation became much more acute. The peace process fomented the perpetration of spectacular terrorist actions inside Israel by hard-line Palestinian organizations. In order to prevent these actions and the consequent erosion of Israeli public support for the accords, the Israeli government implemented a policy of hermetic closure of the borders between Israel and the occupied territories that caused severe labor shortages in the construction and agriculture sectors (Bank of Israel 1994: 180). In the former, the problem was aggravated by the fact that, due to the wave of mass immigration from the Soviet Union that began in 1989, this sector experienced a high level of activity, hence requiring a large and stable labor force. Given these conditions, the employers' organizations intensified their pressure on the government, demanding a solution through the recruitment of foreign workers (State Comptroller 1996: 478).

These circumstances led the government to change its policy and authorize the recruitment of contract workers abroad (Bartram 1998). The number of work licenses for foreign workers provided to the employers jumped from about 10,000 in 1993 to 70,000 in 1995, peaking at roughly 100,000 in 1996 and falling to 70,000 in 1999 (Manpower Planning Authority, Ministry of Labor and Social Affairs 2000: 31). In addition, significant numbers of migrant workers are employed without permits. While it is very difficult to establish the precise number of "illegal foreign workers" employed in Israel, the most reliable estimates range between 50,000 and 100,000.[2] These undocumented workers include foreigners who enter the country on tourist visas and stay to work, and authorized workers who become "illegal" after transgressing the permit conditions by overstaying their visas or by changing their job.

The substitution of Palestinian frontier workers who commuted daily or weekly from their communities to work places in Israel with migrant workers that sojourn in the country for extended periods of time has created a new situation. First, while the maintenance and reproduction needs of Palestinian workers and their families were met in their own communities, the presence of a substantial population of noncitizen residents in the country requires the development of institutional arrangements to provide for these needs. Furthermore, given the political context in which the encounter between the Palestinian frontier workers and the host society occurred, the prospects of their settlement in Israel were practically nonexistent. In the case of migrant workers, by contrast, the probability that they and their families might permanently settle in the country is quite significant. Since the potential emergence of new non-Jewish minorities is perceived by large segments of Israeli society as a threat to the Jewish ethno-national character of Israel, concern over the settlement of this population has become an important issue on the public agenda.

This situation contradicts the fundamentals of the Israeli migration regime, which has as its most basic principle the explicit and formal demarcation between Jews and non-Jews.[3] While Jewish immigration is actively encouraged, the immigration of non-Jews is strongly restricted. This principle is reflected at the ideological, institutional and policy levels. Historically, the Zionist project of state and nation building was founded on Jewish migration flows. Albeit less intensively than in the past, the immigration of Jews to Israel is still conceived of as a crucial component of Zionist ideology and as the raison d'être of the state. State and quasi-state agencies are directly involved in the encouragement of Jewish immigration and in the execution of migration operations. Jewish immigrants are granted Israeli citizenship automatically upon their arrival in the country, and they are entitled to special programs of social and economic assistance.

With respect to non-Jews, by contrast, the state's migration policy is highly restrictive. In fact, until recently the possibility that substantial numbers of non-Jewish immigrants would settle in Israel was a nonissue. Two recent developments, however, have made this possibility real. First, the enormous migration flow from the former Soviet Union brought significant numbers of non-Jews who, due to their familial links with Jews, are entitled to immigrate and settle in Israel. The second development concerns the topic of this article, the continued presence of both documented and undocumented migrant workers.

In accordance with the Israeli migration regime, the recruitment of migrant workers was conceived as a temporary solution to the labor force shortages caused by the closures of the occupied territories, and the persistent presence of this population in the country is generally viewed as a negative phenomenon that the state has the duty to eradicate. Therefore, the state's declared goals are to reduce the number of migrant workers in the country and, especially, to prevent their permanent settlement. Reflecting these goals, the recruitment of documented migrant workers is based on quotas determined by the government, rotation, and strict impediment of family reunification. In the case of the undocumented migrant workers, the state's aims are to prevent their entry to the country and to repatriate those already living and working in Israel.[4] Nevertheless, significant institutional and political constraints impede the effective implementation of this policy (see Rosenhek 1999b).

The failure of the state's attempt to prevent the presence of migrant workers yields important questions regarding the provision of social services and the eventual granting of social rights to that population. Given the restrictive character of the Israeli migration regime for non-Jews, it could be expected that migrant workers would be absolutely excluded from the welfare state. Indeed, the social policy toward them is marked by strong exclusionary practices. Interestingly, however, some state agencies endorse and implement partially inclusionary practices. The existence of these contradictory trends makes it necessary to consider the state as a heterogeneous apparatus, calling for the study of the tensions and conflicts between different state agencies regarding the issue of inclusion of migrant workers into the Israeli welfare state. These intra-state conflicts and tensions[5] appear mainly at two axes: the vertical axis, between the central and the local levels of the state apparatus; and the horizontal axis, between the professional and bureaucratic staffs of agencies charged with the provision of social services—such as the Ministry of Health and the division of welfare in the Ministry of Labor and Social Affairs—and those of agencies functioning mainly as carriers of the Israeli migration regime and as gatekeepers—the Ministry of the Interior and the Authority for Foreign Workers in the Ministry of Labor and Social Affairs. In the following sections I specify these conflicts and the institutional interests that underlie them.

Exclusion and Inclusion of Migrant Workers in the Israeli Welfare State

Documented Migrant Workers

The basic principle guiding the policy on documented migrant workers is to keep the state's direct involvement with their living conditions minimal. In line with this policy, the state has defined the provision of basic social services—housing and health insurance—to the workers as the employers' exclusive responsibility, limiting its role to stipulating some formal regulations. In the legal undertaking employers sign with the Employment Service to obtain the permit to hire foreign workers, it is specified that they are responsible for providing them with adequate accommodation and with private health insurance equivalent to the coverage granted to Israeli residents by the national health insurance program. The state, however, does not implement effective enforcement measures to guarantee that the employers fulfill their legal obligations. In the case of workers' accommodation, for instance, the Ministry of Labor and Social Affairs is supposed to inspect the housing conditions provided by employers and verify that they are of adequate standards. However, the ministry has not established a suitable control apparatus to enforce the regulations (State Comptroller 1996: 493f.; State of Israel 1997: 32). It is not surprising, therefore, that in numerous cases, especially in the construction sector, workers are accommodated in extremely harsh conditions of overcrowding and lack even minimal sanitary facilities.[5] Although the ministry has the authority to revoke employers' permits to hire foreign workers if they violate the regulations, such disciplinary action has never been implemented (State Comptroller 1996: 493f.).

A similar situation exists with respect to the employers' obligation to provide comprehensive health insurance. Many employers provide their workers with health insurance that covers only limited medical services, thus paying lower premiums to the private insurance companies.[6] Furthermore, it was reported that in many cases insurance companies offer employers discounts on the premiums if their workers do not require medical treatment frequently.[7] Since even in those cases the employers deduct from the workers' salaries the full price of around $1 (U.S.) per day for their health insurance, these discounts function as an economic incentive to employers not to send their workers to receive medical treatment, lowering the level of health services to which the migrant workers have access. Although these facts are well known to officials in the Ministry of Labor and Social Affairs and in the Ministry of Health, these agencies have not taken effective measures to prevent these violations of the regulations.

An interesting illustration of the politics of documented foreign workers' exclusion from the Israeli welfare state is the debate over a proposal to include them in the national health insurance program. This proposal was advanced by several nongovernment organizations advocating migrant workers' rights, and although it gained the support of the professional staff of the Ministry of Health, it was eventually rejected.[8] First, it is worth referring to the sources of the support for the proposal by part of the state apparatus. The main considerations were of a professional-bureaucratic character, especially the concern for the threat to public health implied by the existence of a significant population not covered by appropriate health insurance.[9] According to this approach, comprehensive health insurance must be provided to migrant workers primarily in order to protect the ministry's clientele—the Israeli population—and to avoid a problematic situation from the point of view of the ministry's institutional logic.

As for the reasons for the proposal's rejection, one could expect that the main argument would be that the Israeli public health system, which is already in deep financial crisis, might be required to bear the financial burden if the national health insurance program is extended to the documented migrant workers. But this was not the case. Officials in the ministries of health and of finance realized that, from a budgetary perspective, the inclusion of a young and healthy population into the national health insurance program would not be a burden, and could even assist in reducing the system's deficits.[10] The reasons for the proposal's rejection were of a broad political nature and linked to the pattern of relationships, or lack thereof, that the state aims to institutionalize with migrant workers. The major argument was that their inclusion in the statutory health insurance might imply a de jure recognition by the state of their social rights, having implications therefore for their legal and political status.[11] Such recognition would contradict the basic principles of the state's policy, which seeks to impede the institutionalization of binding ties of responsibility and accountability for the migrant workers' living conditions.

In the realm of contributory social security programs the state assumes a very limited responsibility. As in the case of Palestinian workers, migrant workers are covered by only three of the social insurance schemes operated by the National Insurance Institute—work injuries, employer's bankruptcy and maternity—and they are excluded from important social security programs, such as unemployment insurance, old age and survivors' benefits, and children's allowances. Of the three programs that cover migrant workers, the most pertinent is the work injuries insurance. The occupational sector in which most of these workers are employed—construction—is characterized in Israel by a low level of occupational safety and by a concomitant high incidence of accidents. Yet there are clear indications that bureaucratic obstacles seriously reduce the ability of migrant workers who suffered work accidents to effectuate their formal rights.[12]

The examination of the institutional mechanisms in operation and of the political processes shaping them indicates that the basic principle of the state's policy concerning the provision of social benefits and services to the documented migrant workers is to avoid any direct involvement with their living conditions. It is understood that such involvement might create a situation in which the state is perceived as legally and politically accountable to them. This situation, in turn, might encourage the articulation of claims-making by the migrant workers, legitimizing the eventual emergence of social rights-based politics around the issue of labor migration in Israel. The alternative adopted by the state has been to define the provision of social services as belonging to the private sphere of employer-employee relations, keeping the topic outside the political sphere of definition and actualization of entitlements and the state's relations with the population resident in its territory.

Undocumented Migrant Workers

In the case of undocumented migrant workers, state agencies have to confront a situation even more complex than in the previous case. Since the arrival of these immigrants is not based on formal recruitment by employers and they are incorporated mainly in the informal sector of the labor market, the state cannot define the employers as legally responsible for the provision of basic social services. Moreover, in the case of spontaneous undocumented migrants, the state lacks the institutional capabilities to prevent the immigration of married couples, the marriage in the country of new couples, and the birth of children. The presence among this population of families and children makes it more difficult for the state agencies to completely ignore their maintenance and reproduction needs regarding medical, educational and welfare services. It is within this context that significant differences emerge between the modes of operation of different state agencies, and the provision of social services to the undocumented migrant workers becomes a focus of intra-state tensions.

The basic declared principle guiding policy formulation and implementation is the nonrecognition of the undocumented migrant workers as legitimate clients of the Israeli welfare state. Rather, they are considered only as a population that must be repatriated.[13] For instance, the head of the Authority for Foreign Workers in the Ministry of Labor and Social Affairs defines the duty of the agency with respect to the undocumented migrants as "their deportation in humanitarian ways."[14] The government's official stand is that the recognition of that population as legitimate clients of the Israeli welfare agencies would imply the legitimization of their illegal presence in the country, thus encouraging their permanent settlement and attracting more undocumented migrants. Reflecting this logic, in 1996 the minister of internal security urged Tel Aviv Municipality to cease providing social services to undocumented migrants and "to make their life in Tel Aviv miserable."[15]

Officials in the Ministry of the Interior and the Ministry of Labor are well aware of the broad political implications of the provision of social services: granting social rights to migrant workers and their families implies their recognition as members of the society, eventually creating openings for claims-making upon the state. In their strong opposition to even the most minimal inclusion of the migrant workers into the welfare state, they clearly reflect the basic premise of the Israeli migration regime: "Israel is not an immigration country,"[16] meaning of course the immigration of non-Jews. This approach is explicitly articulated in the following statement by a Ministry of the Interior official: "The granting of any status to illegal foreign workers might create the delusion among them that they can stay here permanently. If we give services, we encourage them to stay.... When the foreign children study Israel's heritage in our schools, we make them feel that they are part of us. We are actually hurting them because they are not going to be part of us. It would be better if those children would not go to school and would watch TV all day instead."[17]

With this exclusionary approach as background, it is surprising that the undocumented migrants and their children have certain access to some social services provided by state agencies, particularly in the domains of education and preventive medicine. Tel Aviv municipality, in whose jurisdiction the undocumented migrant workers are concentrated, has emerged as a central actor in the field, and the financing of the social services it provides to them has become a major point of contention with the central government. With respect to education, significant numbers of undocumented children attend kindergartens and schools administered by the municipality.[18] Since the Ministry of Education does not recognize these pupils, the schools in which they study do not receive any special budgetary assistance.[19] The municipality's Department of Education requested that the ministry grant these children the status of "new immigrants,"[20] so they would be entitled to special assistance teaching hours for Hebrew instruction, but in accordance to the government's policy of nonrecognition the Ministry of Education refused.[21]

The same pattern of provision of services by the municipality without official recognition and budgetary participation by the central government characterizes the field of preventive medicine.[22] The municipal centers for family and infant health provide preventive and basic medical services to undocumented pregnant women, babies and infants.[23] Although the duty of these health centers is to provide only preventive medical services, it has been reported that in the case of undocumented migrants, nurses and doctors also treat cases belonging to the field of corrective medicine.[24] Also public hospitals in the Tel Aviv area provide medical services to this population.[25] According to Israeli law, hospitals are obliged to provide emergency medical services to patients in critical condition, whether they are covered by health insurance or not. Frequently, it has been noted, doctors in the hospitals apply "flexible" definitions of life-threatening situations in order to provide treatment to undocumented foreign workers with no health insurance, even if they are not in real danger.[26] A significant part of the costs of these services are considered by the hospital administration as irreclaimable debts.[27]

An additional manifestation of the relatively inclusionary policy implemented by Tel Aviv municipality is the opening in 1999 of an aid and information center for the migrant workers residing in the city. The center provides information and counseling concerning social services, education, health and personal security. It is important to remark that this center—the motto of which is "Tel-Aviv-Yaffo is no stranger to you!"—is the only state agency that explicitly and officially recognizes undocumented migrants as its legitimate clients, representing a significant departure from the policy dictated by the Israeli migration regime.

The conflict with the central government arises mainly around the question of which government level should be politically and financially responsible for the provision of basic social services to the undocumented migrant workers. One of the central arguments advanced by the municipal officials is that as a signatory to the UN Convention on the Rights of the Child, Israel is compelled to provide basic social services to migrant workers' children.[28] These officials emphasize that while the government ministries do not recognize the undocumented migrant workers and the needs of their families, and therefore do not allocate resources for the provision of basic services, the municipality needs to confront the concrete budgetary, social and political implications of their presence within its jurisdiction.[29] This allegation is clearly expressed in the following statement by the Tel Aviv deputy mayor: "For the government the foreign workers resolve a problem, but the municipality has to deal with the troubles caused by their stay in the country."[30]

From the local government's perspective, the presence of the undocumented foreign workers represents not only a technical or bureaucratic problem of social services provision, but mainly a political burden regarding its relationships with its clientele: the Israeli residents of Tel Aviv. According to the view of the municipality's apparatus, the social deterioration that could result if the undocumented migrant workers are deprived of basic social services might damage its image in the eyes of the city's residents. Since these residents see the municipality as responsible for preventing such a situation, officials assert, it must show them that it is doing its utmost to prevent the presence of migrant workers from negatively affecting their quality of life.[31] In the words of a senior municipal official: "We must help the foreign workers in order to resolve the problems of the veteran residents who are our clients."[32]

An inclusionary approach that supports the provision of at least basic social services to the undocumented migrant workers is also expressed by the professional staffs of the Ministry of Health and of the social services division of the Ministry of Labor and Social Affairs. This support is framed mainly in terms of concrete problem-solving and professional idioms. In their view, the presence of a population with no access to basic social services represents a serious threat to the Israeli population.[33] For instance, officials in the Ministry of Health stress that it is absolutely necessary to provide the undocumented migrant workers with medical services, not only for their own good, but also to prevent the public health hazard implied in the existence of a significant population with no access to preventive and corrective medical services.[34] It is important to emphasize that the officials, both at central and local agencies, who claim that migrant workers should be provided with basic social services, do not challenge the premises of the Israeli migration regime at the ideological level. Their approach is basically instrumental, reflecting the institutional and professional logics of the state agencies in which they are located. Nevertheless, they present an alternative to the broad exclusionary policy dictated by the Israeli migration regime. As expressed by one of these officials: "It would be preferable not to have foreign workers in Israel, but if they are already here we must give them social services."[35]

Conclusions

The basic character of the policy formulated and implemented by the Israeli welfare state toward both documented and undocumented migrant workers is one of noninvolvement with their living conditions. In the case of documented migrant workers, the provision of basic social services is defined as belonging to the private sphere of employer-employee relations. Concerning the undocumented migrant workers, the official position is not to recognize them at all as residents and potential clients of the welfare agencies. The inner logic of this exclusionary policy becomes clear when considered against the link between the migrant workers' entitlement to social rights and the chances for the articulation of legitimate demands upon the state illustrated by their inclusion in Western welfare states. It reflects the restrictive character of the Israeli migration regime toward non-Jews and it is mainly directed at preventing the migrant workers' permanent settlement in the country and their gradual recognition as members of Israeli society. Its rationale is to avoid a situation in which, through the granting of social rights to migrant workers, the state assumes direct responsibility for their living conditions. Such a situation, the state agencies acting as gatekeepers realize, might encourage the articulation by this population of a legitimate politics of claims-making, leading to the transformation of their status from "foreign workers" to "denizens" with rights to access to societal resources.

The analysis indicates, however, that the state apparatus does not function in a homogeneous mode. Intra-state tensions between agencies with different institutional interests play a major role in the politics of exclusion and inclusion. Due to their specific location within the state apparatus and their professional-bureaucratic considerations, some agencies endorse and implement at least partially inclusionary courses of action. Local agencies provide basic social services to undocumented migrant workers and their families, although without recognition and budgetary participation by the central government. It is not my intention to assert that this inclusionary approach would necessarily lead to a complete extension of social rights to migrant workers in Israel, yet it indicates the existence of fissures in the exclusionary policy dictated by the Israeli migration regime. If the presence of the migrant workers in Israel assumes a more permanent character, these inclusionary practices based on professional idioms could develop as apertures with significant effects on the mode of incorporation of migrant workers.

Some general conclusions can be drawn from the Israeli case. Even in cases—such as Israel—in which the migration regime is strongly associated with a restrictive ethno-national conception of membership, it is still potentially vulnerable to fissures. These fissures do not originate only from the political activity of actors in civil society presenting ideological alternatives, but can also emanate from the institutional heterogeneity of the state apparatus itself. Inclusionary approaches can be presented by agencies that, because of their location in the state apparatus and their specific clienteles, develop interests that depart from the exclusionary migration regime. While articulated in professional and bureaucratic idioms, these approaches can create openings leading to the partial inclusion of migrant workers in the welfare state.

Notes

This article is part of a research project on labor migration in Israel carried out jointly by Erik Cohen and the author, and supported by grants from the Harvey L. Silbert Center for Israel Studies at the Hebrew University of Jerusalem, The Israel Foundations Trustees, and the Revson Foundation at the Jerusalem Institute for Israel Studies. A more extensive version of the article was published in *Social Problems* (vol. 47, no. 1, 2000). Thanks are due to Erik Cohen, Michael Shalev, and Vered Vinitzky-Seroussi for their comments.

1. This approach is clearly illustrated by Proposition 187, passed in California in 1994, which denies the access of undocumented migrants to most basic social services (Smith and Tarallo 1995).
2. Internal Report of the Manpower Planning Authority, Ministry of Labor and Social Affairs, "Foreign Workers in Israel: Statistics for 1997," June 1998; Internal Report of the Central Bureau of Statistics, "Statistics on Foreign Workers," November 1996. The topic is politically charged, as it is linked to the moral panic that has been developing around the presence of migrant workers in Israel. In this context, exorbitant numbers such as 200,000 or 300,000 of "illegal" foreign workers, have been touted by some politicians and echoed in the media (*Globes*, 28 October 1997; *Ha'aretz*, 6 September 1996, 14 November 1996).
3. The distinction is legally manifested in the Law of Return, and finds expression in the terminology used in Israel to refer to immigration. The term *aliyah* (literally, "ascension") refers to the immigration of Jews to Israel, while the immigration of non-Jews is designated with the neutral term *hagirah* (literally, "migration").
4. "Policy Proposal Regarding Foreign Workers," submitted to the government by the minister of labor and social affairs, August 1996.
5. Letter from the Association for Civil Rights in Israel and Workers' Hotline to the minister of labor and social affairs, 16 January 1995; interview with a senior official in the Tel Aviv municipality, 8 December 1996.
6. Dana Alexander, the Association for Civil Rights in Israel, and the director of a private insurance company, at the seminar "Foreign Workers in Israel: Human Rights and Economic Aspects," Jerusalem, 5 November 1996; Ran Zafrir, Ichilov Hospital Administration, at the seminar "Foreign Workers and the Health System," Tel Aviv, 28 May 1998.
7. "On Foreign Workers and Rights," the Association for Civil Rights in Israel, September, 1997, 9; Newsletter of Physicians for Human Rights, No. 4, April 1997.
8. Letter from the Association for Civil Rights in Israel and Workers' Hotline to the minister of labor and social affairs, 16 January 1995; the Association for Civil Rights in Israel, annual report, June 1996–May 1997, 54.
9. Interview with a senior official in the Department of Public Health Services, Ministry of Health, 28 August 1997; Dr. Itzhak Berlowitz, director of the Department of Medical Services Administration, Ministry of Health, at the seminar "Foreign Workers and the Health System," Tel Aviv, 28 May 1998.
10. Interview with a senior official in the Ministry of Finance, 26 February 1997; interview with an official in the legal department of the Ministry of Health, 10 April 1997.
11. Interview with a senior official in the Ministry of Finance, 26 February 1997; interview with an official in the legal department of the Ministry of Health, 10 April 1997; interview with the head of the Authority for Foreign Workers, Ministry of Labor and Social Affairs, 6 November 1997.
12. Officials in the National Insurance Institute recognize that the number of reports of work accidents in which migrant workers are involved is much lower than could be expected. They explain this by the fact that many employers refrain from reporting accidents to avoid official investigations of occupational safety conditions (interview with a senior official in the division of Work Injury Insurance program, National Insurance Institute, 17 July 1997); see also letter from the Association for Civil Rights

in Israel and Workers' Hotline to the minister of labor and social affairs, 16 January 1995; interview with the director of Physicians for Human Rights, 26 June 1997.

13. "Policy Proposal Regarding Foreign Workers," submitted to the government by the Ministry of Labor and Social Affairs, August 1996; "Proposal for the Establishment of an Authority for Foreign Workers," Ministry of Labor and Social Affairs, 6 May 1998.

14. Interview with the head of the Authority for Foreign Workers, Ministry of Labor and Social Affairs, 6 November 1997.

15. *Ha'aretz*, 18 September 1996.

16. Interview with a senior official in the Ministry of Labor and Social Affairs, 5 January 1997.

17. Commissioner of visas, Ministry of the Interior, in meeting of the Knesset sub-committee on infants, 30 June 1997.

18. Meir Doron, director-general, Tel Aviv municipality, at the seminar "The National and Social Prices of the Employment of Foreign Workers," 19 February 1998. Other undocumented children attend private Christian schools in Jaffa and in Jerusalem.

19. Letter from the director of the Department of Education and Culture, Tel Aviv municipality to the Tel Aviv deputy mayor, 11 July 1996; interview with a senior official in the Tel Aviv municipality, 8 December 1996.

20. The term "new immigrant" refers to a legal category applicable to those immigrating within the framework of the Law of Return.

21. Director of the division of elementary education, Tel Aviv municipality, Summary of the meeting of the Committee on Foreign Workers, Tel Aviv municipality, 18 September 1996.

22. Interview with a senior official in the Tel Aviv municipality, 8 December 1996.

23. Meir Doron, director-general, Tel Aviv municipality, at the seminar "The National and Social Prices of the Employment of Foreign Workers," 19 February 1998.

24. Letter from the director of the Department of Public Medicine, Tel Aviv municipality to the Tel Aviv deputy mayor, 20 January 1997.

25. Another important source of medical services are Palestinian hospitals and clinics in East Jerusalem, where undocumented migrant workers pay much lower prices than in Israel (director of the Tel Aviv District Health Bureau, Ministry of Health, summary of the meeting on Foreign Workers in Tel Aviv, Tel Aviv Municipality, 24 July 1996). In addition, in May 1998 an Israeli NGO—Physicians for Human Rights—opened a special clinic to provide immigrant workers and their families with medical services.

26. Interview with the director of Physicians for Human Rights, 26 June 1997.

27. Ran Tzafrir, Ichilov Hospital Administration, at the seminar "Foreign Workers in Israel: Human Rights and Economic Aspects," Jerusalem, 5 November 1996.

28. Letter from the director of the Department of Education and Culture, Tel Aviv municipality to the Tel Aviv deputy mayor, 11 July 1996; summary of the meeting of the Committee on Foreign Workers, Tel Aviv municipality, 19 August 1996.

29. Report, "Foreign workers in Tel Aviv," Michael Ro'e, member of Tel Aviv City Council, 9 June 1996; Tel Aviv deputy mayor, summary of the meeting of the Committee on Foreign Workers, Tel Aviv municipality, 19 August 1996; memorandum submitted to the chairperson of the Knesset Labor and Social Affairs Committee by Tel Aviv municipality in January 1997; interview with a senior official in the Tel Aviv municipality, 25 March 1997; assistant of the Tel Aviv municipality director-general and director of the South District, Department of Welfare, Tel Aviv municipality, meeting of the Knesset sub-committee on infants, 30 June 1997.

30. Tel Aviv deputy mayor, summary of the meeting of the Committee on Foreign Workers, Tel Aviv municipality, 19 August 1996.

31. Tel Aviv deputy mayor, summary of the meeting of the Committee on Foreign Workers, Tel Aviv municipality, 19 August 1996; interview with senior officials in the Tel Aviv municipality, 8 December 1996, 24 May 1998.

32. Interview with a senior official in the Tel Aviv municipality, 24 May 1998.

33. Report, "Foreign Workers," director of the Department of Social Services, Ministry of Labor and Social Affairs, 31 July 1996.

34. Director of the Department of Public Medicine, Tel Aviv municipality, director of the Department of Public Health Services, Ministry of Health, and director of the Tel Aviv District Health Bureau, Ministry of Health, meeting of the Knesset sub-committee on infants, 30 June 1997; interview with a senior official in the Department of Public Health Services, Ministry of Health, 28 August 1997.
35. Interview with a senior official in the Tel Aviv municipality, 25 March 1997.

References

Bank of Israel. 1990. *Bank of Israel Report, 1989*. Jerusalem. [Hebrew]

———. 1994. *Bank of Israel Report, 1993*. Jerusalem. [Hebrew]

Bartram, David V. 1998. "Foreign Workers in Israel: History and Theory." *International Migration Review* 32 (2): 303–325.

Bommes, Michael. 1995. "Migration and Ethnicity in the National Welfare-State." In *Migration, Citizenship and Ethno-National Identities in the European Union*, ed. Marco Martiniello, 120–143. Aldershot. Avebury.

Calavita, Kitty. 1992. *Inside the State—The Bracero Program, Immigration, and the I.N.S.* New York: Routledge.

Castles, Stephen. 1986. "The Guest-Worker in Europe—An Obituary." *International Migration Review* 20 (4): 761–777.

Dorr, Silvia, and Thomas Faist. 1997. "Institutional Conditions for the Integration of Immigrants in Welfare States: A Comparison of the Literature on Germany, France, Great Britain, and the Netherlands." *European Journal of Political Research* 31 (4): 401–426.

Evans, Peter B., Dietrich Rueschemeyer, and Theda Skocpol. 1985. "On the Road Toward a More Adequate Understanding of the State." In *Bringing the State Back In*, ed. Peter B. Evans, Dietrich Rueschemeyer, and Theda Skocpol, 347–366. Cambridge: Cambridge University Press.

Faist, Thomas. 1994. "Immigration, Integration and the Ethnicization of Politics." *European Journal of Political Research* 25: 439–459.

———. 1995a. "Boundaries of Welfare States: Immigrants and Social Rights on the National and Supranational Level." In *Migration and European Integration: The Dynamics of Inclusion and Exclusion*, ed. Robert Miles and Dietrich Thranhardt, 177–195. London: Pinter Publishers.

———. 1995b. *Social Citizenship for Whom?* Aldershot: Avebury.

Freeman, Gary. 1986. "Migration and the Political Economy of the Welfare State." *The Annals of the American Academy of Political and Social Siences* 485: 51–63.

———. 1992. "The Consequence of Immigration Policies for Immigrant Status: A British and French Comparison. " In *Ethnic and Racial Minorities in Advanced Industrial Democracies*, ed. Anthony Messina et al., 17–32. New York: Greenwood Press.

Heinelt, Hubert. 1993. "Immigration and the Welfare State in Germany." *German Politics* 2 (1): 78–96.

Jacobson, David. 1996. *Rights Across Borders—Immigration and the Decline of Citizenship*. Baltimore: Johns Hopkins University Press.

Manpower Planning Authority. 2000. *The Labor Market in Israel—Statistical Data*. Jerusalem: Ministry of Labor and Social Affairs. [Hebrew]

Marcelli, Enrico, and David Heer. 1998. "The Unauthorized Mexican Immigrant Population and Welfare in Los Angeles County: A Comparative Statistical Analysis." *Sociological Perspectives* 41 (2): 279–302.

Miller, Mark J. 1981. *Foreign Workers in Western Europe—an Emerging Political Force*. New York: Praeger.

Ministry of Labor. 1990. "Training of Israeli Work Force to the Construction Sector." *Avoda V'Revaha V'Bituach Leumi* 42 (1–2): 5–8. [Hebrew]

O'Connor, Julia. 1996. "From Women in the Welfare State to Gendering Welfare State Regimes." *Current Sociology* 44 (2): 1–124.

Quadagno, Jill S. 1994. *The Color of Welfare*. New York: Oxford University Press.

Rosenhek, Zeev. 1999a. "The Exclusionary Logic of the Welfare State: Palestinian Citizens in the Israeli Welfare State." *International Sociology* 14 (2): 195–215.

———. 1999b. "The Politics of Claims-making by Labour Migrants in Israel." *Journal of Ethnic and Migration Studies* 25 (4): 575–595.

Sainsbury, Diane. 1996. *Gender, Equality and Welfare States*. Cambridge: Cambridge University Press.

Schmitter Heisler, Barbara. 1992. "Migration to Advanced Industrial Democracies: Socio-economic and Political Factors in the Making of Minorities in the Federal Republic of Germany (1955–1988)." In *Ethnic and Racial Minorities in Advanced Industrial Democracies*, ed. Anthony Messina et al., 33–48. New York: Greenwood Press.

Schönwalder, Karen. 1996. "Migration, Refugees and Ethnic Plurality as Issues of Public and Political Debates in (West) Germany. " In *Citizenship, Nationality and Migration in Europe*, ed. David Cesarani and Mary Fulbrook, 159–178. London: Routledge.

Schuck, Peter. 1987. "The Status and Rights of Undocumented Aliens in the United States." *International Migration* 25 (2): 125–138.

Semyonov, Moshe, and Noah Lewin-Epstein. 1987. *Hewers of Wood and Drawers of Water*. Ithaca: ILR Press.

Smith, Michael, and Bernadette Tarallo. 1995. "Proposition 187: Global Trend or Local Narrative? Explaining Anti-Immigrant Politics in California, Arizona and Texas." *International Journal of Urban and Regional Research* 19 (4): 664–676.

Soysal, Yasemin. 1994. *Limits of Citizenship—Migrants and Postnational Membership in Europe*. Chicago: Chicago University Press.

State Comptroller. 1996. *Year Report No. 46, 1995*. Jerusalem. [Hebrew]

State of Israel. 1997. *Combined Initial and Second Report of the State of Israel Concerning the Implementation of the United Nations Covenant on Economic, Social and Cultural Rights*. Jerusalem.

Chapter 9

Ethnicity and Citizenship in the Perception of Russian Israelis

Dimitry Shumsky

Introduction

The chronological overlap between the massive wave of immigration from the Commonwealth of Independent States and the heightened erosion of the dominant status of "Israeli culture" and the rise of cultural pluralism in Israel would appear to have shaped the course of research into the Russian community's influence on Israeli politics and society. In other words, most of the scholars investigating this issue, who closely monitor the process of collective development or "crystallization" of migrants from the former Soviet Union in Israel over the last decade, tend primarily to emphasize the separatist, Russo-ethnocentrist component of their identity. As a result, they highlight only the segregationist dimension of their contribution to the nature of the host society (Lissak and Leshem 1995: 24f.; Shuval 1998: 19; Leshem and Lissak 1999: 162f.; Leshem and Sicron 1999: 512). Hence, in these researchers' opinion, the formation of the Russian cultural enclave in Israel constitutes an integral part of the multicultural fabric, even strengthening the sectorial nature of society all the more forcefully.

This distinction, in particular when it is raised in the framework of the general aspiration to smash the myth about the uniqueness of immigration to Israel compared with migration to other countries, is indeed important in and of itself, as well as being accurate to some extent. However, the one-dimensional picture that is painted in the given concrete case is oversimplistic, both when analyzing the identity of the Russian-speaking migrants, and when assessing their influence on the politico-cultural reality in Israel. Thus the argument about the centrality of the separatist foundation within the migrants' collective identity does not match the findings of the comprehensive survey that was recently published by the University of Haifa's Center for Multiculturalism and Educational Research. These findings support a more complex picture of the situation. It therefore seems that in addition to expressing basic support for institutionalizing their separate culture within the emergent multicultural society, the migrants express great interest in preserving the ethno-nationalist political culture that treats its Jewish citizens with such exclusive favor (Al-Haj and Leshem 2000: 67). This two-dimensional picture coincides with Baruch Kimmerling's view of the nature of contemporary Israeli society and the role of the autonomous cultures within it. In Kimmerling's opinion, while each of these new cultures is striving in its own way for institutional autonomy on different levels, at the same time they wish to emphasize their "Jewish" common denominator. The result is the reinforcing of the primordial identity and attachments that are widespread among broad sectors of the Jewish population, a reinforcement that prevents the ideological legitimation of multiculturalism. Hence, the internal dynamic at work in Israeli society is characterized by Kimmerling (1998: 269) as a form of interplay between a centrifugal tendency and a centripetal tendency, with the new cultures, including the Russian Israeli one, accelerating both of these tendencies. Thus this dynamic creates a unique sociocultural structure—"a plurality of cultures without multiculturalism." Kimmerling does not, however, discuss the nature of the migrants' primordial identity, and he further refrains from engaging in a clarification of their contribution to the centripetal tendency, albeit while hinting at the existence of these phenomena. Like other researchers, he prefers to focus on a more visible separatist ethno-cultural dimension of the migrants' identity. In his opinion, their activities in the centripetal direction amount to their political leadership's declaration of general slogans in a mainstream patriotic style, tantamount to pure lip service in return for the possibility of entering the Israeli political system, solely in order to promote sectorial interests (Kimmerling 1998: 290f.).

I wish to present a complementary view of the identity of Russian Israelis and their influence on the image of the state of Israel, as part of an attempt to relocate them within Kimmerling's model of Israeli society ("a plurality of cultures without multiculturalism"). Without denying the strength of the segregationist tendency among the migrants, I shall try to indicate the unique nature of their national understanding, which structures their civil perception of national minorities generally and the Arab minority specifically. The development of the argument will be divided into the following three areas: (1) analysis of the background of the emergence of the migrants' national-civil outlook, which, as will be seen, is tainted in a special understanding of the relationship between ethnicity and citizenship that was standard in the USSR and is still widespread in its successor states; (2) a review of the expressions of this outlook in the Russian Israeli press and in the opinions of the politicians and intellectuals who are admired by the community, with special emphasis on the development of an ethno-national identity in light of the process of transforming the migrants themselves from the status of a national minority in their country of origin to a national majority in the Jewish nation state; and (3) a discussion of Russian Israelis' approach to the concept of a national minority's civil status generally and their attitude to the Arab minority in particular, as well as a reevaluation of Russian Israelis' influence on politics and society in Israel, with all the implications for questions regarding the nature of the state as a Jewish nation-state, the conferring of ideological legitimation on multiculturalism, and the extension of autonomy to Israel's Arab citizens.

The Roots of the Migrants' National-Civil Outlook: The Relationship between Ethnicity and Citizenship in the Former Soviet Union

The tendency to refrain from any systematic discussion of the question of the existence of a centripetal tendency among the Russian Jewish community is undoubtedly the upshot of a general consensus among researchers as to the complete absence of any inherent national awareness among Soviet Jewry. According to this view, which constitutes the basic assumption of practically all researchers examining the self-identity of Russian-speaking migrants, Jews of the former Soviet Union had no attachment to Jewish nationalism in any of its known forms as are common throughout the world, whether secular nationalism in the East European version of secularism, or a traditional nationalism among the religious of the Oriental (Mizrahi) communities (Ben-Rafael 1998: 125). Above all, their indifference to Zionist matters, with the exception of a relatively small group of immigrants from the 1970s (Lissak and Leshem 1995: 31; Shuval 1996: 2f.; Horowitz 1996: 96), is generally emphasized. This fact was therefore sufficient on its own to render irrelevant a discussion about the relationship of the immigrants of the 1990s to Israel's national agenda and a Jewish-primordial common denominator.

The roots of this viewpoint, which is also common among migration researchers from the former Soviet Union to Israel, can be readily determined as lying in a concept that was until recently dominant in the circles of Western Sovietologists: that the Soviet regime was by nature belligerently antinationalist and consistently strove throughout its entire existence to uproot all manifestations of any authentic national awareness by the non-Russian peoples. In so doing, the regime tenaciously promoted the Soviet "national" doctrine, which was in fact grounded in the Russian language and the history of the Russian people, camouflaging its real intentions by establishing completely fictitious multinational frameworks known as "Soviet Republics" and "Autonomous Soviet Republics" (Barghoorn 1986: 31f.; Brzezinski 1989/1990: 6f.; d'Encaausse 1995: 12; Khazanov 1995: 4f.). Under this policy, Jewish nationalism was also suppressed, and as a result Soviet Jewry became a kind of "muted" ethnicity, without a language, without Jewish tradition and education, and without historical roots: in other words, a "Judaism of silence." The only thing Jewishness meant was the fact that it was formally recorded in the "nationality" section in the Soviet Union's internal passports. The cultural identity of the Jews had become utterly Russian, while their Jewish self-awareness was being wiped out (Gitelman 1995: 23, 29; Leshem and Lissak 1995: 138, 143; Horowitz and Leshem 1998: 294).

Without for the moment focusing on the validity of this claim, I wish to first revisit the issue of the national question in the former Soviet Union, a theme that has surfaced onto the research agenda of recent years. I am referring to the new and mutually complementary approaches of two researchers: the Russian anthropologist Valery Tishkov, and the American sociologist Rogers Brubaker, both of whom have recently contested the traditional views of nationhood in Sovietology, which continue to inform research assumptions about immigrants from the former Soviet Union to Israel. As we shall see later, adopting these two theories as a reworked basis for discussing the issue of national identity of Russian-speaking migrants can provide new theoretical tools for addressing it.

Each of these scholars, in his own way, objects to the dichotomous and simplistic presentation of the interaction between the Soviet regime and the nations subject to it, a presentation that paints a picture of a constant battle between Communist supranational ideology and ethnicity in its different forms. We will first examine the arguments of Valery Tishkov, who, coming from the ethnographic establishment of the Soviet Union and post-Communist Russia, provides us with a rare insider's viewpoint of the continuity of Soviet national policy. He reveals that despite the basic adherence to the formula of "fraternity between the Soviet peoples" and the attempt to create a new supranational species of "Soviet man," the Soviet regime in fact promoted a primordial ethnic awareness among a considerable proportion of the peoples it ruled throughout all the years of its existence. Time and again generations of ethnographic scholars, enlisted by the authorities to promote this undertaking, consistently expressed the idea of an "ethnos" as an eternal biological entity, rooted in a particular territory since time immemorial, thereby continuing the Slavophile ethnographic tradition about the nature of the Russian people that evolved in Czarist Russia in the course of the nineteenth century (Tishkov 1997: 1f.). These "scientific" efforts were not, of course, confined to academic debates, but were actually applied in the political domain. While Soviet ethnography strove to construct and even to invent all kinds of "ethnoses," the government developed multinational frameworks according to the accepted data. The upshot was the creation of entire ethnic entities, each with its own age-old pedigree. When Tishkov comes to demonstrate the results of this undertaking, which he calls "ethnic engineering," he makes an instructive comparison between the names of certain nations recorded in the 1897 census and the names of the same nations as known to us today. As a result, he discovers that in the course of the seven decades of the Communist regime, a number of entirely new national identities appeared on the ethnic map of the Soviet Union. Thus for example, the Turks who settled in the area of Azerbaijan at the end of the nineteenth century became Azerbaijanis, Kirghizis became Kazakhs, while Kara-Kirghizis became Kirghizis (Tishkov 1997: 15). Furthermore, numerous subsidiary particularist ethnic identities, which were spread throughout the entire vast area of the Soviet state, were artificially joined into and with both new and old "ethnoses" and united around the myths concerning their joint ancient origins (Tishkov 1997: 16–20).

It is therefore not difficult to identify the motives that led the Communist authorities to adopt such a policy. The construction of "ethnoses" anchored in myths about their early roots was designed to achieve maximum simplification of the complex multiethnic reality, and to guarantee relative national stability by institutionalizing ethnicity in separate frameworks of regions defined as "ethnic territories." It was not possible to deal with such extreme ethnic heterogeneity simply by means of straightforward repression. Consequently, the most important component identified by Tishkov in the mythology of the "ethnoses" is the principle of the "indigenous nation," which has exclusive ownership of "its" ethnic territory that it possesses by virtue of its ancient and unqualified attachments (Tishkov 1997: 8). Furthermore, this criterion of "indigenousness" constituted a vital condition for defining a particular people as an "ethnos," while other peoples resident in "its" ethnic territory were defined as "*ethnikoses*," in other words ethnic entities not sharing ownership of that territory. For example, when the Armenians resident in Armenia were considered an "ethnos," in Georgia or Azerbaijan they became "*ethnikoses*" (Tishkov 1997: 3). This fundamental distinction between the "indigenous nation" and an "ethnikos"—in other words, between a national majority and a national minority in terms of a majority's primordial right to the ownership of the ethnic territory ascribed to it—will be of decisive importance to our discussion. In the meanwhile, we will simply make the point that these primordial ethnic identities, which were constructed by the regime over decades, came into sharper focus during the perestroika period and following the breakup of the Soviet Union, as they become extremely effective propaganda instruments in the hands of nationalist politicians. This is an age of the perfecting of myths about the "indigenous nations" and the growth of incitement toward the "*ethnikoses*" living in their midst (Tishkov 1997: 7), and attention must be focused on the overlap of circumstances between this atmosphere and the major wave of immigration to Israel.

While Tishkov discusses in detail the circumstances and substance of Soviet and post-Soviet ethnic policy, Brubaker provides a theoretical framework for the latter, exposing its consequences in the sphere of citizenship. He objects to the tendency to perceive any given nation as a collective that exists in reality (whether as an immutable given, or the upshot of development or imagination). Instead, Brubaker suggests treating the nation as an institutionalized phenomenon and a cognitive model. The Soviet regime's policy constitutes in his eyes a manifest example of such nation-institutionalization activities. In his opinion, despite the suppression of nationalism, the Soviet regime institutionalized a territorial nationhood on the one hand, and a personal ethnic nation on the other, as basic social categories and cognitive maps of collective self-understanding. In other words, in addition to dividing the state into over fifty regions, each of which was defined as the homeland of a particular ethno-national group, all citizens were classified on the basis of nations, which were entered in the appropriate heading in personal identification documents (Brubaker 1996: 17f.). Unlike most Sovietologists, who see this establishment of the nation on the level of the individual as possessing merely formal significance, Brubaker identifies far-reaching ramifications for the area of citizenship. As he understands the situation, the personal nation category was a basic practical component of the individual's civil status: while members of the people belonging to an "indigenous nation" enjoyed preferential status in their ethnic homeland in various areas (such as admission to higher education institutes or employment in certain jobs), members of national minorities frequently suffered discrimination in those same areas (Brubaker 1996: 31). Thus the dual institutionalization of ethnicity on both the territorial and private level made the relationship between individuals' ethnic origin and the national definition of the area of their domicile into a paramount factor in determining the scope of their civil rights.

If we now combine Tishkov's approach with Brubaker's, we can say that the primordial view of ethnicity, as promoted in the Soviet state, not only established and maintained an exclusive attachment between the "indigenous nation" and "its" ethnic territory, but also constituted a fundamental basis for the inequality of opportunities between a national majority and a national minority within the borders of that territory. The inferior social status of a member of the minority was perceived as an axiomatic state of affairs, while the very concept of a national minority was also considered an inferior and negative category. This is above all testified to by the following fact: in spoken Russian, the abbreviation of the concept "national minority" became a standard derogatory term ("*Natsmen*," which stood for "*Nats[ionalnoye] men[shinstvo]*"), which was primarily encountered by people from the Caucasus and Central Asia when they came to the Slav republics. Furthermore, just as the attachment between the "indigenous nation" and the national homeland was an unchanging given, so too the individual's nation was defined in determinist concepts, i.e., by origin. This means that members of the national minority were also fully aware of their national affiliation, even if they were sometimes cut off from the locus of their homeland and their culture for generations, since their registered nationality became a central parameter of their civil existence.

Primordial Identity in Transition

The Foundations of Russian-Speaking Migrants' Ethno-national Identity

How did "ethnic engineering" affect Jews in the Soviet Union and no less important for our interests, how did this policy shape Jewish perceptions of majority-minority relations and nationhood in general? With the exception of the "Jewish Autonomous Region" in Birobidzhan in the Far East, where the Jews were an insignificant minority, the Jews did not possess a single area or region anchored in the myth of the "indigenous nation," while their very existence was comprehensively excluded both from books about the history of Russia and the USSR, and from the studies of world history. And indeed the surveys on which researchers studying migration from the former USSR to Israel rely confirm the supposition about the muted nature of national and Jewish awareness among most of the migrants. Moreover, the surveys would also appear to strengthen the argument about the migrants' extremely weak attachment to their Jewish identity. For example, in the above-mentioned survey carried out by the Center for Multiculturalism and Educational Research of the University of Haifa, one of the questions that respondents were asked—"If you had the chance, would you want or not want to be reborn a Jew?"—was intended to reveal to the researchers the extent of the migrants' innate commitment to their Jewish identity. Since only 31 percent of the 707 respondents replied categorically in the affirmative, the authors of the study concluded that the migrants were only weakly connected to their Jewishness (Al-Haj and Leshem 2000: 29).

However, it seems to me that the respondents' negative and hesitant responses to this question reflect a more complex phenomenon than mere indifference to their Jewishness. Even if the migrant did prefer not to be born again as Jewish, this does not invalidate the complexity of his or her existence as a Jew. On the contrary, the migrants' internal conflicts over this question are highly indicative of difficulties in coping with a Jewishness that they did not consciously choose, but which was imposed upon them from birth in their country of origin and then perpetuated in their identity. True, this is a form of Jewishness devoid of real substance in all matters relating to those manifestations of Jewish identity that are widespread in the world nowadays, but at the same time this is a Jewishness that is perceived by those who carry it as primordial and deterministic, in terms of imposing a fate that cannot be modified: a situation that is undoubtedly accompanied by all kinds of different ways of self-understanding.

One of the researchers who directs our attention to the primordial nature of the Jewish identity of the migrants from the Soviet Union is the American scholar, Zvi Gitelman. According to him, this identity is buried deep in the migrants' soul, on the level of their inner psyche, and its behavioral expressions may be concealed from sight (Gitelman 1995: 29).

The Jews of the former Soviet Union do not generally need to explain to themselves what "being Jewish" means, since their existence as Jewish is perceived by them as axiomatic, and consists of an aggregate of subjective experiences. Thus Gitelman describes the upset reaction of one of the respondents, a woman who was extremely surprised by the question "What does it mean to be a Jew?" and replied in a short but complete response: "Whoever is a Jew knows that he's a Jew, and that's that" (Gitelman 1995: 31). At the same time, despite the subjective and ambiguous nature of such a Jewish identity, there is nothing to prevent us from trying to elucidate its main foundations, while constantly relating to the significance of its being an identity in transition.

Before proceeding to analyze sources that are relevant to this approach, I must make a methodological point that relates to the question of whether, when discussing Russian Israeli identity, it is a good idea to focus exclusively on the migrants of the 1990s. Research has indeed made clear distinctions between the immigrants of the 1970s and the migrants who came to Israel in the last decade. Apart from emphasizing the general differences in the images of these two different waves of immigration, such as the manifest Zionist attachments of the immigrants of the 1970s in contrast to their absence among the present migrants, or the presence of an accepted leadership among the former lacking in the case of the latter (Lissak and Leshem 1995: 31; Shuval 1996: 3; Leshem and Lissak 1999: 142), emphasis is also placed on the widespread phenomenon of intense mutual criticism and stresses in the relationship between these two groups on the level of day-to-day existence (Siegel 1998: 41f.). At the same time, it seems to me that all these distinctions, even if inherently correct, do not comprehensively reflect the dynamics of the interaction between the two waves of immigration that have evolved over the last decade.

True, the majority of the members of the first wave, who from the outset wanted to integrate into Israeli society, did not approve of the determination of the immigrants of the second wave to maintain their communal identity. And yet outstanding figures from among the immigrants of the 1970s and 1980s—first and foremost former Prisoners of Zion, refuseniks and a range of intellectuals who only recently were advocating the vision of integration—have begun to actively contribute to the Russian community's effort to achieve collective consolidation. According to Kimmerling's opposite argument, the two "waves" have ultimately complemented each other: and of all people, it is the representatives of the first wave's elite who laid the institutional infrastructure for the growth of the sociocultural and ethnic enclave (Kimmerling 1998: 280f.). This can be seen primarily in the creation of the Russian community's two most significant institutions: the Zionist Forum, headed by Natan Sharansky, and the Russian-language press. The forum, which was set up in 1988 in order to represent the interests of the migrants, very quickly became an umbrella organization embracing a range of both countrywide and local "Russian" associations, and in 1995 it provided the organizational infrastructure for the establishment of the Yisrael Ba'aliya party (Kimmerling 1998: 280f.), which in the last two parliamentary electoral campaigns (1996 and 1999) won seven and six Knesset seats respectively. The Russian-language press has demonstrated enormous influence on the Russian public in all matters related to determining its limits and emblems. *Vesti*, the paper with the highest circulation and the most respected in comparison with other dailies such as *Novosti Nedeli* and *Vremia*, is factually subject to the Forum's leadership (Leshem and Lissak 1999: 136, 146) and today reflects the positions of Yisrael Ba'aliya. Consequently, if we wish to unequivocally look at the nature of Russian Israelis' identity, and not simply state its nebulousness as a categorical fact, we must not limit ourselves to examining the data of surveys about the rank-and-file migrants of the 1990s. Undoubtedly we may and indeed must examine the content of what is said by the opinion setters among the "Russian" community, i.e., party leaders, journalists, and intellectuals who are close to the leadership, a majority of whom belong to the first wave of immigration.

One of the outstanding personalities among the "Russian" intellectuals, whose writings I wish to discuss in depth, is Alexander Voronel. Voronel immigrated to Israel in 1975, after three years during which, together with a group of refuseniks, he had "published" a clandestine samizdat series of essays on "Jews in the Soviet Union." After coming to Israel, he and his wife Nina, a well-known Russian-language writer and playwright, were instrumental in setting up the magazine "22," whose editor-in chief he became in 1994. This magazine, defined today as a "sociopolitical and literary magazine of the Jewish intelligentsia from the Commonwealth of Independent States in Israel," undeniably has a limited circulation compared with popular "Russian" newspapers. However, many of its editorial staff have ties with the forum leadership and the editorial personnel of *Vesti*, and first and foremost Eduard Kuznetzov, one of the best known Prisoners of Zion, who in 1970 led a group that tried to hijack an aircraft in order to fly it to Israel, and who until recently was the newspaper's editor-in-chief. A physicist by profession and a professor of physics at Tel Aviv University, Voronel has over the last thirty years written extensively about Jewish topics, including various issues in Jewish philosophy and history. As a self-taught person in these fields of knowledge, Voronel represents a widespread phenomenon among Russian-Jewish circles: the technological intelligentsia with a special interest in art, literature, and philosophy. In him we therefore have a typical representative of that broad-based intelligentsia, which in addition to authors, poets, artists, and journalists also include scientists and engineers who are interested in the arts. According to Lissak and Leshem they constitute the leadership of the Russian community in Israel (Lissak and Leshem 1995: 25).

If we now turn to the collection of Voronel's essays, which appeared in 1998, and focus on what he has written over the last fifteen years, we can see that the leitmotif of all his writing is the intellectual endeavor to provide Israeli society, which is undergoing a process of disintegration, with a consolidating glue and a common basis for continuing Israel's national existence, a kind of "common network of axes" as Voronel calls it in his mathematical terminology (Voronel 1998: 61). The most instructive example of constructing a national common denominator that is available to the author and guides him along his path is the national thinking of Alexander Solzhenitsyn, among the most admired contemporary Russian writers. He is a faithful adherent of the "back-to-the-soil" tradition (whose nineteenth-century founders included Fyodor Dostoevsky and his brother Mikhail), which was close to the Slavophile outlook. Solzhenitsyn's efforts to reimbue Russian self-awareness with the imperial idea, as based on the triply symbolic combination of "God, Czar, and homeland," are viewed by Voronel as fostering a historical mythology of vital importance for healing breaches—a mythology that unfortunately has no counterpart in today's Israel (Voronel 1998: 68). It should be noted that it is not Solzhenitsyn's monarchistic formula as such that attracts the author, but rather the Russian writer's general method for restoring his people's national awareness, as interpreted by Voronel. In his opinion, this rediscovery of the Russian monarchistic heritage is just one of the more tangible foundations of Solzhenitsyn's national theory, while the author's overall plan is designed to revive the totality of the "ancient beliefs" that constitute Russians' common existence as an age-old nation. Similarly, and despite Israeli society's extreme multiculturalism, in Israel too the "ancient beliefs" provide a national infrastructure for Jewish existence. However, this infrastructure is increasingly being crushed by the Israeli intellectuals, unceasingly battling the "ancient beliefs." Voronel sees their destructive undertaking as utterly opposed to Solzhenitsyn's restorative quest (Voronel 1998: 82). This gloomy state of affairs is only likely to change if there appears a responsible group with a national vision on the scene, such as the pioneers (*halutsim*) and the religious settlers from Gush Emunim. Only the Russian Jews, who in Voronel's opinion adhere to the vital "ancient beliefs" more than any other community in Israel, are capable of filling this role (Voronel 1998: 195).

In order to understand the specific traits of their contributions, which in Voronel's opinion are exclusive to the Russian Jewish community, we must examine the meaning of the notion of "ancient beliefs," which is undoubtedly a key expression in the national outlook. It is an extremely positive category, an aggregate of all the primordial attributes that characterize a nation. The neutral and amorphous nature of the concept enables Voronel to also include in it manifestly universal values, imbuing them with ethnic overtones. Thus from among the aggregate of the Russian people's "ancient beliefs," which Solzhenitsyn aspires to restore, Voronel cites a sense of spirituality, being responsive to one's fellow man, and fairness, all of which as he sees as emanating from the ability of the Pravoslav religion to informally grasp the significance of the Bible (Voronel 1998: 61f., 122). On the other hand, Russian Jews have been successful in borrowing from Russian culture its best spiritual attributes, such as a universal understanding of religion, an incessant striving for absolute truth, and a tendency toward philosophical thinking (Voronel 1998: 130f., 149, 241). In doing so, they have imparted their own original ethnic character to these attributes, adding a Jewish intellectual flair and Jewish creative openness (Voronel 1998: 151). In the process they have become a community possessed of an immense spiritual strength, whose Jewishness is not the upshot of rational factors but comes straight from the heart (Voronel 1998: 240). Voronel has no problem offering proof from the past for this noble tradition, in the form of the Russian Zionists' steadfast opposition to the Uganda scheme at the Sixth Zionist Congress (Voronel 1998: 290). Hence, he has no doubt that the successors to those heroes will today be able to lead the struggle against the disintegrative tendencies in Israeli society and to contribute specifically to internal stability. As a result, this is what he expects of the Yisrael Ba'aliya party (Voronel 1998: 170). This amorphous picture of Jewish "ancient beliefs," which according to Voronel are the exclusive province of Russian Jews, would appear to neatly coincide with the vague character of how the rank-and-file migrants of the 1990s perceive Jewish identity, as shown by Gitelman's surveys. The response by the woman who said, "Whoever is a Jew knows that he's a Jew, and that's that" came "straight from the heart," even though it may well conceal countless "ancient beliefs," such as subjective and arbitrary definitions of Jewishness à la Voronel. However, it is nevertheless possible to identify in his chaotic model two central and apparently complementary foundations: on the one hand, the particularist Russian foundation, i.e., the totality of the noble "ancient beliefs" characteristic solely of Russian Jews' Weltanschauung; and on the other hand, the general national-Jewish foundation, i.e., Russian Jews' specific ability to halt the ideological degeneration of Israeli society and make their unique contribution to healing the breaches affecting it. In general terms, this duality is highly reminiscent of Majid Al-Haj's and Elazar Leshem's conclusion concerning the identity structure of Russian Israelis, which they present as a combination of a "Russian" ethnic consciousness of determination to preserve the Jewish nature of the state of Israel (Al-Haj and Leshem 2000: 67). However, what I wish to argue is that, while this view of identity is depicted by Voronel as a structured, static vision, it is actually the outcome of a dynamic development indissolubly linked to the fact of the migrants' move to a Jewish nation-state. In the framework of this development an ongoing interaction exists between the Russian particularist foundation and the general Jewish one.

The Development of Russian-Jewish Identity in the 1990s

I wish, therefore, to distinguish between two critical stages in the development of the collective identity of the Russian-speaking immigrants in Israel: the first stage (1993–99) in which the particularist identity component clearly predominated over the general-national Jewish foundation;

and the second stage (1999 and onward), which we are in the midst of nowadays. Of these two, it is the latter foundation that is constantly becoming stronger. The first stage began in 1993, when as a result of the first democratic elections for the leadership of the Zionist Forum, this organization managed to beat a path to the "Russian" grass roots in Israel, bringing under its auspices dozens of the migrants' voluntary associations, which until then had had practically no dealings whatsoever with the forum. This process of reorganization in turn led to the marked decline of the rival organization, the "Association of Immigrants from the Soviet Union," headed by Sofa Landver, which had the support of the Labor Party, while its affiliated *Nasha Strana* newspaper became embroiled in economic difficulties and was ultimately transferred to private ownership. At the same time, the circulation figures of the *Vesti* newspaper continued to climb (Leshem and Lissak 1999: 157ff.). Thus, during the period from 1989 to 1992, the Russian community was characterized by its anarchic and fragmented nature (Leshem and Lissak 1999: 153f.), but from 1993 onward we see it enjoying relative institutional unity, at the same time as conferring broad-based legitimacy on the consolidation of a particularist "Russian" identity.

This process, which led to the setting up of the Yisrael Ba'aliya party in the summer of 1995, was indeed characterized by the strength of the centrifugal tendency, and was also accompanied by a momentous unification between the outstanding representatives of the immigrants of the 1970s and the new migrants, based on the notion of a Russian-Jewish ethnic community. Thus for example, one of the prominent intellectuals of the first wave, the celebrated poet and journalist Mikhail Gendelev, who had long been a determined opponent of the idea of the "Russian" party, in 1994 suddenly declared his support for this step. Gendelev identifies two reasons for this change in his views. Firstly, he argued, the last wave of immigration had culturally absorbed people from the 1970s wave of immigration, resulting in the emergence of a "Russian Israel" as a new cultural entity, which now needed its own political representation. Secondly, given the erosion of Zionist ideology, to which he, Gendelev, had undoubtedly been utterly loyal, and given the strengthening of other ethnic parties, such as Shas and Arab parties, the founding of the "Russian" party was the upshot of the need of the day and tantamount to accepting new rules of the game. When this new party comes into existence, Gendelev predicted, it will undoubtedly have marked influence in the Knesset (he also predicted that it would gain eight seats), so that it would be able to promote Russian Israelis' common interests. However, Gendelev qualified his post-Zionist vision by implying that the "Russian" party would also be involved in the general process of political decision making, which it will try to influence along the lines of its constituency's disposition. This means that the new party would contribute to the conducting of an assertive and uncompromising policy toward Israel's Arab neighbors, as the "Russian" public fundamentally wishes, in the author's view.[1]

Once the Yisrael Ba'aliya party was established, Gendelev's reservations about the centrifugal tendency were regularly expressed by the party leadership. Thus once Natan Sharansky decided to head the "Immigrants' Party," he declared that his goals would lie in the general national domain, as is clearly evident from the party's platform (Siegel 1998: 160, 171). However, in the period from 1995 to 1999, declarations of this kind were of symbolic importance only, tantamount to doing one's duty toward Israeli society, while the central place in constructing the self-image of the party and the community was given over to highlighting those particularist attributes of the Russian Jews that are largely reminiscent of Voronel's "ancient beliefs." Outstanding professionalism, spiritual strength, Jewish brains (Siegel 1998: 173)—all these "Jewish-Russian" virtues were mentioned only as evidence of the migrants' power to take the initiative in promoting their collective interests.

In 1999, an abrupt about-face took place, when two far-reaching changes can be identified in the life of the Russian-speaking community, swinging things in the centripetal direction. The first change ties in with the long-term results of the split among the "Russian" grassroots and the establishment of the "Yisrael Beitenu" party headed by Avigdor Lieberman. Two former Yisrael Ba'aliya leading figures—Yuri Stern and Mikhail Nudelman—joined the new party. The new "Russian" party, although also having ethnic overtones, advocated clear-cut general national political goals. In the 1999 elections, it won four Knesset seats, gaining itself a prominent position in the Israeli right-wing camp. Moreover, Yisrael Ba'aliya itself also, having ostensibly retained its sectorial image during the 1999 campaign for the elections to the Knesset and the prime ministership, actually behaved in Barak's coalition as a party with a general national orientation in all respects. After the Camp David conference it even resigned from the coalition before the National Religious Party did, which had an even more clearly defined general national platform. Finally, in the run-up to the 2001 prime ministerial elections, Yisrael Ba'aliya entirely dropped its former sectorial neutrality by joining forces with Yisrael Beitenu in supporting the right-wing candidate, Ariel Sharon. What is extremely interesting in this context is the new stance of Natan Sharansky, the leader of Yisrael Ba'aliya, according to whom the "Russian" community is aware of its special obligation to contribute to the uniting of the "entire Jewish people against the foes of the state."[2] That being the case, instead of the rift among the "Russian" grass roots aggravating the disagreement between sectorialism and a mainstream approach, a new amalgamation of these two foundations took place: general national slogans serving collective vested interests were replaced by the promotion of mainstream interests, which the "Russian" community considered vital to the country as a whole.

Another change came about in mid-2000 in the Russian-language press. Eduard Kuznetsov, who had been editing *Vesti* for eight years, left the paper and set up a weekly called *Mig-news*. This magazine, which openly represents the Yisrael Beiteinu line, very soon acquired a fairly respectable position among the "Russian" community. According to a series of surveys carried out on the Russian-Israeli "Israel Today" political site, *Mig-news* is even more popular than *Vesti* itself, at least as far as the younger generation is concerned.[3] Unlike other Russian-language periodicals, the weekly is marked by a clear-cut trend toward shifting the emphasis from topics that relate solely to the needs of the migrants toward issues concerning the whole of Israel society and the future of the country. This difference is particularly visible in the readers' letters section. Whereas in other "Russian" papers this section conveys the voices of migrants who are discriminated against and insulted because of their "Russian" origins, the readers' letters in the *Mig-news* paint a completely different picture. Here the writers, including migrants who by their own admission are "greenhorns," express profound fears about the communal-cultural plurality of Israeli society, which they consider to be bordering on final disintegration in the face of threats by the country's Arab foes. An example of this is provided by a reader who is unable to hide his amazement at the very use of expressions such as "Russian Jew," "Moroccan Jew," or "Georgian Jew." For him, this is a contradiction in terms, an invention of the Israeli press, which is operated by a traditional ruling elite whose nature the writer of the letter, who has been in Israel for just one year, still finds difficult to grasp. On the other hand, he has no problem identifying the Israeli people's unifying symbols: East Jerusalem, the Western Wall, and the common biblical heritage.[4] In contrast to this confused reader, there are many "veterans" who are able to produce a clear definition in more specific terms of this "ruling elite" as maliciously causing division among the people, along with the advancement of all kinds of solutions. One of the most common proposals is to initiate dialogue with representatives of the other groups among the Jewish people, such as Mizrahim and ultra-Orthodox (*Haredim*), with the goal of presenting a common front to the oligarchic establishment, which is trying to rule different communities (*edot*) by means of a divisive post-Zionist ideology.[5] Various communities' representatives would then be able to overcome divisiveness and to expand the common elements, accompanied by the concomitant passing of appropriate legislation.[6]

Thus the question of "combating post-Zionism" gradually becomes one of the key issues in the Russian press in Israel, where the concept of "post-Zionism" includes not only the political process, but also cultural pluralism and the "de-Zionization of education." Gradually, articles on maltreatment of the children of immigrants in schools and the difficulties of integrating with native-born Israelis (sabras), give way to impassioned criticism of the new history curriculum for ninth-graders (World of Change), in which in addition to the story of Zionism and Israel's War of Independence, reference is also made to the Palestinian national movement and Palestinian refugees.[7] A few years ago the Russian newspapers were attacking their Hebrew-language counterparts for charging immigration with responsibility for prostitution, alcoholism, and organized crime, while nowadays they tend to spotlight the appearance of new charges leveled against the migrants, such as extreme nationalism and anti-Arab incitement.[8]

A qualification is called for here: the strengthening of the national-centripetal foundation among the body of Russian-speaking migrants does not mean the elimination of the ethnic "Russian" component in their identity. Undoubtedly, it is precisely those primordial attributes and specificities which are ostensibly unique to the Russian Jews that confer upon them a mission in the form of a general national task to unite the people. After all, is it not the Russian Jews' courage that makes them come out into the streets and battle the Arab rioters in Upper Nazareth[9]; is it not representatives of Yisrael Ba'aliya and Yisrael Beitenu, steadfastly adhering to national principles, who spearhead those who condemn the "de-Zionization" of education[10]; and finally, is it not Russian Jews, steadfast in the virtue of self-respect, who will first and foremost throw themselves into the effort to achieve national reconciliation, along the lines advocated not only by politicians and journalists, but also the grass roots?[11]

Hence, what we are witnessing is a unique development in perceiving national identity, in the course of which Jewish-Russian ethnic consciousness has gradually become stronger concurrently with its perception of the state of Israel as a Jewish nation-state. As summed up by Yuri Stern, in Israel the Russian Jews have come to understand that they are no longer "Natsmen" (members of a national minority), but belong to a national majority in a country of their own, and that same Russian-Jewish internal strength that they acquired in their country of origin in their constant confrontation with the hostile majority is now something that they are prepared to contribute to strengthening the state of Israel as a Jewish state with all its historical national markers.[12] To put it another way, whereas in the former Soviet Union the institutionalization of the Jewish nation as nationally bereft of "its own" ethnic territory made the "nationality" section a mark of Cain for the Jews, in Israel their joining an institutionalized national majority that officially has roots in an ancient land makes the nationality section of an ID card a sign of prestige of which they can be proud. Consequently, despite the unique nature of its development, in outline this national outlook is reminiscent of the kinds of primordial identity that took shape in the former Soviet Union under the inspiration of the Soviet regime and Soviet ethnography.

Between "Indigenous Nation" and National Minority

National Minority and Arab Minority as Perceived by Russian Israelis

It may be stated that just as the researchers addressing the migration of the Jews of the former Soviet Union to Israel have frequently erred in interpreting the nebulousness of the migrants' national identity as sufficient proof that it was actually absent, so too have they failed to express the requisite interest in the question of how the Russian Jews related to the Palestinian minority. Generally, the immigrants' reservations about Arabs were identified as a predetermined fact, an axiomatic state of affairs, at most stemming from immigrants' empirical experience. It therefore comes as no surprise that the systematic ignoring of the existence of an innate national awareness among the migrants led to failure by researchers to look for any structural reason for the phenomenon. Consequently, most of them provided external explanations "from the field" such as immigrants were "… showing 'Jewish patriotism' and a feeling of competition with the other leading sectors of the Israeli state," (Kimmerling 1998: 287) or they made reference to the loathing for the tens of thousands of Arab students who studied in the Soviet Union as a counterreaction to the well-known Soviet slogan of "international brotherhood" (Gitelman 1995: 58ff.). My contention is not that these arguments are invalid, but rather that they are secondary in light of the fact that they do not sufficiently account for the national predispositions that guide the views of most Russian Israelis. We have shown above how, in the former Soviet Union, the supranational slogans of "international brotherhood" concealed the institutionalized activity of "ethnic engineering," which imbued primordial ethnic identities with notions of national majority and national minority as value-laden categories on which the scope of civil rights depended both formally and informally. We have also demonstrated how Russian Israelis' national awareness developed throughout the 1990s on the basis of primordial foundations, being in part grounded in their Soviet experiences (a particularist Russian-Jewish foundation) and in part through their existence in Israel (a general Israeli foundation of the "indigenous nation"). Given all of this, and in light of the presence of the Arab national minority that the majority in Israel does not view as an "indigenous nation," I will explore whether the Russian-Israeli national outlook also perceives the concepts of majority and minority as two different value-laden categories.

Before attempting to explain the attitude of the Russian-speaking migrants about the Arab minority, there are two more general questions that should be addressed. First, how do Russian Jews understand the concept of national minority as such, and how do they relate to the issue of civil rights for minorities? Second, how do they see their own position as a national minority in the former Soviet Union? It seems to me that the answers to these two questions might well provide us with a broad theoretical basis for continuing the discussion of the subject in question.

It would be presumptuous to advance any generally applicable, exhaustive answers given the diversity of the migrants' current views on this particular issue. We have no statistical data on such a general matter. However, we can concentrate on those forces that, according to researchers, to a considerable extent shape "Russian" public opinion—that is to say, the press and the intelligentsia (Kimmerling 1998: 286f.). In order to try to present as broad a picture as possible, I will discuss two sources that address different audiences among the "Russian" community. The first source is again Alexander Voronel, one of the community's leading intellectuals. The second source is the sensationalist weekly *Secret*, which enjoys high circulation figures among the rank and file of migrants from the former Soviet Union.

In one of his most acerbic essays, Voronel describes a joint Soviet-American meeting on human rights that took place in Seattle in the summer of 1990. With great irony the author depicts what took place before his very eyes: a series of representatives of small, remote peoples, including a spokesman for the Yukon Indians from Alaska, getting up and resolutely demanding that the Great Powers recognize their national independence. These claims, particularly that of the Indians' spokesman, aroused in Voronel's heart feelings of contempt mixed with fear of the claimants. For him, this phenomenon is simply an inordinate and inflated expansion of the principle of self-determination, which from the outset was supposed only to be realized in the European cultural reality, while now it is increasingly being transferred to the most ignorant tribes in Africa and Asia, who lack any authentic national history (Voronel 1998: 173–176).

Let us now examine an article by the political commentator for *Secret*, Leonid Borisov. The main hero of the article is Jörg Haider, the Austrian leader, and the author rallies to his defense in the wake of the wave of anti-Austrian protests that engulfed Europe following his party's victory in the polls. To Borisov, Haider's ideas seem to make sense and even to be on the clever side, since all the Austrian leader wants to do is to restore to the European continent its true image, as it was before it became a "paradise for Africans and Asiatics."[13]

It is not hard to identify the common aspects of these two passages in all matters relating to the African-Asian image of the despised minority figure. But can we infer from this that we appear to have two racist approaches, reflecting nothing other than these two men's private opinions? It does nevertheless seem to me that the picture is more complex than would appear at first sight. Let us therefore examine our second question, which concerns the way in which Jews of the former Soviet Union perceived their existence as members of a national minority. It turns out that the inferiority of their status as a Jewish minority, as reflected in certain restrictions imposed on the admission of Jews to institutions of higher education or the blocking of personal promotion to diverse positions, was seen by the Jews themselves as a natural state of affairs (Konstantinov 1991: 17). It is instructive to see that the selfsame Jewish refuseniks and dissidents, although apparently part of a civil movement of protest against the Soviet regime in the 1970s and 1980s, were fighting first and foremost for the Jews' right to leave the Soviet Union. Their pledge seemed utterly divorced from both the image of the nature of the regime itself, and the question of the civil status of the Soviet

Jews within the state (Kimmerling 1998: 278). Moreover, members of the Jewish-Zionist intelligentsia even viewed the existing state of affairs favorably, since in their opinion discrimination against Jews was inhibiting the widespread assimilation of Soviet Jewry. In the 1970s Voronel, for example, extolled the "special national character" of the Russian people, which reminds the Jews that they are alien to it and hence contributes to preserving their ethnic identity (Voronel 1998: 102). While Jews with a clear national awareness may have perceived the regime's anti-Semitic approach as a natural and self-evident phenomenon, all the more so can be said of the Jewish rank and file. The "fifth section"—referring to the nationality section in passports—has become a synonym among Jews for the curse of fate, which only their children, if born of mixed marriages, will be able to avoid (Zaslavsky and Luryi 1979: 149). From this it may be deduced that the Jews' wretched situation was not brought about by the perverted regime, but was decreed by fate, in other words the outcome of history in its primordial meaning.

Hence these two authors' negative attitude to national minorities should not be seen as an expression of purely racist views, just as the reservations about Arabs held by most Russian-speaking migrants (including many left-wing supporters) should not be ascribed, as the surveys show (Gitelman 1995: 60; Al-Haj and Leshem 2000: 39), to just a knee-jerk reaction. Undoubtedly, this phenomenon constitutes a basic element of the ethnic-civil outlook within whose framework a national minority, which is not part of the "indigenous nation" and has no "historic roots," is fundamentally perceived in negative terms.

And indeed, if we now focus on discussions of the "Arab problem" in Israel, as expressed in the "Russian" press, we can see that arguments that are grounded in that "historic reality" occupy a key position there. One of the historians who has a permanent platform in the press, and whom the "Russian' intelligentsia consider an authority on the history of the Israeli-Arab conflict, is Valery Smolensky. Before immigrating to Israel at the beginning of the 1990s, he had spent some twenty years lecturing at the University of Baku, and within his first three years in Israel he published some two hundred articles, many on Arab topics. As a loyal pupil of primordial Soviet ethnography, Smolensky tries to demonstrate to his readers why the concept of the "Palestinian people" has no basis in reality "from the historical viewpoint," and to explain nevertheless the factual presence of Arab inhabitants on the soil of the "Land of Israel"—Eretz Israel. As part of these efforts, he develops a theory about the systematic "conquest" of Eretz Israel by Arab migrants from neighboring countries, which gradually took place during the 1882–1914 period, paralleling Zionist settlement activities.[14] This view is undergoing refinement in the Russian-language press, and nowadays articles appear stating that the first mass "invasion" of the country by these Arab migrants occurred as early as the 1830s, with the "invasion" continuing apace under the British Mandate.[15]

Generally, historical comments of this nature are not confined to the domain of theoretical debate. Thus Pinchas Polonsky, who among the "Russian" public in Israel enjoys the reputation of a first-class religious-national philosopher, is also of the opinion that non-Jewish peoples—who, as he puts it, were defeated by the Jewish people—are present in his homeland as a result of a historical mishap. However, he also states unequivocally that the requisite conditions for the continued existence of any non-Jewish people on the soil of Eretz Israel is their absolute political subordination and close economic supervision by the Jewish majority. While Polonsky fails to specify the meaning of this economic supervision, regarding the political subordination he explains that it is the minority's obligation to accept the Jewish nature of the state without reservation, since in the absence of this, as Polonsky puts it, the minority will not be allowed to live in Israel.[16] It should be noted that the author does not explicitly refer to the Arabs, an omission that is not the result of oversight, since he is presenting the general model of the configuration of relationships between the Jewish "indigenous nation" and the non-Jewish minority as such. If, however, we remove the fundamental "sting" from this model, it can be readily applied to the ethnic republics of the former Soviet Union, and even more so to the latter's successor states, in which the principle of the supremacy of the "indigenous people" over the "*ethnikoses*" is developing with even greater vigor.

The growing prominence of this position is reflected, among other things, in Polonsky's recent appointment to an extremely senior position in the Zionist Forum, which, as we have explained, functions as the institutionalized infrastructure of Yisrael Ba'aliya. Given this fact, we are justified in assuming that views such as Polonsky's about the relationship between a Jewish majority and an Arab minority are becoming more common in circles close to this party's leadership.

While Yisrael Ba'aliya may still in theory be focusing on matters relating to the "Russian" community, Yisrael Beitenu attaches paramount importance to the "Arab question." It is instructive to see that in this connection, Israeli Arabs receive even greater attention than the population of the West Bank and Gaza Strip. Thus the party's leader, Avigdor Lieberman, expresses profound apprehension at the expansion of protest action by the Arab minority, the spreading of illegal Arab construction in Jewish localities within the "green line," and the demands by the Arab leadership to change Israel from a Jewish state to a "state of all its citizens." For Lieberman, the only way to deal with these phenomena, which in his view constitute an existential danger to the state, is to establish a forceful government that will make the Arabs' staying in Israel unequivocally conditional on an unqualified declaration by them of their loyalty to the Jews who are owners of the country. Anyone who refuses to accept this condition will be forced to lose his Israeli citizenship and to leave the country.[17]

This opinion, which is particularly prevalent among supporters of the Yisrael Beitenu party and is also acquiring a foothold in Yisrael Ba'aliya, is becoming more widespread among the general "Russian" public, as can be seen from the increasing popularity of the *Mig-news* weekly, the organ of Lieberman's party. However, the main indicator of the spreading of Lieberman's ideas among the "Russian" community (and in particular among its younger members) is provided by the regular opinion polls conducted at the "Russian" political site, "Israel Today." Thus during November 2000, scores of surfers every day declared that they prefer the Yisrael Beitenu leader to all other Israel politicians.[18]

If this is the case, we can draw the following conclusion: the Russian Israelis' ethno-national perception of identity that evolved during the 1990s out of a combination of an ethnic Russian-Jewish foundation and a national Eretz Israeli foundation embraces a view of the non-Jewish national minority as a natural target for discrimination. Moreover, any action of the minority whose purpose is to change the existing situation is perceived as an existential danger to the Jewish majority, and therefore enables it generally to take all and any necessary defensive measures, including expropriating the civil basis for the continued residence of the minority in the country. This perception is further bolstered in direct relation to the strengthening of the centripetal tendency among Russian Israelis, the overall model being reminiscent of the model of the relationship between ethnicity and citizenship that evolved in the former Soviet Union, although the process of its development, as we have seen above, is more complex than the Soviet "ethnic engineering."

The Post-Soviet Ethno-national Legacy and the Image of the State of Israel: Possible Scenarios

In the conclusion to the section on Russian-speaking Jews in his article, Kimmerling outlines three possible scenarios for the "Russian" community's future development in Israel: 1) absorbing the future generation of migrants within the Ashkenazi middle class, whom the migrants resemble in terms of their various attributes; 2) institutionalization of the "Russian Israeli" as one of the Israeli "types" and varieties of "Israeli characteristics," if the trend toward cultural and class-based subdivision in Israeli society continues; 3) the continued segregation within their enclaves of a considerable portion of "Russians" of future generations, assuming that the tendencies of subdivisions take extreme forms. One way or the other, Kimmerling (1998: 291f.) rightly concludes that the very presence of this cultural group within the Israeli state has already brought about changes in its general, cultural, political, and social fabric. The impression is that one of the significant implications for Israeli society with which Kimmerling credits the "Russian" community is the migrants' contribution to its multiculturalism, an indirect result of which has been the possibility, inter alia, of an expansion in the autonomy and an increase in the involvement of Arab citizens within the state (Kimmerling 1998: 269; Ben-Rafael, Olshtain and Geijst 1997: 386).

Nevertheless, given the exposition of the nature of the migrants' ethno-national identity and the revealing of its civil image, it can no longer be stated that the tendency to the institutionalization of autonomous "Russian" culture (i.e., what Kimmerling calls the centrifugal tendency) plays a dominant role in the life of the "Russian" community, whereas the centripetal tendency is restricted to the merely formal demonstration of "Jewish patriotism" in accordance with the nature of the primordial rhetoric, which is still prevalent in the state of Israel and applies to all the Jewish players within the Israeli political system. True, in the early stages of the migrants' political consolidation, arguments in the general national spirit served the community's leaders primarily as a means of promoting sectorial interests. However, as the Russian Jews' view of themselves as the "crème de la crème" has grown stronger, together with their feeling of belonging to the "indigenous nation," an opposite dynamic has been revealed. During the last two years, we have seen that manifestly ethnic "Russian" institutions constitute a base for the dissemination of the Russian-Jewish ethno-national outlook among "Russian" public opinion, and its application to practical politics, centered round vociferous complaints about the "post-Zionist" plurality of cultures and efforts to curb manifestations of civil demands by Israeli Arabs.

It should be noted that the outlook of the migrants' leadership with respect to the relationship between an "indigenous nation" and a "non-indigenous national minority" coincides with the nature of the state of Israel's system of government. Whether we define the Israeli political system as an "ethnic democracy" in Sammy Smooha's phrase (1999: 34–48), or characterize it as an "ethnocracy" following Oren Yiftachel (2000: 98), its key markers—the principle of the primordial attachment of the Jewish "ethnos" to "its" ethnic territory and the practice of discrimination against the Arab minority—are likely to remind the Russian-speaking migrants of a Soviet and post-Soviet ethno-national reality, which, as detailed above, was considered in their eyes to be a perfectly normal situation. Even if the migrants contest the Zionist ethos by pushing their particular Russian-Jewish identity to the fore (Lomsky-Feder and Rapoport 2001: 10), they are nonetheless adopting one of its important components, namely, the very negation of Palestinians' "indigenousness." Consequently, the Russian Jews' involvement in a general national effort to preserve the state of Israel's Jewish character will grow in direct proportion to the expansion of the Arab civil protest against this "normal" situation. Despite the official nature of this task, the "Russian" autonomous institutions will not die out: on the contrary, they will be harnessed with greater vigor in order to engage "Russian" public opinion and continue to promote the "Russian" self-image as an advance guard of the Jewish people in its battle against the Arabs and all kinds of "post-Zionists." Indeed, we recently witnessed this subordination of the community's communal "Russian" apparatus to national goals, with the two "Russian" parties playing not insignificant roles in the right-wing camp and the Russian-language press brandishing the flag of the struggle against "post-Zionism."

In light of these circumstances it therefore becomes clear that the formula of "plurality of cultures without multiculturalism" conceals within it a catch for the Arab minority and the advocates of cultural pluralism. In the absence of ideological legitimation for institutionalized multiculturalism, and given the continuing maintenance of primordial identities among broad sectors of the Jewish population, institutionalized "plurality of cultures" is likely to become a tool in the hands of certain cultural groups, such as the "Russian" community, which are interested in strengthening the ethnocratic markers of the Israeli political system.

Conclusion

The first conclusion to be drawn from our discussion is the importance of examining the issue of Russian Israelis' identity in the light of new trends in modern Sovietology. Hence, even if we continue to define the Russian-speaking migrant as "Soviet man," this concept must be given a different meaning from that widespread in research until recently, at least in all matters relating to ethno-national aspects. It seems that "Soviet man" was not a creature devoid of ethnic views, just as the Soviet regime itself was not a supranational regime, except for its ideological claims to such a status. Indeed the opposite applies: throughout all the years that it existed the regime fostered primordial ethnic identities, institutionalizing their mythological attachment to a particular territory, which was defined as an "ethnic territory" belonging exclusively to an "ethnos," in other words an "indigenous nation." This policy of "ethnic engineering" had significant ramifications in the civil area, with the individual's ethnic affiliation with an institutionalized "indigenous nation" guaranteeing him preferential social status over a nonindigenous national minority.

As this process continued over time, the Jewish people therefore became institutionalized as a national minority bereft of any ethnic territory, perceived in terms of their ethnic origin only, resulting in the constant erosion of the Jews' civil status relative to the "indigenous nation" in whose midst they lived. As far as the Jews themselves were concerned, this state of affairs put its stamp on both their ethnic identity and their understanding of themselves as citizens. On the one hand, the upshot of daily confrontations with manifestations of discrimination was the evolution of the Jews' self-image as a group possessing mental and intellectual attributes, as a form of substitute for common national consciousness. On the other hand, the practice of civil discrimination of a national minority as such by the indigenous majority was viewed by the Jews as a self-evident and even legitimate state of affairs.

Coming to Israel, Russian-speaking migrants encountered a complex cultural-political reality that confronted them with the dual challenge of the interaction between a centrifugal tendency and a centripetal one. Despite this complexity, the migrants did not find it difficult to understand the rules of the game, and even managed to make use of both these tendencies in constructing their ethno-national identity and conducting pro-identity group policies that are showing an impact on the political culture of Israel. This overall process can therefore be divided into the following two stages:

1. From 1993 to 1999: Following the centrifugal tendency of institutionalizing diverse autonomous cultures within the Israeli state, "Russian" migrants also managed to establish manifestly ethnic institutions, first and foremost a political party (Yisrael Ba'aliya) and a varied Russian-language press. In this stage, their self image as an educational and intellectual elite serves primarily as a tool for promoting sectorial interests. Thus the particularist ethnic component of identity becomes ever more prominent, while the general national component is still nebulous, amounting to patriotic rhetoric only.
2. From 1999 and onward: Following the centripetal tendency, collective identity becomes identified with a Jewish primordial attachment to Eretz Israel. The salient feature here is the migrants' recognition of similarities between Soviet ethnic policy and the Israeli system of government in all matters relating to the supremacy of the "indigenous" majority over the "nonindigenous" ethnic minority. In this context, the migrants' determination becomes clear to act to strengthen the ethnocentric markers of the Israeli political system, in the framework of opposition to multiculturalism as such. At the same time, "Russian" ethnic institutions have not been abolished, but on the contrary are proliferating, the most decisive proof of which is the founding of the second "Russian" party, Yisrael Beitenu. Nowadays, however, most of the "Russian" institutions are involved in promoting general national political goals, including the struggle against "post-Zionist" cultural pluralism, and the preservation of the ethno-national Jewish character of the state of Israel, and the blocking of the expansion of Israeli Arabs' civil and collective rights.

The accomplishment of these tasks is perceived by the leadership of the "Russian" community as a matter vital to the entire Jewish state. In this view, it is an undertaking to which the Russian-Jewish public, prominent by virtue of its attributes, must make a pivotal contribution.

Notes

1. *Vesti*, 4 August 1994, suppl. "Okna," 14.
2. *Vesti*, 28 December 2000, 7.
3. Info@is2day.co.il, 16 November 2000.
4. *Mig-news* 20, 13 September 2000, 48.
5. *Mig-news* 21, 20 September 2000, 51.
6. *Mig-news* 24, 11 October 2000, 51.
7. *Vesti-2*, 28 September 2000, 2–9; *Mig-news* 32, 6 December 2000, 26–28.
8. *Mig-news* 25, 18 October 2000, 16–19.
9. Ibid.
10. *Mig-news* 32, 6 December 2000, 28–29.
11. *Mig-news* 21, 20 September 2000, 51.
12. *Vesti*, 14 December 2000, 9.
13. *Secret* 302, 13 February 2000, 1.
14. *Kaleidoskop*, 20 June 1997.
15. *Vesti-2*, 28 September 2000, 14.
16. *Vesti*, 11 August 1994, 7.
17. *Novosti Nedeli*, 21 September 2000, 14.
18. Info@isday.co.il, November 2000.

References

Al-Haj, Majid I., and Elazar Leshem. 2000. *Immigrants from the Former Soviet Union in Israel: Ten Years Later*. Haifa: University of Haifa, The Center for Multiculturalism and Educational Research.

Barghoorn, Frederick C. 1986. "Russian Nationalism and Soviet Politics: Official and Unofficial Perspectives." In *The Last Empire: Nationality and the Soviet Future*, ed. Robert Conquest, 30–77. Stanford: Hoover Institution Press.

Ben-Rafael, Eliezer. 1998. "The Israeli Experience in Multiculturalism." In *Blurred Boundaries: Migration, Ethnicity, Citizenship*, ed. Rainer Bauböck and John F. Rundell, 111–141. Vienna: European Centre Vienna.

Ben-Rafael, Eliezer, Elite Olshtain, and Idit Geijst. 1997. "Identity and Language: The Social Interaction of Soviet Jews in Israel." In *Russian Jews on Three Continents: Migration and Resettlement*, ed. Noah Lewin-Epstein, Yaacov Ro'i, and Paul Ritterband, 363–388. London: Frank Cass.

Brubaker, Rogers. 1996. *Nationalism Reframed: Nationhood and the National Question in the New Europe*. Cambridge: Cambridge University Press.

Brzezinski, Zbigniew. 1989/90. "Post-Communist Nationalism." *Foreign Affairs* 68 (5): 1–25.

D'Encausse, Carrere H. 1995. *The Nationality Question in the Soviet Union and Russia*. Oslo: Scandinavian University Press.

Gitelman, Zvi Y. 1995. *Immigration and Identity: The Resettlement and Impact of Soviet Immigrants on Israeli Politics and Society*. Los Angeles: Wilstein Institute of Jewish Policy Studies.

Horowitz, Tamar. 1996. "Between Interweaving and Isolation: Patterns of Absorption of Migrants from the Former Soviet Union in Israel in the First Five Years of their Immigration." *Bitachon Sotziali* 45: 95–111. [Hebrew]

Horowitz, Tamar, and Elazar Leshem. 1998. "The Immigrants from the FSU in the Israeli Cultural Sphere." In *Profile of an Immigration Wave: The Absorption Process of Immigrants from the Former Soviet Union 1990–1995*, ed. Moshe Sicron and Elazar Leshem, 291–333. Jerusalem: Magnes Press. [Hebrew]

Khazanov, Anatoli M. 1995. *After the USSR: Ethnicity, Nationalism and Politics in the Commonwealth of Independent States*. Wisconsin: The University of Wisconsin Press.

Kimmerling, Baruch. 1998. "New Israelis: A Plurality of Cultures without Multiculturalism." *Alpayim* 16: 264–308. [Hebrew]

Konstantinov, Viacheslav. 1991. "Jewish Population of the USSR on the Eve of the Great Exodus." *Jews and Jewish Topics in the Soviet Union and the Eastern Europe* 3 (16): 5–23.

Leshem, Elazar, and Moshe Lissak. 1999. "Development and Consolidation of the Russian Community in Israel." In *Roots and Routes: Ethnicity and Migration in Global Perspective*, ed. Shalva Weil, 135–171. Jerusalem: Magnes Press.

Leshem, Elazar, and Moshe Sicron. 1999. "The Absorption of Soviet Immigrants in Israel." *American Jewish Year Book* 99: 484–522.

Lissak, Moshe, and Eli Leshem. 1995. "The Russian Intelligentsia in Israel: Between Ghettoization and Integration." *Israel Affairs* 2 (1–2): 20–36.

Lomsky-Feder, Edna, and Tamar Rapoport. 2001. "Homecoming, Immigration, and the National Ethos: Russian-Jewish Homecomers Reading Zionism." *Anthropological Quarterly* 74 (1): 1–14.

Shuval, Judith. 1996. "Two Waves of Russian Immigration: Comparative Reference Groups." *Israel Journal of Psychiatry* 33 (1): 1–3.

———. 1998. "Migration to Israel: The Mythology of 'Uniqueness.'" *International Migration* 36 (1): 3–23.

Siegel, Dina. 1998. *The Great Immigration: Russian Jews in Israel*. New York: Berghahn Books.

Smooha, Sammy. 1999. "The Status Quo Option: Israel as an Ethnic Democracy—a Jewish-Democratic State." In *Seven Ways: Theoretical Options for the Status of the Arabs in Israel*, ed. Sarah Osatski-Lazar, Asa'd Ghanem, and Ilan Pappe, 23–77. Givat Haviva: The Institute for Peace Studies. [Hebrew]

Tishkov, Valerii. 1997. *Ethnicity, Nationalism and Conflict in and after the Soviet Union: The Mind Aflame*. Oslo: International Peace Research Institute.

Voronel, Aleksandr. 1998. *V plenu svobody* [The Prisoner of Freedom]. Moscow/ Jerusalem: Nevo Art. [Russian]

Yiftachel, Oren. 2000. "'Ethnocracy,' Geography and Democracy: Notes on the Politics of the Judaization of Israel." *Alpayim* 19: 78–105. [Hebrew]

Zaslavsky, Victor, and Yuri Luryi. 1979. "The Passport System in the USSR and Changes in Soviet Society." *Soviet Union* 6 (2): 137–153.

Part Four

Citizenship and Identity

Chapter 10

NATIONALISM, IDENTITY, AND CITIZENSHIP

An Epilogue to the Yehoshua-Shammas Debate

Baruch Kimmerling

A Non-Platonic Dialogue

On the eve of the Jewish New Year, on 13 September 1985, Anton Shammas—the Israeli-Arab writer, essayist, translator, journalist, and the author of *Arabesque*,[1] an autobiographical Hebrew novel of a youngster growing up as a hybrid of Jewish-Arab culture and identity in the village Fasuta—aroused bitter controversy among the Israeli elite. In a brief article he accused Israel of excluding Israeli-Palestinians from participation in the common political, cultural, and collective identity or nationality (Shammas 1985).

His accusations of extreme discriminatory policy against Israel's Arab citizens were by no means a new issue on the Israeli political agenda. Between 1949 and 1966, Israeli Arabs had been subject to crass military rule, which served as a useful umbrella for land confiscation, exclusion from the labor market, and de facto deprivation of most citizen and human rights. Since 1966 their condition has gradually improved; yet still no Jewish intellectual would deny that Israeli-Palestinians have remained an underprivileged ethnic or national minority. Shammas's claim, however, went far beyond the regular complaints and protests against discrimination of a minority group within a supposed democratic and humanistic polity. Shammas called for space and participation for the "Israeli Arabs" within the holy of holiest of Israeli collective identity and Israeli culture.[2]

Faced with such a provocation, even the liberal, "leftist," and dovish writer A. B. Yehoshua, was unable to restrain himself. Although he was not the only respondent to Shammas, he was one of the most strident and certainly the most prominent. "I am suggesting to you," shouted Yehoshua, "that if you want to exercise your full identity, if you want to live in a state that has a Palestinian character with a genuine Palestinian culture, arise, take your chattels, and move yourself one hundred yards eastward, into the independent Palestinian state, that will be established alongside Israel." [3] Alluding to God's commandment to Abraham to leave his home and go forth into the land God will show him, the land of Canaan, Shammas angrily responded: "I have no intention to leave my motherland and my father's home, for the country Yehoshua will show me."[4]

Another respondent to Shammas's challenge was the writer of Mizrahi origin, Sami Michael (1986). He wrote that "Many Jews from every [ideological] camp understand his pain and identify with his suffering as a member of a minority. Many are ready to pay a price in order to make it more comfortable for him [to be a minority], but not to the point where they [the Jews] make themselves into a minority." Here the claim for equal civil and symbolic rights for Israeli Arab citizens was promptly transformed into the restoration of the situation in which Jews were a minority in Palestine (or in fact anywhere in the world) and the Jewish nation-state would be dismantled.

Nonetheless, Anton Shammas never intended to dismantle the state, but rather to challenge its constructions as a homogenous ethno-national entity and identity. He wanted to invent and create a new local national identity, or nationality, common to Jews and Arabs of the country, and based solely on state citizenship and territory.

He stated explicitly, "What I'm trying to do—mulishly, it seems—is to un-Jew the Hebrew language, to make it more Israeli and less Jewish, thus bringing it back to its Semitic origins, to its place. This is a parallel to what I think the state should be. As English is the language of those who speak it, so is Hebrew; and so the state, should be the state of those who live in it, not of those who play with its destiny with a remote control in hand" (Shammas 1989). And he added, "the State of Israel demands that its Arab citizens take their citizenship seriously. But when they try to do so, it promptly informs them that their participation in the state is merely social, and that for the political fulfillment of their identity, they must look somewhere else (i.e., to the Palestinian nation). When they do look elsewhere for their national identity, the state at once charges them with subversion; and, needless to say, as subversives they cannot be accepted as Israelis" (Shammas 1989).

The controversy between Yehoshua and Shammas over the meaning and boundaries of Israeli identity was reopened six years later, in a debate held in 1992. This time Shammas was much more articulate in his arguments and Yehoshua was more defensive.[5]

"My problem and debate with Anton," suggested Yehoshua, "are not about equality, but about identity. Because as a national minority in an Israeli state...."

"What's an Israeli state?" Shammas shot back. "There's no such thing!"

"What do you mean there's no such thing? ... For me, 'Israeli' is the authentic, complete, and consummate word for the concept 'Jewish.'

Israeliness is the total, perfect, and original Judaism, one that should provide answers in all areas of life."[6]

"You see Israeliness as total Jewishness, and I don't see where you fit me, the Arab, into that Israeliness. Under the rug? In some corner of the kitchen? Maybe you won't even give me a key to get into the house?"

"But, Anton, think of a Pakistani coming to England today, with a British passport and telling the British, 'Let's create the British nationality together. I want Pakistani-Muslim symbols....'"

"Buli [Yehoshua's nickname], the minute a man like you does not understand the basic difference between the Pakistani who comes to England and the Galilean who has been in Fasuta for untold generations, then what do you want us to talk about? I always said that the Zionist state's most serious mistake in 1948 was that it kept the 156,000 Arabs who did not run away and were not expelled. If you really wanted to establish a Jewish state, you should have kicked me out of Fasuta, too. You didn't do it—so treat me as an equal. As an equal in Israeliness."

"But you won't receive one single right more for belonging to the Israeli nation. On the contrary. I'll take away your special minority rights.... For instance, you'll have to study Bible, just as in France all citizens study Molière and in England Shakespeare."

"But as a literary text..."

"What do you mean?! We have no Shakespeare or Molière. We have the Bible, the Talmud, and Jewish history, and you will study them, and in Hebrew...."

"If that's the case, then Judaism also has been separated from Israeliness, and you'll oppose that by force of arms."

"But how is that possible? Try, for instance, separating France from Frenchness—it is impossible."

"France and Frenchness come from the same root. But Judaism and Israeliness are a different matter. That's why I advocate the de-Judaization and de-Zionization of Israel.... I'm asking you for a new definition of the term 'Israeli,' so that it will include me as well, a definition in territorial terms that you distort, because you're looking at it from the Jewish point of view.... [However,] ultimately we are dealing with the question of identity; the identity that is given to us by those who have the power to do so."

"... I'm not excluding you. My Israeliness includes you and all the Israeli Arabs as partners in the fabric of life here. Partners in that you vote for the Knesset [Israeli parliament], on creation of Israeli citizenship as a whole...."

"You want me to vote for the Knesset so you can show off your democracy to the enlightened world. I'm not willing to be a party to that. I know that all I can do here is to vote and nothing else. I know that my mother would never be able to see me become Israel's Minister of Education."

Shammas had already demonstrated several years before this exchange that he possessed a comprehensive and sweeping understanding about the past, present, and what should be done in the future. Zionism, as a national movement, Shammas argued, achieved its historic role with the establishment of the state. Every person currently living within the "green line,"[7] who is a citizen of the state of Israel, should be defined as an "Israeli." The time has come to transform the Law of Return into a regular immigration law, as exists in Western secular and democratic states. This state will have the authority to decide who may be called Israeli, but Israeliness should no longer be automatic or self-evidently granted only to Jews. All Israelis should be equal with regard to rights and duties. As the bottom line of his argument, he proclaimed that "we, the members of the Israeli nation, should then wait, with Levantine patience, for the first Jew to proclaim at the head of the camp: 'Zionism is dead, long live the Israeli nation!' That in the hope that the entire [Jewish] camp will follow after him."[8]

Subjects and Citizens

We may grossly divide the states of the world into two categories: subject-states and citizen-states. As was argued by T. H. Marshall (1983), subject-states emphasize the obligations of the individual toward the state and its rulers, while citizen-states emphasize the rights that the state is obliged to grant to its citizens. Between these two ideal types exist a considerable number of mixed types. Subject states are characterized by the unconditional status of the state's population as the state's property, lacking a true basis or claim to any rights based on universal and egalitarian membership in the state. Relations between the state and its subjects are patronage-like: different groups (such as class, ethnic, gender, religious, racial, or occupational groups) receive favors and privileges according to their closeness to the state's rulers and ruling strata in exchange for loyalties to the state's ruler. This loyalty is usually constructed and camouflaged as patriotism, nationalism, and commitment to the state as "motherland."

The citizen-state, in contrast, represents a kind of sociopolitical order based on an unwritten conditional contract between the state and each individual member. The state promises to grant a package of citizen rights that go beyond those self-evident human rights, as defined by the Charter of the United, whose inclusion as self-evident citizen rights and internalization by the state and its legislative and social welfare systems are inviolable. All these citizen rights are provided in exchange for a package of citizen obligations toward the state. The state's minimal obligations are to provide law and order and defense from external threats on the citizen's life, to insure property and freedoms, and to supply some basic needs, such as health services, schooling, and subsistence. In addition, the state possesses a legitimate monopoly on the exercise of violent power within its sovereign territory, that is, the right to make war and peace with other states and external entities. In exchange, the citizen's obligations toward the state are to obey the law, to pay the imposed taxes, to answer the call to military service, and even to endanger one's own life as the ultimate sacrifice to the state's demands.

No wonder that Charles Tilly defined these state-citizen relationships in terms of Mafia-client relations: the citizen has to pay the "organization" protection fees. Beyond these reciprocal relationships, any expansion of the state's role (for example the scope of the welfare offered by the state or its redistributive agencies) is the subject of perpetual negotiation and bargaining between the state and various groups of citizens.

An additional major principle of the notion of citizenship is its universalistic character, or more simply put: all citizens of the state possess equal constitutional rights. This means that the same criteria for access to both material and symbolic common goods are indiscriminately assured for the entire citizenship population and that the same duties are demanded of all.

The scope and validity of rights and obligations imply the inclusion of an individual or social category within the boundaries of the state. The definition of citizenship as a personal status—even if the status symbolizes membership in a collective of equal citizens or in the nation-state as a "membership organization" in Brubaker's (1992) terms—presumes the existence of an individual to whom rights and obligations are "naturally" determined by an invisible social contract. The definition of citizenship as a legal-personal status according to Tilly (1995), is a series of continuing exchanges between persons of a given state in which each has enforceable rights and obligations "by virtue." These virtues or traits are based on an individual's membership as an exclusive category, that is, native-born or naturalized, and on the individual's relation to the state rather than to any other authority the agent may enjoy. This equation is reversed in a situation of an active mass immigrant-settler society, in which the natives are not a part of the "nationality" of the nation-state.

This definition of citizenship in terms of the individual-state relationship, focuses attention on the juridical, political, and symbolical levels of the mutual relationships between individuals and the state (Turner 1983; 1997). It presumes at least a legal membership in the polity. In fact, this is apparently congruent with liberal theory and its approach to citizenship, which defines it as a "set of normative expectations specifying the relationship between the nation-state and its individual members which procedurally establish the rights and the obligations of members and a set of practices by which these expectations are realized" (Peled 1992). Under such definition, individuals are not committed to each other and in fact lack "communal" responsibility toward their fellow citizens. Rights and duties are fulfilled without the help of intermediaries such as institutions and communities, but rather as a direct link between each person and the state (Roche 1987).

More precisely, the state relates and constructs citizenship as individual or collective categories according to its various interests and internal power structure. Thus, some states tend to delimit different types and degrees of citizenship, for example, ethnic-, class-, or gender-based citizenship (Vogel 1991; Walby 1992, 1994; Hindess 1993: 19–21; Yuval-Davis 1997). Thus, within the same state different patterns of citizenship may coexist, according to differential access to the rights and obligations of citizenship. The question is how much the underprivileged or passive citizens consider their lowered level of obligations to the state[9] as a privilege that compensates them for their lowered rights in other spheres, and not as a symbol of their total exclusion from membership in the state. Are "individual-minority rights" a worthy compensation for a lower degree and quality of citizen rights, as hinted by A. B. Yehoshua in equating "citizen rights" with "minority rights"?

Theoretically, the problem should be even more acute: Can a claim that is based on the liberal dogma of unalienable equal citizen rights, which is itself based on the right of an individual, legitimately profess claims for equal collective rights? Can individual citizen rights be separated from collective religious, ethnic, or cultural rights? This whole problematic sounds somewhat familiar, and indeed resembles the nineteenth-century French and German Enlightenment and Emancipator movement slogans that a Jew as a person should enjoy full citizen rights, but Jews as a collective—nothing. Rightly, the Jews considered this formula as covert anti-Semitism and as an attempt to dissolve Jewish identity, culture, religion, and community.

Nonetheless, various patterns and qualities of citizenship that grant differential scopes and degrees of rights reflect how states use citizenship to incorporate social groups (such as gender, class, ethnicity, religion, and nationality) into their structures and to redefine or re-create social categories. As a consequence, patterns of citizenship and diverse cultural, ethnic, and political identities are shaped, created, or reinforced. In the case at hand, the identity of "Israeli Arabs," or even "Israeli-Palestinians" was created rather successfully. This seems to fit with Harrison C. White's (1992) and Jacques Derrida's claim that self-imposed identity, not to mention that imposed by others, is an act of violence. This is because "the rapport of self-identity is itself always a rapport of violence with the other; so that the notions of property, appropriation and self-presence, so central to logocentric metaphysics, are essentially dependent on an oppositional relation with otherness. In this sense, identity presupposes alterity" (Derrida 1984). On the other hand, Dahlia Moore and I have shown how the maneuvering of different definitions of self-identity in different social and political contexts can be employed as a survival strategy for minority groups (Kimmerling and Moore 1997; Moore and Kimmerling 1995).

Different positions within the holy civic communion of the state prescribe what Yasemin Soysal (1994) has conceptualized as "models of membership," or "institutionalised scripts and understandings of the relationships between individuals, the state, and the polity as well as the organizational structures and practices that maintain that relationship." These "scripts and understandings" include cultural assumptions that shape the boundaries of the citizens' collectivity, the different positions within it, and the ways in which access to citizenship is interpreted. These cultural assumptions may be conceptualized as national projects. They are national projects not because they constitute a desire for a separate political and cultural representation for a collectivity, but because they are shaped through narratives and discourses of the state's interests in the discursive space of citizenship (Habermas 1997).

The convention is that historical processes shape national projects. These processes and constraints explain the type of ties between citizenship and national identity that national projects promote. As such, they frame the conception of the links between citizenship and nationality, and envision the exclusivity or inclusiveness of those ties as well as their primordial or civil character.

Moreover, the patterns or degree of inclusion (full, partial, differential, or exclusion) in the community of citizens, and the arenas through which inclusion is concretized and symbolized, are central to the understanding of how individuals and social groups react to the state's practices. Patterns of inclusion are central to the understanding of the patterns of social action and identity mobilized in transactions (bargaining or conflict) between individuals, social groups, and the state's agents. These negotiations and bargaining over citizenship are not only related to "who gets what," but also to "who is what" and "who can decide who is what." The kinds of identities and narratives raised in the process of claims making and negotiations over citizenship, including the terms and degree of participation and membership demanded, are thus central to the understanding of those identities that claim recognition (Yeatman 1994).

The Israeli State and Identity

As was already demonstrated, citizenship includes a basic and inherent contradiction. On the one hand, it is a legal status granted by the modern state to its members. On the other hand, the state is not just a rational-bureaucratic and identity-indifferent organization, but also the embodiment of ethnic and national, and sometimes also religious, attachments. The Israeli state takes this contradiction to its logical and sociological end. By its own constitutional definition, Israel is "Jewish and democratic." At first glance, nothing is wrong or contradictory in this definition. After all, it sounds precisely like "French and democratic" or "German and democratic." After all, a Jew who was entitled to French or German citizenship, but needed to keep his or her ethnic or religious identity, became a "French-Jew" or "Jewish-French," etc. The same goes for "Turkish-German" or even "Muslim-French." Nevertheless, taking into account that Israel is a "Jewish state," can we even consider a fusion of "Jewish-Christian," "Jewish-Muslim," or "Jewish-Buddhist"? These "impossible combinations" are almost inconsiderable to the "Jewish-Israeli" ear—and by the way why not a "Jewish-Jew"? But if Israel is a "Jewish nation-state," implying that the Jews are a nation and "Judaism" is actually "Jewish national identity," why does the existence of "Jewish citizenship" in the Jewish nation-state sound so weird?

In fact, for most of us the answer is taken to be self-evident. It is not accidental that the inscription on the rubric of my official ID card is "nationality (*leom*): Jewish" and not "citizenship: Jewish" or even "Israeli." This is simply because neither Jewish nationalism in its Zionist incarnation nor the Israeli state were able to invent or construct a purely secular or a civil national identity. [10] Zionist nationalism was generally not constructed as a pure ideology, but was intermingled with other ideologies, such as classical liberalism, or with varieties of socialism, including communism (Kimmerling 1985). It is also necessary to remember that the beginnings of Jewish national thought and activity were shaped at the end of the colonialist era, when Jewish migration was intertwined with large scale intercontinental population movements. During this era, the formation and construction of immigrant-settler nations was still at its height. European colonialism was the dominant world order, and Eurocentrism was the hegemonic cultural approach.

Jewish-religious nationalism, which approximated this approach from a religious outlook, was a negligible and marginal minority within the Jewish religious collectivity since religious principles did not permit "forcing the End,"[11] or achieving collective salvation without divine intervention. In spite of this, the religious worldview looked positively on ascendance (*aliyah*) to the Holy Land. But the religious-national mixture was a relatively marginal phenomenon, which demanded a very great intellectual-interpretive effort. Even today its theological standing within Judaism is quite shaky and problematic.[12] Thus, for example, the first rabbi who can be classified as a "Zionist," Samuel Mohilever, was more concerned with convincing secular Jews to consider the sensitivities of fervently observant Jews than he was with the theological problems of a return to Zion in his day. Practically speaking, Mohilever failed in his mission to bring about an understanding among the founding fathers of Zionism, and played a part in starting the split between religious and secular components of the movement. This laid the foundations for the beginnings of the Mizrahi movement (short for *mercaz ruchani* or "spiritual center"), which in 1902 incorporated the group of Rabbi Isaac Jacob Reines.[13]

Even the absence of distinction between religion and nation is not however, the primary cause for, but itself flows from, the basic nature of the Israeli state, which cannot be understood apart from its historical-sociological context. Israel was formed as a society of settler-immigrants, and is still an active immigrant society, engaged in the settlement process to this very day. Two mutually complementary political practices are involved. The first is what we like to call Israel's existence as an "immigrant-absorbing state"; the second involves the view that its bound-aries are still in the process of formation with regard to their expansion and contraction. Israeli Jews therefore belong to the category of "immi-grant-settler" nations, similar to the nations formed in North and South America, in North Africa (French Algeria), and in white South Africa, Australia, and New Zealand. Despite the tremendously fast and constant transformation that this society is undergoing, its fundamental character as a settler-society—which must consolidate itself in a given territory, liv-ing by the sword and with a need to create a space for itself—remains constant. The Arab inhabitants, in whose midst the Jewish immigrants settled, have, almost from the beginning of Jewish settlement, consis-tently resisted the process with great determination. The Jewish-Arab conflict flows from this. Indeed, it is true that Zionism, the national move-ment that motivated Jewish immigration and settlement but that was also formed by it, was clever enough to distance itself from the global colonial context—the matrix out of which it was born. Zionism emphasized the uniqueness of the "Jewish problem," anti-Semitism, persecutions, and, later, the Holocaust, and presented itself as the sole realistic and moral solution. Thus, the Jewish immigration movement was successfully rep-resented as a "return to Zion" correcting an injustice that had lasted for thousands of years, and as totally disconnected from the movements of European immigration to other continents. Nonetheless, the fact that Jew-ish immigration and settlement were construed in these terms was not enough to change their basic social-cultural character.

In reality, Israeli society was established mostly by immigrants from an ethnic, religious, and cultural background that differed from the broad local population, and who thought of themselves as part of "West-ern society." In the political culture of the postcolonial world order, this society has been plagued by the problem of existential legitimacy. It has had to repeatedly explain to itself and to the international community why it chose Palestine, the land retitled as "The Land of Israel," as its tar-get territory for settlement. For behold, Palestine was not chosen for its fertile soil, its natural treasures, the presence of a cheap labor force, nor for its potential markets; rather, it was chosen on the basis of ideological-religious motives (Kimmerling 1983: chap. 7). This caused the Zionist project to be not only unable to support itself from an economic point of view, but also, as an essentially religious project, unable to disconnect itself from its original identity as a quasi-messianic movement. The essence of this society and state's right and reason to exist is embedded in symbols, ideas, and religious scriptures, even if there has been an attempt to give them a secular reinterpretation and context. Indeed, the society was made captive from the beginning by its choice of target ter-ritory for immigration and nation-building. For then neither the nation nor its culture could successfully be built apart from the religious con-text, even when its prophets, priests, builders, and fighters saw them-selves as completely secular.

At least three basic laws[14] and one additional regular law state that Israel is a "Jewish and democratic state." The definition of "Jewishness" that the state itself has adopted, however, transforms these two concepts—"democracy" and "Jewishness"—into mutually exclusive ones in certain areas (Kimmerling 1999). As a result, a major part of the practices engaged in by the state hardly conform to usually accepted notions of Western-liberal and enlightened democracy. Israel inherited what is known as the *millet* system from both the Ottoman Empire and the British colonial administration.[15] This system provides that "religious-ethnic" communities should enjoy autonomy from the state and have sole jurisdiction in matters of personal status litigation. Even before its establishment as a sovereign entity, the Israeli state decided to preserve the institution of the *millets* and to construct a *millet* form of citizenship. Therefore, citizens have been subjected to two separate legal and judicial systems that operate according to different and even opposing principles. One is secular, "Western," and universalistic; the other is religious and primordial, and is mainly run—if we are speaking about Jews—according to the Orthodox interpretation of Halacha. The minorities, who were thus defined ab initio as religious minorities, were also forced to conduct their "autonomous" lives in accordance with this dual system. The Israeli parliament has so far given up its authority to legislate in crucial areas and has recognized a parallel legal and judicial system outside its control. In fact, the state has obligated itself to relate to rules of Halacha, *shariya*,[16] and diverse Christian denominational rules as if they were its own law.

Jewish-religious elements have been incorporated into other areas of legislation as well, such as the Work Hours and Days of Rest Law, the Freedom of Occupation Law, and the like. In contrast to these, the Law of Return and Law of Citizenship, immigration laws, which were intended as a sort of "affirmative action" (or corrective discrimination) on behalf of world Jewry after the Holocaust, are relatively liberal ordinances. One must of course qualify this characterization, since these laws were indeed discriminatory against both those Palestinians who were uprooted from the territory that fell under the rule of the new state and those who remained and were for the most part denied family reunification. Although the Law of Return and the Law of Citizenship are not based on the theological definition of Judaism,[17] and in practice these laws grant Israeli citizenship (and define the boundaries of Judaism) more or less in accordance with the broader definition of the Nuremberg Laws, the logic underlying them is internally consistent and justified. These laws were intended to grant citizenship to almost everyone who suffered persecution as a Jew, even if the individual case did not correspond with the halachic definition of Jewishness. If the Law of Return and the Law of Citizenship have been among the most problematic laws in Israel until now, they have nevertheless preserved relatively open "Jewish" boundaries. The currently proposed "Conversion Law"[18] however, has apparently been intended to "heal" the breach and give the orthodox a monopoly on this essential domain of determination of the boundaries of the collectivity. Complementing the laws of return and citizenship is the Law on the Status of the World Zionist Organization (of the Jewish Agency), which also facilitates the allocation of particularistic benefits to Jewish citizens of the state alone. Yet another constitutional arrangement is inherent in the Social Security Law, which for many years has been complemented by a set of welfare laws, in which the only eligible beneficiaries are "former soldiers" and their families. This most unsubtle code phrase is intended to construct a broad separation between Jewish and Arab citizens. Similarly, the agreement between the Jewish National Fund and the Israel Lands Administration prevents the leasing of state lands, 93 percent of the territory inside the "green line," to non-Jews.

Conclusions

Israeli national identity is based on a mixture of both religious-primordial symbols and orientations and civil and universalistic orientations. These two components of Israeli Zionism complement each the other, but also introduce strains, contradictions, and distortions into the democratic regime. The primordial component is exclusionary and emphasizes Jewish ethnocentrism, while the civil component is inclusive and based on the modern notion of citizenship. On the one hand, the primordial orientation envisions the state as a homogenous Jewish nation-state, in which ethnic or national minorities have some "protected" individual rights as citizens. In this view, citizenship is regarded as a legal status granted to individuals but limited to certain fields. On the other hand, the civil orientation regards citizenship not as a mere legal status, but also as an all-encompassing dominant cultural and political metaidentity, common to all citizens of the state.

According to the primordial orientation, "the people" constitute a state, which is entitled to grant different kinds of "membership cards" to the population under its control, ranging from "full citizenship" to partial rights for those who are seen as "subjects" under state control. The opposite approach perceives citizenship as an absolute right, granted at birth to any member of a state with a democratic regime. This citizenship and the rights it supplies are considered the ultimate base for a common national identity and as the necessary condition for a state's very existence.

The debate between A. B. Yehoshua and Anton Shammas over the fundamentals of Israeli society centered around this primordial-civil and symbolic axis. The liberal Jewish Yehoshua was anxious to preserve the exclusive Jewish ethno-national identity of the state, while the Arab-Palestinian Shammas demanded, for his own interest, equal symbolic and cultural shares for his local Arabness under a reshaped universal Israeli nationality based on citizenship. Conceptually speaking, Shammas fused the liberal-individualistic approach to citizenship and the communitarian construction of citizenship (Daly 1993; Oldfield 1990). Basically, his hidden argument is that citizenship can be shaped and reshaped by an interaction between the individual (as a part of a community) and the community (that makes individuals), and that individuals have the right to equal representation within the national identity as a part of a minority community.

Notes

1. Published in 1986 by the mainstream Hebrew-Zionist publishing house Am Oved. Shammas is also well known for his Hebrew translations of Emil Habibi's powerful novels and stories that depict, through satire and irony, the life of Arabs under Israeli control and the destruction and uprooting of the Arab community during the 1948 War.
2. Arabs are in a continuous dilemma between demanding equal and full (not separate) participation in the common material and cultural goods of the Israeli state and society and demanding autonomous spaces within the state. Recently, some Arab intellectuals suggest a binational state within the whole land of colonial Palestine instead of the two-state solution proposed by them before. For a historical analysis of the Arab Palestinian identity, its crystallization and development, see Kimmerling 2000.
3. Yehoshua 1985. Also see idem 1986. For an excellent overview and analysis of the controversy in its wider context, see Silberstein 1999: 127–165. Yehoshua's response was incredibly harsh, because it resembled the far-right fringe claim of expulsion ("transfer") of all the Arabs from the "Land of Israel."
4. As a matter of fact, Shammas did it. About ten years ago he left the country and settled in Ann Arbor (Michigan), where he accepted a permanent post of professor of Arabic and Hebrew cultural studies.
5. This took place in a private meeting in 1992, when Shammas, who had since moved to the U.S., returned to Israel for a visit. He and the writer David Grossman met with Yehoshua at the latter's home in Haifa. The debate is reported in Grossman 1994: 250–277. The book was first published in Hebrew in 1992. The conversation has been edited and adapted for print.
6. Here Yehoshua adopted the conventional Israeli Zionist belief that Judaism in exile, or diaspora, can only be a partial identity, while the complete or total fulfillment of Jewishness, whatever it might mean, can be expressed only within the framework of a territorial nation-state, or Zion. Thus, the "Israeli" is the Jew who has returned to Palestine ("Eretz Israel"—the "Land of Israel") to constitute the sovereign Jewish nation-state.
7. The armistice border with the Arab states from 1949 to the 1967 War.
8. Shammas 1987. One can read the debate between Shammas and Yehoshua as one of conflicting interpretations of culture and cultural identity. On the one hand, in contrast to Yehoshua's ethnocentric definition of Israeli identity, Shammas's antiessentialistic position resembles the recent strongly contested conceptions of identity that have been espoused by thinkers such as Edward Said, Homi Bhabha, Stuart Hall, and the feminist critic Judith Butler. In their writings, cultural identity is perceived as a dynamic process that can best be understood in relation to the "cultural others" over and against which a group defines itself. See Butler 1990.
9. Such as, for example, exemption from military service in a system that still exercises a universal and obligatory draft. Horowitz and Kimmerling 1974. The "active versus passive" citizenship is Bryan Turner's (1990) concept.

10. Or, as was stated by Anton Shammas: "My nationality, according to the Israeli Ministry of the Interior, is 'Arab'; and my Israeli passport doesn't specify my nationality at all. Instead, it states on the front page that I'm an Israeli citizen.... If I wrote "Arab" under *Nationalité*, in the French form, I would be telling the truth according to the state that had issued my identity card and my passport, but then it might complicate things with the French authorities. On the other hand, writing "Israeli" under *Nationalité* is worse still, because in that case I would be telling a lie; my passport doesn't say that at all, and neither does my I.D." Shammas continued: "I do not know many people in the Middle East who can differentiate between "citizenship," "nation" (*leom*), "nationalism" (*leumiut*), "nationalism" (*leumanut*), "people" (*Am*), and "nation" (*umah*). In Arabic, as in Hebrew, there is no equivalent for the English word 'nationality.'" See Shammas 1995.
11. See, for example, the appendix of Ravitzki 1996.
12. See, for example, Friedman 1989.
13. Reines (1839–1915) was an orthodox rabbi of the community of Lida who called for some adaptation of the Halacha to the modernizing world in order to prevent the secularization of the Jews. He first joined the Lovers of Zion movement and later Herzl's "political Zionism." His major approach was that Zionism should be a genuine religious movement.
14. See "Basic Law: Knesset," "Basic Law: Freedom of Occupation (1992)," and "Basic Law: Human Dignity and Liberty (1992)." The additional "regular" Law is the Parties' Law. A basic law is one passed by a special majority of the Knesset, and intended to be incorporated in any future written constitution (Israel lacks a complete written constitution at present).
15. Since 1948, the Israeli government has recognized certain established religious groups, whose leaders are granted special status even when they are tiny minorities. These communities are entitled to state financial support and tax exemptions. According to Israeli legislation, all residents must belong to a religious denomination whose rules they are obliged to follow with regard to marriage, divorce, and burial. British colonial rule recognized ten *millets* (i.e., Jews and nine Christian denominations). The Israeli state added to these the Druze in 1957, the Evangelical Episcopal Church in 1970, and the Bahai in 1971. Muslims have not been officially recognized, but their religious courts de facto have similar authority to a *millet* institution. All other groups from conservative and reform Jews to "new religious" groups (i.e., cults) are not recognized.
16. Islamic religious law.
17. One born to a Jewish mother or "converted according to Halacha." However, the law does not include this crucial last phrase, thus allowing non-Orthodox converts (abroad) and even family members who are not converts to enter and enjoy the privileges granted according to the immigration law known as the Law of Return.
18. This proposed law states that only Orthodox conversions to Judaism will be recognized by the state.

References

Brubaker, Rogers. 1992. *Citizenship and Nationhood in France and Germany.* Cambridge, Mass.: Harvard University Press.

Butler, Judith F. 1990. *Gender Trouble: Feminism and Subversion of Identity.* New York: Routledge.

Daly, M. 1993. *Communitarianism: Belonging and Commitment in a Pluralist Democracy.* London: Watsworth.

Derrida, Jacques. 1984. "Deconstruction and the Other." In *Dialogues with Contemporary Thinkers,* ed. Richard Kearney, 105–126. Manchester: University of Manchester Press.

Friedman, Menachem. 1989. "The State of Israel as a Theological Dilemma." In *The Israeli State and Society: Boundaries and Frontiers,* ed. Baruch Kimmerling, 163–215. Albany: The State University of New York Press.

Grossman, David. 1994. *Sleeping on a Wire: Conversations with Palestinians in Israel.* London: Picador.

Habermas, Jürgen. 1975. *Legitimation Crisis.* Boston: Beacon Press.

Hindess, Barry. 1993. "Citizenship in the Modern West." In *Citizenship and Social Theory,* ed. Bryan S. Turner, 19–35. London: Sage.

Horowitz, Dan, and Baruch Kimmerling. 1974. "Some Implications of Military Service and the Reserves System in Israel." *European Journal of Sociology* 5 (2): 252–276.

Kimmerling, Baruch. 1983. *Zionism and Territory: The Socioterritorial Dimensions of Zionist Politics.* Berkeley: Institute of International Studies, University of California.

———. 1985. "Between the Primordial and the Civil Definitions of the Collective Identity." In *Comparative Social Dynamics,* ed. E. Cohen, M. Lissak, and U. Almagor, 286–292. Boulder: Westview.

———. 1999. "Religion, Nationalism and Democracy in Israel." *Constellations* 6 (3): 339–363.

———. 2000. "Process of Formation of Palestinian Collective Identities: The Ottoman and Colonial Periods." *Middle Eastern Studies* 36 (2): 41–82.

Kimmerling, Baruch, and Dahlia Moore. 1997. "Collective Identity as Agency, and Structuration of Society: Tested by the Israeli Case." *International Review of Sociology* 7 (1): 25–50.

Marshall, Thomas H. 1983. "Citizenship and Social Class." In *States and Societies,* ed. David Held et al., 248–260. New York: New York University Press.

Michael, Sami. 1986. "The Arabesques of Zionism: Footnotes on the Debate between A.B. Yehoshua and Anton Shammas." *Moznayim* 160: 17. [Hebrew]

Moore, Dahlia, and Baruch Kimmerling. 1995. "Individual Strategies of Adopting Collective Identities: The Israeli Case." *International Sociology* 4: 387–408.

Oldfield, A. 1990. *Citizenship and Community: Civic Republicanism and the Modern World.* London: Routledge.

Peled, Yoav. 1992. "Ethnic Democracy and the Legal Construction of Citizenship: Arab Citizens of the Jewish State." *American Political Science Review* 86 (2): 433.

Ravitzky, Aviezer. 1996. *Messianism, Zionism and Jewish Religious Radicalism.* Chicago: University of Chicago Press.

Roche, Maurice. 1987. "Citizenship, Social Theory and Social Change." *Theory and Society* 16: 363–399.

Shammas, Anton. 1985. "A New Year for the Jews." *Kol Ha'Ir,* 13 September. [Hebrew]

———. 1986. *Arabesque.* Tel Aviv: Am Oved. [Hebrew]

———. 1987. "We? Who Is We?" *Politika* 17: 25–30. [Hebrew].

———. 1988. "A Stone's Throw." *New York Review of Books,* 29 September: 9.

———. 1989. "Your Worst Nightmare." *Jewish Frontier* 56 (4): 10.

———. 1995. "Palestinians in Israel: You Ain't Seen Nothin' Yet." *Journal of the International Institute* 3 (1):24–25.

Silberstein, Laurence J. 1999. *Postzionism Debates: Knowledge and Power in Israeli Culture.* New York/London: Routledge.

Soysal, Yasemin N. 1994. *Limits of Citizenship.* Chicago: Chicago University Press.

Tilly, Charles. 1995. "Citizenship, Identity and Social History." *International Review of Social History* 40: 8.

Turner, Bryan S. 1990. "Outline of a Theory on Citizenship." *Sociology* 234 (2): 189–218.

———. 1993. "Contemporary Problems in the Theory of Citizenship." In *Citizenship and Social Theory*, ed. Bryan S. Turner, 1–18. London: Sage.

———. 1997. "Citizenship Studies: A General Theory." *Citizenship Studies* 1: 5–18.

Vogel, Ursula. 1991. "Is Citizenship Gender-Specific?" In *The Frontiers of Citizenship*, ed. Ursula Vogel and Michael Moran, 58–86. London: Macmillan.

Walby, Sylvia. 1992. "Women and Nation." *International Journal of Comparative Sociology* 33: 81–100.

———. 1994. "Is Citizenship Gendered?" *Sociology* 28: 379–395.

White, Harrison C. 1992. *Identity and Control: A Structural Theory of Social Action*. Princeton: Princeton University Press.

Yeatman, Anna. 1994. "Beyond Natural Right: The Conditions for Universal Citizenship." In *Postmodern Revisioning of the Political*, ed. Anna Yeatman, 57–79. London: Routledge.

Yehoshua, A. B. 1985. "The Quilt of the Left." *Politika* 4: 8–9. [Hebrew]

———. 1986. "An Answer to Anton." *Kol Ha'Ir*, 31 January.

Yuval-Davis, Nira. 1997. *Gender and Nation*. London: Sage.

— *Chapter 11* —

THE FUTURE OF ARAB CITIZENSHIP IN ISRAEL

Jewish-Zionist Time in a Place with
No Palestinian Memory

❦

Hassan Jabareen

Introduction

On 8 March 2000, Israel's Supreme Court granted the petition of the Qa'dan family—Palestinian citizens of Israel—who wanted to buy a house in a new community-based village called Katzir.[1] The respondents—the Israel Lands Administration, the Jewish Agency, the Katzir Cooperative Association, and others—had rejected their application on the grounds that the locality was intended for Jews only. The Supreme Court determined that this constituted discrimination on the basis of nationality, and it ruled that the state is prohibited from using "national institutions" to perform these discriminatory acts on its behalf. An important precedent, this decision sparked considerable public reaction. Until the handing down of the *Qa'dan* judgment, Palestinian citizens, who make up nearly 20 percent of Israel's citizens, were absolutely excluded from localities established by the state in conjunction with Zionist bodies such as the Jewish Agency and the Jewish National Fund.

Since its establishment, Israel has pursued a lands and rural settlement policy under which Arab ownership of the land has been transferred to the Jewish population for its use. These transfers have been based on sophisticated legislative and political mechanisms. Prior to 1948, only around 7 percent of the some 20.5 million dunams, which constituted the area of the new state, was in the hands of the Jews. Today, the state of Israel controls over 93 percent of the lands that make up its territory. The government body that administers the state's lands is the Israel Lands Administration.

The *Qa'dan* judgment exposes one of the many mechanisms of Jewish control over the land. The Israel Lands Administration transferred land to the Jewish Agency, which claims to represent the aggregate of Jewish interests both worldwide and in the state of Israel. The Jewish Agency decided to construct a rural community village called Katzir on the land that it had received from the state. When the Qa'dan family applied to buy a housing unit in the new village, they were told that they did not meet the criteria of the Jewish Agency, which was promoting Jewish interests only, and hence the residents would be exclusively Jewish. The Israel Lands Administration endorsed the Jewish Agency's position, arguing that the policy of the Jewish Agency was grounded in an agreement between the latter and the state.

In fact this mechanism, which involves nongovernmental Zionist bodies such as the Jewish Agency and the Jewish National Fund on the one hand, and the state of Israel, through the Israel Lands Administration, on the other, in the process of settling the "state's lands," helped to exclude the Arabs from living in localities that were established as joint projects (as opposed to towns). Since 1948, some six hundred Jewish localities have been established, while the Arabs have not been allowed to set up a single locality.

This chapter discusses the *Qa'dan* judgment as a model, which outlines the issue of Palestinian citizenship in the state of Israel. This judgment constitutes a tangible application of a doctrine, which advocates the implementation of the state of Israel's values as a "Jewish" and "democratic" state. Many Israelis argue that the Supreme Court, which in *Qa'dan* highlighted the state's Jewish-Zionist characteristics, has also successfully implemented the state's commitment to the principle of equality between all its citizens against a nationality-based background.

In this presentation, I shall critique this civil model of *Qa'dan*. I will argue that this model presents a new form of "Israeliness," a form that is "future-oriented" and will also include Palestinian citizens of the state. However, such inclusion is made conditional on their renouncing components of Palestinian identity, instead assuming the "Israeli Arab" identity, which is characterized by its Zionist components, including acceptance of the ideological values of Zionism. This model, which is underpinned by numerous judicial decisions as well as primary legislation, is at most prepared to relate to those Palestinians who are citizens of the state as possessing a status that is similar to that of diverse ethnic migrant groups, whose rights are limited to the civil-political sphere, with only a limited willingness to grant recognition of cultural aspects, on condition that such recognition will not adversely impact on the ideological structure of the state. It will be my contention that this model's problematic nature in respect to equality is an upshot of the failure to recognize Palestinians who are Israeli citizens as persons indigenous to their homeland or "patrials": a group that is in the process of founding a people and is entitled to self-determination in the framework of the state, in contrast to an ethnic group not living in its own homeland.

In the first part of this chapter, I will start by distinguishing between the characteristics of homeland groups, which constitute a people or a national minority, and other ethnic groups, discussing the differences of their various demands and how countries relate to them. Then, based on a textual reading of the *Qa'dan* judgment, I will analyze the model of citizenship outlined in the judgment as it applies to the collective rights of the Palestinians in Israel. I will attempt to reveal deep ideological structures that are represented and activated through the judicial choices made, based on a disclosure of the narrative structures expressed in the judgment. I will further attempt an analysis of their impact on those affected by them.[2] In the second part, I will analyze the rights accruing to an individual Palestinian under the *Qa'dan* model. I will scrutinize the argument that while the "Jewish state" confers national rights on the national majority group, it is the "democratic state" that implements the principle of equality in the area of civil-political rights. In this context, I will critique those commentators who advocate making a distinction between civil-political rights and collective national rights.

The Qa'dan Model: Israel's Palestinian Citizens as a Migrant Ethnic Group

A group that is defined as a people (or part thereof) is a historical community, which is resident in a defined area, normally its homeland, and is distinguished by possessing its own language and culture. Due to invasion or colonial occupation by other peoples and as a result of force or manipulation, the status of a number of national groups of this kind has changed, so that they have become nondominant national groups called national minorities (Steiner and Alston 1996: 987–1020; Kymlicka 1995: 11).

This involuntary change made the history and collective memory of these groups into pronounced and salient elements in shaping national awareness. The homeland (patria or territory) becomes the locus of national time, where the past, history, and collective memory have forged a distinct national identity. It is for this reason that residence in the homeland has continued to strengthen the claim to a different future for the territory, a future bound up in the political or diplomatic past that once prevailed in the homeland. Such a claim is tantamount to a refusal to accept a present or future that diminishes the groups' political status. The involuntary change in the status of these groups in their own homeland does not, therefore, prevent them from demanding a different status — one that is identical with their sovereign status, a status that is undergoing change, i.e., that recognizes their right to self-determination. This demand for self-determination is made both because they constitute a people, and also by reason of the destruction and the historical oppression that they have experienced as a people living in and on their own land. This is a demand made because of the present and the past alike, and it is also a demand made because of the locus or place—the homeland (see Sack 1986; Smith 1981).

Residence in and ties with the homeland have contributed to the sta-bility of the national identity of indigenous people or natives, whose struggle focuses primarily on issues bound up with the selfsame territory, such as self-determination, land claims, and demands over language (which in their eyes is the language of territory, i.e., of the homeland). The homeland shapes and re-creates the relationship of members of the home-land group with those who are not present in the homeland, namely the displaced group. Among other things, this relationship thwarts and in cer-tain cases prevents the making of particular kinds of civil-political demands such as those relating to integration and assimilation.[3] Such de-mands are likely to create a new "we" identity of a different nature from the "we" identity of the homeland group: an identity that will agree to legitimate the denial of rights to those resident in the diaspora. The rights demanded by the diaspora take the form of recognition based on pre-dominantly historical arguments. Nonrecognition of these arguments constitutes a denial of the history of the homeland group. Furthermore, self-perceptions such as "we" and "they," which are shaped by the power relationship and control over history, call forth difficult questions over demands for civil equality. From the outset, the situation has been such that a very marked perceptual gap has existed between the two groups, making it impossible to address the "language of rights" properly, as a language that will enable the principle of equality between them to be strengthened. The homeland group, which sees itself as a victim of the dominant group's powers of control, will call into question the purpose of the new and dominant "language of rights," implying that it is merely providing an "umbrella" to improve and promote the minority's interests. At the same time, the dominant group, justifying its hold over the terri-tory by means of diverse moral arguments, which in turn provide justifi-cation for its supremacy over the homeland group, bolsters the ideological reasons for the continuation of the unequal situation.[4] The umbrella pro-vided by the "language of rights" can, nevertheless, be used in order to promote legitimate interests of the homeland group, but these will be of limited scope, and the principle of equality will be of restricted applica-bility only (Abel 1995). Furthermore, civil-political demands under the umbrella of the dominant "language of rights" are, in certain cases, likely to perpetuate the cultural supremacy of the dominant group (i.e., the use of the dominant language) over the homeland group. Looking at how the homeland group relates to itself—as a group that is founding a people, and refusing to accept another people's supremacy—some might call this effort a question of "national honor" on the part of the homeland group.[5]

In contrast, any group of immigrants necessarily shapes its political agenda within the host country at a distance from its homeland. Unlike the homeland groups, which have claims on the country in all homeland contexts (such as self-determination, the acknowledgment of historical wrongs, language and land claims), immigrant groups who are distant from their homeland bring their main demands to bear in the area of civil-political rights and antidiscrimination measures in the area of resource allocation. Assimilation and integration sometimes constitute an aspiration on the part of the immigrants themselves, and they are acceptable options. Immigrants perform an individual act of transition. They move from their homeland to a new country in search of their own personal happiness. This is also the unwritten agreement between them and this new homeland: they come to it, and they are absorbed as individuals who wish to be integrated in it, and not as a national community, which wishes to establish a national existence in a new territory.[6] Nevertheless, some immigrant ethnic groups that have accepted the host country's political and ideological structure do sometimes express demands for the recognition of symbolic cultural components that do not conflict with the economic, legal, and political foundations of the receiving or host country.[7]

The Palestinians in Israel are a national group that is resident in its homeland and is part of the Palestinian people who are partially located outside its homeland. As a result of the 1948 war, those Palestinians who are now citizens of Israel were transposed, for the first time in their history, from a dominant national community in Palestine into a national minority, which belongs to a defeated nation, in the new state—the state of Israel. Matters relating to the homeland constitute a paramount component in the demands of Palestinian citizens of Israel, such as the return of expropriated land; the right of return to the villages from which they were displaced; recognition of unrecognized villages; return of absentees' assets; extending the areas of jurisdiction of Arab localities, and so on. The concept of "land" has become a national symbol in this struggle. The first Land Day on 30 March 1976 in which six Palestinians from the village of Arrabe and Sakhnin in the Galilee were killed, is the first and most important national event in the history of the Palestinians as a national collective in the state of Israel. Its significance lies in the fact that the national minority managed, for the first time since 1948, to organize its struggle collectively, declaring a general strike from the Negev in the south to the Upper Galilee in the north, in protest against the policy of land expropriation (Bishara 1993).

Residence in their homeland has strengthened and stabilized Palestinian citizens' national awareness and has shaped their refusal to consider their status as being on the same footing as that of a minority ethnic group fighting solely for civil-political rights. This is despite the fact that, particularly in the 1990s, a variety of issues could be identified over which civil demands were made, especially with regard to budgetary matters, in which such demands were limited to matters of vital importance to the Palestinian citizens' development in the economic and social spheres. Nevertheless, the dogged and fundamental struggles of the Palestinian citizens, struggles in which they were prepared to take to the streets undeterred by the use of force on the part of the security forces, were over national rights, i.e., as sons and daughters of the Palestinian people. In April 1998, during the protests in the Shefa'amr area against the background of the destruction of two houses in an unrecognized village, Umm al-Sahali, dozens of Palestinians were injured by shots fired by local security forces.[8] In September 1998, at the protests by residents of Umm al-Fahem and the Arab localities in Wadi 'Ara over land expropriations in the al-Roha area, more than 450 Palestinian citizens were injured as a result of shots fired by the Israeli police and the border police (Kernochan 1999). In June 1999, a clash took place between Palestinian citizens and the security forces following the destruction of a Palestinian house in Lod (Lydda), and sixteen people were injured.[9] The background to the eruption of al-Aqsa Intifada, which began in late September 2000 and during which thirteen Palestinian citizens were killed by police, derived from the national affiliation of the Palestinians in Israel to the Palestinian people. The same applied in September 1982 to the protests against the Sabra and Shatilla massacres of Palestinian refugees in Lebanon. The list is a long one. In all of these cases, what is involved is a kind of demand that is characteristic of a homeland group that sees itself as part of a people with claims to that homeland, as opposed to the type of struggle typically waged by immigrant ethnic groups.[10]

Is the *Qa'dan* petition characteristic of the struggle by Palestinian citizens of Israel as a national group resident in its homeland? The answer to this question might well also help explain the differences in how the two national groups in Israel related to the *Qa'dan* judgment. Specifically, the "conservative-Zionist" group argued that the judgment constituted an impediment to the Zionist enterprise, while the "liberal-Zionist" group explained that the judgment was a historic breakthrough for Arab rights. Nevertheless, a large proportion of the Arab public expressed indifference to the outcome, while others came out with intense criticism directed against the "jubilation" of the "liberal-Zionist" groups.[11]

The *Qa'dan* judgment is about admitting and including the non-Jewish others in the state of Israel in a project defined as a strictly Zionist-Jewish enterprise. In the judgment, this project is embodied in the image of the locality of Katzir, which was founded jointly by the Israel Lands Administration and the Jewish Agency with the aim of settling Jews in the Wadi 'Ara area (referred to in the judgment as Nahal "Iron"—the "Iron" Valley). The Qa'dan family, the petitioners, represented a challenge to this project through its claim to be able to join and be part of it. This was no easy thing. The Israeli public has understood the judgment as an important and revolutionary document because despite the project's declared goal, it nevertheless enabled "non-Jews" to be included and integrated in it.

The *Qa'dan* judgment adopts an antidiscriminatory approach, which seeks to remove obstacles caused by exclusion. All citizens are entitled to equal treatment so that they can gain entry to this ideological domain. National or racial origin makes no difference. Those who are admitted are individuals who are "set apart" by virtue of their standing as citizens.

Although the Qa'dan family represented not only the Arabs but also all those for whom the project was not intended, i.e., the "non-Jews," the "Arab" aspect of the judgment was particularly salient because of the Jewish Agency's presence in the legal text. It was this presence that in turn underscored the ideological presence of the Arab-Palestinian identity, because of the nonneutral relationship between Palestinian and Zionist identities constructed on relationships of rejection and negation: because the Zionist identity delimits and defines Israeli identity as a Jewish-Zionist identity, it by definition rejects the constituent elements of the importunate Palestinian identity. Azmi Bishara (1999) has provided a very cogent explanation of this attitude: "Israeliness does not distinguish the Arabs in Israel from the rest of the Arabs in the same way that it distinguishes the Jews in Israel from the rest of the Jews, because from the very outset Israeliness has been Jewish-Zionist and rejected the Arab, and even perceives itself as such. In order to be Arab-Israeli, the Israeli Arab has to be part of his rejection."

Prohibiting discrimination involves what Isaiah Berlin dubbed the "negative freedom" of individuals, according to which individuals' freedom shall not be vitiated or denied because they belong to this or that particular group. In other words, the state seeks to act neutrally, without *arbitrariness*, as it were, following a policy of "collective blindness." In contrast, a claim for equal treatment against the backdrop of group membership seeks to establish a positive right, which requires the state to adopt positive or affirmative measures so as to treat the group's legitimate interests with respect and concern.[12] In other words, in an antidiscrimination suit, the demand is for revocation of the institutions' *arbitrary* policy, which attaches weight to the collective or group difference of individuals. In contrast, in a suit for equal treatment against a group background, it is precisely the group's difference that should constitute the decisive factor. However, as will be explained below, antidiscrimination policy will not succeed, and discrimination will continue to exist without the guarantee of "positive" or affirmative equality.

Despite its importance, the *Qa'dan* type of suit is not characteristic of the principal actions and claims made by an indigenous national minority. Rather, it typifies the actions of diverse ethnic groups seeking to integrate in a new society. Nevertheless, its importance in terms of removing obstacles in the way of all individuals must not be downplayed, particularly when the exclusion is institutionalized by legislation or declared policy with the goal of maintaining the supremacy of the dominant group. However, a vast abyss separates this from any characterization of these suits as principal claims of an indigenous national minority.[13] This is not saying that a homeland minority should remain detached and refrain from all and any kind of integration. Clearly, at the very least, economic needs such as employment and academic studies will require the minority to strive for inclusion (Bruner and Peled 1998: 107).

However, in matters involving the historical reality of the homeland, the demand for inclusion is problematic from the homeland group's viewpoint, because it is likely to undermine the legitimacy of the claims of the homeland groups, possibly giving the impression that their struggle is one of an ethnic group fighting for civil-political rights only, instead of a struggle by a homeland group seeking equality between two national groups. Does the *Qa'dan* case fall into this category?

The settlement of Katzir was established at the initiative of the Jewish Agency, which, according to the judgment, "took as its goal the settling of Jews throughout the whole of the country, and in particular in border regions including areas with a sparse Jewish presence."[14] According to the Jewish Agency's perception, a sparse Jewish presence is defined in terms of the Arab presence. In Wadi 'Ara, the Arab presence is on a large scale, and hence the presence of the Jews, according to the Jewish Agency's understanding, is sparse. The Arab presence, according to the Jewish Agency, constitutes a threat to the area's Jewishness. To put it more delicately, the Arab presence is not legitimate and hence solutions to this presence must be found. The settlement of Katzir was established with the goal of negating the presence of the Arab identity in Wadi 'Ara through the intermediary of settling Jews. In the eyes of the Qa'dan family, this is said to be a goal that lacks legitimacy. Furthermore, most of the settlement of Katzir was established on expropriated Arab land.[15] As a result, in the context of Katzir, "Jewish" and "Arab" identities are not neutral matters: the relationship between them is constructed on the basis of negation. This is through no fault of the Qa'dan family, but because of the goals of the Jewish Agency.

In this way, an enormous yawning gulf has been created between the request of the Arabs, as a homeland group, for the return of its expropriated land and the application of an Arab to purchase a house on expropriated Arab land, and also to present the success of this request as an Arab "victory." Does not this attempted purchase confer legitimacy and validation on a policy that is directed against someone who is not present on the land, i.e., the original owners of the land? Does it not convey an attitude embodying neutrality, and perhaps capitulation by the homeland group with regard to the illegitimate goals in establishing the settlement of Katzir? Is there not here a new association, resulting in the creation of a different "we" (including individual Arabs and the Jewish Agency) that negates and rejects the right of other displaced people who are the original owners of the land (in this context, they might be outside Katzir but not necessarily outside the entire homeland)? How legitimate is the fragmentation of the national "we" of the patrials when it comes about, not for internal reasons, but rather as a result of external intervention by those threatening it (viz., the Jewish Agency)? Are the petitioners not placing themselves in a hostile situation that negates their very identity as Palestinian Arabs? It is also of interest to examine how the legal text relates to the collective rights of the national minority in Israel. What historical narratives were referred to in the text, what form was given to the image of the petitioners, and what are the limits of the dialogue of collective rights that emerge from it?

From the viewpoint of the homeland group, these questions point to the problematic nature of civil-political claims of the *Qa'dan* type. Notwithstanding the antidiscrimination policy, which professes to be at the heart of the judgment, the text related to the ideological aspects of the petitioners, members of the Qa'dan family. The *Qa'dan* text presents us with petitioners who do not raise historical claims, and do not contest the legitimacy of the Jewish Agency's actions, accepting the ideological values of the state of Israel as a Jewish-Zionist state, and expressing loyalty to the "Jewish people." In the first few pages of the judgment, Chief Justice Aharon Barak discloses the petitioners' credo by observing: "The petitioners do not discount the Jewish foundations of the state of Israel's identity, nor the history of settlement in Israel. Their petition is future-oriented. In their opinion, the Jewish foundations of the state's identity are of decisive weight only in matters involving the very essence of the Jewish nature of the state—such as the Law of Return, 5710–1950."[16]

What we have here is an extremely important and interesting disclosure. Despite the petitioners' national identity, they concur with the primary objectives of Zionism, which has broad support among Supreme Court justices. But it goes further than this. Specifically, the petitioners concur with that entire body of literature that supports efforts to achieve the greatest possible harmony between "Jewish" and "democratic," emphasizing the importance of the Law of Return, which is practically the only component designed to continue granting national preference to Jews in Israel (Gavison 1998: 213; Saban 1998/1999: 79). The legal text depicts the image of the petitioners as individuals who have no historic ties whatsoever with the territory, the land, the soil, or the place. Were such components to appear in the text, they would immediately create associations with the petitioners' indigenous Palestinian identity, which threatens the historical legitimacy of the Zionist project. The petitioners in *Qa'dan*, according to the text, are not seeking recognition of the historic wrong done to them and members of their people as a result of the policy of expropriating land, nor are they seeking recognition of their collective memory. What they are propounding contains nothing that in the slightest way identifies them with Palestinian national identity, such as the return of expropriated land or a partnership in managing the land of Katzir. But it goes further than this. The text presents them as, unexpectedly, accepting the national identity of the state as a Jewish state, conferring legitimacy on the "rural settlement enterprise," or to use Chief Justice Barak's words, "the issue in this petition is not the entire panoply of the Jewish Agency's actions."[17] The petitioners have no arguments or criticisms of the past. Their suit "is oriented toward the future"—an expression that is emphasized on a number of occasions in the text.

Apart from the ideological aspects of the petitioners as highlighted and propounded in the text, we have no information about them apart from the following attributes: "The petitioners are a married couple who have two daughters. They are Arabs who are currently living in an Arab locality."[18] The reader is provided with no information, for example, about the Arab locality—which is the Arab village of Baqa al-Garbiyeh in the Triangle. This information could perhaps have been added in order to indicate the proximity of this village to Katzir, which according to the judgment is located in "Nahal 'Iron" (instead of calling the area by its standard Arabic name of Wadi 'Ara), and perhaps also in order to provide a comparative view of the standard of living in the two localities. We have not been afforded a glimpse into the personal lives of the couple who brought the petition in their quest for a different standard of living, and a better future for their children.

So what was it that the petitioners wanted in Katzir? This is something that the text does disclose to us: "They sought—and are still seeking—to live in a place with a different quality of life and standard of living from those where they are currently living."[19] This is a neutral request that has absolutely nothing to do with the national cleft. It could apply equally to any nationality, and is not specific to Arab identity. In practice, this is a request that completely neutralizes the fact that they are members of a homeland group, presenting them as people belonging to a (non-Jewish) migrant ethnic group, whose sole concern is better quality of life. Just as we do not care where immigrants have come from, the text does not provide us with the name of the Arab village from which the petitioners have come: the main thing is that they are citizens. Nor did the petitioners contest the respondents' argument that in Katzir the festivals and holidays would be Jewish-Zionist, and the schools would teach in Hebrew, following Zionist values. Like most immigrants, they will be unhesitatingly willing to accept the local language and values.

The implicit assumptions that allowed the judges to vote in favor of the petitioner in the *Qa'dan* case become even more transparent when we compare it to the case of *Bourkan*.[20] In this case, the petitioner underscored his membership in a group resident in its homeland, presenting a competing historical narrative for the purpose of recovering his home in Jerusalem—possibly the reason why the petition was turned down. *Qa'dan* presents petitioners who did not "confuse" the text with a threatening historical narrative and came in the guise of new citizens concerned to ensure that their children would be educated in "good" schools in a quality location. True, in both judgments the petitioners were seeking to purchase an apartment in a Jewish residential area, but there is a major difference between them. Firstly, Katzir does not resemble the Jewish Quarter of Jerusalem's Old City, as the purpose for which Katzir was established was specifically directed against Arab identity, while the Jewish Quarter had also existed in the homeland prior to 1948, for centuries constituting an integral, harmonious part of Arab culture. Secondly, the location is per se Jewish, and hence does not generate problems that resemble those of Katzir, which by its very nature and purpose is directed against the patrials. Thirdly, the petitioner in *Bourkan* was subversive, challenging the legitimacy of his removal from the Jewish Quarter. In contrast, the Qa'dan family was presented in the text as conferring legitimacy on this denial of identity. Fourthly, and most importantly, the petitioner in *Bourkan* was using the trial to recover his own house, as opposed to the Qa'dan family, who had applied to Katzir in order to purchase a house built in the area on expropriated Arab land. The *Qa'dan* narrative was that of an "Israeli Arab," as opposed to *Bourkan*, who sought to present a Palestinian narrative.

In contrast to the meager narrative figure of the petitioners in the text of the *Qa'dan* case, the Jewish Agency looms large as a richly detailed literary figure in all its variety, with everything it has contributed, a moral, national figure possessing an abundant past and a history filled with deeds. The legal text presents its readers with a single history that played a starring role throughout the entire judgment: the history of the Jewish Agency as the executive arm of the Zionist movement in the area of rural settlement, immigrant absorption, and control of the land.[21] Despite the court's finding that exclusion on the basis of nationality is invalid, the text made no critical references whatsoever to the Jewish Agency's policies over the years. In parallel, there was no reference at all to the historical discrimination against Arabs in Israel in all matters relating to planning and land policy. The absence of these references occurred despite the fact that counsel for the petitioners enclosed an expert opinion on the matter, addressing the dearth of land and housing among the Arabs, an issue of which the text made no mention whatsoever. There was no expression in the text of the historical injustice done to them. The word "Arab" appeared just three times, in the context of the petitioners themselves. Were this a historical text to be read by historians of the future, they would not know whether or not there is an Arab population with historical roots in this country. It therefore comes as no surprise that the "we" of the text is also exclusively Jewish.

"Emptying" the judgment of the Arab-Palestinian presence made it easier to deal with the ethnic part of the judgment, starting with the ideological voiding of their presence from the homeland, as is expressed in Israel's Declaration of Independence: "The values of the state of Israel as a Jewish, democratic state are based, inter alia, on the right of the Jewish people to have an independent existence in its own sovereign state." In the words of Dr. Orit Kamir (2000): "The brief statement 'Eretz Israel was the birthplace of the Jewish people' therefore erases facts, opinions.... It thereby negates the possibility of the existence of any form of an Arab national entity whose 'birthplace' was also the territory in question. In this way, the opening sentence of the Declaration of Independence expresses that which is called by some the (ideological) 'emptying' of the land of its non-Jewish inhabitants, and certainly of any 'people' other than the 'Jewish people.'" Thus, anyone who expected this important judgment to acknowledge the Arabs as patrials, as natives and members of a people, will be disappointed. The text concludes resolutely that this land is "Eretz Israel," the Land of Israel, not Palestine and not Palastina, that there is only one exclusive historic right, and that it belongs to the "Jewish people."

The Jews are the only ones in the judgment to be called a "people," as opposed to an ethnic or a religious group. The others are simply "minorities" within the Jewish state, and at most they are defined negatively as "non-Jews." The Arabs constitute part of these "members of minorities," possessing no distinctive markers whatsoever such as membership of a people or nation, with their own language, comprising a high percentage of the population; being indigenous or native, etc. In the state of Israel, many minorities are recognized: Muslims, Christians, Druze, Bedouin from the North, Bedouin from the Negev. Although they are all Arab-Palestinians, neither legislation nor judicial rulings are prepared to relate to them as a single national group, instead treating them as small ethnic communities. Recognizing them as members of a given people and a nationality, as opposed to different ethnic groups, would threaten the view of the state as a Jewish nation-state (Nafa'a 1999).

Along these lines, the initial starting point, according to *Qa'dan*, is the finding that the state of Israel is a Jewish state, but even a Jewish state has rights and duties in respect of non-Jewish individuals as well, as propounded by Barak: "Indeed, the return of the Jewish people to its homeland is the result of the values of the state of Israel as a Jewish and simultaneously a democratic state.... But the values of the state of Israel as a Jewish and democratic state in no way require the state to discriminate between its citizens. Jews and non-Jews are citizens with equal rights and duties in the state of Israel."[22] The homeland group is required to accept these trenchant findings regarding the Jewishness of the state. Members of this group have no edge whatsoever over the other non-Jewish groups in the state of Israel when it comes to this subject. In this sense, they are all equal. They are all supposed to accept the state's characteristics without protest. Here, too, this is a requirement made of all of Israel's non-Jewish citizens and residents, just as it is made of all immigrant groups that accept the basic characteristics of the host state. However, this does not mean that they are devoid of rights. According to the text, they are entitled to equal civil rights like any ethnic group in a nation-state, on condition that these demands do not impair the political-constitutional structure of the state.[23]

The judgment in *Qa'dan*, as well as other cases, is an adoption of a similar stance, prohibiting discrimination on the basis of group affiliation.[24] They come out against the *arbitrary policy* of those administrative authorities, which prevents individuals from realizing their personal freedom. In these cases, the civil-political right had to be balanced against the "values of the state" as a Zionist-Jewish state, i.e., the realization of the civil right is made conditional on the characteristics of the state itself. Collective rights were replaced by civil-political rights. The court recognized just one set of collective rights—those of the Jews. Only the Jews appeared as a "people," contrasted with "the others" who appear as ethnic minorities and foreign groups.

However, even the granting of civil-political rights is not self-evident in the Jewish state, but predicated on the recognition that the petitioner's claim will not undermine Jewish-Zionist dominance, be it in terms of land control, Arab language usage or any other realm that is potentially contested. The realization of civil-political rights will depend on Jewish-Zionist time and the strength of its enterprise. It may be noted then, with the utmost caution, that the rationale of the *Qa'dan* case and others is to enable individuals within the state of Israel to conduct their lives as they see fit, without interference, as long as this does not harm the political-constitutional framework of the state. This rationale ignores the fact that the country's Palestinian citizens belong to a homeland people and pop-ulation, and that it seeks to relate to them using only the "umbrella" of civil-political rights. This rationale makes it possible to recognize cultural aspects of the Arab population, particularly in its private sphere, as long as these do not threaten the ideological-political structure of the state. And in fact, this is the situation in the state of Israel. The Arabs use their language in Arab localities, and Arabic is the language of education at Arab schools. The state recognizes their religious groups with regard to personal status, recognizes their religious festivals, enables them to have freedom of religion and of worship, and supports forms of their culture in the realm of folklore. Recognizing the Arabs as religious groups and different ethnic communities or groups, as opposed to recognizing them as a national minority, does not constitute an ideological threat to national exclusiveness over this land.

Ethno-national versus Multicultural States

Those states that respect the freedom of immigrant groups with respect to symbolic ethnic-cultural subjects are defined as polyethnic states, as opposed to states that comprise more than one nationality, which are defined as multinational states (Kymlicka 1995: 11; Saban 2000: 29–32). Accordingly, the state of Israel is a binational state. The fact that the state defines itself differently does not make it a nation-state. The test is the ter-ritorial principle, the homeland. Nevertheless, the principle of "emptying the land and giving precedence to the Jews" defines the state of Israel as a Jewish state despite the Arab-Palestinian presence within it, the Arabs constituting only an ethnic group within it. As has been pointed out, the difference between a national group and an ethnic group is, inter alia, that the former is resident in its homeland, while the latter is not. In this case, the state of Israel is Jewish, despite the Arabs who "came and migrated" to "Eretz Israel"—the Land of Israel—because the function which determines that the Jews are the "people" who arrived here earlier is that of time, and not place or abode in the territory. At the very most, the territory may create a "Jewish people" or an "Israeli nation," but not a "Jewish people" that includes all Jews, even those who are not resident in the territory. Consequently, the absence of any recognition of the Pales-tinian Arabs as part of the homeland people and group leaves only one alternative, which allocates to the Arabs a status similar to that of migrants. And thus you will find many Israelis who will readily draw the following parallel: just as the foreigners and migrants who came to France did not make it un-French, so the foreigners, the goyim, the aliens, the migrants in the state of Israel are not making it non-Jewish, even though Frenchness is a matter of territory (see Shammas 1995: 19).[25] But this is an Israeli specialty—looking for models of comparison in order to come up with forms of justification; many of them have defined the state as a nation-state, thereby shifting the debate to the question of the legitimacy of this model, which exists in many countries. But the problem lies not in the model, but in the very definition of the state of Israel as a nation-state, a definition that contradicts the fact that it is a binational state.

In conclusion, the *Qa'dan* model, which is based on the conception of the nature of the state as a "Jewish-democratic" state, demonstrates an Israeliness that is "future-oriented": an Israeliness involving, on the one hand, recognition of the past and the history of the Jews as the only people in this land who are entitled to self-determination in this state, and on the other hand, the Arabs, who have no history, and are not founding a people or a homeland group that is also entitled in turn to self-determination in this state. This Israeliness is "future-oriented" insofar as it grants conditional recognition to some of the civil-political rights and obligations of its "non-Jewish" citizens, while at the same time it asks them to accept the ideological "umbrella" of the state as a Jewish-Zionist state. According to this model, the Palestinian Arabs in the state of Israel are migrants in their homeland.[26]

The Personal Autonomy of the Individual: "Israeli Arab" versus "Palestinian in Israel"

So far, I have related the *Qa'dan* case to the group rights of Palestinian citizens. In this section, I will briefly discuss the personal autonomy of the Palestinian individual according to the *Qa'dan* judgment. Many Israelis argue that while the Jewish state does indeed grant national precedence to the Jews, nevertheless it implements the principle of equality in the area of civil rights. In this context, I will consider whether this is in fact the case, and whether the rights of the Palestinian individual who holds Israeli citizenship are indeed equal to those of his Jewish counterpart, despite the collective precedence enjoyed by the population of the national majority.

The legal rhetoric and outcome of *Qa'dan* embody a civil model in which the Arabs can be included in a future-oriented form of Israeliness. In this Israeliness, the Arab's national identity must be drained away at the same time as it is negated. This identity is required so as to demonstrate loyalty to the basic values of Zionism. Loyalty of this variety is not a neutral loyalty to shared civil values, but rather loyalty to a nonneutral ideology toward the Arabs (Yiftachel, Ghanem, and Rouhana 1999/2000: 67–68; Rouhana and Ghanem 1998; Smooha 1993: 325–326). The only thing that will satisfy it is demonstrating a national identity, which does not contest its legitimacy. This is obviously not a question of loyalty to the state—nothing like this is to be found in Israeli reality because of the lack of any distinction between Zionism and Israeliness. And it is clear that the Palestinian national identity, which by definition requires an acknowledgment of the past, of history, of a collective memory, of a historical wrong, of the right of return, contests the legitimation of the ideological foundations of Zionism. Consequently, the integrationist model of *Qa'dan*, seeking to secure the stability of these Zionist foundations, requires renunciation of these Palestinian elements, which are to be replaced by integration in a nonthreatening identity, devoid of its own past or history, while at the same time this identity is supposed to accept the history of the Zionist side.[27] In other words, the Arab's identity is required to be Arab-Zionist, but because Zionism does not include the Arabs, this identity will assume the form of the "Israeli Arab" instead of the Palestinian who is an Israeli citizen (see Bishara 1996: 312). The Arab is required to demonstrate that he has stepped back a certain distance from his national identity, lest ideological positions be attributed to him, which will expose him as a Palestinian Arab. His national identity is the motivation and the reason for laying down conditions of loyalty of the type stipulated in *Qa'dan*, on the one hand, is also the reason, which requires him to act in opposition to it, on the other hand. The Arab individual cannot, within the framework of this model, identify with the longings of his people.

In contrast, the personal autonomy of the Jewish individual will benefit from broader freedom of choice. He enjoys a more diverse range of options, allowing him to be "himself." Generally, the Jewish individual's ideological affiliation, with rare exceptions, does not taint him with the suspicion of threatening the very existence of the project, the reason being that, through his very presence, he embodies the project's intrinsic goals. Accordingly, in most instances, the Zionist ideology does not attach great significance to the Jewish individual's ideological aspects because, as far as it is concerned, the main thing is that Jewish individual's ethnic affiliation. This enables the Jewish individual to enjoy broad freedom of action and self-expression: he may be Zionist, non-Zionist, anti-Zionist ultra-Orthodox (*haredi*), leftist, extreme right-wing, and so on. In contrast, the Arab individual, because of his national identity, is required to act like a conservative Zionist. Otherwise, and even if he appears to be a left-wing Zionist, the suspicion will arise that the position has been adopted because of his national affiliation, and not because of his ideological beliefs.[28]

Furthermore, the state, which sets itself a single goal—the self-determination of the Jewish people—is per se assuring the collective rights of the Jewish individual, thereby providing a cultural environment supportive of the personal autonomy of the Jewish individual. The Jewish individual does not need, for example, to fight for the status of the Hebrew language and Hebrew culture in the state of Israel, because these are assured by the state. This supportive environment provides the Jewish individual's personal autonomy with multiple possibilities of choice. Things are very different for the Arab individual, who is required to struggle for collective rights in order to secure broader personal autonomy. Nevertheless, according to the integrationist model of *Qa'dan*, he will find himself in a different cultural setting, which in many instances constitutes the negation of his culture as a Palestinian.

In the *Mahameed* case, the issue before the Supreme Court concerned the connection between the rights of the Palestinian individual and his cultural rights.[29] The petitioner, a citizen and resident of Umm al-Fahem, obtained a B.A. in Arabic studies and Islam, graduating cum laude from An-Najah University in Nablus, West Bank. After being accepted for a second degree in this area at Bir Zeit University in Ramallah, West Bank, the respondent issued a restraining order prohibiting him from entering the territory of the West Bank on the grounds that the petitioner belonged to the Hamas leadership, and therefore constituted a risk "to the security of the region." The respondent did not deny the fact that the petitioner was never arrested or questioned concerning his involvement in any political activity, and that he does not have a criminal record. In parallel, the petitioner argued in his petition, inter alia, that the order prejudices his right to continue his studies, particularly given the fact that there is no university in Israel that provides Arabic-language facilities in his academic field. In his affidavit, the petitioner acknowledged that he is a religious person without any interest in political factions, and that his friends at An-Najah University belong to the Hamas movement. He explained that the university campuses on the West Bank are known for the political activities of the various Palestinian movements, and practically the entire student body belong to these movements; no Meretz, Labor, or Herut are to be found there, but instead Hamas, Islamic Jihad, Fatah, the Popular Front, the Democratic Front, and others. Because he is a religious person, not secular and not a Marxist, who attends the mosque on campus, it is natural for his friends to be involved in the more religious movements. However, these friendships in no way imply that he is involved in illegal activities, the petitioner declared. The Supreme Court justices rejected his petition out of hand, ruling, in just a few lines, that they saw no grounds to interfere in the respondent's decision.[30]

From the outset, the petitioner did not have the option of choosing between studying at a university in Israel or studying at a university outside the country; given his academic field, he had just one option, i.e., to study at an Arabic university, which does not exist in the state of Israel. Even if he had opted to study at another university outside the West Bank, this would not have helped him, because all the Arabic universities in the area (in Jordan or Egypt) are known for their political culture, which is neither favored by, nor acceptable to, the dominant political culture in Israel. Moreover, neither did he have the option of being an "Israeli Arab" at An-Najah University, since this identity is perceived there as suspect and unacceptable. The only option open to the petitioner at An-Najah University, given the prevailing Palestinian sociopolitical culture, was to make a social choice that was acceptable in the context of Palestinian culture. Any other choice would not have been accepted there as normal. However, this normalcy constitutes an extreme aberration in the eyes of Israeli culture. The whole of Palestinian space or locus, in this instance, surrendered to Israeli culture. And in this way the petitioner lost his chance to pursue his academic studies.

The thesis of Canadian philosopher Will Kymlicka identifies a close tie between the individual's capacity to make choices and his personal autonomy on the one hand, and his cultural membership on the other. This cultural membership provides the supportive setting, which enables the individual to shape and realize his choices. Kymlicka (1995: 105) makes the following observations about the connection between the individual's rights and the collective context:

> [L]iberals should recognize the importance of people's membership in their own societal culture, because of the role it plays in enabling meaningful individual choice and in supporting self-identity. While the members of a (liberalized) nation no longer share moral values or traditional ways of life, they still have a deep attachment to their own language and culture.... [Na]tional identity lies "outside the normative sphere" ... that it provides a secure foundation for individual autonomy and self identity. Cultural membership provides us with an intelligible context of choice, and a secure sense of identity and belonging, that we call upon in confronting questions about personal values and projects.[31]

It would appear that according to the *Qa'dan* model, the personal autonomy and self-identity of the Arab individual are not accorded equal treatment with that of the Jewish individual in the state of Israel. Many researchers, such as Sammy Smooha (1999), Ruth Gavison (1998), Yoav Peled (2000), and Ilan Saban (1998/1999: 79) argue that despite its ethnicity, the Jewish state manages, to a marked degree, to provide a firm footing for civil-political rights in the area of the individual. Hence some of them argue that it is possible to reconcile the "Jewish" with the "democratic." However, these approaches fail to provide answers to the question as to whether these individual rights put into practice the principle of equality between Jewish individuals and Arab individuals. The problematic character of these studies is to be found in two areas: the first is the perception of the dichotomy between individual and collective rights; while the second and main one involves the way that they relate to the rights of the Palestinians who are Israeli citizens as an ethnic minority rather than as indigenous inhabitants. As is made clear in this part of the article, the lack of equality in the practice of civil-political rights in the individual sphere arises from the ethnic definition of the state of Israel, which confers national rights on the majority group only. Hence, in my opinion, antidiscrimination policy also fails to implement the principle of equality in the individual sphere in the absence of any recognition of positive equality, i.e., recognition of collective rights.

Ruth Gavison (2000) is aware of the problematic situation created by the *Qa'dan* model in the sphere of assuring collective rights. She is critical of the approach of the court, which she argues, ignores national differences and opts for a policy of "national blindness." There is no doubt, in my opinion, that the failure to take account of national differences, as Gavison argues, will perpetuate the discriminatory situation against those groups which are denied justice in the name of a policy of "national blindness." Nevertheless, Gavison's criticism also suffers from the same logical flaw of "blind equality." She too argues that the policy is also supposed to provide expression of the state's Jewish-Zionist uniqueness, and hence "providing the possibility to the Jew who so wishes to live in Israel in a Jewish locality is not ... necessarily unwarranted discrimination." The impression given by Gavison's suggestion is that the Jews in the state of Israel are also founding a group comprising a national minority, which, unhesitatingly, justifies the assuring of exclusive rights for special requirements. Gavison tries to apply her alternative without distinction in terms of dominance and weight between a national-majority group and a national-minority group. This approach ignores the basic rationale, which underlies the granting of exclusive rights to groups of minorities. This rationale seeks to counteract a camouflaged policy involving a dictatorship of the majority. It is no coincidence that international law has seen fit to relate to the rights of minorities, as opposed to dominant groups, as exclusive rights, and many democratic constitutions have sought to lay down special protection for minorities, such as in the area of language or affirmative action. The Jewish nature of the state will be maintained as Jewish without any need for privileges or special legislation, for no other reason than because this culture is dominant. The danger in this approach is concealed in the legitimation it confers on a twilight zone, which will lead to a dictatorship of the majority. In my view, a fundamental problem in Israeli Supreme Court decisions relating to Arabs' rights lies precisely in the way that they relate to the national-majority group as a group with special needs, justifying special treatment, without examining issues on the basis of a majority-minority relationship.[32]

Conclusion

In this chapter, I have tried to examine the relevance of the homeland group's civil status in a state that negates its national existence. The discussion has focused on the homeland group, not on the issue of whether it is possible to reconcile the two expressions "Jewish" and "democratic."[33]

As indicated in this presentation, most Israeli critics have attached no weight to a distinction between an ethnic minority and a homeland minority. This has blurred the distinctions, shifting the debate to a different fundamental question, which addresses the status of ethnic minorities in a nation state. This blurring has led to a situation in which characteristics of the state of Israel are presented as characteristics of a nation-state, even though (de facto) it is a binational state, and Palestinian citizens are presented as an ethnic minority group although they are a homeland minority. This, then, is the explanation of the source of the capitulation to the hegemonic dialogue, the dominant dialogue having created a model for itself, which is presented as a normal model of a similar type to standard models in many democratic countries, i.e., a model of a nation-state containing ethnic minorities within it. The dominant dialogue has also ordained that this comparison constitutes a defined area lying within the borders of the dialogue.

In order to subvert this dialogue, a different kind of attitude is required: one that refuses to discuss the degree of openness and tolerance of the "Jewish state" in respect of liberal rights of "non-Jews," but instead strives to focus on the relevance that must arise out of relating to the homeland group as a group that is in the process of founding a people. This approach is required because of its ability, at the very least, to pose a different question: is the definition of the state as a "Jewish" state a matter of *"cultural violence"*?

This violence, as presented in this article, embodies a negation of the national existence of the homeland group, the collective memory, history, demands for acknowledgment of the historical injustice it has suffered, language, and so on. Instead, it proposes relating to the homeland group as an ethnic group. In other words, this "cultural violence" is asking that the status of a people be turned into one of immigrants in its own homeland. In addition, it is asking this people to surrender to Jewish national "supremacy." The relevance of "cultural violence" is the demand for a change in the status, in actual fact, of the Palestinian citizen as an "Israeli Arab" to the status of a non-Jewish migrant in the Jewish state. The Palestinian citizen and the non-Jewish Anglo-Israeli are supposed to accept the state's Zionist values and to seek their national identity somewhere else, outside the "Jewish homeland." However, as opposed to the civil status of the non-Jewish Englishman, these values are not neutral to the Palestinian's identity, but rather negate its existence, and furthermore, the Palestinian has not left his homeland but is still living in it. The dialogue between authors A.B. Yehoshua (Buli) representing the "liberal Zionist" stream and Anton Shammas, from the Galilee village of Fasuta, throws into sharper relief the degree of "cultural aggression" of the Zionist dialogue in the eyes of the Palestinian citizen. Yehoshua, like many Zionists, draws a parallel, which at the same time encompasses a suggestion. He compares Shammas's insistence on seeking recognition of his national-Palestinian identity in the state of Israel with a Pakistani who comes to

England on an English passport and insists on being involved in fashioning English national identity by including Pakistani and Muslim symbols and language in English nationality. Shammas responds to this aggression as follows: "Buli, the minute a man like you does not understand the basic difference between the Pakistani who comes to England and the Galilean who has been in Fasuta for untold generations, then what do you want us to talk about?"[34]

Notes

I would like to thank the following people for their helpful comments and assistance: Samera Esmeir, Oren Yiftachel, Jamil Dakwar, Ilan Saban, Ronen Shamir, Shulamit Almog, Eyal Gross, Gadeer Nicola, and Rina Rosenberg. I am, of course, solely responsible for the content of the chapter.

1. High Court (H.C.) 6698/95, *Qa'dan v. Israel Lands Administration et al. Piskei Din* (P.D.) 54 (1): 258.
2. Such an examination is influenced by critical approaches that seek to expose the narratives of judicial writing, analysis of the rhetoric revealed by judgments, and how judicial writing influences the shaping of reality. On this research, see Brooks and Gewirts 1996; Delgado 1989; Williams 1987; Farber and Sherry 1993; and Almog 2000.
3. "The homeland, as a concept and a set of practices, has played a major role in the persistence of groups against threats of assimilation or against domination by alien rulers and cultures … ethno-national mobilization and identity formation is associated with a specific territory. This territory is the ethnic homeland around which ethno-national identity is framed and reproduced…. Homeland ethnicity, as noted, is held by groups that reside on the territory they believe to be the cradle of their identity and history." (Yiftachel 2000: 359).
4. Minow 1997: 347; see also Brown 1997: 85: "Minority people committed themselves to these struggles [for rights], not to attain some hegemonically functioning reification leading to false consciousness, but a seat in the front of the bus, repatriation of treaty-guaranteed sacred lands, or a union card to carry into the grape vineyards," citing Robert A. Williams, Jr., "Taking Rights Aggressively."
5. It should be noted that the symmetry or parallel that is drawn between the patriotism of a homeland group and that of the dominant group is misleading. The patriotism of a homeland group is a desirable response to a policy of oppression and discrimination, constituting an instrument of empowerment for members of the nondominant group, the outcome of the principle of equality and dignity. Equality, in this context, seeks not to detract from the status of the homeland group and to relate to its members with respect or dignity, and hence is the rationale underlying the international declarations and the international conventions on the recognition of such groups' self-determination. Consequently, treatment of this patriotism (as opposed to nationalism) constitutes a fundamental part of the conception of human rights. In the terminology of "rights," the concept of group rights replaces the concept of patriotism, but in fact the reference is to one and the same perception with different names.
6. I am aware of the dichotomy, which I am outlining in terms of the differences between the two groups. However, this dichotomy can be helpful in managing to see the overall picture, throwing the differences between the groups into sharper relief. It is obvious that some of the demands by the homeland groups relate also to the civil-political domain, but do not constitute the focal point of their struggle. On the other hand, the

dichotomy between the struggle for self-determination and civil-political rights is also problematic, since in certain cases one sustains and is related to the other. Moreover, there are immigrant groups that, because of protracted residence, have come to relate to their struggle as a struggle by a national minority, such as French-speakers in Canada. Ilan Saban (2000: 19) notes that in practice, cases and circumstances are too diverse to be combined in the apparent dichotomy of an indigenous/immigrant distinction. The indigenous/immigrant characterization "is present in the eye of the beholder." It is not a simple matter of chronology, but rather a psychological and historical combination performed on the basis of a continuous comparison with the characteristic perception of the other community.

7. In the words of the Canadian philosopher, Will Kymlicka (1995: 14): "It is now widely (though far from unanimously) accepted that immigrants should be free to maintain some of their old customs regarding food, dress, religion, and to associate with each other in order to maintain these practices. This is no longer seen as unpatriotic or 'un-American.' But it is important to distinguish this sort of cultural diversity from that of national minorities. Immigrant groups are not 'nations,' and do not occupy homelands. Their distinctiveness is manifested primarily in their family lives and voluntary associations, and is not inconsistent with their institutional integration. They still participate within the public institutions of the dominant culture(s) and speak the dominant language(s)." See also Baker 1994.

8. *Washington Times*, 26 April 1998.

9. *Ha'aretz*, 23 June 1999; *New York Times*, 24 June 1999.

10. The major gap between the positions of the "liberal-Zionist" trend and the Palestinian minority is the upshot of the quality of the Zionist treatment of and attitude toward the Palestinian minority as an ethnic minority and not a homeland minority, as I shall explain subsequently. On this basis, it is possible to explain the disparity in positions between the Jewish-Zionist public and the Palestinian minority over subjects such as military service or (alternative nonmilitary) national service, for example. See also Jabareen 2000.

11. Jamil Dakwar, "To what extent is it an achievement," *Ha'aretz*, 15 March 2000 (Hebrew); The Editors, "Introduction," *Adalah's Review* 2 (fall 2000): 5.

12. Dworkin distinguishes between "the right to equal treatment" and "the right to treatment as an equal." In the former, the citizen is entitled to equal distribution of goods, and it is here that the antidiscrimination issue arises, as opposed to the latter, which relates not to this distribution of burdens and benefits, but rather to the attitude of respect and concern, and I believe this is what involves the issue of group equality. As Dworkin (1978: 227) puts it, it is "the right to treatment as an equal, which is the right, not to receive the same distribution of some burden or benefit, but to be treated with the same respect and concern as anyone else."

13. The American ruling in *Brown*, for example, which adopted the principle of "group blindness," raises a serious problem among the American Indians and native Hawaiians, since according to *Brown* they must be treated as racial minorities instead of national groups. As a result, their autonomous institutions were eliminated on the grounds that they were acting as for racial segregation. In 1969, the Canadian government, basing its arguments on the rationale in *Brown*, dropped the proposal requiring constitutional protection for the Indians. In the same spirit, the Canadian Supreme Court overturned legislation granting exclusive rights to the Indians. Thus, the use of antidiscrimination policy justified the overriding of claims for equality in these cases on the basis of group diversity. *Regina v. Drybones* [1970] *Supreme Court Review* (S.C.R.) 282; Kymlicka 1995: 58–60.

14. Paragraph 10 of the judgment.

15. A considerable proportion of the Katzir locality land originally belonged to the Yunes family from the village of Ar`ara. See The Editors, "Introduction," *Adalah's Review* 2: 2.

16. Paragraph 7 of the judgment.

17. Paragraph 28 of the judgment.

18. Paragraph 4 of the judgment.
19. Paragraph 4 of the judgment.
20. H.C. 114/78, *Bourkan v. Minister of Finance et al.*, P.D. 32 (2): 800.
21. Dalal 2000. On the history of anti-Aborigine discrimination in Australian land policy, cf. Australia's *Mabo v. Queensland* judgment, which acknowledged the injustice inflicted on the indigenous people of that country and recognized their forms of acquisition in Shamir 2000.
22. Paragraph 31 of the judgment.
23. The loyalty required of the Arabs who are citizens is a loyalty to the Jewish people. As I shall show in detail in the second part of this chapter, this is made perfectly clear in legislation and the rulings of the Supreme Court. An extreme illustration of this is to be found in Section 7 (A) (1) of the Basic Law. The Knesset prevents a political list of candidates from participating in elections if that list rejects "the existence of the state of Israel as the state of the Jewish people."
24. See, for example, the case of *Re'em*, which is also an excellent example of the limits of the civil rights dialogue in the Jewish state. If *Qa'dan* was about the right to choose a place of residence, the *Re'em* case was about the right to use a language (Arabic in this case) on the basis of choice. H.C. 105/98, *Re'em Contracting Engineers, Ltd. v. Natserat Illit Municipality et al.* P.D. 47 (5): 189.
25. For a detailed discussion, see Shammas (1995).
26. The major reservation in drawing a parallel between the Palestinian citizens and the status of the non-Jewish migrants attaches to the issue of the status of the Arabic language in Israel. This is because, generally speaking, the original mother tongue of ethnic groups of migrants is not recognized as an official language in the host country. However, in the state of Israel, Arabic has a special status. On the other hand, given the judicial rulings, which have been handed down and the indecisive attitude of the government to the status of the Arabic language, this differentiator may be considered to be anything other than a primary differentiating factor.
27. This is manifest when it comes to the inclusion of Arabs in national Zionist institutions, where the identity of the institution is a critical aspect of the function it plays. It can also be felt in political positions and in government ministries where the expression "we" and "them" is based on national limits, such as the army, the Israel Lands Administration, the police, Knesset committees (this is striking in the foreign affairs and security committees), some government corporations, senior positions in government organs including the judiciary, etc. On this matter, see Jabareen 1999, 2000.
28. Judicial rulings on the highest level in a number of judgments have underscored this approach. In *Yardor*, Justice Haim Cohen in a minority opinion observed: "... even when it comes to that group of Jews who repeat time and time again, in words and deeds, that they do not recognize the state, the learned Attorney General has admitted, in response to my question, that no one would consider preventing them from presenting a list of candidates in the Knesset elections, if they so wish." H.C. 1/65, *Yardor v. Chairperson of the Central Election Committee*, P.D. 19 (3): 365, 380. In *Ben Shalom*, Justices Menahem Elon and Dov Levin observed in a minority opinion that an electoral list must demonstrate loyalty to Zionist values and, first and foremost, the Law of Return. H.C. 2/88, *Ben Shalom v. Central Election Committee*, P.D. 43 (4): 211. However, this requirement has never been demanded of ultra-Orthodox (*haredi*) non-Zionist movements and parties. The reason, in my opinion, is that these parties do not represent the Arab other, which threatens the Jewishness of the state. In fact, the very presence of the ultra-Orthodox per se strengthens the Jewish majority and the Jewish aspect of the state. In the *Zichroni* judgment, Justice Kahan based the importance of positions not on their content, but on the identity of the person expressing them. He observes that "... a statement containing opposition to the settlements in the area of Judea, Samaria and the Gaza Region constitutes a legitimate expression of an opinion, if it is made by an individual who seeks for the good of the state," (i.e., a Jew, H.J.) "but the same words, when said by a public personality who is identified

by the residents of the area with the PLO, can have an inflammatory and subversive effect...." H.C. 243/83, *Zichroni v. The Board Committee of the Broadcasting Authority,* P.D. 37 (1): 757, 787. In the *Jiryis* judgment, the petitioner was asked to declare his loyalty to the Zionist ideology as a condition proving that he had ceased to believe in the national Arab way. H.C. 253/64, *Jiryis v. Haifa District Commander,* P.D. 18 (4): 673. See also Shamir 1991.

29. H.C. 1964/00, *Mahmoud Mahameed et al. v. Moshe Ya'alon, IDF Chief Commander of the Central Division* (unpublished).

30. It is interesting that in respect of the petitioner, it is argued that he constitutes a security risk because he is part of the Hamas leadership. However, he was allowed to move about Tel Aviv and Haifa freely and even be present in a Supreme Court courtroom entirely without restriction or impediment.

31. See also Margalit and Halbertal 1998: 93; Bruner and Peled 1998: 107.

32. It would appear that this approach, as it is found in various judicial rulings and in Gavison, originates in historical sources that view the history of world Jewry as the history of minorities within sovereign states, resulting in an absence of Jewish historical experience in how to behave as a national majority group in a democratic state. The first and only—at the time of writing—petition in which the Supreme Court recognized equality (as opposed to an antidiscriminatory approach) in the group domain is *Adalah v. Minister of Religious Affairs et al.* In this case, the Court held that the principle of equality is to be applied when allocating budgetary resources to cemeteries. Here, the petitioner had no choice other than to argue that "the Arabs and the Jews are all mortal, and they have an equal need to be buried with dignity ... the subject of cemeteries and death is not an exclusive need of one group or another." H.C. 1113/99, *Adalah v. Minister of Religious Affairs et al.* P.D. 54 (2): 104. It is regretful that only in connection with the subject of death has recognition so far been granted to the issue of equal needs between Jews and Arabs. On the politics of differences in Supreme Court decisions, see *Legal Violations of Arab Minority Rights in Israel,* Adalah, March 1998, 23–29.

33. Jewish and democratic is a pairing that is widely debated among Israeli scholars. They have managed to create a legal-political dialogue around the ethnic perception of the state of Israel, in which the key issue is its being a "Jewish" state on the one hand and "democratic" on the other. They have argued that there exists a genuine possibility of reconciling "Jewish" and "democratic" conceptions, while acknowledging the inherent contradictions. The main point here is that the dichotomy is set up in such a way that the Zionists have defined (rather than problematized) the state as a "Jewish" state and accepted its democratic nature at face value, rather than making it the subject of their study. True, the criticism that the critics bring to bear is trenchant and profound, but it still remains within the preset borders and limits of this dialogue: "Jewish" versus "democratic."

34. The quotations appear in Silberstein 1999.

References

Abel, Richard L. 1995. *Politics by Other Means: Law in the Struggle Against Apartheid, 1980–94.* New York: Routledge.

Almog, Shulamit. 2000. *Law and Literature.* Jerusalem: Nevo. [Hebrew]

Baker, Judith, ed. 1994. *Group Rights.* Toronto: University of Toronto Press.

Bishara, Azmi. 1993. "On the Question of the Palestinian Minority in Israel." *Theory and Criticism* 3: 7.

———. 1996. "The Israeli Arab: Reflections in a Split Political Dialogue." In *Zionism: A Contemporary Controversy,* ed. Pinchas Ginossar and Avi Bareli, 312. Sde Boker: Ben Gurion University of the Negev Press. [Hebrew]

────, ed. 1999. *Between the Me and the We: Constructing Identities and Israeli Identity.* Jerusalem: Van Leer Institute. [Hebrew]

Brooks, Peter, and Paul Gewirts, eds. 1996. *Law's Stories: Narrative and Rhetoric in the Law.* New Haven: Yale University Press.

Brown, Wendy. 1997. "Rights and Identity in Late Modernity: Revisiting the 'Jewish Question.'" In *Identities, Politics, and Rights,* ed. Austin Sarat and Thomas R. Kearns, 85–130. Ann Arbor: University of Michigan Press.

Bruner, Jose, and Yoav Peled. 1998. "On Autonomy, Abilities, and Democracy: The Liberal Multicultural Critique." In *Multiculturalism in a Democratic and Jewish State,* ed. Menachem Mautner, Avi Sagi, and Ronen Shamir, 107–131. Tel Aviv: Ramot Publishers. [Hebrew]

Dalal, Marwan. 2000. "A Reading in the Unread in the Qa'dan Decision: The Guest, the House, and the Judge." *Adalah's Review* 2: 44–49.

Delgado, Richard. 1989. "Storytelling for Oppositionists and Others: A Plea for a Narrative." *Michigan Law Review* 87: 2411–2441.

Dworkin, Ronald. 1978. *Taking Rights Seriously.* Cambridge, Mass.: Harvard University Press.

Farber, Daniel A., and Suzanna Sherry. 1993. "Telling Stories Out of School: An Essay on Legal Narratives." *Stanford Law Review* 45: 807.

Gavison, Ruth. 1998. "A Jewish and Democratic State: Challenges and Risks." In *Multiculturalism in a Democratic and Jewish State,* ed. Menahem Mautner, Avi Sagi, and Ronen Shamir, 213–278. Tel Aviv: Ramot Publishers. [Hebrew]

────. 2000. "Jewish and Democratic." *Adalah's Review* 2: 32–38.

Jabareen, Hassan. 1999. "On the Oppression of Identities in the Name of Civil Equality." *Adalah's Review* 1: 26–28.

────. 2000. "Towards a Critical Palestinian Minority Approach: Citizenship, Nationalism, and Feminism in Israeli Law." *Plilim* 9: 53. [Hebrew]

Kamir, Orit. 2000. "The 'Declaration' Has Two Faces: The Strange Tale of 'The Declaration of the Zionist State' and 'The Declaration of the Democratic State.'" *Iyouni Mishpat* 23 (2): 473–482. [Hebrew]

Kernochan, Julia. 1999. "Land Confiscation and Police Brutality in Um El Fahem." *Adalah's Review* 1: 49–53.

Kymlicka, Will. 1995. *Multicultural Citizenship.* Oxford: Clarendon Press.

Margalit, Avishai, and Moshe Halbertal. 1998. "Liberalism and the Right to Culture." In *Multiculturalism in a Democratic and Jewish State,* ed. Menachem Mautner, Avi Sagi, and Ronen Shamir, 93. Tel Aviv: Ramot Publishers. [Hebrew]

Minow, Martha. 1997. "Rights and Cultural Differences." In *Identities, Politics, and Rights,* ed. Austin Sarat and Thomas R. Kearns, 347–365. Ann Arbor: University of Michigan Press.

Nafa'a, Hisham. 1999. "Justice Zamir's Comment: Who is a Druze?" *Machbarot Adalah* 1: 18–20. [Hebrew]

Peled, Yoav. 2000. "Strangers in Utopia: The Civil Status of Palestinians in Israel." *Theory and Criticism* 3: 45. [Hebrew]

Rouhana, Nadim, and Asa'd Ghanem. 1998. "The Crisis of Minorities in Ethnic States: The Case of Palestinian Citizens in Israel." *International Journal of Middle East Studies* 30: 321–345

Saban, Ilan. 1998/1999. "The Option of the Limits of the Zionist Paradigm." In *Seven Ways: Theoretical Options for the Status of the Arabs in Israel,* ed. Sarah Ostzaki-Lazer, Asa'd Ghanem, and Ilan Pappe, 79. Givat Haviva: The Institute for Peace Research.

────. 2000. "The Legal Status of Minorities in Democratic Deeply Divided Societies." J.S.D. thesis, University of Haifa. [Hebrew]

Sack, Robert. 1986. *Human Territoriality: Theory and History.* Cambridge: Cambridge University Press.

Shamir, Ronen. 1991. "Legal Discourse, Media Discourse, and Speech Rights." *International Journal of the Sociology of Law* 18: 45.

────. 2000. "Zionism 2000: Past, Future and the Qa'dan Family." *Adalah's Review* 2: 27.

Shammas, Anton. 1995. "The Day After: 'Palestinians,' 'Israelis,' and Other Innermost Thoughts." In *Arab Politics in Israel—at a Crossroads*, ed. E. Rekhass and T. Yagnes, 19. Tel Aviv: Tel Aviv University.

Silberstein, Laurence J. 1999. *Postzionism Debates: Knowledge and Power in Israeli Culture.* New York: Routledge.

Smith, Anthony. 1981. *The Ethnic Revival.* Cambridge: Cambridge University Press.

Smooha, Sammy. 1993. "Political Culture and Social Cleavage." In *Israeli Democracy under Stress*, ed. Ehud Sprinzak and Larry Diamond, 325–326. Boulder: Lynne Rienner Publishers.

———. 1999. "The Status Quo Option: Israel as an Ethnic Democracy—a Jewish-Democratic State." In *Seven Ways: Theoretical Options for the Status of the Arabs in Israel*, ed. Sarah Osatski-Lazar, Asa'd Ghanem, and Ilan Pappe, 23–77. Givat Haviva: The Institute for Peace Research. [Hebrew]

Steiner, Henry, and Philip Alston. 1996. *International Human Rights in Context: Law, Politics, Morals.* Oxford: Oxford University Press.

Williams, Patricia J. 1987. "Alchemical Notes: Reconstructing Ideals from Deconstructed Right." *Harvard Civil Rights-Civil Liberties Law Review* 22: 401–433.

Yiftachel, Oren. 2000. "The Homeland and Nationalism." In *Encyclopedia of Nationalism*, ed. Alexander Motyl et al., 1:359–361. San Diego: Academic Press.

Yiftachel, Oren, Asa'd Ghanem, and Nadim Rouhana. 1999/2000. "Is an 'Ethnic Democracy' Feasible? Jews, Arabs, and the Israeli Regime." In *Jama'ah*, ed. Haya Bambaj-Sasportas, 67–68. Beer Sheva: Ben Gurion University.

Chapter 12

THE TRANSFORMATION OF GERMANY'S ETHNO-CULTURAL IDIOM

The Case of Ethnic German Immigrants

Daniel Levy

Introduction

This chapter explores how changing national self-understanding in the Federal Republic of Germany is related to immigration and concomitant debates about citizenship. Most of the scholarly literature on the question of immigration and nationhood in Germany has focused on labor migrants (so-called guest workers). I examine the issue of German nationhood by focusing on a very different group of immigrants, namely, ethnic Germans from East and Central Europe. They have enjoyed privileged access to citizenship on the grounds of Germany's descent-based laws. The literature commonly presents this privileged access of ethnic Germans and the persistence of *ius sanguinis* as expressing Germany's ethno-cultural understanding, at the expense of a civic-territorial conception of nationhood (Bade 1990, 1999; Fulbrook 1999). In a comparison of citizenship and nationhood in France and Germany, Rogers Brubaker focuses on the prevalence of the ethno-cultural idiom in German national self-understanding. He argues that "particular cultural idioms, ways of thinking and talking about nationhood—ethno-cultural and differential-ist [i.e., exclusionary] in Germany—were reinforced and activated in specific historical and institutional settings…" (Brubaker 1992: 6). According to Brubaker, the expansive approach toward ethnic Germans "reflects the pronounced ethno-cultural inflection in German self-understanding (Brubaker 1992: 4)."

This essay builds on the idea, in Brubaker's terms, that "citizenship in a nation-state is inevitably bound up with nationhood and national identity" and that "proposals to redefine the legal criteria of citizenship raise large and ideologically charged questions of nationhood and national belonging" (Brubaker 1992: 182).[1] However, in contrast to Brubaker, the focus is on those circumstances in which Germany's ethno-cultural idiom has been challenged. I analyze how ethnic Germans, who are formally part of the collective self, are transformed into "others." Ethnic Germans exemplify the notion of the ethno-cultural nation, an idea of nationhood not bound by the territorial limits of the state but expressed by shared language and culture (*Kulturnation*) and the principle of descent (*Ethnonation*). The politics that surround them—that is, the politics they pursued, and the politics pursued with them in mind—played a key, but underappreciated, role in the history of the FRG. Rather than presupposing that the inclusion of ethnic Germans expresses an essentialist ethnocultural self-understanding, this study describes a historical process in which the ethno-cultural idiom itself is remade. I examine how changing policies and perceptions of ethnic German immigrants have affected, and in turn been affected by, emerging forms of national self-understanding in Germany since 1945.[2] Representations of ethnic Germans over time reflect both ethnic and civic conceptions of nationhood. The balance between ethnic and civic understandings of nationhood is shaped on a background of political contingencies and crucial historical turning points. Here our focus will be on reunification and the growing prominence of immigration in public and political discourse during the 1990s.

Ethnic Germans and the Reconfiguration of National Categories

The Potsdam Treaty sanctioned large population transfers after the Second World War, which led to the flight and expulsion of about ten million ethnic Germans from Eastern and Central Europe. They are commonly referred to as expellees (*Vertriebene*). Two million followed between 1950 and 1988, referred to as *Aussiedler* (late resettlers or ethnic German immigrants). Over two million *Aussiedler* have come to Germany since 1989. However, they are not a culturally homogeneous group. Indeed, ethnic German minorities are a rather heterogeneous group, who over the last two centuries have developed different cultural attributes and a variety of German dialects. Some have maintained ethnic traits and preserved German traditions while others have been highly assimilated (Münz and Ohliger 1997). It is a legally sanctioned ethno-national self-understanding that defines them as German—no matter how feeble their "ethnicity" in terms of culture or language—rather than a set of uniform cultural practices. It was the legally privileged access of ethnic Germans to Germany that institutionalized descent as a definition of Germanness, independent of culture and ethnicity.[3]

West German national self-understanding has been shaped in the context of three historical junctures during which the place of ethnic German immigrants in the articulation of ethno-cultural nationhood was transformed. The empirical focus of this essay is on the post–Cold War period.[4] Findings are based on three categories of data covering a wide range of Germany's political discourse about ethnic Germans. Memories of the past and emerging perceptions of ethnic Germans are established and interpreted through a variety of social institutions that involve the official-political sphere. Here the analysis consists of an examination of parliamentary speeches and keynote speeches that refer to ethnic Germans (e.g., *Berichte zur Lage der Nation,* or state of the nation addresses, and *Regierungserklärungen,* or governmental declarations and inaugural addresses). In addition, the official governmental stance toward ethnic Germans, as expressed in a monthly publication called *Info Dienst Deutsche Aussiedler,* is analyzed. The government distributes it to state agencies, the press, policy makers and voluntary organizations involved with the integration of ethnic Germans. The institutional-legislative sphere reflects how the memory of ethnic Germans has been institutionalized in citizenship regulations and how legislation, in turn, shapes public perceptions. Finally, public-cultural discourse about ethnic Germans is particularly salient in the post–Cold War era when the number of ethnic German immigrants rose dramatically. Key editorials from leading national newspapers are examined. The analysis of these editorials is complemented with relevant opinion surveys. This allows one to distinguish between public and publicized modes of representation. Together, these three kinds of data encompass a wide range of perceptions, and delineate the discursive possibilities to imagine and talk about the nation.

The Postwar Period

In the first postwar decade, Germany's ethno-cultural self-understanding remained largely intact. However, questions of political legitimacy rather than ethnic attachments explain this persistence. After World War II, West Germany faced the problem of salvaging aspects of German nationhood not tainted or defined by the Nazi regime. Rather than focus on the active participation and widespread consent of the German population in the Nazi regime, Germans portrayed themselves as victims. This image of victimization dominated the first postwar decade and provided a consensus around which a sense of nationhood was reconstructed. The expulsion of Germans from territories east of the Oder-Neisse line was a major basis for the collective claim to victim status. Ethnic Germans were the primary carrier of this ethno-cultural notion. The strength of this understanding of suffering was underscored through the widespread institutional power ethnic Germans had at the time (Levy 2002a). Perceptions of the suffering of ethnic Germans—sustained through social memories and promoted by published autobiographies and official commemorative occasions—played a significant role in the rehabilitation of German nationhood and the reproduction of an ethno-cultural self-understanding.

No less important was the institutionalization of extensive legislative measures on behalf of ethnic Germans. The Federal Republic adopted descent-based citizenship legislation that relied on the 1913 Imperial and State Law (*Reichs- und Staatsangehörigkeitsgesetz*) and modifications made by the Nazi regime. Why would this liberal postwar constitution adopt citizenship regulations based on *ius sanguinis*? One possible answer lies in Germany's powerful ethno-cultural traditions and their hold on the national imagination (Brubaker 1992; Fulbrook 1999). However, the choice of *ius sanguinis* as the basis of citizenship in 1948 was not a simple adoption of the preexisting ethno-cultural German citizenship law dating back to 1913. There was nothing "natural" about this initial adoption and the continuous reliance on the Imperial Law of 1913. It was determined by social policy concerns and political calculations shaped in specific circumstances of the postwar period.

It was, first and foremost, a matter of social policy. That is to say, only a generous interpretation of German citizenship law could provide legal equality between ethnic Germans and the resident population. Legal equality for expellees and refugees from the former Eastern territories within the borders of 1937 was established through the Basic Law (*Grundgesetz*) in 1949. This status was extended to *Aussiedler* in the Federal Expellee law of 1953. A second consideration was largely of a political nature. The reproduction of an ethno-cultural understanding was instrumental in sustaining West Germany's claim to embody German unity, despite its actual division and loss of its eastern territory to another sovereign German state. The main point here is that it was those political and social considerations that were institutionalized in the citizenship law, not a preexisting understanding of Germanness.

The Discrediting of the Ethno-cultural

The second historical turning point emerged during the 1960s against the backdrop of new foreign policy considerations (Cold War détente) and Willy Brandt's reconciliatory *Ostpolitik* (politics toward Central and Eastern Europe). Expellee organizations objected to these changes and their rhetoric against the East—a resource during the earlier phases of the Cold War—now appeared retrograde and disruptive. Brandt marked them as radical and dangerous. Negative public perceptions of expellees contributed to the gradual demise of the ethno-cultural idiom. The discrediting of the ethno-cultural theme was intensified in the conflict between Germany's first postwar generation and its predecessors. The revolt against the elder generation by the "68ers" was also a revolt against the ethno-cultural understanding of Germanness since it was associated with Nazism. The outcome was a reevaluation of Germany's national past, resulting in public and official representations that increasingly associated expellee organizations, and, by extension, ethno-cultural nationhood, with outdated traditions, historical revisionism or even the legacies of the Nazi past. Ethno-cultural ideas were weakened and relegated to the fringes of political discourse, but not forgotten. However, official attempts to revive ethno-cultural references during the early 1980s by stressing historical memories of the postwar decade were futile.

The Post-unification Period

The end of the Cold War and the concomitant process of German unification constitute an important historical juncture during which questions of national self-understanding were pushed to the fore. Renewed debates about the role of the nation, Germany's nationalistic aspirations and its position in the European Union, have since been dominant themes. According to some, reunification revived a traditional sense of the ethno-cultural nation. Mary Fulbrook (1999) rightly points out that some of the ethno-national tropes persisted in the German Democratic Republic. In contrast to its discrediting in the Federal Republic, East Germany never divested itself of this conception and it was readily available once the opportunity for reunification presented itself. This dynamic is frequently illustrated by a shift in emphasis during the demonstrations that led to the opening of the Wall: from the democratic emphasis of *"Wir sind das Volk"* (We are the people) to the more nationalistic *"Wir sind ein Volk"* (We are one people).

However, looking at the reception of ethnic German immigrants in the aftermath of unification and the ongoing antagonism between West and East Germans, one has to cast doubt on this interpretation. The preservation of ethno-cultural tropes in East Germany does not imply their incorporation into unified Germany. On the contrary, in light of the negative attitude Westerners harbor toward the East (in part as a result of the financial burdens unification imposed through their taxes), the association of the ethno-cultural with the East, further contributed to its discrediting. This process is part of a broader attempt to associate racism, neo-Nazism and violence against strangers as an East German problem. To be sure, this is not to say that these issues are not a real and pervasive problem in both parts of Germany. Instead, my argument is that xenophobia and other exclusionary measures, for the most part, no longer rely on descent. As I will show in the following section, anti-immigrant sentiments are primarily addressed in the context of new and broad debates of monocultural and multicultural conceptions and utilitarian considerations about immigration. In this context, I argue, ethnic German *Spätaussiedler* are no longer perceived as co-nationals but as just another group of immigrants. On this view, reunification has not led to a re-nationalization (at least not along ethnic lines) but to a further decline of the ethno-cultural idiom.[5]

From Volk *to Immigrants*

The weakness of the ethno-cultural code is thus underscored on the backdrop of crucial historical junctures (i.e., the opening of the Iron Curtain and German unification) and related political contingencies (i.e., the inclusion of ethnic Germans in a highly politicized debate about immigration). My findings of this period show how official ethno-cultural rhetoric about ethnic Germans has been replaced with social and economic references and how their integration has increasingly been situated within a broader debate about immigration. The permanent recognition of Germany's eastern borders was formalized in the unification treaties, but the symbolic boundaries of the nation were far from settled. Negotiations over who should be considered part of the German nation assumed a new quality after 1989. In addition to a growing number of asylum seekers, the sudden influx of "national ethnics" from the GDR (so-called *Übersiedler*) and the dramatic rise in *Aussiedler* numbers sharpened the public debate. In 1989 the number of asylum seekers reached 121,318; from East Germany 343,854 *Übersiedler* came to West Germany; and the number of *Aussiedler* rose from 78,523 in 1987 to 202,673 in 1988 and almost doubled to 377,055 in 1989.

Official celebrations of the political unification of Germany did little to alleviate the growing resentment of resident Germans toward the influx of these "fellow Germans."[6] *Aussiedler* were thrust into a highly politicized debate about immigration, in which previously held distinctions between German newcomers (*Zuwanderer*) and nonnational immigrants were fading. Ethnic Germans would no longer confirm Germany's official ethno-cultural self-understanding. On the contrary, state practices and official governmental declarations about *Aussiedler* greatly contributed to the decline of ethno-cultural references and, eventually, the legal redefinition of German nationality.

Let me briefly illustrate the context and content of this transformation. The government's initial response in 1988 to the growing number of *Aussiedler* was to declare the integration of ethnic Germans a "national goal."[7] Presenting a special program for the integration of *Aussiedler*, Chancellor Helmut Kohl declared:

> It is my desire that we receive our fellow-countrymen (*Landsleute*) with open arms....Our new fellow citizens (*Mitbürger*) from the regions of outer settlement (*Aussiedlungsgebiete*) are a gain for our country and our society....A notable problem that many *Aussiedler* have—particularly the younger ones— is that they don't have any or very little knowledge of German. That is not their fault. We have to be aware that it was not possible for most *Aussiedler* to learn our language...As the numbers of *Aussiedler* grows the federal state has already increased the resources for their integration (Pressemitteilung des Presse- und Informationsamtes der Bundesregierung, from here on: PPI, Nr. 301/88, 8/31/1988).

At first, the state mobilized material and symbolic resources to communicate the national importance of *Aussiedler* integration to the larger native population. This was also part of Kohl's *Geschichtspolitik* (politics with history) and his attempt to revive traditional conceptions of German nationhood. Historical memories of the postwar period were frequently invoked and played a significant role in the government's attempts to promote support and understanding for its policies toward *Aussiedler*. Comparisons between the postwar and the post–Cold War period abounded. However, appeals to ethno-cultural values and memories of ethnic Germans no longer resonated with the collective self-understanding of the majority of the population. Consequently, historical memories of expulsion and postwar economic reconstruction remained largely ineffective in generating support for the integration of *Aussiedler*. Memories of ethnic German suffering contended with more recent accounts of victimhood that emphasized memories of the Holocaust. Moreover ethno-cultural references were publicly associated with Nazism and the government's open approach toward *Aussiedler* was often dismissed as *"Bonner Deutschtumspolitik,"* (a politics of Germandom) implying that the immigration of ethnic Germans was related to ethno-national motives. As the Social Democrat Peter Conradi put it: "Many *Länder* are opting out of the consensus of the 'national goal' [proclaimed by Chancellor Kohl]. Only at the end of last year the Prime Minister of Saarland Oskar Lafontaine (SPD) was attacked because he criticized this unconditional immigration as *'Deutschtümelei'* (Germanocentric outlook). Now politicians in almost all *Länder* speak openly about how to resist the *'Heim-ins-Reich-Politik'* from Bonn (BT, 1/15/1990)."[8] The association between the immigration of ethnic Germans and discredited ethno-national motives was not confined to polemics. It was strengthened through recurrent reports about how ethnic Germans were granted *Aussiedler* status based on written evidence drawn from Nazi documents.[9] Kohl's attempts at dissociating ethno-cultural values from the ethno-racial policies of the Nazis were weakened by recurrent press reports about how official documents from the Nazi period (such as membership in the SS) served as sufficient evidence for their citizenship entitlement.

The second aspect that distinguished the public perception of *Aussiedler* immigration from the historical memories of expellees' postwar integration related to the absence of shared social memories and the lack of institutional power. From a simple quantitative point of view, the comparison with the postwar period is instructive. About ten million ethnic Germans came to West Germany in the aftermath of the Second World War, every sixth citizen of the Federal Republic (Münz and Ohliger 1997). The post–Cold War scenario differs significantly. Between 1988 and 1996, about 2.25 million *Aussiedler* came to Germany (approximately every twenty-fifth citizen).[10] However, their weakness is not only a matter of demographics. In contrast to the shared social memories of the 1950s and the presence of expellees in all realms of German politics and society, *Aussiedler* have no institutional power and lack the cultural capital to influence public discourse. Those who have arrived during the last decade have little command of the German language and their cultural and social habits greatly differ from West Germans. Instead of shaping policies, they are merely subjects of decisions that are made in response to social and economic considerations rather than with respect to "national priorities." Post–Cold War Germany offers few economic opportunities for *Aussiedler* and many depend on various measures of state support. In light of structural economic problems and chronic unemployment rates, *Aussiedler* remain at the margins of society.[11] They are treated as a policy problem by the state and are perceived as welfare recipients by the wider public.

Realizing that ethno-cultural appeals were insufficient to generate public support for the integration of ethnic Germans, the government complemented its organic rhetoric with an emphasis on the economic contributions of ethnic Germans. However, this "utilitarian" approach, portraying ethnic German immigration as economically beneficial, contradicted the government's own arguments about the economic costs of other migratory movements. For years, the Kohl government had warned against immigration, associating it with a socioeconomic burden for the wider population. Ultimately, this utilitarian approach contributed to the conflation by the public of ethnic Germans and other groups of immigrants.[12] Once the public perceived of ethnic Germans as just another group of immigrants, representations relied on the same negative symbolism previously reserved for labor migrants or asylum seekers (Levy 1999). The majority of the population showed little interest in ethno-cultural considerations when assessing the economic benefits the participation of specific groups would yield.[13] Most resident Germans perceived of ethnic German immigrants in terms of social envy (*Sozialneid*). A majority favored a more restrictive approach regarding the immigration of ethnic Germans.[14] With the backdrop of high unemployment rates, housing shortages and a charged public debate, arguments used against the immigration of foreigners now also shaped public opinions on ethnic Germans.

Concomitant with the absorption of the ethnic German theme into the broader debate about immigration, official ethno-cultural references were minimized and the hitherto expansive approach toward these fellow ethnic Germans was replaced with increasingly restrictive legislation.[15] Conversely, restrictive legislation and administrative practices toward ethnic Germans were reflective of, and contributed to, the ways in which they were addressed in public discourse. Although some politicians in the government continually insisted on the special status of ethnic Germans, control and regulation of ethnic German immigration became the primary policy objectives. With ongoing revisions to the expansive legal framework from the 1950s, discrepancies between public proclamations of ethno-cultural solidarity and restrictive administrative practices were apparent to the public. The focus here is not on the procedural rules, but on the larger normative implications these legislative changes carry. "A strongly institutionalized system of official ethno-national identities makes certain categories available for the public representation of social reality, the framing of political claims, and the organization of political action" (Brubaker 1998: 288). In this case, we are observing the reverse, that is, a deinstitutionalization of ethno-cultural categories and their effect on claim-making activities.

Early legislation between 1989 and 1992 was aimed at the regulation of integration and the amelioration of social tensions between resident Germans and ethnic German immigrants.[16] After 1992, these regulatory efforts continued, but legislative changes also involved redefining Germanness. If postwar legislation for ethnic Germans was generous and justified in social and ethno-cultural terms, new legislation after 1989 was recast in social terms only. In both periods, integration was a central policy objective. However, in the postwar period, expellees exerted a strong influence on the legislative process and the need for integration led to an expansive approach that provided "positive discrimination" for ethnic Germans. In comparison, the need for integration in the post–Cold War period has been framed in the context of "social envy" (*Sozialneid*), precluding preferential treatment of ethnic Germans in the absence of a grand narrative of suffering. On the contrary, reduced integrative measures were deemed necessary to ameliorate social tensions with long-time residents. Paradoxically, financial cuts have exacerbated their dependency on welfare measures, which, in turn, has made "social envy" even more salient.

After 1992, these regulatory measures were complemented by legislation that essentially will put an end to privileged immigration of ethnic Germans within the next decade. In the process, the criteria for belonging to the German nation were also redefined. In contrast to previous administrative adjustments aimed at the regulation and restriction of ethnic German immigration, this legislation explicitly inscribed the end of ethnic German suffering into the Law for Settling the Consequences of the War. Political transformations in Eastern Europe—democratization processes and the recognition of minority rights—weakened the appeal of ethno-cultural rhetoric and undermined the central rationale for ethnic German immigration, namely the postwar assumption of an ongoing *Vertreibungsdruck* (expulsion pressure).

Not only was the ethnic German theme absorbed into the heated debate about the so-called *Asylkompromiss* (asylum compromise), but fundamental ethno-cultural assumptions about their automatic right to immigrate were undermined or altogether eliminated. The government and administrative courts actively redefined what it means to be German. Descent and commitment to the German *Volk* had always been ambiguous criteria. It was precisely because of the vagueness of these criteria that administrative guidelines enjoyed a certain room for maneuver. This left many decisions about who is legally German to the discretion of administrative bodies, which had been remarkably expansive toward ethnic Germans (Brubaker 1992). Prior to 1989, ethnic Germans who had minimal or no command of German and who had been fully assimilated were recognized as *Aussiedler*. Their forced assimilation—that is, their inability to preserve the German language and culture—was interpreted as discrimination and thus reason enough to grant them citizenship. It was precisely because of their inability to display any of those criteria that they were legally recognized as a persecuted ethnic minority. If the absence of language skills for years counted as evidence for repression and an argument for the inclusion of ethnic Germans, lacking German language skills were now a ground for exclusion. Analysis of the legislative process reveals that the justifications for these changes were not made with reference to concerns over nationhood but were absorbed into the broader debate of integration and social envy. Language was no longer discussed as an ethno-cultural signifier and its relationship to a narrative of victimhood, but as a prerequisite for the successful integration into the Federal Republic.

In sum, changes in public perceptions and the inclusion of ethnic Germans into highly politicized debates about immigration in conjunction with widely publicized restrictive state measures contributed to the official and popular decline of an ethno-cultural self-understanding. After years of highly politicized debates and governmental rhetoric about the economic and social downsides of immigration, Germans were more concerned with their socioeconomic well-being than with the smooth integration of their "fellow ethnic Germans." Nonethnic criteria complemented descent as desirable conditions for membership in the German nation. Official ethno-cultural rhetoric was gradually replaced by a discourse that situated nationhood in distinctively nonethnic terms revolving around social norms.[17] They were now perceived as immigrants rather than as bearers of a particular sense of Germanness.

Conclusions

The changing status of ethnic Germans expressed in restrictive policies, negative perceptions and a broad recognition that they are part of a debate about immigration rather than a privileged group, have informed a discourse where ethno-cultural criteria no longer carry symbolic or political weight. Evidence for this trend arises from recent controversies about new citizenship regulations. In the fall of 1998, a new center-left coalition of Social Democrats and the ecological Green Party was elected. Their first policy decision was to introduce a bill that would reform citizenship legislation and be more inclusive toward millions of labor migrants (*Gastarbeiter*) who have been living in Germany since the 1950s, essentially introducing elements of *ius soli*. The new law came into effect on 1 January 2000.[18] The proposal also contained a provision for "dual citizenship," allowing new German citizens to keep the citizenship of their countries of origin. Without dual citizenship, earlier administrative easing of naturalization procedures remained insignificant since the majority of eligible foreigners were unwilling to give up their original citizenship. The dual

citizenship provisions became a topic of heated political and public controversy. It reinforced the view that attempts to redefine citizenship in
Germany are about national self-understanding and the imagined
boundaries of the national community. This citizenship controversy was
not about potential immigration but rather about what the criteria for
becoming German should be for those foreigners already in Germany.
The controversy illuminates the ways in which the ethno-cultural code
has become bereft of its political and cultural relevance.

The citizenship initiative was strongly contested by the conservative
CDU/CSU. Shortly after the government announced its plans, the CDU/
CSU initiated a campaign against the "dual citizenship" provision. It lit-
erally took its objections to the street, collecting signatures against the
proposed measure.[19] One could surmise that the rejection stance on "dual
citizenship" is a sign of the persistence of ethno-cultural conceptions.
And, to be sure, some far right members of the CDU and the Bavarian
CSU openly expressed concerns about the possibility that millions of
Muslims would become German citizens, a sentiment certainly shared by
a significant portion of the population. However, the official arguments
of CDU/CSU objections to the citizenship proposals did not refer to any
of the ethno-cultural tropes that had earlier characterized debates on citizenship. During the 1980s and early 1990s, opponents of dual citizenship
for Germany's Turkish immigrant minority ritualistically invoked the
formula that "Germany is not a country of immigration."

Since the mid 1990s, mainstream objections to the incorporation of
Turks have no longer been conducted with reference to an ethno-cultural
vocabulary but have been absorbed into a functional approach that centers on the conditions of successful integration.[20] Reliance on language
skills as a prerequisite for labor-market integration rather than language
as a cultural marker of nationality is reminiscent of the argument that is
used to determine whether people from Eastern Europe are granted the
status of ethnic German immigrants. Concerns over the social effects of
immigration rather than ethno-cultural attributes of immigrants inform
debates about citizenship. Successful integration into the social fabric is
perceived as the primary issue for becoming a member of the nation, and
language rather than descent its chief expression.

A second objection to dual citizenship revolves around the question of
alleged loyalty conflicts and speaks to the theme of belonging. Opponents of dual citizenship invoke scenarios in which dual loyalties stand
in contradiction to the idea that one's primary collective commitment
should focus on the country of which one is a citizen. The question of
civic and political loyalty is an important and legitimate concern for the
sovereign nation, though it seems that immigrants, when forced to
choose usually display political loyalty to their country of settlement (Rex
1994). Once immigration is predicated on integration and loyalty rather
than on descent, choices can be made, both by immigrants themselves
and by the state. This is the decisive political aspect of the controversy

rather than the xenophobic subtext and popular anti-immigrant senti-ments of the signature campaign. Debates about dual citizenship have deflected attention from the real incision into Germany's body politic. Ethno-cultural considerations have been relegated to the fringes of Ger-many's political discourse as debates about immigrants, including ethnic Germans, have shifted from a national rhetoric to preoccupations with social integration. Occasional ethno-cultural references continue to exist as a mechanism of exclusion against immigrants. But since it also tends to exclude ethnic Germans—not to mention the continuously antagonistic relationship between West and East Germans—the ethno-cultural code remains a weak category for collective identification let alone mobilization.

The case of ethnic Germans shows how conceptions of otherness are evolving in the context of historical junctures, and how politically con-tingent they are. Different representations of ethnic Germans and chang-ing legislation for *Aussiedler* illustrate the malleability of nationhood and the struggles around the formation of new modes of collective identifica-tion. The absence of geopolitical and demographic considerations, on the one hand, and the political, cultural and economic centrality of Ger-many's European embeddedness, on the other, indicates that inclusion into the collectivity is no longer based on formal criteria of descent. Instead, it is narrated through a history that is shaped by a new national iconography (economic reconstruction, democratization) that resonates with the resident majority and tends to exclude those who are newcom-ers. To be sure, citizenship remains a mechanism of social closure, but the conditions for participation in the German polity have changed.

Notes

This essay is a revised and expanded version of an article entitled "The Politicization of Eth-nic German Immigrants: The Transformation of State Priorities" (Levy 2002b).

1. As such, Germany is part of a broader phenomenon in postwar Western Europe, where controversies about immigration have replaced conflicts between states as the primary arena for the articulation of nationhood (Schain and Baldwin-Edwards 1994; Tilly 1995). Most of these debates on collective identification have been triggered through the cultural, economic, and political effects of migration giving rise to widespread pol-itics of belonging and reassessments of collective boundaries (Geddes and Favell 1999). National identity is perceived here as a changeable product of collective self-identification, "not as its stable underlying cause" (Brubaker 1994: 9). In this view, national identifications are continually constructed, contested, and negotiated as his-torically contingent, path-dependent projects, arising in politically charged settings.
2. The claim is not that ethnic Germans are the only force acting on national identifica-tion. The ways in which official political discourse has addressed them in the last fifty years is not identical with nationhood but a symptomatic illustration of the reforma-tion of Germany's ethno-cultural self-understanding.

3. It should be noted that this was not merely a German decision but also a praxis promoted by the Soviet Union, which deported ethnic Germans and enforced various measures of discrimination against them.

4. This essay is part of a larger project that examines political debates about ethnic Germans in three distinctive periods including the first postwar decade, the late 1960s and early 1970s. For a more detailed analysis of the postwar period, see Levy 2002a.

5. Another example of this trend is the recent controversy about the so-called *Leitkultur* (dominant culture). On the surface, one could easily interpret the demand for a dominant culture as a return to traditional ethno-cultural tropes. However, what is striking about the debate is that its conservative proponents are stressing such general aspects as the command over language and full integration into society. To be sure, the underlying motivation might well be guided by deep-seated convictions of innate Germanness, but their public articulation shifts the attention to aspects that, at least theoretically, provide choices and the option to participate in the German collectivity. It thus becomes part of a more generic majority-minority conflict.

6. Ongoing tensions between "Wessis" and "Ossis," as West and East Germans refer to each other, are widely acknowledged. For an overview of the various facets of this antagonism, see Welsh 1997.

7. Pressemitteilung des Presse- und Informationsamtes der Bundesregierung (PPI), Nr. 301/88, 8/31/1988

8. The *Heim-ins-Reich* term originally refers to Nazi policies to resettle ethnic Germans from Eastern Europe within the boundaries of the Third Reich.

9. As part of its expansionist policy and the need to rule over a docile population, the Nazis compiled so-called *Volkslisten* in the conquered territories in Eastern Europe. While Nazis used their ethno-racial ideology to disenfranchise people and strip them of their citizenship within the German Reich, they were more inclusive toward certain segments of the populations that they conquered.

10. The figures for 1997 and 1998 are below 150,000; since 1999, the numbers have dropped below 100,000.

11. The assessment of their actual unemployment rate is problematic since the Bundesanstalt für Arbeit (Federal Agency for Employment) does not keep records of *Aussiedler* beyond a five-year limit, after which *Aussiedler* are treated as ordinary Germans (Mammey and Schiener 1996). These limitations notwithstanding, assessments of unemployment figures for *Aussiedler* can be made. Official estimates are in the range of 30 percent, but this number is far higher if we include those who are excluded from the unemployment statistics because they partake in such state-sponsored programs as language courses or job-retraining measures.

12. Public surveys during the early 1990s reveal that ethnic Germans were publicly identified as Russians, Poles, and Romanians. Thus, when asked whether ethnic Germans were true Germans, only 31 percent answered affirmatively, with 40 percent not sure; for 29 percent they were clearly not (Noelle-Neumann and Köcher 1993: 520).

13. In 1990, questioned about the advantages and disadvantages of labor-market participation of different ethnic groups, 46 percent saw the presence of labor migrants as advantageous (17 percent as disadvantageous), whereas only 13 percent responded affirmatively for ethnic German immigrants (53 percent thought of it as disadvantageous) (ALLBUS 1990).

14. In a 1990 survey, public opinion indicates that 83 percent wanted to restrict immigration access for ethnic Germans, of which 20 percent wanted to end their immigration altogether. Only 17 percent thought ethnic Germans should continue to enjoy privileged access to citizenship. This is even more striking when we compare these figures with the relatively high level of approval for employees from EU countries (almost one-third) and for *Übersiedler* from the GDR (almost one-fourth) (ALLBUS 1990). In a 1996 survey, the number of people who wanted to restrict the immigration of ethnic Germans rose to 85 percent (ALLBUS 1996).

15. The main legislative changes are expressed in the law on the allocation of housing, the Law for Establishing a Provisional Place of Residence for Late Resettlers (*Gesetz über die Festlegung eines vorläufigen Wohnortes für Spätaussiedler – Wohnortzuweisungsgesetz*), 1989; the Integration Adjustment Law (*Eingliederungsanpassungsgesetz*), 1990; the Law Regulating the Reception of Resettlers (*Aussiedleraufnahmegesetz*), 1990; the Law Dealing with Late Consequences of World War II (*Kriegsfolgenbereinigungsgesetz*), 1992. In addition, many administrative guidelines were changed in the aftermath of unification, most notably the institution of stringent language tests for applicants for ethnic German immigration status in 1996.

16. Despite its attempts to separate ethnic Germans from the larger immigration question, the government ultimately yielded to public and political pressures and initially instituted a yearly quota of approximately 200,000. The government has been jubilant about its ability to reduce the number of ethnic German immigrants ever since, and the quota has been reduced to 100,000.

17. When asked in 1996 which criteria Germans deem as the most important condition for naturalization, not having a criminal record was listed first by 86 percent, followed by concerns that those to be naturalized can provide for their own livelihood (78 percent), have long lived in Germany (73 percent), speak German (66 percent), have adjusted to a German lifestyle (62 percent), and are born in Germany (60 percent). Only then was German descent listed (54 percent) (ALLBUS 1996).

18. The law affects up to three of the seven million resident "foreigners." Immigrant children born in Germany qualify temporarily for dual citizenship if one parent was under fourteen upon entering the country and has remained a resident, or if one parent, at the time of the child's birth, had lived in Germany for at least eight years and is in possession of a residence permit. Between age eighteen and twenty-three they have to opt for one of the two passports. In addition, foreign residents who have lived for eight years in Germany can claim naturalization. Foreigners eighteen or older who wish to naturalize have to pass a German language test and must have no criminal record.

19. By March 1999, the opposition had collected over two million signatures. Dual citizenship remains controversial. According to surveys, 53 percent were against it and 39 percent in favor of it (EMNID January 1999). There are clear differences based on age. Among those under thirty, 50 percent were in favor as opposed to only 28 percent among those over fifty years of age (Newsletter 1999: 3).

20. To be sure, the argument is not that all Germans subscribe to a multicultural vision of society or that tolerance levels are higher, but rather that a multiethnic society frames the mnemonic experience of nationhood for the majority of the population. West Germany's postwar generations have not known anything but a multiethnic society. With the institutionalization of *ius soli* this demographic fact is invested with an official normative power. Hence, the shift from an officially sanctioned "we are not a country of immigration" as an expression of a *Volksgemeinschaft* to the popular standpoint that "we do not want any more immigrants" is interpretively and politically important.

References

Allgemeine Bevölkerungsumfragen in den Sozialwissenschaften (ALLBUS). 1990–1996. Mannheim: ZUMA.

Bade, Klaus J., ed. 1990. *Neue Heimat im Westen. Vertriebene, Flüchtlinge, Aussiedler.* Münster: Verlag Westfälischer Heimatbund.

———. 1999. *Aussiedler. Deutsche Einwanderer aus Osteuropa.* Osnabrück: Universitätsverlag Rasch.

Brubaker, Rogers. 1992. *Citizenship and Nationhood in France and Germany.* Cambridge, Mass.: Harvard University Press.

———. 1994. "Rethinking Nationhood: Nation as Institutionalized Form, Practical Category, Contingent Event." *Contention* 4: 3–14.

———. 1998. "Myth and Misconceptions in the Study of Nationalism." In *The State of the Nation: Ernest Gellner and the Theory of Nationalism,* ed. John A. Hall, 272–306. New York: Cambridge University Press.

Fulbrook, Mary. 1999. *German National Identity after the Holocaust.* Cambridge: Polity Press.

Geddes, Andrew, and Adrian Favell, eds. 1999. *The Politics of Belonging: Migrants and Minorities in Contemporary Europe.* Avebury: Aldershot.

Levy, Daniel. 1999. "Coming Home? Ethnic Germans and the Transformation of National Identity in the Federal Republic of Germany." In *Immigration and the Politics of Belonging in Contemporary Europe,* ed. Andrew Geddes and Adrian Favell, 93–108. Avebury: Aldershot.

———. 2002a. "Refugees, Expellees, and Aussiedler in the Federal Republic of Germany: Social, Political, and Legal Dimensions of the Integration Process." In *Coming Home to Germany? The Integration of Ethnic Germans from Central and Eastern Europe in the Federal Republic,* ed. David Rock and Stefan Wolff. Oxford: Berghahn Books (forthcoming).

———. 2002b. "The Politicization of Ethnic German Immigrants: The Transformation of State Priorities." In *Ethnic Migration in 20th Century Europe: Germany, Israel and Russia in Comparative Perspective.* ed. Rainer Münz and Rainer Ohliger. London: Frank Cass (forthcoming).

Mammey, Ulrich, and Rolf Schiener. 1996. "Das BiB-Aussiedlerpanel – Methodische Überlegungen zur Repräsentativität." *Zeitschrift für Bevölkerungswissenschaft* 22: 145–170.

Münz, Rainer, and Rainer Ohliger. 1997. "Long-Distance Citizens: Ethnic Germans and their Immigration to Germany." In *Paths to Inclusion: The Integration of Migrants in the United States and Germany,* ed. Peter H. Schuck and Rainer Münz, 155–201. Providence: Berghahn Books.

Münz, Rainer, Wolfgang Seifert, and Ralf Ulrich, eds. 1997. *Zuwanderung nach Deutschland. Strukturen, Wirkungen, Perspektiven.* Frankfurt am Main: Campus.

Newsletter. 1999. *Migration und Bevölkerung.* February. Berlin: Humboldt-Universität.

Noelle-Neumann, Elizabeth, and Renate Köcher, eds. 1993. *Allensbacher Jahrbuch der Demoskopie 1984–1992.* Munich: Saur.

Rex, John, and Beatrice Drury, eds. 1994. *Ethnic Mobilisation in a Multi-cultural Europe.* Avebury: Aldershot.

Schain, Martin, and Martin Baldwin-Edwards. 1994. "The Politics of Immigration: Introduction." *West European Politics* 17: 1–16.

Tilly, Charles. 1995. "Citizenship, Identity and Social History." *International Review of Social History* 40 (Supplement 3): 1–17.

Welsh, Helga A., Andreas Pickel, and Dorothy Rosenberg. 1997. "East and West German Identities: United and Divided?" In *After Unity: Reconfiguring German Identities,* ed. Konrad H. Jarausch, 103–137. Providence: Berghahn Books.

PART FIVE

REVISITING CITIZENSHIP AND IDENTITY: THE JEWISH EXPERIENCE

Chapter 13

THE JEWISH CHALLENGES IN THE NEW EUROPE

~~~~~~

Diana Pinto

Introduction

In early March 1999, three weeks before the war in Kosovo began, an international conference was held in Budapest on "Southeastern Europe: A New Agenda for the Twenty-First Century." There were of course no Jewish topics on the program, for Europe no longer has a "Jewish question" and Israelis were not present. Yet the Hungarian keynote speaker, as well as many local activists working for transnational dialogue, borderless harmony, and a more civilized European space, were all Jewish. They would of course have recoiled in horror if someone had defined them as "Jews" as a way of relativizing or perhaps even disqualifying their statements. A commanding Jewish presence thus remained invisible on the continent as though the very idea of saying publicly "As a Jew in Europe, I would like Europe to be or to do such and such" had continued to be an impossible proposition after Auschwitz just as it had been before—an identity sacrilege in our universal and highly individualist democratic societies.

The issues raised by the presence/absence of so many Jews at that Balkan conference lie at the core of this essay. Have Jews in Europe today become exclusively a group that has turned the horrors of the past into an identity icon? Or do they have a future-oriented role to play in a continent coming to grips with democratic, pluralist and multicultural challenges? It is my belief that Jews across Europe today, and particularly so in united Germany, are not only central actors of the continent's new political and cultural stakes, but also inevitable mirror images for Israel's own identity debates. What Jews have won for themselves from their respective European states in rights and identity recognition will inevitably spill over into what Israel will one day be expected to give to its own "others." Hence lies the need to understand the transformations in Jewish life in Europe in the last decade.

In this essay we will examine five transformations, in reality the over-coming of five postwar obstacles, which have effectively given a new centrality to Jewish life in Europe. The first is a fundamental internal transformation: the slow lifting of the profound (and not wholly unjustified) antipathy for the very concept of "Europe" in a post-Shoah Jewish world dominated by American Jewry and Israel. The second is a major international transformation: the end of the Cold War divide symbolized by the fall of the Berlin Wall in 1989. Only when the two halves of the continent were reunited could the Jews within them, with their multiple and clashing pasts, be reunited as voluntary Jews. And nowhere was this more true than in Germany. The third is a most important European transformation: the "coming home" of the Holocaust in the national memory of each country, beyond guilty Germany. The fourth transformation has been the coming to the fore of "new Jews" in Europe with a very different outlook and identity compared to those of the pre-Shoah world. The fifth transformation, which is only just beginning, can be defined as the formation of a new American-Israeli-European triangle involving both Jews and non-Jews. The combined weight of these transformations is giving Jews in Europe a new central role to play both inside Europe and in the Jewish world at large.

The Postwar Ambiguity of the European Jewish Reference

After the near extermination of European Jewry, most Jews in the world were convinced that Europe had become, after Auschwitz, the equivalent of post-1492 Spain: a place with a spent Jewish past no longer harboring significant Jewish life. On this count, ideology seemed to back history. Zionism, well before Nazism and the creation of the state of Israel, delegitimized a Jewish presence in incurably anti-Semitic Europe and prodded the return of all the Jews to their historic homeland, Eretz Israel. American Jews shared, along with so many other immigrants to the New World, a similar reading of Europe as a continent of intolerance and injustice. They considered America instead as an exceptional land of tolerance and harmony, the equivalent of a "terrestrial Jerusalem," and therefore did not consider themselves to be living in exile. Thus did the two poles of post-Holocaust Jewish life share a common revulsion for Europe and a common belief that Jews had no business being on the continent of death.

This anti-European vision was also shared by most Jews in Western Europe. They could personally feel at home in their respective home-lands, but this did not prevent them from condemning "Europe" as a concept and value. The only difference was that the dividing line between "possible" and "impossible" countries for Jewish life shifted according to the nationality of the Jews making the evaluation. This vision contained, however, some certitudes. The Jews of Eastern Europe were all dead, the ultimate victims of the godforsaken lands of *Yiddishkeit*, the few survivors with a Jewish soul having all managed to migrate to Israel immediately after 1948. The others, diehard communists, were assumed to be relapsed Jews. Truly captive Jews were to be found only inside the Soviet Union.

Furthermore, across Europe, the majority of Jews also perceived themselves (through Zionist eyes) as a disappearing species. Vicarious Zionists were confident that their children and future generations of Jews born in Europe would settle in Israel. Assimilated Jews were assumed to be on the way out, their "Jewishness" a mere humanistic and ethical residual trait. Communist Jews were, of course, militant internationalists who considered all religion and particularist ethnic identities (including the Jewish) as antiquated and useless. While the Ultra-Orthodox Jews lived in special enclaves in a few selected cities, above all London and Antwerp, and retained a crystal clear identity that minimized ties to the host countries or to Europe.

The ambivalence of the links between Europe and the Jews was also prevalent among non-Jewish Europeans who more than willingly accepted the Zionist vision of the Jewish future as existing only in Israel. Thus Europeans and Israelis (and American Jewry) seemed to agree on one point: there could no longer be any significant collective Jewish life in Europe.

The Sea Change of 1989

This rather comfortable state of mind both on the Jewish and the non-Jewish side came to an end, as so much else linked to the postwar period, with the fall of the Berlin Wall in 1989. Already in the second half of the 1980s, Jewish life had begun simmering once more below the surface throughout Eastern Europe, as supposedly fully assimilated Jews and, even more, their postwar children sought their Jewish roots inside the communist camp. In the context of glasnost and perestroika, Gorbachev allowed Jewish life to resume inside the former Soviet Union, while slowly liberalizing travel and the right of all Jews to emigrate. As a result, throughout the Communist bloc, even before the Berlin Wall tumbled, Jewish communities were either reactivated from the top or given new freedoms. The former took place in East Germany where Honecker used the fiftieth-anniversary commemorations of *Kristallnacht* in 1988, to put "his" loyal Jews to good use to win favor with the United States through what he considered its all-powerful Jewish lobby. The latter took place in Hungary where the community was simply allowed to live freely.

Jews around the world however, including those in Western Europe, assumed that the fall of the Wall would lead to only one outcome: the departure of all the Jews from the Communist bloc and thus the final closing of accounts in the painful chapter of Jewish life in Eastern Europe.

Rather unexpectedly, instead of turning into a definitive graveyard, Eastern Europe was suddenly aglow with a numerically small, but qualitatively vital, revival of Jewish life, as those who chose not to go to Israel did not turn their back on their Jewish origins, but on the contrary, actively pursued them. Thus did the demise of Communist regimes across Europe set the ground for an emerging European Jewish identity. For it was only when "captive Jews" were finally free to leave for Israel that one could identify and count the "voluntary" Jews. These Jews were coming back to the fold out of forced or voluntary total assimilation, precisely at the same time that Jews in Western Europe were also disassimilating and taking on a more confrontational attitude toward their countries' respective pasts, especially during the Holocaust.

But on both sides of the ideological divide, Jews were turning to Jewish life in the context of full political and even cultural belonging, for the search for such an identity implied that one no longer possessed it, having blended inside wider national settings. Today's Jews thus combine both an *Ostjuden* understanding of a Jewish ethnic specificity and a Western assimilated notion that they belong in their respective democratic settings. And nowhere have both tendencies combined more powerfully than in the Jewish reaction to, and participation in, the coming home of the Holocaust to Europe.

The Holocaust Comes Home

Renewed Jewish life in Europe is becoming conceivable above all because the taboo of the Holocaust has been lifted from the collective history of the continent. The Holocaust has now spilled over beyond guilty black Germany and dark gray "anti-Semitic" Poland to penetrate the identity and history of all other European nations on Jewish terms. From Norway to Turkey, from Portugal to Russia, the specificity of what happened to the Jews during the Holocaust is finally standing out with respect to the far more classic stories of wartime suffering, resistance, antifascist struggle and national liberation. Confronting the Holocaust across Europe meant transcending the ultimate symbol of Birkenau to confront the far more prosaic multiple administrative, political-cultural, and economic measures that inexorably isolated and later cut off Jews from the rest of the population, turning them into pariahs before they became victims. This process has been gaining strength in the last two decades, as the last trials of collaborators shed new light on the Jewish specificity of the horror, while also showing how eager bureaucrats across Europe performed their own sinister tasks with postwar impunity. The trial of Maurice Papon, a high civil servant in the Vichy-France era, and also in the postwar period, is perhaps exemplary on this count. The role played by neutral countries, most notably Switzerland, but also Sweden, in indirectly helping the Nazi war effort has changed previously favorable evaluations of their wartime record. Similarly, in-depth studies on the anti-Semitic prejudices of heretofore victorious countries such as Great Britain (whose immediate postwar coldness toward the survivors who wanted to reach Palestine undid its previous heroic stance in Jewish eyes), can be matched with the rereading of "nice" little Italy's own record toward its Jews starting in 1938, or Holland's record of collaboration in the extermination of 80 percent of its Jewish population. And historians are only beginning to delve into the dossiers concerning the occupied parts of the former Soviet Union, especially Belarus and the Ukraine where apparently collaboration with the Nazis against the Jews was not uncommon in the local populations and their political cadres. The outcome of all of this Holocaust research, internal questionings and confrontations with each nation's war past has been most salutary for all, not only the Jews, for it points the way to a better understanding of the power of state-enforced racism, and the dangerous reliability of administrations to follow orders and crush individual lives and group destinies with the utmost facility.

The spotlight placed on Jewish themes throughout Europe has had one primordial consequence for Europe's own Jews. It has in a sense freed them from the existential burden of being the vestals of the Holocaust in the name of the murdered and on behalf of the survivors. Thus, with time the Holocaust should cease to be an abyss between Jews and non-Jews in Europe and should instead become a bridge. Its "coming home" has not only lifted an oppressive silence but has permitted long-needed national debates to take place, thus liberating and enriching political and cultural agoras throughout Europe. Nor should one forget that Jews in Europe are the only Jews who conjugate their verbs in the future within the continent. The descendants of the victims live their daily lives alongside with the descendants of the perpetrators or the bystanders. Such a rubbing of shoulders in no way minimizes the horror of the past but it does lead to a more tolerant perception of how peoples and societies can change. If Jews can live voluntarily in Europe then it means that there is no essential historical and un-washable European "evil" for which the only response can be Zionism. European Jews in this context offer the living proof that the Holocaust, while never being forgotten, can be transcended, and this stance more than any other, may set them apart from their Israeli or American cousins, for whom the Holocaust has become a terrifying frozen memory.

Jews in Europe can build a calm identity for themselves by interpreting the pre-Shoah Jewish world in a positive manner (and not as a prelude to Auschwitz) while also perceiving to what a degree the Europe of today is qualitatively new and better (because open and democratic) with respect to that same rediscovered past. Thus in "Jewish Europe" positive transnational and creative poles will supplant a Holocaust memory only used to square accounts with the past. Furthermore, such a memory will be enriched by the double interaction with the continent's majorities as well as its traditional or new minoritarian "others." In the process, it will take on a far stronger emblematic quality. The difference with America and Israel on this count is crucial.

Europe's "New Jews"

In the Israeli and the American imaginations, naturally enough, Europe's Jews today are perceived very much as the inheritors of their pre-Shoah forefathers. Yet nothing could be further from the truth. Today's Jews in Europe are qualitatively different and very much "new" compared to those of the prewar past. First of all, in Western Europe, many are simply geographically new, thanks to the important migrations of the postwar period. French Jewry was renewed through the arrival of North African Jews, above all those from Algeria in the early 1960s. The same was true for Italian Jewry that received Jews, as Great Britain and Switzerland also did, from Lebanon, Syria and Egypt, plus its own Lybian Jews. Scandinavian countries received Jews from Poland, Austria received many Jews from Hungary while West Germany welcomed Jews from Poland, Hungary and Romania, and also for more or less permanent stays, from Israel. Most recently and most spectacularly as a reunited country, Germany has received many Jews from the former Soviet Union.

Equally important, those Jews who were the descendants of the long established pre-Holocaust Jewries of Europe were themselves transformed by historical events into a new type of Jew. The old assimilated Jewries of Western Europe may have retained a national loyalty but they could no longer muster the same kind of unconditional patriotism as in the past, especially after the "coming home" of the Holocaust. In Eastern Europe, communism led to the forceful assimilation of Jews, turning them into citizens like everybody else at the expense of their own often fragile identities. The postwar Polish Jews had little in common with their prewar predecessors, just as few postwar French Jews continued to be the equivalent of the assimilated "Israelites" of the past. Furthermore, in France, the survivors of the *Ostjuden* who had immigrated after World War I and who were never part of the old French Jewish elites, have taken up their own identity in the postwar period with a vengeance, along with the Sepharad Jews. In countries with virtually no Jewish populations, such as Spain or Portugal, new Jews arrived who were a mixture of German exiles, Ashkenazi immigrants from Latin America, and local Jews who often emerged from clandestinity, true Marranos, although the term was now also used to evoke Poland's "new Jews."

To these Jews must be added the "cohorts" of Jews stemming from mixed marriages who were actively choosing to espouse a Jewish identity whereas in the past, they would have fallen out of the Jewish world. These half or quarter Jews pose a most disturbing historical question. Indeed, many of today's active and voluntary Jews in Europe would not even have been born had their own parents not survived because they were the children of mixed marriages. To this mix must also be added two other categories of Jews not native to Europe: American Jews living as expatriates in Europe who played a crucial role in introducing grass-roots community organization; and Israelis abroad who aspire to deepen a Jewish (as opposed to just Israeli) identity.

If with the opening of Eastern Europe American Jewry has gone into an immense nostalgia trip for their roots in the world of *Yiddishkeit*, Jews in Eastern Europe, coming out of assimilation, feel no similar need. Their search is for viable modern roots inside the Judaism of their forefathers, for a usable, as opposed to a mythical, past. These "new Jews" are living Jews, who are conquering for themselves places within civil society, no longer confining themselves in niches within the protective (or often stifling) structures of the state. One can no longer speak of "Anglo-Jewry," French Jacobin Jews, or Jewish-Italian patriots, much less of old German Jews as in the past. But neither can one continue to consider the postwar Jews of Europe as an entirely new "breed" with nothing in common with their pre-Holocaust equivalents. We are witnessing the emergence of new personae: Jews with multiple loyalties who are rather like free electrons inside newly defined state and cultural perimeters. Theirs is an identity challenge that will no longer brook pigeon-holing in the categories defined by the dominant Christian world or by the majority "others" as had been the case throughout European history, but instead is being defined by Jews who themselves adamantly belong inside their respective societies—but on their own terms.

Toward a New America-Israel-Europe Triangle

In the immediate postwar period, the situation seemed starkly clear. Jewish life in Europe was finished. Israel constituted the future, along with America, even though the two poles of world Jewry lived in an uneasy balance. American Jews had the security and the clout, Israelis the historical legitimacy and the universal "meaning." The latter needed the former but the opposite was also true. Jewish irritation and even hatred toward Europe did not need artificial cultivation. Occasions to display it abounded as a weak and fragile continent compounded all possible errors toward the Jewish state, particularly after its victory in the Six Day War in 1967. Henceforth, relations between Europe and Israel were characterized by an infernal spiral of suspicion and disdain on the part of the Israelis toward the continent. Conversely, Europeans seemed to be bogged down vis-à-vis Israel in a psychologically repressed and most unhealthy blend of silence, guilt, realpolitik considerations vis-à-vis the Arab world, misplaced international morality and legalistic punctiliousness, all of which also wrought havoc with the very idea of Jewish life in Europe. As a result, even today, the Jewish world feels paradoxically more at ease with Germany, Israel's European "protector" and ally, than with Europe as a whole.

Yet this black-and-white vision of each side of the triangle, with problematic Europe in the middle, is blurring, as each side confronts its own identity demons. American Jewry, so proud of its power, has turned inward to contemplate its own inherent diasporic fragility: declining numbers, mixed marriages, a loss of commitment and ideals as its members moved up the social ladder, virtually disappearing into a WASP elite condition in the space of just three generations, from ghetto to national power. In the great multicultural jockeying for power, America's Jews stand uneasily in society at large, having still barely recovered from the struggles and tensions of their relations with the black community after the initial honeymoon of the civil rights period. Europe's historical victims could not make a similar claim for "victimization" inside the American body politic, thus missing out on the multicultural realignment of America's symbolic politics.

Similarly, Israel also has experienced a major transformation that has eroded its original ideological credos, historical purity, and progressivism. As the most powerful country in the region, Israel has experienced the reality of state power with its concomitant realpolitik choices, errors and injustices, in particular toward the Palestinians. More important, the tiny democracy in the Middle East has developed its own internal enemies in the ultra-orthodox nationalist camp, whose beliefs are at the antipodes of social democratic Zionism, bordering on a Jewish version of "blood and soil" fascism, religious intolerance and ethnic purity. Internal strife, deadly tensions, and a growing feeling that Israel, like all of the Western world, but Europe in particular, still has democratic lessons to learn, has given Israelis a new humility. A major role was played in this sense by the revisionist historians who underscored the inherent European-like ethnic nationalism that underlay the foundations of the Jewish state in its behavior to its historic "others," the Arabs. In other words, Israel was much more a part of Europe than its Zionist ideology claimed. It, too, has to retool its national identity to take democratic pluralism into account. Thus, its challenges are far closer to those of Europe at present. The gap between the old world and the new Israel is narrowing rather than expanding, even after the return of hostilities in the Middle East since the fall of 2000.

Furthermore, since 1989 Europe has begun to define itself in terms of democratic and human rights values and with respect to what has become its self-proclaimed (but also true) postwar specificity, national and historical reconciliation—all values that Israel also needs, both internally and externally. Internally, this need is expressed in the context of growing cultural, ethnic, and political religious cleavages, which eerily echo the historic battles for separation of church and state in European history; while externally it must search for solutions vis-à-vis its Arab neighbors to bring to an end what is becoming the equivalent of a "Hundred Years War." Israel will thus need to confront its European roots on both counts. Another reason for the changed setting is of course the fall of communism, which brought half of Europe back into direct contact with the Israeli state. Slowly but surely, Israelis will also head back to Europe in the search for their own political and democratic roots, but less with a sense of nostalgia American style as with a sense of future oriented priorities and rapprochements of their country with its natural cultural and historical hinterland.

The relativization of the three sides of the Jewish triangle is only slowly emerging today but it will have an undoubtedly crucial impact on future European Jewish life and on Israel itself. For the Jewish state will need a strong diaspora in Europe not just as a messenger but far more importantly as a democratic and pluralist counterweight to its own inevitable realpolitik priorities. In this context, it will be neither in the interests of Israelis nor of European Jews to speak of poor or even "dying" European cousins at the hands of a haughty (or now anguished) historically self-contained Israel. The relationship should be mutually beneficial and reciprocal. In the future, European Jewry may well end up being a point of equilibrium between the Israeli and the American poles of world Judaism. Paradoxically, the different transformations outlined above inside the European stage can actually turn Europe's "new Jews" into those who have the greatest creative tensions, identity solutions, and forward-looking syntheses that neither the Jewish ethnic heterogeneity of Israel nor the increasingly multicultural American context can offer. With this perspective in mind, one should turn to the challenges that European Jews will have to confront in the twenty-first century in a revamped continent: the pluralist challenge, the multicultural challenge, and the challenge of filling "Jewishly" Europe's Jewish space.

The Pluralist Challenge

Post-Holocaust Jews in Western Europe were able to live in dignity, because their countries allowed them implicitly what would have been unimaginable in the past: uncontested full citizenship with the implicit right to multiple loyalties through extremely strong ties and links to another state, Israel, and through extensive contacts with Jews elsewhere in the diaspora, even when, as was the case for Soviet Jewry, such a cause was not really compatible with the foreign policies and interests of their respective countries. As a proof of the radical newness of this implicit contract between Western democracies and their Jews, one needed simply to look at what was happening to the Jews in nondemocratic environments. Any form of Jewish collective cultural and even religious life was considered dangerous and potentially traitorous in the right-wing authoritarian regimes of the postwar period. Jews in Spain under Franco and in Portugal under Salazar were the subjects of police files, possessed limited community privileges and rights, and were surrounded by a taint of suspicion. Under communism, they were always at the mercy of the label of "Zionist" traitor, and were ideal candidates, despite the presence of stalwart Communist Jews, for the charge of "cosmopolitan" counter-revolutionary activity or its opposite, ethnic "particularism."

Now that most of Europe is no longer under the sway of ideological regimes, the challenge Jews must confront is far more internal than external: how to develop inside their communities the same pluralist tolerance that they have come to expect of the outside world. Anti-Semitism and vicarious Zionism are no longer the mainstays of Jewish life on the continent. Jews express their "Jewishness" in other far more positive ways, be they religious or cultural, and these expressions are in all cases voluntary. They now bring the openness of their pluralist and even postmodern surroundings inside their Jewish life and increasingly expect the two sides of their identities to conform.

As a result, most communities with a sufficient critical mass of Jews now have ultra-orthodox, orthodox, liberal and even radical religious Jewish groups plus an equivalent amount of cultural lay Jews. All of these groups contest the legitimacy and hegemony of established community structures, which in response to the pressure of the ultra-orthodox have strengthened their religious rigor. A collective type of democratic individualism has penetrated Jewish life. In a European context, such a pluralist choice has major political implications. Most of the official community structures of European Jewry were institutional inventions of the respective states whose rulers wanted to have only one official Jewish interlocutor. Bringing pluralism inside Jewish life implies transforming the very mental categories of the state toward religion, i.e., bringing it into civil society and away from the vortex of power.

Communities in the future can hope to remain united only if they transform themselves into umbrella-like institutions housing very different ways of being Jewish. This will spell the end of a monolithic Jewish link to the state via a personality or a small group of men in power. Two other issues fall also in this pluralist challenge: the redefinition of the role of women and the inclusion of new types of Jews who in the past were neither considered Jewish by the religious authorities nor sought to define themselves as Jews. The debate over gender equality is destined to amplify, as is that surrounding the key question "Who is a Jew?" On both counts, the egalitarian and the voluntaristic assumptions of our respective societies are impinging inside Jewish community life, for in democracies all walls are ultimately transparent.

The Multicultural Challenge

As European societies increasingly take into account the many different types of "others" in their midst, whether they be older ethnic minorities or more recent immigrants, Jews will increasingly have to decide how they define themselves inside a transformed continent. In an increasingly voluntary manner, Jews seems to cover all possible definitions ranging from

British lords to Turks in Germany. In Great Britain, where the Jewish elites occupy the highest levels of power, many Jews paradoxically feel comfortable with the idea of being part of a multicultural, even ethnic, definition of Jewishness. The more orthodox Jews even go so far as to feel closest to the Muslims in Britain with their dietary and educational imperatives, fighting the same identity battles. French Jews on the other hand, as France itself, will not hear of any multicultural or minority status for themselves or for anyone else for that matter. Swedish Jews have opted for such a status but not their Danish equivalents. Hungarian Jews refused to be labeled as a minority while the Poles have accepted this. Sometimes the two converge in dramatically ironical contexts as for instance in Russia where some Jews now want to cling to an ethnic national definition of themselves, even inside their passports, a label they had eschewed for decades for its discriminatory consequences.

One thing is certain. Across the continent, being Jewish has ceased being a simple matter of private religious practice for otherwise indistinguishable patriotic citizens of a given nation. There has been a vast homogenization of a Jewish cultural identity combining ethnic references and religious practice. *Yiddishkeit* and Sephardi references have entered mainstream Judaism, which is now conjugated through a vast array of world and regional movements in what has become a Jewish global village.

But can one really think of Jews as obvious members of a multicultural society? Can they be equated to Turks or North Africans or the increasing number of truly distant foreigners (such as for instance the Filipinos) to be found across wealthy and even not so wealthy Europe? Can Jews really be perceived as multicultural "others" when they were often at the very heart of their respective, even if often historically anti-Semitic, societies? Does the partial cultural disassimilation of the younger generations amount to their claiming to be of a different culture? Hardly. It is rather the proof of how well integrated they really are in their own national contexts. Only "insiders" can step outside.

Delving inside the Jewish past inside Europe thus becomes less an exercise in multiculturalism than in historical and cultural symbiosis—the very opposite of the current ideological fashion. One may ask European societies today to respect the Jewish "dignity" and "difference" but the essential lies elsewhere. The cutting edge is to make Europeans understand the degree to which their own culture was influenced by the Jewish presence, not just to stress its own separate dignity. The true challenge entails evaluating the Jewish component of what can still be called "high culture," unraveling the symbiotic threads, fostering new interactions, stressing creativity over predictability, in a complex juggling of identities. And nowhere is this more visible than in today's Germany where the children of the postwar *Ostjuden* immigrants are increasingly taking on the intellectual and cultural mantle of their prewar (non)equivalents.

Paradoxically, any Jewish claim to multiculturalism is strongest not in the ethnic but in the religious realm. For one needs to dismantle the all too comfortable, even ritual, references to the Judeo-Christian tradition. The hyphen between the two adjectives must be interpreted as an equal sign, not as an implicit arrow pointing to a final product in a chemical reaction. The challenge of presenting Judaism in its richness and complexity to a wider public is integrally before all Jews, who have been too used to regarding non-Jewish interest in Jewish matters with suspicion. In this sense, Judaism does present the ultimate multicultural threat to established Christianity if it were to reclaim what is its due in the construction of the latter religion (for example, how many Christians know the Jewish origins of their most sacred holidays?) or, more importantly, to hold its own in the contemporary supermarket of spirituality.

Jews must confront the multicultural challenge head on because, despite its many attractive and even noble features, multiculturalism contains vicious seeds and perverse effects that can lead to a renewed marginalization of Jewish life in Europe, this time around in a self-imposed ghetto. Jews "belonged" on the European continent from the first, even though they were often internal outsiders whose presence was very much on the margins of European life and whose center of gravity remained steadfastly collective and inwardly oriented until modern times.

Today, it is the nature of "belonging" that must be reappraised, not its validity. Ideally, Jews should serve as two-way plugs in redefining a wider notion of belonging for Europe's "others," but in redefining it from within and not from without. The multicultural challenge, therefore, must be confronted in an enriching and not impoverishing manner, all the more so that Jewish life contains its own multiculturalism. But one must be aware that Jews are now "insiders" who wish to retain an "outsider" status, the very opposite of their pre-Shoah forefathers.

The Jewish Space

One of the results of the European sea change and above all of the Holocaust's "coming home" to Europe has been the exponential growth of interest in Jewish themes in the non-Jewish world. Novels and films written by non-Jews with Jewish characters in them (the most notable being of course, Roberto Benigni's *La vita è bella*), memoirs and histories, Jewish traditions ranging from the Torah to cuisine, Jewish jokes, Jewish museums, memorials, and exhibits now fill Europe's cultural agoras. This interest in Jewish "things" has no historical precedent in European history and constitutes the greatest challenge of all for Jews in Europe. First of all there is a banal objective reason, which is that there are not enough Jews across the continent to fill by themselves this growing Jewish space. Unlike Israel, which is its own vast Jewish-Jewish space, or America where Jewish space is filled by Jews themselves, in what can be called a sociological and cultural triumph, Jews in Europe are only one part of this new space. This is particularly true in Germany where in the Jewish study programs at the universities, inside museums, in the realm of publishing, as well as in every other Jewish manifestation (except for religion), non-Jews constitute the majority of the "users" and even implementers of this space. But this is also true elsewhere, with the possible exception of France and Great Britain with their large communities. Rather than perceiving this numerical reality as an impoverishment, Jews should consider this structural condition as a major positive challenge, indeed, as a challenge unique to Europe. For if Jews now live in Europe in a voluntary manner it means that they share a series of complex affinities with "others" and it is this link that must be deepened and turned into a creative dialogue, starting with the non-Jews who choose to enter the Jewish space.

Jewish spaces across Europe should not be predicated uniquely on the past, and definitely not in a past read as so many steps on the road to Auschwitz. Indeed, one of the still unsolved questions is how to define Auschwitz in terms of the Jewish space, for it lies both at its black apex but also outside of its realm as a locus for Polish, Roma or even Soviet memory. This is why it is important to reconsider the Jewish pre-Holocaust past in Europe not just as a murdered chapter. It should be perceived as a living source of existential dignity, cultural creativity, religious depth but also civic involvement, all of which contain universal implications for the identity stakes of the future.

The Jewish space cannot exist without Jews, but neither can it exist only with them, for the space is not the equivalent of a community. It is an open cultural and even political agora where Jews intermingle with others qua Jews, and not just as citizens. It is a virtual space, present anywhere Jews and non-Jews interact on Jewish themes or where a Jewish voice can make itself felt. Such a space is the crown jewel of a democratic pluralist space, and as such is a useful model for other ethnic, religious, and cultural spaces that must still come into being.

It is therefore not surprising that the tectonic plates of identity clash above all in this space, as proven by the major debates surrounding the Berlin *Mahnmal* or the autonomy of the Jewish Museum in Berlin. But it is equally important to stress that the Jewish space can also strengthen Jewish cultural life. This is particularly true in Germany. The heirs of the old German Jewry to be found mainly in America and in Israel are increasingly attracted to this growing space in Germany, claiming their "rights" to it and making their voices heard. They come to it not only for the sake of their own past, but very much as a stake for the future. And this is true everywhere across Europe from Portugal to Russia. Never has the timing been more propitious both in terms of the interest of the outside world and the possibilities of the world within, but with one proviso. Jewish life can fully blossom in an open Europe only if Jews learn to master the fear of freedom and the lack of external constraints.

Ultimately, the greatest challenge Jews must confront in the future is Judaism's links to "others." In an age of human rights, of international references to democracy and to the respect of cultures, Judaism cannot afford to close itself off from the world in the name of a hallowed speci-ficity, thus failing to assume its rightful place in the agora of universal values precisely at the time when the outside world is at last willing to listen to Jewish voices. Jews in Europe should avail themselves fully of the new opportunities of a continent that is remolding itself. They should infuse Jewish life, given the numbers they have, and welcome inside the Jewish ranks those who want to join the Jewish people. By the spreading of Jewish religious values, history, philosophy and ethics, and culture (well beyond its facile ethnic components), Jews should take on a leading role in Europe's coming to terms with itself. The invisible voices at the conference on the Balkans should at last feel free to express their own multiple identities and values. For the ultimate victims of yesterday have become Europe's most impressive postwar success story. They are increasingly towering over the crossroads of the continent's past, present, and future, very much on center stage. May they have the collective wis-dom to use this symbolic power with openness, modesty, and justice.

— Chapter 14 —

FROM CITIZEN WARRIOR TO CITIZEN SHOPPER AND BACK

New Modes of Cosmopolitan Citizenship

Natan Sznaider

Introduction: Citizenship and the State

Debates regarding citizenship are framed around the state. It is very difficult to think about citizens without a state. Just the opposite, a state of statelessness is a state of limbo, a state of misfortune, a state without rights. Not only a Jewish problem, but very much informed by Jewish fate, statelessness became the central problem for Jews in the twentieth century (see Arendt 1951). The strongest manifestation of this statelessness was, of course, caused by German politics. Only Zionism could allegedly make whole what the German Nazis broke; to give the Jews a state; to make a stateless people a people with a state and a home. The tension between nationhood and statelessness has some parallels with the German case. As the introduction of this volume points out, "their respective laws of return are legal-normative reactions to their historical 'incompleteness' as nation-states: *ius sanguinis* (i.e., descent-based citizenship) comes in response to two interrelated aspects: one, a long condition of statelessness—in both cases, the nation concept is prepolitical insofar as it antedates the formation of the state; and two, dispersion—that is, not all members of the nation reside in the nation-state." As their fates are connected, it is no surprise that debates regarding citizenship take on similar features. The terms of these debates are "civic nationalism" versus "ethnic nationalism," both at the same time empirical as well as normative criteria of belonging.

Both of these criteria are closely entwined with a well-known tension between two fundamental definitions of nationhood: the first, territorial and political with its roots in Western Europe; the second ethnic, typical of the historical experience of Eastern and Central Europe. Both are conceptualized through the boundaries of the state. The Western type, which, according to Boaz Evron (1995), lost the struggle in Israel, also forcefully reinvigorated by many so-called post-Zionists, is associated with the "rational" principles of citizenship and democratic virtues. The second type, the victor in the Israeli context, is organic and associated with "irrational" beliefs that supercede the voluntaristic character of the Western type. In this view, a developmental approach is involved as well. "Enlightened" political nationalism was gradually replaced by organic forms of nationalism that were embraced in Central and Eastern Europe and went on to become the origins of the Jewish nation in Israel. But are these the only alternatives?

In what follows, I would like to propose an alternative conception of citizenship, a citizenship not based on solidarity, war, memory and blood, but a citizenship based on something frequently perceived as counter-productive to citizenship, namely the global market and its features of consumption and indifference. I will propose a new citizen, "the citizen shopper," as a model that points to new features of solidarity and belonging. The Western world has been changing since the fall of the Wall. The heroic narrative of nationhood upon which nation-state formation processes in the nineteenth century relied has largely been replaced by a more skeptical narrative of collectivities (Levy and Sznaider 2001) that is based on individuals and personhood, which has resulted in a decoupling of rights and membership (Soysal 1994). I explore the historical and ideological origins of this transformation by juxtaposing two ideal-typical conceptions of citizenship: namely the national warrior and the cosmopolitan consumer.

War and ethnic strife do still exist, but among an increasing number of "citizens of the world" there seems to be tacit agreement that internal processes of democratization (and globalization) go hand in hand with the pacification of relations between peoples and states. That does not mean that world peace has broken out, but it means that there is a new cultural base for peace rooted in a new kind of citizenship, which can be called "cosmopolitan," challenging state-centered notions of belonging. However, by "cosmopolitan citizenship" I do not mean one who is a rootless citizen of the world, a man or woman who belongs only to a universal community of spirit, whose place of birth is merely accidental. Revived by eighteenth-century Enlightenment thinkers, this universal sense of belonging puts enormous demands on its followers: a feeling of membership of humankind expressed in responsibility for all, regardless of origin and place, and the creation of international institutions and laws safeguarding these principles (Heater 1999: 134–154). Based on notions of "moral cosmopolitanism" (it is no accident that the major foundational text of this view is Kant's 1795 *On Perpetual Peace*) it leaves out the market and individual desires as spurious and nonrelevant to these views. However, it stresses the notion of "rights" and "obligations" within a universal community of world citizens. One of the leading proponents of "cosmopolitan democracy," David Held (1998: 24) talks about "overlapping communities of fate" where the fates of countries are becoming more and more entwined. However, Held also does not cross the borders of the national. He just enlarges them.

Globalization does provide a serious challenge to state sovereignty. So do new notions of citizenship. Isin and Wood (1999) suggest new forms of cosmopolitan citizenship: they mention "urban citizenship" based on membership in increasingly globalizing cities with its increasing transnational classes, youth cultures, minority cultures etc., "technological citizenship" dealing with new forms of communication mediated by the new digital technology (like the internet), and "ecological citizenship" based on transnational concern for the environment. I would like to add another form of citizenship, one based on the enjoyment of consumption. I will first explore the historical, ideological and sociological origins of this conception. I will then illustrate its various manifestations in the context of a set of competing ideals of Jewish identity and state-centered visions of political Zionism.

Consumers versus Knights

If we take the long historical view, the fundamental meaning of consumption for both its proponents and its antagonists is a sign of civilization. In my opinion, this view has never been expressed more clearly than in Leon Feuchtwanger's novel called *The Jewess of Toledo*.

The story is set in the Spain of the twelfth century. It is a country on the frontiers between Christianity and Islam, and thus on the front-lines of the original Crusades and Jihads, when those words were more than metaphors. And in the interpenetration of those frontiers lives Feuchtwanger's main protagonist, Jehuda Ibn Esra. He accepts the post of finance minister under King Alfonso—essentially the post of an economic czar, who takes a cut of the overall profit in return for personally putting up capital and bearing huge risks—because he sees this Christian country as full of productive potential that he can bring to fruition, if, and only if, he can keep the country out of war. The king, a knight of the old stamp, wants to go to war as soon as possible, of course, for that is the only sure road to glory. He only grudgingly accepts that he must build up the economic strength of his exhausted country first, and with the same grudgingness, he accepts that Ibn Esra has a genius for peacetime management that he himself lacks. And so the two struggle with and against each other for many years, in a partnership and a rivalry with very high stakes. It is not an accident that Feuchtwanger wrote this book just after the Nazis and World War II destroyed his German-Jewish world of educated and wealthy "burghers." For Feuchtwanger, the knightly ideals that would destroy everything that other people have built up for the sake of glory were all too close to home. He opposes them to the strivings for wealth and commerce that are carried on by the citizens of towns, by Jews and by women, who counteract the destructive force of knights and barons with the quiet pleasures of enjoying material things.

But Ibn Esra is not only fictional. The anthropologist and writer Amitav Gosh (1992) tells the story of the Jewish Arab Ben-Yiju of the twelfth century, a time when being a Jewish Arab was no contradiction in terms as it is in today's Israel. Ben-Yiju was a merchant travelling the Orient, in communication with peoples of all cultures and worlds. What holds them together is their common desire to trade and get rich. And if we look at Weimar Germany for instance, we can find several Ibn Esras and Ben-Yijus each trying to work out economic and political arrangements that would connect Germany to England and avoid war. Rathenau, Oppenheimer and Schwarzschild are all good examples, and there were more. Like Ibn Esra and Ben-Yiju, they were between cultures and regarded with suspicion. And they saw themselves playing the same dangerous game for the same high stakes: for the preservation of civilization and all that they had built.

But it was the virtue of these men that they were between cultures. That is what gave them their sophistication, their breadth of vision and their tolerance. Their culture came from many places and existed mixed with them. All of it felt familiar, as if it belonged together. They embodied the ideal of integration, it was inextricably part of their ideal of individual cultivation. Among men like this, rootedness—being fixed in one place and submerging one culture—was regarded as a limitation. And limited people could extend their boundaries only by war. Modern Zionism turned against this cosmopolitan ideal. It was in some ways an ironic turn back to the ideals of warrior virtue. New trends of consumption in Israel, its desire to become like an image of America, I argue, represent attempts to find a way back into exile, to the secular-Jewish and softening virtues of modern cosmopolitanism.

Toward a New Theory of Citizenship: Citizen Shoppers

So how can we conceive a public sphere that has room for the citizen shopper? Two criteria seem essential. One requires a reassessment of the sociological and cultural implications of consumerism and the concomittant development of indifference; the other necessitates a recognition that conflict is not by definition antithetical to some form of consensus. Citizen shoppers? Is this notion not a contradiction in terms? Is not the citizen the complete opposite of the shopper? Is not "indifference" the polar opposite to citizenship, the ideal of which is engagement personified? Rousseau is the modern source of this idea of citizenship: "The better constituted the state, the more public affairs outweigh private ones in the minds of the citizens.... In a well conducted city, everyone rushes to the assemblies. Under a bad government, no one cares to take even a step to attend them: no one takes an interest in what is done there, since it is predictable that the general will will not prevail, and so finally domestic concerns absorb everything" (1978: 102).

This is what we might call the classical theory of politics. It comes ultimately from the Greeks. Rousseau was the first to try to translate ideas suited to the polis—hence, political ideas—into a form suited to modern life. But he was by no means the last. The twentieth century has seen many such attempts, starting most prominently perhaps with Rousseau's harshest critic, Hannah Arendt, who by the way held Rousseau ultimately responsible for the Holocaust. And yet she agreed with him on this basic point that politics was something separate from, opposed to, and in danger of being swallowed by, too much involvement in economic life. Jürgen Habermas's (1962) influential early work on the changing structure of the public sphere posits a coffeehouse public sphere in the golden age of capitalism that is progressively eaten away as "late capitalism" develops. And communitarians like Amitai Etzioni (1994) and Charles Taylor (1992) also see the market as something that erodes the common project that makes fulfilling politics, and fulfilling lives, possible.

But as brilliantly as these theorists twist and turn it, there is something deeply anti-modern about the classical theory of politics. The Greek notion of politics is different than the theory of gesellschaft and gemeinschaft, because it does not idealize the (good) organic community and oppose it to the (bad) atomized individual. On the contrary, it celebrates the individual. It makes his individual cultivation key to the health of the state, and it makes the healthy functioning of the state key to the cultivation of the individual. On the other hand, the conception of economic life that underlies Aristotle is even more premodern than that of the gesellschaft theorists. The very word for economics derives from "*oikos*," which also means household. For the Greeks, economics is household affairs in patriarchal latifundia. From the viewpoint of a citizen, this consists of the relations one has with slaves and women, with noncitizens. It is thus by definition outside the sphere of politics. As Hannah Arendt pointed out, the classic Greek word for "private" meant "deprived," cut off from the life of the agora. Slaves and women led private lives. Citizens led public ones.

So the democracy of pure participation rested on the base of slavery. When later theorists take up this opposition of pure, ennobling public life, and cramping, constraining private life, they are covertly arguing that modern economics, the realm of private interests, is just as "depriving" as the world of the *oikos* was. But on the face of it, this is nonsense. In a slave economy, economics is isolating, each head of household a king in his own little world. But under an advanced division of labor, every act of production and consumption, from your cup of coffee to your fax machine, links you to thousands of unseen others. The modern word for what the Greeks meant by economic life is really social life. That includes everything concerned with economics and private life. It includes your career and the schooling that prepares your for it, your family life and the circle of modern friendship. Can we really agree with Hannah Arendt when she says that an overinvolvement in social life is limiting? Or do not most of us think of social life as precisely the sphere in which both self-fulfillment and common projects take place?

There is another way in which the politics of the Greeks was opposed to economics—they turned centrally on matters of war, waged not only for defense but for profit and glory. It was not only that war touched on the ultimate political questions, concerning the survival of the polis. It was also that the competition for glory was the soul of Greek public life, and war was therefore not "politics by other means" but politics in its purest form. The virtuous Greek citizen was centrally a citizen soldier.

But if the goal of modern society is not war, but rather peace and the production of material wealth, than we can no longer make any strict division between economic and political interests. I am not arguing that politics can, or should be, reduced to economics. The nation-state, like the polis before it, is centrally concerned with issues that do not just resolve themselves through laissez faire. But the goals of politics and economics can no longer be starkly distinguished as the Greeks did. In the modern world, the telos of both is to increase our security and well-being.

And there is a third way in which the translation of "*oikos*" into "economic," rather than "social," distorts what the Greeks meant by politics. Politics was the public life of the polis. It was not just public affairs, it was every activity that afforded a pursuit of glory, since glory was by nature public. The Greek idea of public life included sports and entertainment, not as adornments, but as central, meaning-giving activities. Poetry, which Plato wanted to ban from his ideal and fairly fascist-looking republic, was the mass media of the Greek city-state. Drama, philosophy, wrestling—all of this was politics to the Greeks. And all of it is social life to us. We do not pursue glory the way they did. We have a very different morality and a very different conception of the self. But we share with them implicitly that being "wrapped up" in these activities is central to the life of the soul, and that through them we express our place in society at the same time as we cultivate our pleasures in a competitive nexus.

When the Greek idea of politics is imposed on modern life, it makes it look as if all the Greeks meant by politics was talking, voting, and the state taking action. But what they really meant was everything that was common and meaningful. They never meant by it, as modern theorists seem to imply, something so pure that everything people cared about was left out. So the classical oppositions between public and private, politics and economics, political life and life, all need to be redrawn if we are to properly apply Greek ideas to modern life. Our society is differently organized; our valuation of war is different; our conception of the self and of glory and of morality has completely changed. In order to understand modern politics, we need a conception that takes these changes into account—that understands the "public life" of a nation as everything that impinges on people in common, and everything that alerts and orients individuals to their place in society. In modern society, social issues, without exception, are politics. And where the Greeks had glory, we have status. It might seem, well, less glorious. But the diminishment of glory is the necessary consequence of thinking war is bad and peace is the good.

Consumerism is the antidote to this glory-based conception of society. It was Simmel who, in his *Philosophy of Money* (1900), first elaborated without prejudice the deep connection between money and monotheism. Both are able to reconcile differences through abstraction, by separating themselves from every particular time and place. It was also Simmel who first made the heretical assertion that consumerism is a worthy replacement for religion. Many Jeremiahs have lamented that the people seem more concerned with commerce than God. Simmel points out that the Jeremiahs are right that consumerism is something that you can get lost in, but thereby, like religion, it enacts a dreamworld with material objects. The cultivation of tastes expresses both our identity and our place in society—our status—just as the practice of religion used to. And it does so through the objects of everyday life, just as religion used to. When left- and right-wing Jeremiahs cry out that "the people worship things," Simmel would have responded that the people worship through things, just as they always have.

Money is identified by Simmel as the means and expression of social abstraction. The abstraction of personal relations results in the much wider nexuses of impersonal relations. Historically, money has been a universal solvent that has replaced personal obligations with services purchased on the market, and thereby freed individuals from particular others by making them more dependent on the whole. This replacement of one large, unbreakable bond by a thousand little bonds is real freedom, it is the history of an increase in the individual's scope of action. At the same time, the extension of the money economy tends to erode inequality through the same process of making people substitutable. It is hard to maintain the ideal of inequality—that some people were born to rule, and others born to serve—when people are functionally interchangeable. Money therefore tends to extend the concept of equality, in so far as the legitimacy of inequality was based upon a perception of essential differences in the person (see Miller 1995; Poggi 1993).

Indifference and Inattention: The Soft Forces of Integration

The hatred of the bourgeoisie and its spirit was clear in the works of German social thinkers like Tönnies, Sombart and Scheler, which was often mixed with anti-Semitism as well. They denounced the modern world as a world of strangers. Simmel characteristically turned their idea on its head and defended strangerhood as one of the most positive features of the modern world. He thought indifference was a great cultural and historical achievement, and thought that strangership made a positive contribution to the social order.

Simmel's point has rarely been picked up by modern sociologists in so many words. But it hides in plain sight in Goffman, only awaiting a historical perspective to bring it to light. He is reductionist about, or at best indifferent to, the historical and institutional setting of his analysis. What we want to do here is rescue Goffmanesque sociology from its ahistorical and apolitical inclinations. In *Behavior in Public Places* (1966), Goffman discusses "civil inattention." This is something that takes place when people are mutually present but not mutually involved. Goffman gives a microsociological meaning to the idea of strangers. When people are strangers, they give each other signs to let the others know that they have recognized their existence, but also signs that make clear in the same instant that the others are not a special target of curiosity or design. Goffman explains that "civil inattention" is a set of signs by which strangers in civil society declare their nonhostile intentions. But we only need to add that concept of "civil society" to see what an epochal turning away this is from warrior society. Now we are in a world where people are constantly, without thinking about it, assuring each other of their nonhostile intentions.

So Goffman, without using the word, is detailing everyday life in a "Gesellschaft"—a society of mutually indifferent people. But to see it as such, we need to place this vision in history, as was done by both Adam Smith and Simmel (see Muller 1993; Silver 1990, 1997). And once we do— once we see by the contrast how society can change its fundamental structures—we raise a question that Goffman never raised, but to which his work in part supplies the answer: what holds everyday life in the modern world together? If warrior society was held together by personal bonds and obligations, what holds a society of strangers together? People's first reaction in warrior society is to identify a newcomer as friend or enemy—and either way, the bonds of the in-group are strengthened. People's first reaction to a newcomer in gesellschaft is to ignore him. What bonds can possibly grow out of this?

For Smith (1988), the virtue of a society of strangers was that it made possible the viewpoint of the impartial spectator. The more the structures of kinship and clanship and hierarchy broke down, the more people could look at each other as equals and wonder how they would feel in each other's place. The strong bonds of inequality were also barriers to sympathy, and as they dissolved, the bonds of sympathy increased. And the more sympathy became generalized—the more one reacted to people's behavior based on how one would act in their place—the more sympathy gave rise to general codes of action, and a general means of enforcement. Because, as Smith puts it so succinctly, in his *Theory of Moral Sentiments*, "sympathy mutually accorded is a pleasure, and sympathy withheld is a pain" (1988: 9) And when this scheme of mutual regulation is internalized, so that we judge our actions in advance from the viewpoint of the impartial spectator, society has been generalized and individualized at the same time. And society has replaced God as the source of conscience.

Simmel (1992) tackles the same problem from a different angle. He distills the essence of premodern society in the "concentricity" of its social circles. One's family, one's village, one's religion, one's class—they all encompassed the one within the other like a nest of concentric circles. In agreement with Smith, he points out that the same mechanism that reinforced social bonds also made them more mutually exclusive. Two people that modern man would see as occupying very similar niches were conceived through the honeycomb of premodern society as being at the center of very different worlds, separated by almost impassable layers of social insulation.

But in modern society, says Simmel, the groups that define us overlap, and this changes everything. It not only means that we are connected with people horizontally rather than vertically. It also means that each person constitutes a unique combination of connections. And this in turn has three consequences. In the first place, it means people are more individualized; the number of possible combinations increases geometrically. In the second place, it means each individual has more in common with a wider group of people. And in the third, it means the lines of division between groups of people are fuzzier because of all of the overlap. The weak bonds of association are enough to hold society together (a) because they are weak bonds to so many; (b) because they erode, through their very existence, the forces used to drive people apart; and (c) because they are anchored in the individual's free expression of his desires. When a person joins groups because he wants to, and not because he was born into them, he is bound by his desires more than by taboos. And when we do what we like, we do not feel bound, a sentiment from which weak social bonds derive their strength. Indifference is not nothing. It is a very subtle something. It means treating everybody exactly the same. It is not corrosive of morality. It is the basis of modern morality. And the institutional form of indifference—of treating everyone the same—is rights.

Consequently, we need a concept of the public where divisions can unite, and where indifference and social distance can contribute to society's integration (Holmes 1987). The key to squaring the circle is to realize that the soul of politics is conflict, and the soul of social life is the production of common norms. What we need is an explanation of how public conflict can be the key to integration—how the clash of conflicting norms can deepen our common norms and make them stronger.

This brings us back to Simmel. The political consequences of his ideas were elegantly formalized in yet another forgotten classic of mainstream social theory, *Conflict Functionalism*, by Lewis Coser (1954). Coser argues that when there are only one or two or three divisions in society, they cut deep; loyalties are strong, and therefore antagonisms are just as strong. But when there are numerous divisions, each of them commands a smaller, more fragmented group loyalty and is opposed by a disorganized and therefore milder opposition. Society coheres because the overall tension has been lessened. This is one reason why a free press, and a freely elected parliament in which all parties participate, is less likely to lead to revolution than the suppression of all dissent. From the individual perspective, not only do people in such a society find they have several overlapping identities, but it is easier for them to choose new groups to which to belong. In a polarized society, one takes up a taste associated with the class or religious or generational enemy at the risk of being ostracized by one's friends. In such a world, many identities that the individual might find satisfying are ringed with taboo. In a society cut by thousands of little divisions, the force of taboo is much lessened. It is easy to mix and match, to discover personal tastes one never would have discovered without experiment, and never would have experimented with if it counted as a costly transgression. Consequently, such a society fosters individuation. And such individuation fosters personal ties that reach across and further knit together social divisions.

What does this mixing and matching of identities have to do with consumption? It is accomplished through their commodification. Anti-modernists often bemoan the fact that ethnic identities today are no longer "authentic," but are rather superficial, made up of musical tropes and clothing styles and exaggerated gestures that are not passed down from generation to generation, but chosen through the influence of the mass media. But it is precisely this commodification that allows people to choose elements from various cultural traditions and blend them into a new identity. The same process also makes it easier for people to stray from their "original" identities—or in conventional terms, to integrate into society.

Uncommodified ethnic identities are closed to outsiders and raise the costs for straying outside one's walls: one either is, or is not. But the more it becomes accepted that identity can be adequately manifested through symbolic gestures—that one can throw out large parts of tradition and still be accepted as part of the group—the more people are free to experiment without the risk of being cut off from their roots. These new ethnic identities are not necessarily weaker than the old ones. But mix and match identities are by definition easier to integrate. They are wholes that can interpenetrate each other through the choices of individuals who belong to more than one group. They are thus group identities that can occupy the same social space. And this is how commodified ethnic conflicts can precipitate a progressively denser common core.

The political principle that links consumption to liberalism is "self-interest." Self-interest is, first and foremost, opposed to self-sacrifice. As Holmes (1995) has shown in his stimulating history of "self-interest," the notion rose to cultural importance in the eighteenth century because of its egalitarian and democratic implications. As we learn from Hirschman's history *The Passions and the Interests* (1977), eighteenth-century thinkers were trying to justify the emergence of commercial society as a counterpassion to the pursuit of glory, a notion again very relevant in the Israeli context. Early liberalism was endeavoring to replace militarism with the unheroic virtues of exchange, commerce and consumption.

Hirschman and Holmes focus on the writers of the Scottish Enlightenment, especially Adam Smith and David Hume. These authors rejected cultural systems based on martial virtues, warfare, and religious piety; instead, they championed a new system of civilization based on commerce. They argued that commerce refined and softened manners. They argued that commerce in the eighteenth century had pacific virtues. More trade was supposed to tame the sovereign and his militaristic, dynastic and tyrannical inclinations. Hume's famous essay *On Luxury* identifies luxury and commerce with "the great refinement in the gratification of the senses" (Berry 1994). This essay has many parallels with the ideal evoked in Israel of the "New Middle East" that was stressed by some of the architects of the peace process.

The countermodel in the eighteenth century was the mythologized conception of Sparta. Its military prowess, its denunciation of pleasure, and its mobilized citizenry for collective purposes became the model for "civic republicanism," for the renunciation of selfish pleasure and the acceptance of sacrifice. In the Israeli context, this notion is symbolized by the famous words of Trumpeldor, when the outpost he commanded was attacked by Arabs during the pre-state period: "It is good to die for my country." But even those critical Israeli thinkers who try to demythologize such notions of self-sacrifice are for some reason not willing to go far enough and accept that the countermodel to it is "self-interest" and "commerce." Elias takes the same process even further back in his study *The Civilizing Process* (1978). He looks at the *"longue dure"* and shows how the pleasure that medieval warriors found in violence was slowly replaced over the centuries by the refinement of manners, and how this was inextricably bound up with distance toward our bodies and an avoidance of pain. On both views, consumption leads to the social taming of the body (see Falk 1994). And this development is the necessary precondition of the modern, feeling, bourgeois self (Sznaider 1996, 1998a).

This point is especially relevant for the current Israeli context. The object of war is to kill and injure people. War needs the ultimate political distinction between "friend" and "enemy" (Schmitt 1932). Consumption, on the other hand, does not know this distinction. In the language of Adam Smith, "in commercial society, everybody becomes a merchant." There are no friends and enemies, only competitors and spectators. Consumption is about the maximization of pleasure, while war is about the maximization of pain (Scarry 1985). Citizens on the edge of the West who, like Israelis, are still divided into "citizen shoppers" and "citizen warriors" are advantageously placed to see the real underpinnings of modernization because they can see them balanced against the necessities of imminent war, just as the Scottish Enlightenment drew so much inspiration from the conjunction of Glasgow and the highland clans.

The alternative to the softening, peace-seeking and compromising characteristics of commerce is a nationalism constantly stoked to be ready to fight, or even to ethnically cleanse. This kind of nationalism is about war, and war is about wearing your poverty and hardship as a sign of virtue—rather than as a sign of shame, as it appears in peace. And the reverse is also true: consumption is about wearing your luxury as a sign of virtue, rather than being ashamed of it as a sign of sinful indulgence. They are thus opposed moral schemes. The key pleasure in nationalism is the pleasure of renunciation (Zizek 1990). Perspectives on consumption who regard it as excess, as waste, even as the destruction of citizenship (see Featherstone 1991), have to be understood critically as the understanding of consumption through the perspective of such nationalism.

In a country where the contrast between the moral order of consumers and warriors is still very much alive, the phenomenon of conspicuous consumption has an entirely different meaning. In countries like Israel, sites of consumption indeed are "dream worlds," in Walter Benjamin's term, but they are dream worlds of order and regularity rather than of abandon. Malls and streets full of boutiques represent the yearning for a rational bourgeois way of life, a nostalgia for a world not yet gained. It is a dream of the quiet pleasures of sitting in a cafe and bathing in the sun without fearing that a bomb will end the dream. It is first of all the desire to avoid pain. The connections between consumption and peace, and the relations between the "citizen shopper" and the "citizen warrior," have therefore to be understood as founded not on mental categories but on the production of modern bodies that express an increased sensitivity to physical pain.

Citizen Warriors and Shoppers: Pioneers into Consumers

In the last decade, the cultural and business elite in Israel tried to cultivate an image of Western secularism and cosmopolitanism. Their objective was to create a permissive, consumerist, high-tech, nontraditional Israel in a "New Middle East." For these new "Yuppies" the prospect of increased consumption was a major incentive to support the Israeli-Arab peace process (see Peled and Shafir 1996). Many Israelis of the middle classes favored a new civil discourse. However, this civil discourse is not only about a discourse of "rights," but also about a discourse of "fun." Liberalism, in Israel as well, was increasingly viewed as the pursuit of individual pleasure and the privatization of social life. In short, the peace process increased consumption for people with money, and their desire for more consumption reinforced their support for the peace process. But increased consumption also increased the divisions in society, and made them more noticeably visible. And when the "have-nots" acted on their resentments, they opposed the whole Weltanschauung of the ruling parties of old: Westernization. Americanization, globalization, and cosmopolitanization (see Beck 2000)—and the consumption patterns that accompany them—result in ethnic identities becoming plural and commercialized. In today's Israel, being an Israeli can mean that one reads Russian papers, goes to a Russian theater and listens to Russian rock music. But being an Israeli can mean equally that one takes one's Jewish Oriental identity seriously and, paradoxically, thanks to the influence of Western multiculturalism, rejects everything Western. And being an Israeli also means that non-Jewish Israelis, Palestinians with an Israeli passport, can claim cultural autonomy for themselves. These are just a few examples that demonstrate how ethnic relations are becoming more plural through consumer goods—and how people are turning into "citizen shoppers."

Conclusion

When a country enters world markets and increases its consumption, it increases existing gulfs at the same time as it begins to share tastes with other countries. Furthermore, these class and cultural divisions reinforce the divisions that exist between Westernizers and traditionalists in every such society (Featherstone 1991; Hall 1992; Miller 1995). So the "Americanization equals homogenization" argument is wrong, but so is the idea that modernization strips away national culture and hence leads to a fundamental loss of national identity. Americanization increases cultural conflicts. But conflict enlivens culture, it does not strip it away. And so long as the conflicts are of a certain sort—multiplicitous and commodified—they integrate society. National culture is not lost. It is transformed, both in its parts and as a whole.

Where does this leave us with our new theory of "cosmopolitan citizenship"? Maybe the new is not that new after all. Maybe this is about rediscovering the roots of liberalism within a Jewish and Israeli context. It is an attempt to complete the historical symbiosis between democracy and capitalism. In this newly conceived global world, there are numerous divisions and each of them is milder and less coercive, unlike the class divisions of old. Society is more firmly bound together because it is more divided; it coheres because the tension has lessened. The alienation and indifference to others is, therefore, a side effect of modernization and something that does not need to be lamented. It is about civil life among mutually indifferent strangers.

Note

This essay is based on two previously published articles that have been revised and rethought for this volume (Sznaider 1998b, 2000). I would like to thank Daniel Levy and Michael Pollak for continuous intellectual dialogue.

References

Arendt, Hannah. 1951. *The Origins of Totalitarianism*. New York: Meridian.

Beck, Ulrich. 1997. *Kinder der Freiheit*. Frankfurt am Main: Suhrkamp.

———. 1998. *Was Ist Globalisierung?* Frankfurt a. M.: Suhrkamp.

———. 2000. "The Cosmopolitan Perspective: Sociology of the Second Age of Modernity." *British Journal of Sociology* 51 (1): 79–105.

Berry, Christopher. 1994. *The Idea of Luxury: A Conceptual and Historical Investigation*. Cambridge: Cambridge University Press.

Campbell, Colin. 1987. *The Romantic Ethic and the Spirit of Modern Consumerism*. Oxford: Basil Blackwell.

Coser, Lewis. 1954. *The Functions of Social Conflict*. New York: Free Press.

Elias, Norbert. 1978 [1938]. *The Civilizing Process: The History of Manners*. Vol. 1. New York: Pantheon.

———. 1996. *The Germans*. Cambridge: Polity Press.

Etzioni, Amitai. 1994. *The Spirit of Community: The Reinvention of American Society*. New York: Simon and Schuster.

Evron, Boas. 1995. *Jewish State or Israeli Nation?* Bloomington: Indiana University Press.

Falk, Pasi. 1994. *The Consuming Body*. London: Sage.

Featherstone, Mike. 1991. *Consumer Culture and Postmodernism*. London: Sage.

———. 1995. *Undoing Culture: Globalization, Postmodernism and Identity*. London: Sage.

Feuchtwanger, Lion. 1956. *Die Jüdin von Toledo*. Frankfurt am Main: Fischer.

Goffman, Erving. 1966. *Behavior in Public Places*. New York: Free Press.

Gosh, Amitav. 1992. *In an Antique Land*. New York: Vintage Press.

Habermas, Jürgen. 1962. *Strukturwandel der Öffentlichkeit*. Neuwied: Luchterhand.

Heater, Derek. 1999. *What is Citizenship?* London: Polity Press.

Held, David. 1998. "Democracy and Globalization." In *Re-Imagining Political Community: Studies in Cosmopolitan Democracy*, ed. Martin Kohler and David Held, 11–27. London: Polity Press.

Hirschman, Albert. 1977. *The Passions and the Interests*. Princeton: Princeton University Press.

Holmes, Stephen. 1995. *Passions and Constraints: On the Theory of Liberal Democracy*. Chicago: University of Chicago Press.

Isin, Engin, and Patricia Wood. 1999. *Citizenship and Identity*. London: Sage.

Levy, Daniel, and Natan Sznaider. 2001. *Erinnerung im globalen Zeitalter. Der Holocaust*. Frankfurt am Main: Suhrkamp.

Lichtblau, Klaus. 1997. *Kulturkrise und Soziologie um die Jahrhundertwende: Zur Genealogie der Kultursoziologie in Deutschland*. Frankfurt am Main: Suhrkamp.

Miller, Daniel. 1995. *Acknowledging Consumption: A Review of New Studies*. London/New York: Routledge.

Mizuta, Hiroshi. 1975. *Moral Philosophy and Civil Society, in Essays on Adam Smith*. Oxford: Clarendon Press.

Muller, Jerry. 1993. *Adam Smith in His Time and Ours: Designing the Decent Society*. New York: Free Press.

Peled, Yoav, and Gershon Shafir. 1996. "The Roots of Peacemaking: The Dynamics of Citizenship in Israel, 1948–93." *International Journal of Middle East Studies* 28: 391–413.

Poggi, Gianfranco. 1993. *Money and the Modern Mind: Georg Simmel's Philosophy of Money*. Berkeley: University of California Press.

Rousseau, Jean-Jacques. 1978 [1762]. *On the Social Contract*. New York: St. Martin's Press.

Scarry, Elaine. 1985. *The Body in Pain: The Making and Unmaking of the World*. New York: Oxford University Press.

Schmitt, Carl. 1932. *Der Begriff des Politischen*. Munich: Duncker.

Silver, Allan. 1990. "Friendship in Commercial Society: Eighteenth-Century Social Theory and Modern Sociology." *American Journal of Sociology* 95: 1474–1504.

————. 1997. "Two Different Sorts of Commerce: Friendship and Strangership in Civil Society." In *Public and Private in Thought and Practice*, ed. Jeff Weintraub and Krishan Kumar, 34–74. Chicago: University of Chicago Press.

Simmel, Georg. 1989 [1900]. *Philosophie des Geldes*. Frankfurt am Main: Suhrkamp.

————. 1992 [1908]. *Die Kreuzung der sozialen Kreise in Soziologie*. Frankfurt: Suhrkamp.

Smith, Adam. 1988 [1759]. *The Theory of Moral Sentiments*. Indianapolis: Liberty Classics.

Soysal, Yasemin N. 1994. *Limits of Citizenship: Migrants and Postnational Membership in Europe*. Chicago: University of Chicago Press.

Sznaider, Natan. 1996. "Pain and Cruelty in Socio-Historical Perspective." *International Journal of Politics, Culture and Society* 10 (2): 331–354.

————. 1998a. "The Sociology of Compassion: A Study in the Sociology of Morals." *Cultural Values* 2 (1): 117–139.

————. 1998b. "Vom Wehrbürger zum Einkaufsbürger. Konsum und Nationalismus in Israel." *Soziale Welt* 49: 43–56.

————. 2000. "Consumerism as Civilizing Process: Israel and Judaism in the Second Age of Modernity." *The International Journal for Politics, Culture and Society* 14 (2): 297–314.

Taylor, Charles. 1992. *Multiculturalism and the Politics of Recognition*. Princeton: Princeton University Press.

Zizek, Slavoj. 1990. "Eastern Europe's Republics of Gilead." *New Left Review* 183: 50–62.

AFTERWORD

Outlook(s)—Citizenship in the Global Era

Daniel Levy and Yfaat Weiss

Between Ethnic and Civic Conceptions

As is evidenced by the findings in this volume, the post–Cold War era constitutes a turning point for migration regimes in Israel and Germany. Both were suddenly confronted with a large influx of privileged immigrants (Jews from the FSU and ethnic Germans). Paradoxically, both the scope and the realization of this ethnic immigration, and the way they have influenced the formation of new political and cultural constellations, have challenged the ethnic presuppositions around which both countries have long defined themselves. Their respective responses to these groups, however, and the subsequent debates about immigration have taken on very different contours. In this overview we present some of the aspects that inform these debates and highlight emerging conditions of possibility that frame the tensions between universalistic and particularistic notions of collective self-understanding. The broad impact of this recent wave of immigration in Germany and Israel puts into sharper relief the factors that prove conducive or detrimental for the expansion of citizenship rights to nonnational minorities and their national inclusion.

In Germany—with the introduction of partial *ius soli* in the year 2000 and the recently published recommendations of a government-appointed commission to institute an immigration system loosely based on the Canadian model—we observe broadly speaking a gradual departure from ethno-cultural assumptions and an official turn toward a more civic-oriented citizenship conception. But these changes have not remained uncontested. Policy reforms easing naturalization and recent proposals to regulate immigration (essentially amounting to the official recognition that de facto Germany has become a country of immigration) have reinforced objections to a multicultural vision of German society and are likely to be thematized during the upcoming federal elections in the fall of 2002.

In the Israeli case, the ethno-national foundations inscribed in its Law of Return remain intact. Occasional discussions about modifying the law retain the character of an inner-Jewish dialogue about the question of "who is a Jew" or rather about who should have the institutional authority to decide this matter. For some, it may be tempting to explain the persistence of this ethno-national trope as a function of primordial attachments. But it seems more fruitful to place it in the context of broader developments revolving around several domestic cleavages: that is, social tensions among Jews along ethnic (Ashkenazim versus Mizrahim) and religious-secular lines, as well as national-religious (Jews versus non-Jews) tensions. These divisions are compounded by negative assessments of the growing presence of nonnational labor migrants and the strengthening confirmation of a Palestinian identity among Israel's Arab citizens. Together, these trends have reinforced an enemy-driven rhetoric of ethno-national (i.e., Jewish) solidarity.

A central difference between the two cases refers to the initial context within which their citizenship laws were implemented. To begin with, they had different demographic compositions during the formative years when their citizenship laws were legislated. Germany was then more or less homogeneous. Israel was heterogeneous from its inception, with the Palestinian minority constituting about 18 percent of the population. This difference is not negligible, given the strong demographic rationale behind Israel's immigration laws. Cohen's essay in this volume reminds us of the enormous demographic significance of immigration for the Zionist project. Between 1948 and 1995 the net migration balance constituted nearly 50 percent of the Jewish population growth. A second difference refers to the distinctive origins of their respective immigration laws. The German law of 1949, to a large extent, is an extension of an ethno-cultural conception that goes back to the Imperial Law of 1913, bracketing the racist modifications of 1933 and 1935. Israel's Law of Return, on the other hand, is a novelty in Jewish history. A third, and related, distinction refers to the ideological underpinnings of these laws. Whereas Germany's laws for privileged immigrants were temporary, Israel's Law of Return was constitutive for the Zionist ideal of a Jewish state (Rosenheck and Joppke 2001). Ethno-cultural provisions in the Basic Law and the Federal Expellee Law were designed as a temporary remedy for the consequences of World War II, namely the division of Germany and the expulsion of ethnic Germans from territories under Soviet control. The temporary character of the law finds its expression in the fact, that after the end of the Cold War and with no apparent oppression of those ethnic Germans who remain in Eastern Europe, the central provisions granting citizenship rights are gradually being dismantled (see Levy in this volume).

By contrast, as a constitutive element of the Jewish state, Israel's Law of Return is a permanent provision. It is expansive and defines the state. To be sure, in Israel too, privileged migration is a deliberate reply to centuries of Jewish dispersion and suffering, and most specifically to the experience of the Holocaust. However, this view does not exhaust the comprehensive ideological underpinnings of this ethno-national conception. The law remains in place even after persecution no longer plays a role. That, of course, is because it was not just a response to persecution, but first and foremost an attempt to institutionalize the Zionist aspiration to "nationalize" Judaism, that is to be a Jewish state and make itself the central political and cultural source of Jewish identification. Hence, all American Jews, for example, remain entitled to automatic citizenship in Israel, while Americans of German descent can, for the most part, no longer claim German citizenship. A second reason for the persistence of privileged Jewish immigration relates to demographic considerations and the Jewish-Arab conflict.

Both issues naturally are closely intertwined. A brief look at the reasons and circumstances for the persistence of Israel's ethno-national self-understanding is illuminating. The tension between Israel's attempt to be at once a (particularistic) Jewish and (universalistic) democratic state, becomes apparent when we consider the de facto exclusion of about 20 percent of its Palestinian citizens. While they enjoy de jure rights, they cannot (and increasingly do not want to) partake in the common good, since the state is defined by Jewish symbols. Their second-class status is further enhanced through various forms of discrimination that are both political (i.e., Jewish parties ultimately show little obligation toward the so-called "Arab sector") and structural (i.e., with the exception of Druze, Bedouins and some Christian Arabs, Palestinian-Israelis do not serve in the army and as a consequence are not eligible for a host of social and economic benefits that are derived from and made contingent upon this service—see also Lustick 1980; Kretzmer 1990; Doron 1991; Cohen 1998). In short, state practices, and legal rules, as well as cultural conventions, create a matrix of citizenship statuses, which allocate a set of differentiating rights and duties to individuals who are formally entitled to equal citizenship rights.

As it is, the state declares itself to be both Jewish and democratic, but proves unwilling to tackle the tensions between the two. Thus the aforementioned contradictions and injustices remain largely obscured and are rarely addressed (Mautner, Sagi, and Shamir 1998; Gavison 1999). At best, this fundamental political and ethical predicament is treated as a problem of socioeconomic inequality requiring a greater allocation of public resources. There is almost no public, let alone political debate, on what is an undeniable quandary. A notable exception relates to scholarly attempts to explain and conceptualize the citizenship status of Israel's Palestinian minority. In an attempt to resolve the aforementioned tension between the particularistic (Jewish) state of affairs and its universal (democratic) declarations of civic equality, Sammy Smooha (1990), for example, has introduced the model of "ethnic democracy." In this view, Palestinian Israelis are guaranteed full citizenship rights but have no access to the "common good," which is defined by the Jewish nature of the state. Yoav Peled

(1992) expresses a similar view when he distinguishes between republican and liberal types of citizenship. Palestinians in Israel are barred from the former, which entails the attendance to the common good, but they do enjoy the latter, which grants them civil and political rights.

Until recently, Smooha viewed Israel as a unique case and "ethnic democracy" as a viable compromise for Arab-Jewish relations. In light of continuous cleavages and growing objections expressed by Israel's Palestinian minority, however, he himself now questions the feasibility of this approach (Smooha 1998). Oren Yftachel (1992, 2000) confirms that the notion of "ethnic democracy" is an unworkable (and undesirable) idea. Instead of viewing the Israeli scenario as unique, Yftachel situates it in a comparative framework and directs our attention to a crucial difference between *homeland* and *immigrant* ethnic groups, comprising two distinct types of ethnicity (1992: 127). He points out that the ethnic democracy model has existed elsewhere, but nowhere has it remained operational in the long term. Ultimately, governments facing a comparable majority-minority situation have resorted to "two alternative approaches to preserve political stability: majority domination or consociation. The latter has been used in Belgium, Switzerland and Canada, entailing genuine minority accommodation emphasizing power sharing, territorial separation and cultural autonomy" (ibid.: 130). In contrast, Israel has attempted to preserve internal political stability by the use of majority domination policies, a central reason why Yiftachel prefers the term "ethnocracy" over the conciliatory sounding "ethnic democracy." Experience from other countries shows that the persistent deprivation of minorities in bi-ethnic countries has resulted in increasing levels of inter-ethnic violence, ultimately leading to a collapse of the democratic order. "Attempts to institutionalize domination over a homeland minority in dual societies have generally failed" (ibid.: 130).

The sustainability of the ethnic democratic model becomes particularly questionable when we consider growing demands by Israeli Palestinians for group recognition and cultural autonomy, on the one hand—Jabareen's contribution to this volume exemplifies the distinction between a national homeland minority and an immigrant group—and the ongoing Middle East conflict, on the other. Gershon Shafir and Yoav Peled (1996) have looked at the impact of this conflict and the so-called peace process. They have pointed to a transition from a colonial to a civil society, and concomitantly the gradual replacement of its republican citizenship discourse, predicated on one's Zionist pedigree, so to speak, with a more liberal discourse, based on a more individualistic conception. A great virtue of their approach lies in the fact that they historicize citizenship, rather than taking it as a formal and static factor. They show how the peace process began producing economic dividends, which in turn, created a climate that was conducive to a more liberal approach to membership and rights (for a similar conclusion see also Sznaider in this volume). Conversely, as much as the agreements of Oslo and the ensuing process to establish peace provided the potential to conceive of a more inclusive polity, the breakdown of this process has contributed to an intensification of ethno-national and exclusive tendencies among the collectivities involved.

Discrepancies between de jure inclusion and cultural exclusion are also part and parcel of the German immigration debate. While the state is moving toward a more inclusive model of naturalization and immigration, social and political developments point in another direction. Controversies about immigration and the integration of long-term resident nonnationals (i.e., guest workers) are salient features of an ongoing public debate that seeks to reconfigure the cultural boundaries of the nation. The most striking example of this split, between formal inclusion and exclusion from the republican foundations of citizenship has been the so-called *Leitkultur* debate. Literally translated as "lead culture," which attributes specific cultural features to Germanness, its advocates on the right have shifted public attention to the alleged incompatibilities of different cultures. It is a veiled critique of Islam and the Turkish minority, which is by far the largest group of nonnationals living in Germany. *Leitkultur* is primarily an attempt to reproduce a monocultural model of Germanness in light of its increasingly multicultural composition and aspirations. Underlying these competing visions are social conflicts that are related to the persistence of high unemployment figures and deepening social cleavages that have dominated Germany since its reunification. Ironically, it is precisely the antagonism between West and East Germans that prevents the application of *Leitkultur* to a homogeneous ethnic conception of nationhood. As is evidenced by Levy's contribution in this book, the ambivalence toward ethnic German *Aussiedler* further undermines an organic vocabulary. The East-West divide is also a salient feature of the trajectories of antiforeigner sentiments. Against the backdrop of unemployment figures reaching almost 20 percent in the East and with no significant past experience with foreigners in the GDR, East Germans are less inhibited in voicing their objections to foreigners. Even though the majority of Germany's nonnational population resides in the West, violence against foreigners, both physical and rhetorical, is more pronounced in the East (e.g., with neighborhoods priding themselves on being *ausländerfreie Zonen*—zones free of foreigners).

Socioeconomic dimensions also frame many of the debates in Israel since the topic of immigration from the FSU was catapulted to the forefront of public attention. Almost one million immigrants from the FSU have arrived in Israel where they now constitute almost 20 percent of the population. Many of these newcomers are not Jewish (up to 40 percent in recent years), neither are the approximately 200.000 foreign labor migrants currently employed in the country. Their arrival has intensified religious and ethnic conflicts in Israeli society. Many Oriental Jews (Mizrahim) and the orthodox Shas Party have raised objections to both the presence of non-Jews and the ethnic divisions that come with it. They have expressed concern about the economic implications this upwardly mobile group of immigrants has for the socioeconomic divide in Israel. Socioeconomic stratification has a strong ethnic dimension: the primary division is between Ashkenazi and Mizrahi Jews, with Israeli Palestinians and guest workers at the bottom of the economic opportunity structure. In both countries immigration and the allocation of citizenship rights thus also relates to broader issues pertaining to the welfare state. Ongoing welfare retrenchments have sharpened social conflicts, which, in turn, are frequently transposed to an ethnic dimension and questions of nationhood.

Globalization and the Fragmentation of Citizenship

This brief excursion accentuates how sharply political contingencies and historical junctures inform changing perceptions of citizenship. Both cases underscore that we cannot simply continue to operate with an ethnic-civic dichotomy (Brubaker 1999), nor can we presume some evolutionary shift from ethnic to civic conceptions. Instead, a broader perspective is required, one that involves the impact of globalization processes on citizenship debates. The comparative framework of this book is also instructive for a number of conceptual points pertaining to exogenous factors: the increasingly transnational character of immigration, the changing legitimacy of diaspora cultures, the importance of supranational institutions, and the weight geopolitical conflicts exert on perceptions of membership and rights.

Though a popular buzzword, globalization remains an undertheorized concept in the context of migration studies. It is recognized that globalization is causing increased migration (Sassen 1998), which, in turn, has reinvigorated debates about membership and border controls. A second set of debates revolves around the aforementioned claim that global migration trends contribute to the fragmentation of allegedly homogeneous nations, which is frequently perceived as a threat to the sovereignty of states (Joppke and Lukes 1999). Overall, globalization cannot be reduced to economic processes and their impact on migratory trends. It is also a source of cultural and political repertoires upon which different groups—including migrants and other nonnationals—within the nation-state can draw. This can help explain why it might be more appropriate to speak about "mixed citizenship conceptions" rather than a simple juxtaposition of ethnic and civic categories.

Let us briefly elaborate on these two points by way of taking a closer look at how globalization affects debates about citizenship. It should be emphasized that globalization does not have a uniform (let alone homogenizing) effect on how different states address questions of immigration and the allocation of rights. Instead, the salience of globalization appears on a continuum that is determined, among other things, by three main factors: one, the degree to which a country is exposed to ideas that are circulating in the global context; two, the extent of its institutional embeddedness in supranational organizations; and three, its geopolitical situation. A quick look at our two cases is instructive. The aforementioned fragmentation of collectivities within the state and the concomitant demands for group recognition in Israel and Germany are greatly influenced by a growing awareness of comparable debates in the North American context. Multiculturalism, cosmopolitanism and attempts to reconcile demands of group rights with individual-centered notions of liberal polities are among the key concepts that are increasingly appropriated into local (i.e., national) contexts. "Mixed citizenship conceptions" are the result of a group's varying responses to a globally available repertoire of rights and membership categories. Division lines run between those who endorse new nation-transcending concepts and those who feel threatened by them and as a consequence pledge their right to emphasize conventional nation-supporting ideas. It would go beyond the scope of this brief overview to provide a full analysis of this division, which is admittedly more complex. Suffice it to say here that globalization facilitates a greater range of mimetic activities. That is to say, minority groups can draw on rhetorical strategies that originated in other places but have relevance for their own experience. The emergence of strong identity politics and the concomitant claims for group recognition are but one example of this process (see Jabareen in this volume). The success of more inclusive policies and the willingness to accept the normative prescriptions that are readily available through processes of globalization largely depends on a country's institutional embeddedness in supranational structures. Germany's involvement in the EU plays a central role in this regard. In contrast to the political and normative interdependencies with which the Federal Republic is confronted, Israel, in part because of its geopolitical isolation, continues to depend on its lateral relationships, primarily with the U.S. As such, Israeli politics (and convictions) are much less vested in adhering to goals and norms that originate outside its own national purview. Hence, a possible shift from ethnic to civic conceptions should not be construed as an inevitable evolutionary process. Rather than conceiving of the replacement of one or the other, we witness an ongoing coexistence of civic and ethnic modes.

The prevalence of one or the other depends, among other things, on the persistence or transformation of "friend-foe" schemata. Germany and Israel reveal a complex range of "others," both citizens and noncitizens. Both share a tradition of nationhood, which arose in the context of a conflict, whereby a negative "other" became a constitutive component of their national self-understanding. Germany's formative national experience took place in the context of French occupation. Israel's self-perception is marred by the duality of historic persecution and Arab antagonism, on the one hand, and the country's colonial activities and the dominating features that accompany those, on the other. These have been the different contexts of "friend-foe" relations that frame their respective debates about nationhood and citizenship. As Sznaider's contribution to this volume indicates, challenges to the "heroic narrative of the nation-state" are highly contingent on the geopolitical situation of a given country. In the Israeli case, the impact of peace prospects and economic liberalization at one point contributed to the liberalization of its citizenship discourse (Peled and Shafir 1996). Conversely, ethnic conceptions (never really extinguished, but rather temporarily bracketed) have regained prominence in the context of deteriorating Jewish-Arab relations. Contemporary Germany, on the other hand, finds itself in a situation where, for the first time, it maintains friendly relations with all of the countries surrounding it. However, this might also partly explain the shifting focus on the "enemy within" and the aforementioned attempts to control the cultural terms of inclusion. Broadly speaking then, the reconfiguration of citizenship conceptions in both countries is taking place in the context of changing perceptions of enemies and victimhood. With the end of the Cold War, the fall of the Iron Curtain and the consolidation of the European Union, Germany faces an entirely new scenario that affords the possibility to rethink the boundaries of nationhood. On the other hand, the ongoing Israeli-Arab conflict is an obstacle and is deliberately exploited to prevent a broader discussion on equal citizenship.

The initial impulse for this book has been the desire for a better understanding of the unique yet comparable nature of German and Israeli citizenship conceptions. By comparing the two cases we have elucidated the distinctive traits of each incorporation regime. Situating both cases in a global context allows us to highlight some of the similarities that owe as much to nation-specific characteristics as to evolving global migration developments. Beyond our immediate interest in the specifics of the two cases, it is, therefore, our hope that this volume will prompt further research exploring the balance of ethnic-civic conceptions and cases of privileged migration in the context of emerging global processes.

As such, this book also serves as a reminder that all processes of citizenship inclusion by definition contain elements of social closure. The global context also accentuates a "cognitive dissonance," where perceptions of immigrants are guided by memories of previous modes of incorporation. For example, Germany's recent desire to recruit software specialists from abroad failed, in part, because popular perceptions were guided by anachronistic conceptions of unskilled workers dating back to the origins of the "guest worker" program. Similarly, perceptions of labor migrants in Israel are still dominated by its thirty-year experience of Palestinian day laborers from the occupied territories. Both apparently have not caught up with Georg Simmel's insight that the modern stranger is the one who comes today and stays tomorrow. This book has tried to direct attention to a more reflexive process recognizing not only the malleability of national self-understandings but also of the very assumptions that guide perceptions of "otherness." One objective of this academic endeavor has been to sketch new options for political discourse, which is frequently circumscribed by populist demands and confined to narrow electoral interests. It is our hope that the findings of this book will provide policy makers and the wider public with alternatives to the ethnocentric tropes that still dominate many of the immigration debates.

References

Brubaker, Rogers. 1999. "The Manichaean Myth: Rethinking the Distinction between 'Civic' and 'Ethnic' Nationalism." In *Nation and National Identity*, ed. Hanspeter Kriesi et al., 55–71. Zurich: Verlag Rüegger.

Cohn, Chaim H. 1998. "Judaism in the State of Israel," *Alpayim* 16: 9–35. [Hebrew]

Doron, Avraham, and Ralph M. Kramer. 1991. *The Welfare State in Israel: The Evolution of Social Security Policy and Practice*. Boulder: Westview Press.

Gavison, Ruth. 1998 "A Jewish and Democratic State: Challenges and Risks." In *Multiculturalism in a Democratic and Jewish State*, ed. Menahem Mautner, Avi Sagi, and Ronen Shamir, 213–278. Tel Aviv: Ramot Publishers.

———. 1999. *Can Israel Be Both Jewish and Democratic?* Tel Aviv: Hakibbutz Hameuchad. [Hebrew]

Joppcke, Christian, and Steven Lukes, eds. 1999. *Multicultural Questions*. New York: Oxford University Press.

Joppke, Christian, and Zeev Rosenhek. "Ethnic-Priority Immigration in Israel and Germany: Resilience versus Demise." (unpublished manuscript)

Kretzmer, David. 1990. *The Legal Status of the Arabs in Israel*. Boulder: Westview Press.

Lustick, Ian S. 1980. *Arabs in the Jewish State*. Austin: University of Texas Press.

Mautner, Menachem, Avy Sagi, and Ronen Shamir, eds. 1998. *Multiculturalism in a Democratic and Jewish State*. Tel Aviv: Ramot Publishers.

Peled, Yoav. 1992. "Ethnic Democracy and the Legal Construction of Citizenship: Arab Citizens of the Jewish State." *American Political Science Review* 86: 432–443.

Peled, Yoav, and Gershon Shafir. 1996. "The Roots of Peacemaking: The Dynamics of Citizenship in Israel." *International Journal of Middle East Studies* 28: 391–413.

Sassen, Saskia. 1998 *Globalization and Its Discontents: Essays on the New Mobility of People and Money* New York: New Press.

Smooha, Sammy. 1990. "Minority Status in an Ethnic Democracy: The Status of the Arab Minority in Israel." *Ethnic and Racial Studies* 13 (3): 389–413.

———. 1999. "The Status Quo Option: Israel as an Ethnic Democracy: A Jewish-Democratic State." In *Seven Ways: Theoretical Options for the Status of the Arabs in Israel*, ed. Sarah Osatski-Lazar, Asa'd Ghanem, and Ilan Pappe, 23–77. Givat Haviva: The Institute for Peace Studies. [Hebrew]

Yiftachel, Oren. 1992. "The Concept of 'Ethnic Democracy' and Its Applicability to the Case of Israel." *Ethnic and Racial Studies* 15 (1): 125–136.

———. 2000. "'Ethnocracy,' Geography and Democracy: Notes on the Politics of Judaizing Israel." *Alpayim* 19: 78–105. [Hebrew]

NOTES ON CONTRIBUTORS

Yinon Cohen is Associate Professor in the Department of Sociology and the Department of Labor Studies at Tel Aviv University. His current research focuses on the economic assimilation of immigrants in Israel and the U.S.; on socioeconomic gaps between ethnic, national, and gender groups in Israel; and on the transformation of the industrial relations system in Israel.

Ralf Fücks is Chairman of the Heinrich Böll Foundation. As a member of the Green Party, he has served in the state parliament of Bremen since 1985. From 1991 to 1995, he was the senator of Bremen for environmental conservation and urban development. His fields of interest include development, the future of employment, and international politics. He is a frequent contributor to newspapers and political journals.

Dieter Gosewinkel is a lecturer at the Free University Berlin. He is also a researcher at the Max Planck Institute (Frankfurt am Main) for European legal history. His research interests include the comparative history of nationality and nation-states, and the history of European dictatorships. His most recent publication is *Einbürgern und ausschließen. Die Nationalisierung der Staatsangehörigkeit vom Deutschen Bund bis zur Bundesrepublik Deutschland* (2001).

Hassan Jabareen is a lawyer. He is the founder and General Director of Adalah: The Legal Center for Arab Minority Rights in Israel. He is a lecturer in various Israeli law schools. Jabareen was the lead counsel for the Committee for Arab Citizens of Israel before the Commission of Inquiry investigating the October 2000 killings of thirteen Arab citizens by the Israeli police. He was the recipient of the Peter Cicchino Award for Outstanding Advocacy in the Public Interest (2000).

Baruch Kimmerling is a George S. Wise Professor of Sociology at the Hebrew University of Jerusalem. He is the author of numerous books in English and Hebrew, including *Zionism and Territory* (1983); *The Interrupted System: Israeli Civilians in War and Routine Times* (1985); *Palestinians: The Making of a People* (1993), with Joel S. Migdal; and *The Invention and Decline of Israeliness: State, Society, and the Military* (2001).

Daniel Levy is Assistant Professor in the Department of Sociology at the State University of New York—Stony Brook. His research interests include the comparative sociology of immigration and political sociology. He has published on the subjects of immigration and collective memory. In a recent book, *Erinnerung im Globalen Zeitalter: Der Holocaust* (with Natan Sznaider, 2001), he explores the impact of globalization on collective memories in Germany, Israel, and the United States.

Gilad Margalit teaches German history at the University of Haifa. His book *Die Nachkriegsdeutschen und 'ihre Zigeuner'. Die Behandlung der Sinti und Roma im Schatten von Auschwitz* was published in 2001. The English version will appear in 2002. Currently, he is engaged in research on the mourning culture of the victims of war and fallen soldiers in the early Federal Republic of Germany.

Rainer Münz is Professor of Demography at Humboldt University in Berlin. His main fields of research are demography, international migration, and ethnic and linguistic minorities. Among his recent books are *Paths to Inclusion: The Integration of Migrants in the United States and Germany* (1998); *Zuwanderung nach Deutschland – Strukturen, Wirkungen, Perspektiven* (1999); *Ost-West-Wanderung in Europa* (2000); and *Diasporas and Ethnic Migration* (2002). In 2000–2001, he was a member of Germany's Federal Commission on Immigration Reform.

Diana Pinto, a historian and writer living in Paris, holds a Ph.D. from Harvard University. She has been a consultant to the Political Directorate of the Council of Europe in Eastern Europe and the former Soviet Union. She is currently finishing a book, *The Wager: Reconciling Europe and the Jews in the 21st Century* (2003), in the context of her interest in pluralist democracy.

Zeev Rosenhek is a lecturer in the Department of Sociology and Anthropology at the Hebrew University of Jerusalem. His fields of research include state-society relations, the political economy of the welfare state, ethnicity and stratification, and labor migration. He has published articles in *Social Problems, International Sociology, Ethnic and Racial Studies*, the *Journal of Social Policy*, and the *Journal of Ethnic and Migration Studies*.

Dimitry Shumsky is a Ph.D. candidate in the Department of the History of the Jewish People at the University of Haifa. He is a research assistant at the Bucerius Center for Research of Contemporary German History and Society. His research interests include the Jewish experience at the Czech-German frontier during the turn of the century and the Bohemian origins of the idea of a binational state in Palestine.

Levent Soysal is Assistant Professor of Anthropology and teaches at the Draper Program in Humanities and Social Thought, New York University. During 2001–2002, he will be in residence as a postdoctoral fellow at the Berlin Program for Advanced German and European Studies, Free University, Berlin. His research interests include youth culture, identity, migration, transnationalism, and city and public performance in Europe.

Natan Sznaider is Associate Professor of Sociology at the Academic College of Tel-Aviv-Jaffa in Israel. His publications focus on the study of moral sentiments, popular culture, and globalization. Among his publications is *The Compassionate Temperament: Care and Cruelty in Modern Society* (2000). He has recently completed a comparative study, *Erinnerung im globalen Zeitalter. Der Holocaust* (with Daniel Levy, 2001), on the relationship of Holocaust memory and globalization.

Yfaat Weiss is a lecturer in German and German-Jewish History in the Department of Jewish History at the University of Haifa. She is also the director of the Bucerius Center for Research of Contemporary German History and Society. Her most recent book, *Deutsche und polnische Juden vor dem Holocaust. Jüdische Identität zwischen Staatsbürgerschaft und Ethnizität, 1933–1940*, was published in Munich in 2000.

INDEX